The Regulated Riparian Model Water Code

Final Report of the Water Laws Committee
of the Water Resources Planning
and Management Division of the
American Society of Civil Engineers

Edited by
Joseph W. Dellapenna
Professor of Law
Villanova University School of Law
Villanova, Pennsylvania

Published by
ASCE American Society of Civil Engineers
345 East 47th Street
New York, New York 10017-2398

Abstract:

The purpose of the Model Water Code Project of the American Society of Civil Engineers (ASCE) was to develop proposed legislation for adoption by state governments for allocating water rights among competing interests and for resolving other qualitative conflicts over water. To this end, input was procured from a variety of people involved with water-related issues such as engineers, government administrators, lawyers, business people and academics. Due to the continued divergence among the water laws of eastern and western States, the development of a single code appropriate for all the States was not possible. In the end, two different Model Water Codes had to be prepared. This one, *Regulated Riparian Model Water Code*, reflects the needs and legal traditions of the eastern States. Since regulated riparian statutes allocate the right to use water on the basis of whether the use is "reasonable," this Code follows this pattern for the allocation of the waters of a State. This Code also addresses the difficult question of multijurisdictional transfers of water, whether across a water basin boundary or across a state line.

Library of Congress Cataloging-in-Publication Data

American Society of Civil Engineers. Water Resources Planning and Management Division.
The regulated riparian model water code : final report of the Water Laws Committee of the Water Resources Planning and Management Division of the American Society of Civil Engineers / edited by Joseph W. Dellapenna.
p. cm.
ISBN 0-7844-0226-4
1. Water--Law and legislation--United States--States. 2. Riparian rights--United States--States. 3. Water rights--United States--States. I. Dellapenna, Joseph W. II. Title.
KF5575.Z95A47 1997 97-158
346.7304'32--dc21 CIP

Library of Congress Catalog Card No: 97-158
ISBN 0-7844-0226-4
Manufactured in the United States of America.

PREFACE

The Model Water Code Project of the American Society of Civil Engineers (ASCE) was begun in 1990 under the direction of Professor Ray Jay Davis of the Brigham Young University School of Law. Its purpose was to develop proposed legislation for adoption by state governments for allocating water rights among competing interests and for resolving other quantitative conflicts over water. Professor Davis enlisted the active aid of a large number of engineers, lawyers, and others interested in improving the administration of water allocation laws in the States of the United States. Input was procured from engineers engaged in working with water in many different ways, from government adminstrators working with water from a variety of perspectives, from lawyers representing development interests and from lawyers representing environmental interests, from business people representing a wide spectrum of industries, from academics from disciplines including civil engineering, economics, hydrology, law, and political science, from environmental activists, and from just plain folks. Several dozen people from such varied backgrounds gave detailed critiques of the several drafts of the project; many of these also attended two or more meetings per year where the drafts were discussed in detail. Probably each person who contributed to this project could pick at least a few points where he or she thinks the end products could be improved–the end products are not any single person's efforts, interests, or conclusions. Those involved in the project agree that overall the end products are carefully balanced to represent a coherent body of law that would markedly improve the law of water allocation as presently found in many States. (The term "State" is used throughout this Code to refer to a State of the United States, and not to states in the international sense, although such states might also find much of use in this project.)

Originally, the hope was to prepare a single Model Water Code appropriate for any or every State. While there has been notable convergence among the water laws of eastern and western States over recent decades, there continues to be more divergence than convergence, a divergence will almost certainly continue for many years. It proved impossible to craft a single code appropriate for all the States. In the end, two different Model Water Codes were prepared, reflecting the different needs and legal traditions of eastern and western States–the Regulated Riparian Model Water Code and the Appropriative Rights Model Water Code. The original goal is reflected in that each Code contains as much language identical to that in the other Code as possible. A legislature consider revising its water laws should examine both Model Codes.

In part because of the decision, made fairly late in the drafting process, to prepare two Model Water Codes, the project remained unfinished when Professor Davis retired from Brigham Young University. In August, 1995, Professor Joseph W. Dellapenna, of the Villanova University School of Law, succeeded Professor Davis as director of the project. Professor Dellapenna had chaired the working group that drafted the Regulated Riparian version of the Model Water Code. The other members of the working group were Robert Abrams, Jean Bowman, Gary Clark, William Cox, Stephen Draper, and Wayland Eheart. This document is the final report of the Regulation Riparian Model Water Code. The final draft of this report was subject to independent review by three prominent experts in eastern water law who had not been actively involved in the drafting of the Model Codes. They were Marshall Golding, a professional engineer from Pennsylvania, and two law professors, Robert Beck of Southern Illinois University and Earl Finbar Murphy of Ohio State University. The remainder of this Preface will explore in more detail why the Water Laws Committee of the ASCE decided that two versions were necessary.

To understand why two complete, separate Model Water Codes proved necessary requires some understanding of the path by which States east of Kansas City created a highly-administered regulatory approach to water allocation within the State, a path quite different from the path followed in the States west of Kansas City. While States to the west of Kansas City experimented with private property systems that coalesced into the doctrine of appropriative rights, States to the east of Kansas City continued to adhere to the common property model of common law riparian rights. *See* Joseph Dellapenna, *Riparianism,* in 1 & 2 WATERS AND WATER

RIGHTS chs. 6-10 (7 vols., Robert E. Beck ed., 1991) ("Dellapenna"), § 6.01(b). Although based on the ideal of sharing, riparian rights proved less than helpful whenever demand for water began to outstrip supplies. The Pacific coast States and the high plains States (from North Dakota to Texas) eventually abandoned riparian rights in favor of appropriative rights, although these States were unable to abolish riparian rights completely through inability or unwillingness to compensate the owners. *See id.*, §§ 8.01, 8.02. The result is those states a dual system combining the worst features of both bodies of law unsuitable to the more hydrologically developed eastern States. Even Mississippi, the only eastern state to adopt a dual system (in 1955), abandoned it in 1985 in favor of what in this Code is called "regulated riparianism." *See id.*, § 8.05; Joseph Dellapenna, *Eastern Water Law: Regulated Riparianism Replaces Riparian Rights,* in THE NATURAL RESOURCES LAW MANUAL 317 (Richard Fink ed. 1995).

No state has adopted a dual system since Alaska in 1966. Instead, eastern States have developed a highly regulated system of water administration based on riparian principles that could best be described as a system of public property. Regulatory antecedents to regulated riparianism go back to colonial times in several States. *See* Dellapenna, §§ 9.01, 9.02. Initially, the transition from extremely limited regulatory intervention to more or less comprehensive regulation resulted from incremental changes in earlier systems rather than a conscious design to revolutionize the system of water rights. As a result, there is disagreement over when to date the emergence of the first true regulated riparian system. Nor is there a fully agreed name for the new system, although regulated riparianism appears to be about as succinctly descriptive as one can hope. Suggested alternative names have serious defects. "Eastern permit systems" or the like tells us nothing about the nature of the legal regime, and leave one more open to the charge that the new system has taken rather than regulated pre-existing property rights. "Non-termporal priority permit systems" is more immediately descriptive than "regulated riparianism" but it is rather too much to expect people to say frequently and also leaves more room for the allegation that property was taken by the legislation. The name "regulated riparianism" both emphasizes that the administrative permit process proceeds on essentially riparian principles, and that the new system is a regulation of rather than a taking of the older riparian rights. *Id.*, § 9.01.

The transition to the true regulated riparian system occurred by 1957 when Iowa adopted a fully regulated system, although the realization that something truly new in water law had emerged did not occur for another several decades. Little has been written about the new system, and most of that has been reportorial rather than analytic. *See, e.g.*, Richard Ausness, *Water Rights Legislation in the East: A Program for Reform*, 24 WM. & MARY L. REV. 547 (1983); Peter Davis, *Eastern Water Diversion Permit Statutes: Precedents for Missouri*, 47 MO. L. REV. 429, 436-37 (1982). Such writers have tended to see the statutes as a mere modification superimposed on the riparian rights that they see still as the core of the law in these States. Others have construed regulated riparian statutes as inartfully drafted appropriative rights statutes. *See, e.g.*, Frank Trelease, *A Water Management Law for Arkansas*, 6 U. ARK.-L.R. L.J. 369 (1983). Neither set of commentators realized that regulated riparian statutes represent a truly different model of water law. *See* Dellapenna, ch. 9.

In part, the emergence of a new form of water law was missed because, as noted above, the regulatory system was not originally introduced as a radical revision of the water law of a particular state. Rather, in most states, it emerged gradually through a process of small legislative interventions that eventually cummulatively did fundamentally change the water law of the state. As a result,it is sometimes difficult to determine precisely when, in a particular state, the transition from riparian rights to regulated riparianism occurred. In several states it still remains unclear whether the law would better be described as still basically riparian rights with limited legislative alterations or as regulated riparianism. As of 1996, about eighteen States have enacted a regulated riparian system for surface water sources, generally including underground water sources as well. Two other States apply a regulated riparian system to underground water sources only. In several instances, these states have not actually implemented the regulated riparian statutes on the books, and in several others the limitations on the reach of regulatory authority allows serious question as to whether this state truly has enacted a regulated riparian statute. With those caveats in mind, the states are (with the approximate date of the transition to regulated riparianism in parenthesis):

Indiana (1955)*

Iowa (1957)

Maryland (1957)

Wisconsin (1959)

Delaware (1959)

New Jersey (1963)

Kentucky (1966)

South Carolina (1969)**

Florida (1972)

Minnesota (1973)

North Carolina (1973)***

Georgia (1977)****

New York (1979)*

Connecticut (1982)

Illinois (1983)**

Arkansas (1985)*

Massachusetts (1985)**

Mississippi (1985)

Hawaii (1987)

Virginia (1989)****

Alabama (1993)*

---

* Less completely developed or implemented than for other regulated riparian States.

** Applicable to underground water only and requiring permits in capacity use areas only.

*** Applicable to critical management areas only.

**** This date refers to the adoption of a regulated riparian statute that applies to surface water sources. These states had adopted similar statutes for groundwater earlier (Georgia, 1972; Virginia, 1973).

In addition, the unusual arrangements of the Delaware River Basin Compact and the Susquehanna River Basin Compact create a regulated riparian system in those basins (stretching across four and three States respectively) under interstate supervision or management. *See id.* § 9.06(c)(2); Joseph Dellapenna, *The Delaware and Susquehanna River Basins,* in 6 WATERS AND WATER RIGHTS 137-47 (1994 replacement vol.).

One might add a few examples of regulated riparian systems in western states. As indicated in the foregoing chart, Hawaii has enacted such a statute for water in that state, although Hawaii does not really share the western legal tradition generally or particularly regarding water. *See* Joseph Dellapenna, *Related Systems of Water Law,* in 2 WATERS AND WATER RIGHTS § 10.1(C). The Arizona Groundwater Management Act of 1980, as well, perhaps, as some other western statutes relating to groundwater, also seem more in the regulated riparian mode than in the appropriative rights mode use for surface sources in the same state. ARIZ. REV. STAT. ANN. §§ 45-401 to 45-655. These statutes, while adopting the sort of public management approach characteristic of regulated riparian statutes, operate against a background of appropriative rights and have some notably different features from otherwise similar statutes found in eastern States or Hawaii. Therefore, the western statutes are seldom referred to in the Regulated Riparian Model Water Code.

The most fundamental departure from common law riparian rights found in regulated riparian statutes is the requirement that, with few exceptions, no water is to be withdrawn from a water source without a permit issued by the State within which the withdrawal occurs. Such a requirement is based on a State's police power to regulate water withdrawal and use in order to protect the public health, safety, and welfare. Regulated riparian statutes allocate the right to use water not on the basis of temporal priority but on the basis of whether the use is "reasonable" (or substitute terms such as "beneficial," "reasonable-beneficial," or "equitable"). The statutes also usually abolish common law restrictions based on the location of the use and require periodic review of the continuing social utility of the permits. Finally, the statutes create mechanisms for long-term planning and for otherwise providing for the public interest in the waters of the State. *See* Dellapenna, §§ 9.03 to 9.05. This Regulated Riparian Model Water Code follows this pattern for the allocation of the waters of a State. While recognizing the necessity of integrating water allocation with regulations designed to protect water quality, it does not attempt to exhaust the latter field. The Code does address the difficult question of multijurisdictional transfers of water, whether across a water basin boundary or across a state line. See Dellapenna, § 9.06.

Today, the main threats to the availability of water in eastern States, both as to quantity and as to quality, are not pollution or withdrawal, but the physical and ecological transformation by human intervention of water sources and the lands on or in which the sources are found. Dams not only "withdraw" water, they disrupt temperature and nutrient patterns on which rivers depend for their ecological diversity–as does the "straightening" of a river. Repeated withdrawals of water from water sources both deplete the quantity of water remaining and alter the waste assimilative and other natural aspects of the water source, often to the detriment of potential users--human and non-human. Sediments from farms suffocate many small forms of aquatic life. Vacationers who cut trees to improve the view from summer homes may erode stream banks or lake shores. As a result, the stream then carries more sediment and becomes wider, shallower, and warmer, making the water unfit for many important organisms and for many significant uses. The Regulated Riparian Model Water Code addresses only direct use of the water. It does provide some provisions for the coordination of the regulation of all human activity relevant to the waters of the State, but it does not address directly human activities other than direct uses that, often unintentionally, despoil the waters of the State.

NOTE: FORM AND SOURCES

Finally, a word about the form of this Code and how that form reflects the goals of the drafters. The Code follows the form commonly used today in the drafting of proposed uniform state laws under the auspices of the National Conference of Commissioners of Uniform Laws. That form consists of a statutory language in bold face that a legislature could enact with or without change. This language is arranged in sections, generally consisting of a single sentence, for ease of citation. The numbering of the sections consists of three parts, indicating the chapter of the Code, the part of the chapter, and the sequential numbering of each section within that part. Each section in this Code also contains an "R" to distinguish it from sections in the Appropriative Rights

Model Water Code (denominated "A"). For example, § 2R-2-02 means section 2 of part 2 of chapter 2 of the Regulated Riparian Model Water Code. Each section necessarily is optional in that a state legislature, even were it to decide to enact the bulk of this Code, could delete or change any particular section. Nonetheless, the drafters of this Code strove to create a complete, comprehensive, and well integrated statutory scheme for creating or refining a regulated riparian system of water law capable of dealing with the water management problems of the twenty-first century. The drafters have concluded that nearly every section of this Code is necessary to achieve that goal. Several sections (§§ 2R-2-21, 3R-1-03, 4R-4-01 to 4R-4-08, 5R-4-09, and 5R-5-03), however, are specifically denominated "optional." This indicates that the drafters consider these sections might not be necessary or appropriate to the needs of a particular state. These sections, therefore, merit special consideration should any legislature consider enacting this Regulated Riparian Model Water Code. A coherent and workable Code would still result were all of the "optional" sections to be omitted.

This Code refers to current *ASCE Policy Statements* and to certain common references. For the eastern tradition of water law, the central source is Joseph Dellapenna, *Riparianism* ["Dellapenna"], in 1 & 2 WATERS AND WATER RIGHTS chs. 6-10 (7 vols., Robert E. Beck ed., 1991) ["WATER AND WATER RIGHTS"]. Other standard sources are FRANK MALONEY, RICHARD AUSNESS, & J. SCOTT MORRIS, A MODEL WATER CODE (1972) ["MALONEY, AUSNESS, & MORRIS"]; LEONARD RICE & MICHAEL WHITE, ENGINEERING ASPECTS OF WATER LAW (1987) ["RICE & WHITE"]; JOSEPH SAX, ROBERT ABRAMS, & BARTON THOMPSON, JR., LEGAL CONTROL OF WATER RESOURCES (2d ed. 1991) ["SAX, ABRAMS, & THOMPSON"]; A. DAN TARLOCK, LAW OF WATER RIGHTS AND RESOURCES (1988) ["TARLOCK"]; A. DAN TARLOCK, & JAMES CORBRIDGE, JR., & DAVID GETCHES, WATER RESOURCE MANAGEMENT (4d ed., 1993) ["TARLOCK, CORBRIDGE, & GETCHES"]; FRANK TRELEASE & GEORGE GOULD, WATER LAW–CASES AND MATERIALS (4th ed. 1986) ["TRELEASE & GOULD"]. To simplify citation throughout, these standard references are cited only in the form indicated in brackets after the reference.

TABLE OF CONTENTS

CHAPTER I

DECLARATIONS OF POLICY

This Chapter sets forth the policies that are to inform the interpretation of the Regulated Riparian Model Water Code in both litigious and administrative settings. These policy statements describe in general terms the goals the administering State Agency and courts are to pursue in carrying the Code into effect. While the goals sometimes conflict, together they express a comprehensive vision of the waters of the State as public property to be administered by the Agency to achieve optimum of social utility. The Agency is given considerable discretion to resolve policy conflicts when they appear in concrete situations.

"Discretion" as used here does not mean "arbitrary." Rather it refers to decision according to legal standards which are to guide the decisions by the Agency. Those standards are carefully delineated in this Code. To call a decision "discretionary," as used in this Code, then is to use a neutral term that describes the nature of the decision-making process; it is not in any sense pejorative.

§ 1R-1-01 PROTECTING THE PUBLIC INTEREST IN THE WATERS OF THE STATE

The waters of the State are a natural resource owned by the State in trust for the public and subject to the State's sovereign power to plan, regulate, and control the withdrawal and use of those waters, under law, in order to protect the public health, safety, and welfare by promoting economic growth, mitigating the harmful effects of drought, resolving conflicts among competing water users, achieving balance between consumptive and nonconsumptive uses of water, encouraging conservation, preventing

excessive degradation of natural environments, and enhancing the productivity of water-related activities.

Commentary: This section sets forth the basic policies of the Regulated Riparian Model Water Code, delineating the central issue to be resolved by the State Agency in managing the water of the State: the need to balance economic growth against other important values. In a general sense, this balance could be described as "the public interest." That term is defined in a more general way in section 2R-2-18. For an analysis of how States have worked out of the several policies expressed in this section, see *generally* Dellapenna, § 9.03. *See also* Linda Butler, *Defining a Water Ethic through Comprehensive Reform: A Suggested Framework for Analysis,* 1986 U. ILL. L. REV. 439. This Code defines the interest of the state in major part through the concept of "sustainable development."

The reference to the ownership of the waters by the State in trust for the public echoes the idea of the public trust doctrine. *National Audubon Soc'y v. Superior Ct.,* 658 P.2d 709 (Cal.), *cert. denied sub nom. City of Los Angeles v. National Audubon Soc'y,* 464 U.S. 977 (1983); *United Plainsmen Ass'n v. North Dakota State Water Conserv. Comm'n,* 247 N.W.2d 457 (N.D. 1976); Douglas Grant, *Western Water Rights and the Public Trust Doctrine: Some Realism about the Takings Issue,* 27 ARIZ. ST. L.J. 423 (1995); Joseph Sax, *The Public Trust Doctrine in Natural Resource Law: Effective Judicial Intervention,* 68 MICH. L. REV. 471 (1970). The public trust doctrine has been invoked with limited success to unsettle apparently settled property rights in several western states. Joseph Sax, *Some Thoughts on the Decline of Private Property,* 58 WASH. L. REV. 481 (1983). The public trust doctrine has had a much lower profile in riparian law than it has assumed in appropriative rights, if only because property notions remain less fully developed in riparian law. Dellapenna, § 7.05(b). In either event, the formulation in the Code is not a direct expression of the public trust doctrine, for this formulation is found in the law even of States that most insistently reject the applicability of the public trust doctrine to the waters of the State. *See* COLO. CONST., art. xvi, § 5. This formulation neither compels the acceptance nor compels the rejection of the public trust doctrine as such. It does serve to underscore the reality that water as an ambient resource cannot be fully subordinated to private rights; water is always a matter of public concern and subject to regulation in the public interest.

Cross-references: § 1R-1-11 (preservation of minimum flows and levels); § 2R-2-06 (consumptive use); § 2R-2-13 (nonconsumptive use); § 2R-2-18 (the public interest); § 2R-2-24 (sustainable development); §§ 3R-2-01 to 3R-2-05 (protection of minimum flows or levels); §§ 4R-2-01 to 4R-2-04 (planning responsibilities); § 6R-3-01 (standards for a permit).

Comparable statutes: ALA. CODE § 9-10B-2; CONN. GEN. STAT. ANN. § 22a-366; DEL. CODE ANN. tit. 7, § 6001; FLA. STAT. ANN. § 373.016; GA. CODE ANN. §§ 12-5-21, 12-5-91; HAW. REV. STAT. § 174C-2(a); IND. CODE ANN. § 13-2-1-8; IOWA CODE ANN. § 455B.262(3); KY. REV. STAT. ANN. § 151.110; MD. CODE ANN., NAT. RES. § 8-801(1); MINN. STAT. ANN. § 105.38; MISS. CODE ANN. § 51-3-1; N.J. STAT. ANN. § 58:1A-2; N.Y. ENVTL. CONSERV. LAW §§ 15-0103, 15-0105(1); N.C. GEN. STAT. § 143-215.12; VA. CODE ANN. § 62.1-11; VA. CODE ANN. § 62.1-44.36, 62.1-44.84; WIS. STAT. ANN. § 144.25(1).

§ 1R-1-02 ASSURING EFFICIENT AND PRODUCTIVE USE OF WATER

> **Pursuant to this Code, the State undertakes, by permits and other steps authorized by this Code, to allocate the waters of the State among users in a manner that fosters efficient and productive use of the total water supply of the State in a sustainable manner in the satisfaction of economic, environmental, and other social goals, whether public or private, with the availability and utility of water being extended with a view of preventing water from becoming a limiting factor in the general improvement of social welfare.**

Commentary: In order to achieve the goals set forth in this section, the Regulated Riparian Model Water Code adopts the basic policy of requiring a permit for all water uses within the State except for those that are exempted pursuant to this Code. Permits are to achieve efficient and productive use of the water by the standard "reasonable use" as defined in the Code. The section acknowledges that efficient and productive use of water includes environmental as well as economic uses, with the ultimate goal of "sustainable development." While those two categories of use might well exhaust the possibilities, the Code leaves open whether there are other social goals that might be included within the purview of the Code. One other goal that might play a significant role is concern about social equity, a policy that is introduced explicitly in the next section and in section 1R-1-05. *See, e.g., Mason v. Hoyle,* 14 A. 786 (Conn. 1888); *See generally* MALONEY, AUSNESS, & MORRIS, at 170-73; RICE & WHITE, at 27, 162; SAX, ABRAMS, & THOMPSON, at 144-47, 307-13; TARLOCK, § 5.16; TRELEASE & GOULD, at 186-87; Robert Beck, *The Uses of and Demands for Water, in* 1 WATERS AND WATER RIGHTS § 2.02.

One particular problem that apparently impedes efficiency and productivity under appropriative rights is a tendency to "overappropriate" in order to capture future rents. In order to discourage speculation in water rights and to preclude the holding of water merely to deny its use by others, the Code authorizes the State Agency to require diligence in putting water to actual use once a permit is issued, and retention of an unexercised right is only authorized for limited periods and for justifiable reasons. One expression of this policy in the Code is the requirement that the State Agency set a time limit for the construction of any necessary facilities as a condition to permits where such construction is contemplated.

Cross-references: § 2R-1-01 (the obligation to make only a reasonable use of water); § 2R-2-18 (the public interest); § 2R-2-20 (reasonable use); § 2R-2-24 (sustainable development); § 2R-2-32 (waters of the State); § 6R-3-02 (determining whether a use is reasonable); § 7R-1-01 (permit terms and conditions); § 7R-1-03 (forfeiture of permits).

Comparable statutes: ALA. CODE § 9-10B-2(5), (6); DEL. CODE ANN. tit. 7, § 6001(a)(6), (b)(1), (c)(1), (4); FLA. STAT. ANN. § 373.016(2); GA. CODE ANN. § 12-5-91; HAW. REV. STAT. §

174C-2(C); ILL. COMP. STAT. ANN. ch. 525, §§ 45/2, 45/3; IND. CODE ANN. §§ 13-2-1-1, 13-2-2-2; KY. REV. STAT. ANN. § 151.110; MISS. CODE ANN. § 51-3-1; N.Y. ENVTL. CONSERV. LAW § 15-0105(2), (4); S.C. CODE ANN. §49-5-20; VA. CODE ANN. §§ 62.1-11(C), (E), 62.1-44.36.

§ 1R-1-03 CONFORMITY TO THE POLICIES OF THE CODE AND TO PHYSICAL LAWS

In order to promote efficiency, equity, order, conjunctive management, and stability in the utilization of the water resources of this State over time, this Code and all orders, permit terms or conditions, or regulations issued pursuant to this Code, are to be interpreted to achieve the policies embodied in this Code and to conform to the physical laws which govern the natural occurrence, movement, and storage of water.

Commentary: Too often, the law relating to water has survived without change despite the emergence of a deeper understanding of the hydrologic cycle that renders older laws virtually obsolete. The Regulated Riparian Model Water Code challenges administrators and courts alike to keep the interpretations of and regulations under the Code not only consistent with the policies in the Code but also abreast of current scientific knowledge in so far as doing so does not directly contradict the express terms of the Code. Generally, doing so will require knowledge of interconnected surface and subsurface systems in a water basin, although many water projects will not be tied strictly to basins and the most important disputes are likely to involve transfers (or proposals to transfer) out of basin. As this analysis suggests, the mandate to interpret the Code consistent with physical laws is directed primarily at ensuring conjunctive management of surface and underground waters, although the mandate is certainly not limited to that goal. It is important to note that this section speaks of all physical laws. The other policy goals mentioned in this section are addressed in more detail in other sections of this Chapter. On the need for the law to conform to physical laws, see RICE & WHITE, at 19-20; Dellapenna, § 6.02. *See also* TARLOCK, §§ 2.01-.06; TARLOCK, CORBRIDGE, & GETCHES, at 4& G; TRELEASE & GOULD, at 39, 385; Robert Beck,

The Water Resource Defined and Described, in 1 WATERS AND WATER RIGHTS § 1.03; Robert Beck, *The Legal Regimes, in* 1 WATERS AND WATER RIGHTS §§ 4.05, 4.08.

Cross-references: § 1R-1-09 (coordination of water allocation and water quantity regulation); § 2R-2-18 (the public interest); § 2R-2-24 (sustainable development); § 2R-2-28 (water basin); §§ 3R-2-01 to 3R-2-05 (protection of minimum flows or levels); §§ 6R-4-01 to 6R-4-05 (coordination of water allocation and water quality regulation); §§ 8R-1-01 to 8R-1-07 (multijurisdictional transfers).

§ 1R-1-04 COMPREHENSIVE PLANNING

> **Recognizing the importance of proper planning and management of the waters of the State to the health, safety, and welfare of the people, the State will develop a comprehensive water allocation plan and devise appropriate conservation and drought management strategies to serve the public interest in the waters of the State through establishing and maintaining sustainable development of the waters of the State.**

Commentary: In order to achieve the policy goals of the Regulated Riparian Model Water Code, the State must undertake comprehensive planning and conservation both for normal conditions and to respond to particular situations when the water available falls below that available under normal conditions. Effective and efficient management of water as a public resource is simply impossible without adequate planning. *See* Dellapenna, § 9.05(a). ASCE support for comprehensive water planning is expressed in *ASCE Policy Statement* No. 308 (revised 1993).

Cross-references: § 1R-1-10 (water conservation); § 2R-2-04 (comprehensive water allocation plan); § 2R-2-09 (drought management strategies); § 2R-2-18 (the public interest); § 2R-2-24 (sustainable development); §§ 3R-2-01 to 3R-2-05 (protection of minimum flows or levels); §§ 4R-2-01 to 4R-2-04 (planning responsibilities); §§ 7R-3-01 to 7R-3-07 (restrictions during water shortages or water emergencies).

Comparable statutes: ALA. CODE §§ 9-10B-2(5), 9-10B-5(1); DEL. CODE ANN. tit. 7, § 6001(a)(7); N.Y. ENVTL. CONSERV. LAW § 15-0105(3); HAW. REV. STAT. § 174C-2(b).

§ 1R-1-05 EFFICIENT AND EQUITABLE ALLOCATION DURING SHORTFALLS IN SUPPLY

The State, in the exercise of its sovereign police power to protect the public interest in the waters of the State, undertakes to provide, through this Code, an orderly strategy to allocate available water efficiently and equitably in times of water shortage or water emergency.

Commentary: Water rights under the Regulated Riparian Model Water Code are subject to the obligation of the State to make suitable provisions for coping with water shortages and water emergencies. Water rights under this Code are not some form of private property which the State is debarred from interfering with without paying full compensation. *See generally* SAX, ABRAMS, & THOMPSON, at 43-49; TARLOCK, CORBRIDGE, & GETCHES, at 104-21; Dellapenna, § 9.05(d); Jan Laitos, *Water Rights, Clean Water Act, Section 404 Permitting and the Takings Clause*, 60 U. COLO. L. REV. 901 (1989). This is emphasized by placing this section immediately before the section on legal security for water rights. The State Agency is charged to allocate water during such periods both to promote economic efficiency and social equity. Efficiency is a relatively objective goal, while equity remains necessarily a subjective goal that the legislature, the State Agency, and the courts will never define in a fully satisfactory way. *See* Guido Calabresi & A. Douglas Melamud, *Property Rules, Liability Rules, and Inalienability: One View of the Cathedral*, 85 HARV. L. REV. 1089 (1972). The open texture of the term "equitable" does not authorize complete discretion in the State Agency. Rather, determinations of equity are to be determined consistently with the general laws and policies of the state and the specific policies and requirements of this Code.

Cross-references: § 2R-2-18 (the public interest); § 2R-2-24 (sustainable development); § 2R-2-29 (water emergency); § 2R-2-32 (water shortage); §§ 3R-2-01 to 3R-2-05 (protection of minimum flows or levels); §§ 7R-3-01 to 7R-3-07 (restrictions during water shortages or water emergencies).

Comparable statutes: ALA. CODE § 9-10B-2(6); ARK. CODE ANN. § 15-22-201(b); ILL. COMP. STAT. ANN. ch. 525, § 45/2; KY. REV. STAT. § 151.110; N.C. GEN. STAT. § 143-215-13(a).

§ 1R-1-06 LEGAL SECURITY FOR WATER RIGHTS

In order to provide legal security for water rights within the constraints provided in this Code, this Code establishes a system of permits that make a water right a matter of legal record entitled to legal protection.

Commentary: One of the most serious problems with traditional riparian rights is the lack of legal security for lawful uses of water or even of any definite record of such lawful uses of water. Permits authorized under the Regulated Riparian Model Water Code are designed to remedy these deficiencies. A permit issued under this Code creates a right to use water (a "water right") that is entitled to full legal protection within the terms and conditions of the permit. Legal security is necessary to foster appropriate investment in water resources. *See generally* Dellapenna, § 6.01 (6).

Permits are required for large users, and some smaller users are required to register their uses in order to create a record of the use. The smallest of users are not required even to register their uses. Some users who are not required to register or to receive an allocation might nonetheless choose to perfect a record of their use through non-mandatory registration as authorized in section 6R-1-06. Furthermore, some users who are not required to obtain a permit might choose to apply for one any way under section 6R-1-03 or section 6R-1-04 as appropriate. The reason for taking this rather expensive step would be to obtain advance approval for a plan for conservation or a conservation credit, both of which are useful in times of water shortage or water emergency. Obtaining a non-mandatory permit could also entitle one to a preference for water developed through conservation measures if one expects to need enough additional water in the foreseeable future that one would cross the volumetric threshold that makes the permit mandatory.

Cross-references: § 2R-1-04 (protection of property rights); § 2R-2-05 (conservation measures); § 2R-2-14 (permit); § 2R-2-17 (plan for conservation); § 2R-2-30 (water right); § 3R-1-03 (small water sources exempted from allocation); § 5R-2-03 (administrative resolution); § 5R-5-02 (revocation of permits); § 6R-1-01 (withdrawals unlawful without a permit); § 6R-1-02 (small withdrawals exempted from the permit requirement); § 6R-1-03 (existing withdrawals); § 6R-1-04 (withdrawals begun after the effective date of the Code); § 6R-1-06 (registration of withdrawals not subject to permits); § 7R-1-03 (forfeiture of permits); § 7R-2-04 (no rights acquired through adverse use); § 7R-3-01 (authority to restrict permit exercise); § 7R-3–05 (restrictions of withdrawals for which no allocation or permit is required); § 7R-3-06 (conservation credits); § 9R-1-02 (preferences to water developed through conservation measures).

§ 1R-1-07 FLEXIBILITY THROUGH MODIFICATION OF WATER RIGHTS

In order to attain contemporary economic, environmental, and other social goals, the State shall encourage and enable the sale or other voluntary modification of water rights subject to the protection of third parties and the public interest.

Commentary: Attaining the policies embodied in the Regulated Riparian Model Water Code, including the securing of the advantages that come from holding valid water rights, requires that water be available for new uses matching contemporary needs and values. Unfortunately, the voluntary application of water to new uses has in fact generally been inhibited by the various forms that water law has taken over the years. This Code adopts the policy of encouraging and enabling such changes in water use (as well as other modifications not involving change in ownership). Where the proposed modification results only in no change or immaterial changes in the time, place, or manner of use, the Code directs the State Agency to provide a process for simple and quick approval. If the proposed modification will produce a material change in the time, place, or manner or use, it will in principle be subject to the same public control as would apply were the buyer making an original application for a permit in order to provide security to other private interests and in order to promote the public interest, although even for such material changes the State Agency is authorized to implement simplified procedures for review of the application to modify so long as doing so does not materially impair the rights of the public or of third parties. Exchanges and sales, as well as other modifications of water rights, are included within this policy. *See* Dellapenna, § 9.03(d). *See also* TARLOCK, *supra*, § 5.17.

Cross-references: § 2R-2-11 (modification of a water right); § 2R-2-18 (the public interest); §§ 7R-2-01 to 7R-2-03 (modification of water rights).

Comparable statute: VA. CODE ANN. § 62.1-245.

§ 1R-1-08 PROCEDURAL PROTECTIONS

The State shall provide procedural protection and fairness to parties to disputes over water rights through public proceedings on the allocation or modification of water rights, making available and encouraging formal and

informal procedures for dispute resolution, and encouraging alternative dispute resolution mechanisms.

Commentary: One of the more central aspects of providing legal security to water rights is assuring procedural protections to right holders and others involved in disputes over water rights. If such procedural protections are too rigidly formal, however, the very protections can become a serious impediment to both the legal security the protections are intended to provide and to the flexibility the Regulated Riparian Model Water Code is intended to encourage and enable. In addition to acknowledging the usual legal obligations of due process within the State Agency and judicial review of Agency action, this section expresses the interest of ASCE in fostering alternative dispute resolution regarding disputes over the allocation or use of water. *ASCE Resolution* No. 256 (1989).

Cross-references: § 3R-2-04 (burden of proof); § 4R-1-05 (application of general laws to meetings, procedures, and records); § 4R-1-09 (protection of confidential business information); §§ 5R-1-01 to 5R-3-05 (disputes and enforcement); §§ 6R-2-01 to 6R-2-08 (permit procedures); §§ 7R-3-02, 7R-3-03 (water shortages and water emergencies).

Comparable Statute: ALA. CODE § 9-10B-2(6)(b).

§ 1R-1-09 COORDINATION OF WATER ALLOCATION AND WATER QUALITY REGULATION

The State shall coordinate the plans, laws, regulations, and decisions pertaining to water allocation with those pertaining to water quality.

Commentary: Water allocation is inseparable from the regulation of water quality. Regardless of whether both functions are vested in a single agency or not, water allocation must be coordinated with water quality for effective management of a water source and to comply with federal laws and regulations. The Regulated Riparian Model Water Code fosters efficient and effective administration of the various laws and regulations relating to water usage within the State by directing state and local agencies to undertake such coordination as much as possible. This policy can be seen as a particular expression of the more general policy that the State Agency conform its decisions and regulations to physical laws as well as a means of achieving the pervasive goal of sustainable development.

The quality of water generally is measured by maximum limits on the concentrations of pollutants in the water and minimum limits on the concentrations of dissolved oxygen in the water. These limits are affected by three variables:

(1) the prior pollutant load of the water in a particular source;

(2) the volume of the water in that source; and

(3) the rate and amount of discharge of pollutants into the water source.

The greater the volume of the water relative to prior pollutant load or to polluted effluents being discharged into the water, the greater the waste assimilative capacity of the water source. *See generally* Robert Beck, *Introduction, History, and Overview, in* 5 WATER AND WATER RIGHTS § 52.03; Peter Davis, *Protecting Waste Assimilation Stream Flows by the Law of Water Allocation, Nuisance and Public Trust, and by Environmental Statutes,* 28 NAT. RESOURCES J. 357 (1988).

As these variables suggest, the allocation of water to uses requiring the withdrawal of water from the water source will directly affect the waste assimilative capacity of the source even if, as is often not the case, the withdrawal and use will not return polluted effluent to that or another water source. This reality alone mandates the coordination of the functions of water allocation and water quality regulation to avoid contradictory commands or other inefficiencies. In addition, coordination is necessary as part of a program of coordinating State and federal programs given the large federal role in environmental protection in general and the setting and enforcing of water quality standards in particular. The problem is outlined in DAVID GETCHES, LAWRENCE MACDONNELL, & TERESA RICE, CONTROLLING WATER USE: THE UNFINISHED BUSINESS OF WATER QUALITY PROTECTION 91-120 (1991); SAX, ABRAMS, & THOMPSON, at 917-70; TRELEASE & GOULD, at 728-58; Robert Beck, *The Uses of and Demands for Water, in* 1 WATERS AND WATER

RIGHTS § 2.03; Robert Beck, *The Water Quality Approach, in* 5 WATERS AND WATER RIGHTS § 54.09(d)(2).

Chief among the federal laws with which the State must coordinate its allocations is the Clean Water Act, 33 U.S.C. §§ 1251-1387. Although the Clean Water Act specifically disclaims superseding or abrogating State authority to allocate water, *id.*, § 1251(g), the Act's focus on water quality standards necessarily has a significant impact on State allocation of waters. Under the Act, water quality standards are set as a matter of federal law which the State is required to meet in allocating its water resources. *See* C. Peter Goplerud III, *Technological Controls,* in 5 WATERS AND WATER RIGHTS §§ 53.01-53.04; Robert Beck, *The Water Quality Approach,* in 5 WATERS AND WATER RIGHTS §§ 54.01-54.09.

Two programs, directed to achieving and maintaining "the chemical, physical, and biological integrity of the Nation's water," *id.*, § 1251(a), will particularly affect State water allocation:

(1) ambient water quality standards; and

(2) effluent discharge standards for "point sources."

Ambient water quality standards are based upon the designated uses of the particular segment of a water source (e.g., agriculture, industry, public supply, recreation, etc.). These standards include minimum concentrations of dissolved oxygen, maximum concentrations for bacteria, maximum allowable temperature changes, and defined limits to hydrogen ion concentrations (pH). Effluent discharge standards require each point source to obtain a permit under the National Pollutant Discharge Elimination System ("NPDES"). A point source is the discharge of any effluent into the waters of the United States at a discrete outlet (a "point"). Examples include sewage treatment plants, industrial discharges, and urban stormwater drains. The NPDES permit sets the particular limits on various pollutants authorized for discharges by the point source. *See* SAX, ABRAMS, & THOMPSON, at 16, 918, 928-39.

State allocations will impact on the federal scheme for achieving and maintaining the several integrities of the waters of the United States in three ways. First, the allocation of uses, whether in-place or by withdrawal, affects the designated uses of the waterbody and therefore the ambient water quality standards of the water source. Second, the allocation of withdrawal rights may lower the volume of flow and consequently reduce the waste assimilative capacity of the water source. Finally, the allocation of withdrawal rights normally signals a return flow to the water source, often triggering the National Pollutant Discharge Elimination System permit requirement. *See* TARLOCK, CORBRIDGE, & GETCHES, at 132-35, 577, 740-41, 854-61. Efficient and effective water management requires that these effects be considered in allocating water to particular uses.

In some States, a single agency will administer both water allocation and the regulation of water quality; in others, the administration of the two programs will be vested in different agencies. Regardless of how the administration of water quality and water quantity issues is arranged, failure to coordinate will, at the least, run afoul of the policy of conforming the management of the waters of the State to the relevant physical laws. Furthermore, failure to coordinate and even to integrate the two programs will preclude the efficient and effective management of both programs and create a risk of federal intervention into the State's water management.

Cross-references: § 1R-1-01 (protecting the public interest in the waters of the State); § 1R-1-03 (conformity to physical laws); § 2R-2-02 (biological integrity); § 2R-2-03 (chemical integrity); § 2R-2-15 (person); § 2R-2-16 (physical integrity); § 2R-2-18 (the public interest); § 2R-2-21 (safe yield); § 2R-2-24 (sustainable development); § 2R-2-30 (water right); § 2R-2-32 (waters of the State); § 2R-2-33 (water source); § 2R-2-34 (withdraw or withdrawal); §§ 3R-2-01 to 3R-2-05 (protection of minimum flows or levels); § 4R-3-04 (combined permits); §§ 6R-4-01 to 6R-4-05 (coordination of water allocation and water quality regulation).

Comparable statutes: ALA. CODE § 9-10B-2(7); GA. CODE ANN. § 12-5-21; HAW. REV. STAT. § 174C-2(d); IOWA CODE ANN. §§ 455B.265(1), 455B.267(2); N.Y. ENVTL. CONSERV. LAW § 15-0105(6); WIS. STAT. ANN. § 144.025(1).

§ 1R-1-10 WATER CONSERVATION

The State shall conserve the waters of the State through suitable policies and by encouraging private efforts to conserve water and to avoid waste.

Commentary: In addition to recognizing the need to coordinate water allocation and water quality regulation in order to achieve sustainable development, the Regulated Riparian Model Water Code fosters the conservation of water as a basic policy of the State. Conservation appears at frequent intervals in the Code, but its accomplishment is to be achieved primarily by a two-pronged approach. First, the State and its various agencies are to conform their own activities to sound conservation practices. Second, the State Agency is to encourage, through the terms and conditions it attaches to permits, private efforts to conserve water. Planning will be an essential element to the State Agency's conservation activities. ASCE support for water conservation is expressed in *ASCE Policy Statements* No. 308 (revised 1993) and No. 337 (revised 1994). *See* Robert Beck, *The Uses of and Demands for Water, in* 1 WATERS AND WATER RIGHTS § 2.01. For an example, consider the California approach to conservation, see SAX, ABRAMS, & THOMPSON, at 979-97.

The Regulated Riparian Model Water Code embodies several important provisions designed to assure the minimum necessary conservation and to encourage or promote additional conservation. The Code establishes minimum flows and levels of water that are to be protected from withdrawal or other consumptive uses. *See* sections 3R-2-01 to 3R-1-04. The Code also provides for the State Agency to contract to protect additional flows and levels beyond that minimum. Section 3R-2-05. The Code requires all permit holders to adopt plans for conservation. Sections 6R-2-01(p), 7R-1-01. The Code also establishes a preference for persons who have voluntarily undertaken conservation measures beyond those required by the provisions of the Code and beyond the requirements of any plan of conservation that has been made part of the terms and conditions of their permits. Sections 9R-1-01, 9R-1-02. Finally, the Code creates a system of conservation credits that arise from fulfilling the terms or conditions of a permit or as a response to a water shortage or water emergency, including joint actions taking collectively by two or more permit holders. Section 7R-3-06.

The relationship of these several provisions is complex. For example, the preference for voluntary conservation measures under section 9R-1-02 relates to steps taken neither as a requirement of the permit nor as a direct response to a crisis. Its primary role will be as a preference relating to an application to modify the use made of water under a permit. Conservation credits under section 7R-3-06 relate to preferences in the context of restrictions on water use during a water shortage or water emergency. Either sort of preference, however, might count in determining whether one or another use is reasonable when several permit holders are seeking to renew permits or are otherwise competing for limited supplies of water.

Quantification of the water conserved will involve comparing the amounts of water used before introduction of the voluntary conservation measures with that use afterward, allowances being made to natural variations in the use and occurrence of water. Normally, the Agency will require actual measurements to estimates. In appropriate cases the Agency might rely on estimates based upon sound engineering principles.

A person using water can, to some extent, control which section a particular conservation measure comes under through the manner in which the conservation measures are disclosed to the State Agency (*i.e.*, through a permit application or otherwise). When that is possible, the person undertaking a conservation measure must then consider which sort of preference will be more beneficial. This basically comes down to how frequent are water shortages or water emergencies on the one hand, and how substantial are the opportunities to make another use of the water through a modification of a permit on the other. The risk of not disclosing fully how one intends to use the water does create a risk that the pattern of use, instead of giving rise to a conservation credit under section 7R-3-06, or a modification preference under section 9R-1-02, will be held to have been a waste of water and therefore not only not the basis for either a credit or a preference, but also in fact a basis for forfeiture of part of the water right evidenced by the permit. See section 7R-1-03. In an extreme case, the less than full disclosure could even lead to a criminal prosecution for perjury. Section 5R-5-03.

Although broadly speaking any conservation could be considered the elimination of the waste of water rather than conservation as such, when the initiative comes from the water user rather than from prodding by the Agency and the practices that the person changes were not egregiously wasteful, the activity should be rewarded as a means of encouraging the conservation measures. Some might fear that the sort of preferences provided here in effect negates the social benefits of the conservation by allocating the water levels to the party who conserved it. The Code proceeds on the basis that such a preference provides the best incentive to developing more efficient ways of exploiting water. These several provisions do not, however, overcome the general requirement that a person claiming a preference make a reasonable use of the water. Without some such reward, there is likely to be less voluntary water conservation as there would be no gain for the person undertaking the conservation measures and might well be a net loss if subsequently the Agency were to determine that resumption of the former use patterns would constitute a waste of water. The Code does not recognize a preference if the original permit inadvertently (or otherwise) authorized the waste of water or if the water can be "conserved" because it has not been used for the forfeiture period or is not capable of being used consistently with the terms and conditions of the permit. In other words, water must have been used in order to be conserved; to do otherwise would be to open the door to the possibility of one or a few large users monopolizing the waters of the State.

Cross-references: § 1R-1-04 (comprehensive planning); § 1R-1-11 (preservation of minimum flows and levels); § 2R-2-05 (conservation measures); § 2R-2-06 (consumptive use); § 2R-2-13 (nonconsumptive use); § 2R-2-17 (plan for conservation); § 2R-2-18 (the public interest); § 2R-2-20 (reasonable use); § 2R-2-21 (safe yield); § 2R-2-24 (sustainable development); § 2R-2-27 (waste of water); § 2R-2-29 (water emergency); § 2R-2-31 (water shortage); § 2R-2-32 (waters of the State); §§ 3R-2-01 to 3R-2-05 (protection of minimum flows or levels); §§ 4R-2-01 to 4R-2-04 (planning responsibilities); § 6R-3-01 (standards for a permit); § 6R-3-02 (determining whether a use is reasonable); §§ 6R-4-01 to 6R-4-05 (coordination of water allocation and water quality regulation); § 7R-1-01 (permit terms and conditions); § 7R-2-01 (approval required for modification of permits); § 7R-2-06 (conservation credits); §§ 9R-1-01, 9R-1-02 (conservation).

Comparable statutes: ALA. CODE § 9-10B-2(3); ARK. CODE ANN. § 15-22-201(a); DEL. CODE ANN. tit. 7, § 6001(a)(4), (5), (c)(3); FLA. STAT. ANN. § 373.016(2)(b); GA. CODE ANN. § 12-5-91; HAW. REV. STAT. § 174C-2(C); ILL. COMP. STAT. ANN. ch. 525, §§ 45/2, 45/3; KY. REV. STAT. ANN. § 151.110; N.Y. ENVTL. CONSERV. LAW § 15-0105(6); S.C. CODE ANN. § 49-5-20; VA. CODE ANN. § 62.1-11(D). *See also* Dellapenna, § 9.03, at 446 n. 228.

§ 1R-1-11 PRESERVATION OF MINIMUM FLOWS AND LEVELS

The State shall preserve minimum flows and levels in all water sources as necessary to protect the appropriate biological, chemical, and physical integrity of water sources by reserving such waters from allocation and by authorizing additional protections of the waters of the State.

Commentary: In order to achieve the public interest in the maintenance of a minimal level of biological, chemical, and physical integrity for water sources as a central aspect of sustainable development, the Regulated Riparian Model Water Code authorizes the State Agency to adopt regulations and take other steps to preserve a protected minimum level for each water source. The three forms of integrity mentioned in this policy and defined in this Code reflect the statutory criteria of the Clean Water Act, although that Act does not specifically express its three interrelated concerns as mandatory integrities. 33 U.S.C. § 1314(b). The definitions provided in this Code derived from the policies declared in the Clean Water Act as relevant to the achievement and maintenance of the three integrities. *See* 33 U.S.C. § 1251(a)(1) to (7).

While the aspects of water protected under the term "physical integrity" mostly apply only to surface water sources, the biological and chemical integrities to be protected under this section are relevant to both the surface and underground water sources within the State. The differing characteristics of the several types of water source will be considered by the State Agency in specifying the protected minimum level for each water source. The Safe Drinking Water Act, 42 U.S.C. §§ 300f-300j-11, sets specific federal standards regarding the regulation of underground injections and protection of aquifers that are the sole source of a public water supply. These standards will have a large, and generally controlling, role in setting the protected levels for underground water. *See* Robert Beck, *Introduction, History, and Overview,* 5 WATERS AND WATER RIGHTS § 52.06(c); Robert Beck, *The Water Quality Approach,* in 5 WATERS AND WATER RIGHTS § 54.03.

Like water conservation generally, the Code adopts a two-pronged approach to minimum level protection. First, the Code reserves from allocation the waters necessary for the preservation of the protected integrities of water sources. Second, the Code establishes a mechanism for providing further protection to instream flows. *See* RICE & WHITE, *supra,* at 2; Dellapenna, § 9.05(b). One means for providing further protection to instream flows that has been gaining in importance in recent decades is the regulation of releases from reservoirs. *See, e.g., Confederated Tribes v Federal Energy Regulatory Comm'n,* 246 F.2d 466 (9th Cir. 1984), *cert. denied,* 471 U.S. 1116 (1985); Lydia Grimm, Comment, *Fishery Protection and FERC Hydropower Relicensing under ECPA: Maintaining a Deadly Status Quo,* 20 ENVTL. L. 929 (1990); Michael Pyle, Note, *Beyond Fish Ladders: Dam Removal as a Strategy for Restoring America's Rivers,* 14 STAN. ENVTL. L.J. 97 (1995). In some watersheds, release management significantly mimics the natural cycle of spring floods and summer low flows in order to sustain the biological integrity of the stream. *See, e.g.,* Jon Christensen, *River in Nevada Helps Its Own Restoration,* N.Y. TIMES, Sept. 24, 1996, at C4.

Cross-references: § 2R-2-02 (biological integrity); § 2R-2-03 (chemical integrity); § 2R-2-16 (physical integrity); § 2R-2-18 (the public interest); § 2R-2-21 (safe yield); § 2R-2-24 (sustainable development); §§ 3R-2-01 to 3R-2-05 (protection of minimum flows or levels).

Comparable statutes: ARK. CODE ANN. §§ 15-22-201(b), 15-22-202(6), 15-22-222; FLA. STAT. ANN. §§ 373.0397, 373.042, 373.223(3); HAW. REV. STAT. § 174C-3; MISS. CODE ANN. § 51-3-3(i), (j); N.Y. ENVTL. CONSERV. LAW § 15-0105(6); VA. CODE ANN. §§ 62.1-11(F), 62.1-44.36(5). *See also* Dellapenna, § 9.05 (b), at 529 n.845.

§ 1R-1-12 RECOGNIZING LOCAL INTERESTS IN THE WATERS OF THE STATE

The diverse hydrogeographic, economic, and institutional conditions existing within the State require the State to continue to support the activities of general and special purpose local units of government that address local and regional water resource conditions and problems.

Commentary: In all States, county and municipal governments have long addressed local hydrologic conditions and problems. In most States, there also are various special purpose units of government, such as regional sanitation districts or public supply systems, that have long provided essential services to local (including metropolitan) communities. The Regulated Riparian Model Water Code includes provisions to assure cooperation with such governmental units and support to their activities so far as the resources available to the State Agency allow. The Code further recognizes that many States will choose to administer the permit process provided in this Code, as well as some of the planning and other functions provided in this Code, through Special Management Water Areas covering only particular portions of the States. Other States will choose to have all functions directly covered by the Code performed by a single state-wide agency. States opting for the latter approach will delete the sections dealing with Special Water Management Areas.

Cross-references: § 2R-2-18 (the public interest); § 2R-2-22 (Special Water Management Area); §§ 4R-4-01 to 4R-4-07 (Special Water Management Areas).

Comparable statutes: ALA. CODE § 9-10B-25; ARK. CODE ANN. §§ 15-22-202(9), 15-22-505(9); FLA. STAT. ANN. §§ 373.016(3), 373.026(7).

§ 1R-1-13 REGULATING INTERSTATE WATER TRANSFERS

The State shall maintain the waters of the State both for supplying water requirements within the State and, under appropriate circumstances, for out-of-state transportation and use.

Commentary: Transferring water across state boundaries might raise economic, environmental, and social issues concerning the safety, health, and welfare of the citizens of the state of origin. While the public interest that the State Agency exists to promote is the interest of the public of this State, membership in a federal union precludes anything less than an even-handed treatment of the interests of persons and communities in other States. *Sporhase v. Nebraska* ex rel. *Douglas,* 438 U.S. 941 (1982); *City of El Paso v. Reynolds,* 597 F. Supp. 694 (D. N.M. 1984); Dellapenna, §§ 9.06(b), (c); Douglas Grant, *State Regulation of Interstate Water Export,* in 4 WATERS AND WATER RIGHTS §§ 48.01 to 48.03. *See also* TARLOCK, §§ 9.01-10.07; TARLOCK, CORBRIDGE, & GETCHES, at 746-60; TRELEASE & GOULD, at 671. The Regulated Riparian Model Water Code recognizes the obligation not to impede the flow of interstate commerce but also recognizes the right of the state-of-origin to regulate such transfers in a nondiscriminatory manner and to prevent the loss of the water necessary for the survival, health, or safety of the State's citizens. In those settings where there is no interstate compact or other arrangement for collective decisions relating to interstate allocations, the Code requires the State Agency to balance these concerns to allocate the waters of the State to their proper use.

Cross-references: § 2R-2-18 (the public interest); §§ 3R-2-01 to 3R-2-05 (protection of minimum flows or levels); §§ 8R-1-01 to 8R-1-07 (multijurisdictional transfers).

Comparable statutes: ARK. CODE ANN. § 15-22-303; CONN. GEN. STAT. ANN. § 22a-369(10).

§ 1R-1-14 REGULATING INTERBASIN TRANSFERS

The State shall protect the reasonable needs of water basins of origin through the regulation of interbasin transfers.

Commentary: Transferring water for use outside of its basin of origin with little or no return flow to the basin of origin might pose similar problems to the basin of origin as are likely to arise in interstate transfers even when both the basin of origin and the basin of use are within a single state. The Regulated Riparian Model Water Code recognizes the obligation to protect the needs of basins of origin, but rejects any abstract standard that might prevent interbasin transfers beyond that amount necessary to serve actual or foreseeable needs of the basin of origin. Implicit in this policy is a recognition that interbasin transfers are not to be permitted if it would prevent the basin of origin from meeting any of the environmental or other social and economic objectives set forth in this Code or in related laws and regulations pertaining to water quality. *See generally* RICE & WHITE, *supra*, at 1-2; SAX, ABRAMS, & THOMPSON, at 262-71; TRELEASE & GOULD, at 1-12; TARLOCK, CORBRIDGE, & GETCHES, at 51-66; Owen Anderson, *Reallocation*, *in* 2 WATERS AND WATER RIGHTS § 16.02(c)(2); Robert Beck, *The Water Resource Defined and Described*, *in* 1 WATERS AND WATER RIGHTS §§ 1.02; Dellapenna, § 9.06(a).

Cross-references: § 1R-1-12 (recognizing local interests in the waters of the State); § 2R-1-02 (no prohibition of use based on location of use); § 2R-2-10 (interbasin transfer); § 2R-2-18 (the public interest); § 2R-2-24 (sustainable development); § 2R-2-28 (water basin); §§ 3R-2-01 to 3R-2-05 (protection of minimum flows or levels); § 6R-3-06 (special standard for interbasin transfers); § 7R-1-01(k) (permit terms or conditions involving an interbasin transfer to include compensation to the water basin of origin); §§ 8R-1-01 to 8R-1-07 (multijurisdictional transfers).

Comparable statutes: 42 U.S.C. § 1962d-20; ILL. ANN. STAT. ch. 19, ¶¶. 119.1-119.12; IND. CODE ANN. § 13-2-1-9; MICH. COMPILED LAWS ANN. §§ 323.71-323.76; MINN. STAT. ANN. §§

105.405(4)(a)(2), (3), 105.405(4)4(b); N.Y. ENVTL. CONSERV. LAW §§ 15-1601 to 15-1615; WIS. STAT. ANN. §§ 144.026(5)(b), (c), 144.026(11).

§ 1R-1-15 ATMOSPHERIC WATER MANAGEMENT

> **As the management of atmospheric water through weather modification affects the public health, safety, welfare, and the environment, the State shall subject such activities to regulation and control in the public interest and integrate such activities with surface and underground water resources management in order to improve water allocation and quality.**

Commentary: The Regulated Riparian Model Water Code recognizes that weather modification has become important in a few States and might become important in other States. The Code therefore provides for water rights and liabilities to be associated with weather modification. The Code does not attempt a comprehensive regulation of the practice. ASCE supports programs to develop and apply weather modification. *ASCE Policy Statement* No. 275 (1988). *See* Robert Beck, *Augmenting the Available Water Supply, in* 1 WATERS AND WATER RIGHTS § 3.04; SAX, ABRAMS, & THOMPSON, at 699; TRELEASE & GOULD, at 52.

Cross-references: § 2R-2-01 (atmospheric water management or weather modification defined); §§ 9R-2-01 to 9R-2-05 (atmospheric water management).

Comparable statute: FLA. STAT. ANN. § 373.026(6).

CHAPTER II
GENERAL PROVISIONS

This Chapter sets out a number of general provisions essential to the proper functioning of any code of law, particularly definitions of recurring terms given special meanings within this Code. The Chapter opens with certain basic changes in traditional riparian law that form the premises of a regulated riparian approach to water management. While largely preserving existing riparian and related rights to use water, this chapter does introduce one significant change in the law in that it repeals any limitations on the use of water derived from the location of the use. The chapter then provides the basic definitions for the Code. Finally, the chapter concludes with certain provisions necessary for the transition from prior law to the system enacted in this Code.

Part 1
General Obligations and Prohibitions

This Part reaffirms the basic rule of decision in riparian law that uses of water are lawful only if reasonable and also that vested property rights are to be protected. This Part, however, changes one feature of traditional riparian law that severely constrained the utility of the reasonability premise in operation: that uses on land that were not contiguous to the water source or within the same watershed were inherently unreasonable. *See* section 2R-1-02. This change, coupled with the addition of the requirement of a permit for most withdrawals of water provided in Chapters VI and VII, significantly transforms the manner in which the traditional criterion of reasonableness will be applied even while leaving its substantive content intact.

Some will question whether repeal of the restriction of use to riparian lands contradicts the claim that the Regulated Riparian Model Water Code is a regulation of riparian rights rather than a replacement of those rights. The core of riparian rights, as those rights have evolved in the later nineteenth and twentieth centuries, is not the restriction of use to riparian lands, but the requirement that uses of water be reasonable. *See Harris v. Brooks,* 283 S.W.2d 129 (Ark. 1955); *Lake Williams Beach Ass'n v. Gilman Bros. Co.,* 496 A.2d 182 (Conn. 1985); *Hoover v. Crane,* 106 N.W.2d 563 (Mich. 1960); *Red River Roller Mills v. Wright,* 15 N.W. 157 (Minn. 1883).

The American Law Institute recognized the result of this evolution when it concluded in the *Restatement (Second) of the Law of Torts* (1977) that the use of water on non-riparian lands is to some extent legally protected. If the use is made by a riparian owner, albeit on non-riparian land, the *Restatement* treats the use as "riparian" on the theory that the law of riparian rights protects the interests of the owner of the right rather than simply creating a benefit for certain lands defined as riparian. *Restatement (Second) of Torts* § 855. If a use on non-riparian land is made by someone who does not own any riparian land, the *Restatement* describes the use as a "privilege subject to defeasance by the exercise of riparian rights." *Restatement (Second) of Torts* § 856(1) comment a. This latter notion has been recognized to some extent in several cases. *Dimmock v. City of New London,* 245 A.2d 569 (Conn. 1968); *Pyle v. Gilbert,* 265 S.E.2d 584 (1980). Much the same is true for the view that the "reasonable use" rule for underground water is restricted to land that overlies the aquifer. *Restatement (Second) of Torts* 857(1). *See generally* Earl Finbar Murphy, *Quantitative Groundwater Law,* 3 WATERS AND WATER RIGHTS §§ 20.07(b), 22.01-23.03.

The rationale for the traditional restrictions is to restrict water rights to the land that naturally benefits from the presence of the water. *Tyler v. Wilkinson,* 24 F. Cas. 472, 474 (D. R.I. 1827) (No. 14,312); *Buddington v. Bradley,* 10 Conn. 213 (1834); *Blanchard v. Baker,* 8 Me. 253 (1832); *City of Baltimore v. Appold,* 42 Md. 442 (1875); *Niagara Mohawk Power Corp. v. Cutler,* 492 N.Y.S.2d 137 (App. Div. 1985), *aff'd mem.,* 492 N.E.2d 398 (N.Y. 1986). In a very real sense, all land within a watershed naturally benefits from the precipitation that falls across the watershed that feeds both surface and underground waters. Within the watershed, the Code simply disregards artificial boundaries drawn on the land in favor of allowing all whose lands contribute to the drainage to share reasonably in the natural benefits of the water.

The Regulated Riparian Model Water Code does not entirely abandon the notion of preferences for uses within the watershed for the Code provides protections against interbasin transfers. The Code provides a special standard for interbasin transfers designed to afford real protection to the basin of origin. *See* section 6R-3-06. Even with those preferences in place, however, the Code does not prohibit interbasin transfers. Rather, the Code provides for compensation to the basin of origin through an Interbasin Compensation Fund. *See* sections 4R-1-04(2), 7R-1-01(k).

§ 2R-1-01 THE OBLIGATION TO MAKE ONLY REASONABLE USE OF WATER

No person shall make any use of the waters of the State except in so far as the use is reasonable as determined pursuant to this Code.

Commentary: The traditional criterion for resolving conflicts over water use under common law riparian rights was to determine which use was, in light of all relevant facts, reasonable. *See* Dellapenna, §§ 7.02(d), 7.03; TARLOCK, § 5.16. This section carries that criterion forward as the fundamental criterion for allocating water under the Regulated Riparian Model Water Code. All uses of water, including those not required to have a permit or an allocation, must be "reasonable" as defined in this Code. By so doing, the Code seeks to eliminate or minimize wasteful uses of water, to prevent unreasonable injury to other water right holders, and to assure the allocation of the waters of the State to the uses most consistent with the public interest and sustainable development. *See generally* Dellapenna, § 9.03(b).

Cross-references: § 1R-1-02 (assuring efficient and productive use of water); § 2R-2-18 (the public interest); § 2R-2-20 (reasonable use); § 2R-2-24 (sustainable development); § 2R-2-27 (waste of water); §§ 3R-2-01 to 3R-2-05 (protection of minimum flows or levels); § 5R-2-03 (administrative resolution); § 6R-3-02 (determining whether a use is reasonable).

Comparable statutes: ARK. CODE ANN. § 15-22-217(a) ("equitable portion"); DEL. CODE ANN. tit. 7, § 6010(f)(1) ("equitable apportionment"); GA. CODE ANN. § 12-5-31(e) to (g); ILL. COMP. STAT. ANN. ch. 525, §§ 45/3(c), 45/6; IND. CODE ANN. §§ 13-2-1-3, 13-2-1-8; MASS. GEN. LAWS ANN. ch. 21G, § 7(4), (8) to (10); MINN. STAT. ANN. § 105.45; N.Y. ENVTL. CONSERV. LAW § 15-1503(2) ("just and equitable"); N.C. GEN. STAT. § 143-215.16(e), (f). *See also* CONN. GEN. STAT. ANN. § 22a-373; MD. CODE ANN., NAT. RES. § 8-807(a); N.J. STAT. ANN. § 58:1A-7; WIS. STAT. ANN. § 144.026(5)(d).

§ 2R-1-02 NO PROHIBITION OF USE BASED ON LOCATION OF USE

(1) Uses of the waters of the State on nonriparian or nonoverlying land are lawful and entitled to equal consideration with uses on riparian or overlying land in any administrative or judicial proceeding relating to the allocation, withdrawal, or use of water or to the modification of a water right.

(2) Nothing in this Code shall be construed to authorize access to the waters of the State by a person seeking to make a nonriparian or nonoverlying use apart from access otherwise lawfully available to that person.

Commentary: The Regulated Riparian Model Water Code repeals the common law rule that limited lawful uses of water drawn from a watercourse to riparian lands and from underground sources to land overlying the aquifer from which the water is drawn. There is no reason to believe that limiting the lawful use of water to riparian land is necessarily always either efficient or ecologically sound, let alone that it will necessarily serve the public interest. The Code places non-riparian and non-overlying uses on an equal footing with the formerly favored uses. Location of use is simply one factor of many to be considered by the State Agency in determining whether to issue a permit for a particular use. *See* TARLOCK, § 3.20 [1]-[3]; Dellapenna, §§ 7.02(a)(1),

9.03(a)(2). For the modification of the watershed limitation, see TARLOCK, § 3.20[6][b]; Dellapenna, § 7.02(a)(2). The rationale for this change is further developed in the introduction to this part.

The recognition of a right to withdraw water from a water source when one's land is neither contiguous nor overlying to the source does not, however, authorize trespass or other invasion of private rights to obtain the water for which a permit is issued. The rule announced in this section applies to interbasin uses of water as well as intrabasin transfers to nonriparian or nonoverlying land. Whether a permittee has lawful access to the water source from which use is authorized by a permit will not always be clear. The State Agency should attempt to determine whether there will be lawful access before issuing a permit, but its determination in this regard cannot create a new right of access in the permit holder, nor destroy the right to resist trespass or other unlawful intrusion by an intervening land owner. A contrary rule would contradict the provision in section 2R-1-04 that protects vested property rights from being taken without compensation.

Cross-references: § 1R-1-14 (regulating interbasin transfers); § 2R-1-04 (protection of property rights); § 2R-2-10 (interbasin transfer); § 2R-2-18 (the public interest); § 2R-2-28 (water basin); §§ 3R-2-01 to 3R-2-05 (protection of minimum flows or levels); § 6R-3-01 (standards for a permit); § 6R-3-02 (determining whether a use is reasonable); § 6R-3-06 (special standard for interbasin transfers); §§ 8R-1-01 to 8R-1-06 (multijurisdictional transfers).

Comparable statutes: ARK. CODE ANN. § 15-22-304; FLA. STAT. ANN. § 373.223(2); HAW. REV. STAT. § 174C-49(C); IND. CODE ANN. §§ 13-2-1-6(1), 13-2-2-8.

§ 2R-1-03 NO UNREASONABLE INJURY TO OTHER WATER RIGHTS

No person using the waters of the State shall cause unreasonable injury to other water uses made pursuant to valid water rights, regardless of

whether the injury relates to the quality or the quantity impacts of the activity causing the injury.

Commentary: The Regulated Riparian Model Water Code continues the traditional standard of the common law of riparian rights (and of the reasonable use version of the law relating to underground water) that no use is lawful if it entails unreasonable injury to other lawful uses. Determining whether an injury is reasonable remains a process of balancing the interests of the affected parties and of society generally. *See* Dellapenna, § 7.03. The law is changed in that the primary responsibility for determining when an unreasonable injury occurs is now vested in the State Agency rather than in the courts. The Code proceeds on the premise that there is no injury, reasonable or otherwise, if the affected party is compensated pursuant to a voluntary agreement or pursuant to measures directed by the State Agency under its authority as defined this Code.

Cross-references: § 2R-2-18 (the public interest); § 2R-2-23 (State Agency); § 2R-2-26 (unreasonable injury); §§ 5R-2-01 to 5R-2-03 (dispute resolution); § 6R-3-01 (standards for a permit); § 6R-3-02 (determining whether a use is reasonable); § 7R-2-01 (approval required for modifications of permits).

§ 2R-1-04 PROTECTION OF PROPERTY RIGHTS

(1) Nothing in this Code authorizes the taking of any existing vested property right in the use of water except for just compensation.

(2) Proof of compliance with this Code is not a defense in any legal action not founded on this Code except to the extent that the provisions of this Code expressly supersede prior law on which such claim is founded.

Commentary: The Regulated Riparian Model Water Code proceeds on the theory that while the State cannot take a vested property interest without just compensation, including a vested property interest in the use of water, the State can regulate property rights in the public interest. For this purpose, the State can compel even holders of vested property interests to obtain a permit subject to loss of their property interest if they fail to comply with the permit requirement. This is particularly true for water as the waters of the State are owned by the State in trust for the public, with only the right to use water being owned by particular users. This approach does not deny all protection of property rights even in water as regulation can become so extensive as to amount to a taking, particularly if the regulation deprives a property owner of substantially all economic value or imposes a significant burden not related to activities on the property. *Dolan v. City of Tigard*, 114 S. Ct. 2309 (1994); *Lucas v. South Carolina Coastal Council*, 112 S. Ct. 2886 (1992). *See also* James Audley McLaughlin, *Majoritarian Theft in the Regulatory State: What's a Takings Clause for?*, 19 WM. & MARY ENVTL. L. & POL'Y REV. 161 (1995). Courts thus far have been unanimous that a permit system like the one created by this Code is not a taking. *Village of Tequesta v. Jupiter Inlet Corp.*, 371 So. 2d 663 (Fla.), *cert. denied*, 444 U.S. 965 (1979); *Crookston Cattle Co. v. Minnesota Dep't of Nat. Resources*, 300 N.W.2d 769 (Minn. 1981); *Omernick v. State*, 218 N.W. 2d 734 (Wis. 1974). *See also* Michelle Walsh, *Achieving the Proper Balance between the Public and Private Property Interests: Closely Tailored Legislation as a Remedy*, 19 WM. & MARY ENVTL. L. & POL'Y REV. 317 (1995). Special provisions are made for permits for such persons which will gradually integrate them fully into the State's regulatory system. *See* Dellapenna, § 9.04(a). *See also* TARLOCK, § 3.20[3].

The problem of protecting vested property rights would be more troubling were a legislature attempt to displace a system of appropriative rights with this Regulated Riparian Model Water Code. Appropriative rights are defined in terms of a specific quantity of water applied to a beneficial use. *See, e.g., Imperial Irrigation Dist. v. State Water Resources Control Bd.*, 275 Cal. Rptr. 250 (Cal. App. 1990), *review denied; In re Application for Water Rights.*, 891 P.2d 952 (Colo. 1995); *Hardy v. Higgenson*, 849 P.2d 946 (Idaho 1993); *Romey v. Landers*, 392 N.W.2d 415 (S.D. 1986); *Provo River Water Users Ass'n v. Lambert*, 642 P.2d 1219 (Utah 1982); *State v. Grimes*, 852 P.2d 1054 (Was.1993). Such rights to use water clearly are vested property that could not be abolished without compensation. *United States v. State Water Resources Control Bd.*, 227 Cal. Rptr. 161 (Cal. App. 1986), *review denied*. Nor would a severe crisis forcing the abandonment of many uses due to water shortage invoke the doctrine that the state must choose among those to be destroyed when some uses must be destroyed. *Miller v. Schoene*, 276 U.S. 272 (1928). The state has already made that choice through the temporal priority feature of appropriative rights that have become a part of the vested property right. *Sears v. Berryman*, 623 P.2d 455 (Idaho 1981); *State* ex rel. *Cary v. Cochrane*, 292 N.W. 239 (Neb. 1940). The takings clause thus would probably preclude the adoption of this Code in an appropriative rights jurisdiction.

Some eastern states have accorded a limited protection to the right to use water based upon temporal priority. CONN. GEN. STAT. ANN. § 22a-368; IND. CODE ANN. §§ 13-2-1-8, 13-2-2-5 MASS. GEN. STAT. ANN. ch. 21G, § 7; MISS. CODE ANN. § 5-3-5(2), (3); N.Y. ENVTL. CONSERV. LAW § 15-501(1); OHIO REV. CODE § 1521.16; VA. CODE ANN. §§ 62.1-248(D), 62.1-253. Whether any of these enactments would amount to the creation of such vested rights as would require compensation to change is at least debatable. Probably no temporally-defined rights to use water in eastern states are so developed as to amount to a vested property right requiring compensation before it could be altered. *See* Dellapenna, § 9.03(b)(3).

Most States will choose to exempt some water uses from the permit system. In that case, the Code provides that disputes involving such exempted water uses will be governed by the principle of reasonable use. In most cases, that rule is simply the prior law that already applied to them as the common law of riparian rights or the common law of underground water. The Code also preserves private rights of action arising from injuries caused by pollution or other degradation of the waters of the State.

Cross-references: § 1R-1-01 (protecting the public interest in the waters of the State); § 1R-1-06 (legal security for the right to use water); § 2R-1-01 (the obligation to make only a reasonable use of water); § 2R-2-18 (the public interest); § 2R-2-33 (the waters of the State); § 3R-2-01 (protected minimum flows or levels not to be allocated or withdrawn); § 5R-2-03 (administrative resolution); § 5R-4-09 (citizen suits); § 6R-1-03 (existing withdrawals); § 6R-4-05 (preservation of private rights of action).

Comparable statutes: ALA. CODE § 9-10B-27; GA. CODE ANN. §§ 12-5-46, 12-5-104; HAW. REV. STAT. § 174C-15(C); IOWA CODE ANN. § 455B.270; MD. CODE ANN., NAT. RES. § 8-812; MINN. STAT. ANN. § 105.391(12); N.C. GEN. STAT. § 143-215.22; VA. CODE ANN. §§ 62.1-12; 62.1-253; WIS. STAT. ANN. § 144.026(12)(b).

§ 2R-1-05 APPLICATION OF DEFINITIONS

> **When used in this Code or in any order, permit term or condition, or regulation made pursuant to this Code, the definitions in the following Part shall apply.**

Commentary: The definitions in this Chapter are to be used throughout the Regulated Riparian Model Water Code. Modern possibilities of textual search by computer make it substantially self-defeating to provide the usual out of "unless the context clearly requires otherwise." Definitions are provided if the term appears in more than one section in the Code, but only if the term is used in a precise sense that in some respect would not be self-evident to an ordinary speaker of American English. When the drafters of the Code could not provide a better definition than a simple dictionary definition or when the term used is, and is expected to remain, vague rather than precise, they did not attempt to provide a definition.

Part 2
Definitions

§ 2R-2-01 ATMOSPHERIC WATER MANAGEMENT OR WEATHER MODIFICATION

The phrases "atmospheric water management" and "weather modification" both mean any activity performed with the intent of producing artificial changes in the composition, motions, and resulting behavior of the atmosphere or clouds, including fog, or with the intent of inducing changes in precipitation by use of electrical device, lasers, or alterations of the earth's surface, but not including any activity performed in connection with traditional ceremonies of American Indians.

Commentary: This definition is consistent with the definitions usually used in State and federal laws on weather modification. *See generally* Robert Beck, *Augmenting the Available Water Supply, in* 1 WATERS AND WATER RIGHTS § 3.04; Ray Jay Davis, *Four Decades of American Weather Modification Law,* 19 J. WEATHER MODIFICATION 102 (1987).

Cross-references: § 1R-1-18 (policy of regulating atmospheric water management or weather modification); §§ 9R-2-01 to 9R-2-05 (atmospheric water management).

§ 2R-2-02 BIOLOGICAL INTEGRITY

The "biological integrity" of a water source means the maintenance of water in the source in the volume and at the times necessary to support and maintain wetlands and wildlife (including fish, flora, and fauna) in so far as protection of either is required by federal or State laws or regulations.

Commentary: Water sources are vital to the survival of entire ecosystems, of which humans form only a part. Sustainable development of a water source requires respect for and protection of the biological integrity of the source. The biological integrity of a water source is defined as the preservation of sufficient water in a water source to assure the survival of the ecosystem as such, although human needs necessarily preclude any aim of preserving all ecosystems without change. The term comes from the Clean Water Act where it is one of the three fundamental criteria for setting effluent standards, although the Clean Water Act does not express its mandate in terms of "integrity." 33 U.S.C. § 1314(b). A simple way of expressing the goal is for the agency to prevent the loss of genetic diversity within the ecosystem, although this cannot be taken as an absolute value without utterly precluding human activity involving water.

Rather than attempting an exhaustive definition of how to balance the needs of humans and other participants in the ecosystem, an effort that is probably foredoomed to failure, the Regulated Riparian Model Water Code seeks to achieve the necessary balance by referring to other laws or regulations to define the extent to which ecosystems are to be preserved. This approach is taken in order to provide a measure of certainty to the otherwise vague standards proposed to define minimum flows or levels. The ultimate aim is to prevent permanent impairment to aquatic and other life-forms dependent on a particular water source. *See* The Endangered Species Act, 16 U.S.C. § 1531-1543; *Babbitt v. Sweet Home Chapter of Communities,* 115 S. Ct. 2407 (1995); *Tennessee Valley Auth'y v. Hill,* 437 U.S. 153 (1978); *National Wildlife Federation v. Federal Energy Regulatory Comm'n,* 801 F.2d 1505 (9th Cir. 1986); *Riverside Irrig. Dist. v. Andrews,* 758 F.2d 508 (10th Cir. 1985); SAX, ABRAMS, & THOMPSON, at 599-607; TARLOCK, §§ 5.05(7)(b), 5.07(3), 5,13; TARLOCK, CORBRIDGE, & GETCHES, at 739-43, 746-48; TRELEASE & GOULD, at 758-61; Melissa Estes, *The Effects of the Federal Endangered Species Act on State Water Rights,* 22 ENVTL. L. 1027 (1992); A. Dan Tarlock, *The Endangered Species Act and Western Water Rights,* 20 LAND & WATER L. REV. 1 (1985). *See generally* Hal Beecher, *Standards for Instream Flows,* 1 RIVERS 97 (1990); Dellapenna, § 9.05(b); Andrew Solow, Stephen Polasky, & James Broadus, *On the Measurement of Biological Diversity,* 24 J. ENVTL. ECON. & MGT. 60 (1993).

Cross-references: § 1R-1-09 (coordination of water allocation and water quality regulation); § 1R-1-11 (preservation of minimum flows and levels); § 2R-2-03 (chemical integrity); § 2R-2-16 (physical integrity); § 2R-2-18 (the public interest); § 2R-2-21 (safe yield); § 2R-2-24 (sustainable development); § 2R-2-33 (water source); §§ 3R-2-01 to 3R-2-05 (protection of minimum flows or levels).

Comparable statutes: ARK. CODE ANN. § 15-22-202(6)(C); FLA. STAT. ANN. §§ 373.042(1), 373.223(3); HAW. REV. STAT. § 174C-71(1)(C), (3); MINN. STAT. ANN. § 105.417(3), (4); VA. CODE ANN. § 62.1-246(1), 62.1-248(A).

§ 2R-2-03 CHEMICAL INTEGRITY

> **The "chemical integrity" of a water source means the maintenance of water in the source in the volume and at the times necessary to enable a water source to achieve the water quality standards prescribed for the water source by federal or State laws or regulations in light of authorized effluent discharges and other expected impacts on the water source.**

Commentary: Although the waters of a State continue to be used to dispose of waste materials and probably always will be so used to some extent, sustainable development requires respect for and protection of the chemical integrity of water sources. Today such discharges are extensively regulated under the Clean Water Act, 33 U.S.C. §§ 1251-1387, and other laws and regulations. Such regulations necessarily presuppose some minimum water level or flow regime to enable adequate waste assimilation by authorized discharges. The preservation of that minimum level or flow regime is here defined as the chemical integrity of the stream as defined in other relevant laws or regulations. The term comes from the Clean Water Act where it is one of the three fundamental criteria for setting effluent standards, although the Clean Water Act does not express its mandate in terms of "integrity." 33 U.S.C. § 1314(b). This approach is taken in order to provide a measure of certainty to the otherwise vague standards proposed to define minimum flows or levels. The preservation of the chemical integrity of a water source is necessary so that neither human nor other life-forms are endangered by excessive pollution or low flows. *See, e.g.*, *Arkansas v. Oklahoma*, 112 S. Ct. 1646 (1992); *National Wildlife Federation v. Gorsuch*, 693 F. Supp. 156 (D. D.C. 1982). *See generally* TAYLOR MILLER, GARY WEATHERFORD, & JOHN THORSON, THE SALTY COLORADO 25-31 (1986); SAX, ABRAMS, & THOMPSON, at 923-59, 963-70; TARLOCK, CORBRIDGE, & GETCHES, at 132-38, 576-79, 854-63; TRELEASE & GOULD, at 728-52; Robert Glicksman & George Coggins, *Groundwater Pollution I: The Problem and the Law*, 35 U. KAN. L. REV. 75 (1986).

Cross-references: § 1R-1-09 (coordination of water allocation and water quality regulation); § 1R-1-11 (preservation of minimum flows and levels); § 2R-2-02 (biological integrity); § 2R-2-16 (physical integrity); § 2R-2-18 (the public interest); § 2R-2-21 (safe yield); § 2R-2-24 (sustainable development); § 2R-2-33 (water source) §§ 3R-2-01 to 3R-2-05 (protection of minimum flows or levels).

Comparable statutes: ARK. CODE ANN. §15-22-202(6) (D); GA. CODE ANN. § 12-5-96(d)(3); MISS. CODE ANN. § 51-3-7(4); VA. CODE ANN. § 62.1-243; WIS. STAT. ANN. § 144.026(5)(e)(6).

§ 2R-2-04 COMPREHENSIVE WATER ALLOCATION PLAN

A "comprehensive water allocation plan" is a plan developed by the State Agency for the intermediate and long-term protection, conservation, augmentation, and management of all the water of the State and is designed to promote and secure the sustainable development and reasonable use of the waters of the State taking into account economic, environmental, and other social values.

Commentary: Many states now require comprehensive planning as a necessary precondition to any effective regulation of the use of the waters of the State. Such planning seeks to define the public interest in the waters of the State and to determine the data necessary for decision making to achieve the public interest and the sustainable development of the waters of the State. This section defines the comprehensive water allocation plan as an intermediate- to long-term plan for the overall management of the waters of the entire State. States opting for the Special Water Management Area approach should consider whether those Areas as well as the State Agency should be required to develop intermediate- to long-term plans. *See* Dellapenna, §9.05(a).

Cross-references: § 1R-1-04 (comprehensive planning); § 2R-2-09 (drought management strategies); § 2R-2-18 (the public interest); § 2R-2-24 (sustainable development); § 2R-2-33 (the waters of the State); §§ 3R-2-01 to 3R-2-05 (protection of minimum flows or levels); §§ 4R-2-01 to 4R-2-04 (planning responsibilities); §§4R-4-01 to 4R-4-07 (Special Water Management Areas).

Comparable statutes: ALA. CODE § 9-10B-5(1); MASS. GEN. LAWS ANN. ch. 21g, § 2; N.Y. ENVTL. CONSERV. LAW §§ 15-0107(6), 15-1301(1).

§ 2R-2-05 CONSERVATION MEASURES

"Conservation measures" refers to any measures adopted by a water right holder, or several water right holders acting in concert pursuant to an approved conservation agreement under section 7R-3-05, to reduce the withdrawals or consumptive uses, or both, associated with the exercise of a water right, including, but not limited to:

(a) improvements in water transmission and water use efficiency;

(b) reduction in water use;

(c) enhancement of return flows; and

(d) reuse of return flows.

Commentary: Sustainable development requires steps to conserve the waters of the State. This definition limits the application of the term "conservation measures" to practices relating to a water right by the holder of the right, an important aspect of conservation for which special provision is made in this Regulated Riparian Model Water Code. Specifically excluded from this definition are practices applied to native or naturally occurring waters, return flows from other water rights, or other water sources not associated with the water right holder or sought by the applicant. These exclusions are designed to prevent someone from evading the regulatory and managerial responsibilities of the State Agency through actions not taken under their own permit and thus subject to the terms and conditions of that permit. For example, a person not holding a water right is not permitted to eradicate phreatophytes along a stream and claim the resulting reduction in water consumption as a conservation measure entitling that person to any rights to the water saved. In addition, a person would not be able to develop runoff from an upland irrigator under the guise of water conservation except by procuring a permit pursuant to this Code for such development or pursuant to an agreement with the other water right holder under section 7R-3-06(3), (4). Persons who claim to be conserving water other than their own use under a permit are required to seek a permit for such water (and the practices said to develop or conserve that water) just like anyone else seeking to initiate a new use of water. *See* Robert Beck, *The Uses of and Demands for Water, in* 1 WATERS AND WATER RIGHTS § 2.02; SAX, ABRAMS, & THOMPSON, at 14-15, 199-212, 688-92; TRELEASE & GOULD, at 66-70.

Nothing in this Code attempts to spell out in detail what steps might actually qualify as appropriate conservation measures. Such efforts as improved efficiency in manufacturing processes, the substitution of drip irrigation for sprinklers, or the introduction by a public water supply enterprise of requirement that customers use low flow toilets or showerheads would all be appropriate examples. The Code leaves the precise details regarding the suitability of these or other possible conservation measures to be developed by the regulatory and planning processes prescribed for the State Agency.

Cross-references: § 1R-1-10 (water conservation): §§ 2R-2-06 (consumptive use); § 2R-2-13 (nonconsumptive use); § 2R-2-17 (plan for conservation); § 2R-2-20 (reasonable use): § 2R-2-21 (safe yield); § 2R-2-23 (State Agency); § 2R-2-24 (sustainable development); § 2R-2-27 (waste of water); § 2R-2-29 (water emergency); §2R-2-31 (water shortage); § 2R-2-32 (waters of the State defined); § 4R-1-06 (regulatory authority of the State Agency); § 4R-2-01 (the comprehensive water allocation plan); § 4R-2-02 (drought management plans); § 6R-3-01 (standards for a permit); § 6R-3-02 (determining whether a use is reasonable); § 7R-1-01 (permit terms and conditions).

§ 2R-2-06 CONSUMPTIVE USE

> **A "consumptive use" is any use of water which is not a "nonconsumptive use" as defined in section 2R-2-13 of this Code, including, without being limited to, evaporation or the incorporation of the water into a product or crop.**

Commentary: A consumptive use is one that diminishes the quantity or quality of water in a water source. Excessive consumptive use impairs the sustainable development of a water source. By defining "consumptive use" as any use that is not a "nonconsumptive use," the Regulated Riparian Model Water Code resolves all instances of water use where the obligation to obtain a permit from the State Agency might be in doubt in favor of the permit obligation. *See* RICE & WHITE, at 147, 169; Robert Beck, *The Uses of and Demands for Water, in* 1 WATERS AND WATER RIGHTS § 2.01; Dellapenna, §§ 6.01(a)(4), 7.03(c).

Cross-references: § 2R-2-13 (nonconsumptive use); § 2R-2-20 (reasonable use); § 2R-2-21 (safe yield); § 2R-2-24 (sustainable development); 2R-2-33 (water source).

Comparable statutes: GA. CODE ANN. § 12-5-92(3); HAW. REV. STAT. § 174C-3 ("noninstream use"); N.J. STAT. ANN § 58:1A-3(b); N.C. GEN. STAT. §143-215.21(3); WIS. STAT. ANN. § 144.026(c).

§ 2R-2-07 COST

"Cost" means direct and indirect expenditures, commitments, and net induced adverse effects, whether compensated or not, incurred or occurring in connection with the establishment, acquisition, construction, maintenance, or operation of any facility or activity for which a permit is required by this Code.

Commentary: The Regulated Riparian Model Water Code uses the term "cost" in the sense of "opportunity costs," referring to the value of foregone opportunities made necessary by the project or activity for which the cost is to be determined. Opportunity costs include the actual out-of-pocket expenditures the necessary action or forbearance will entail, but also include the adverse effects on others regardless of whether those effects are compensated.

Cross-references: § 5R-2-03 (administrative resolution); § 6R-3-01 (standards for a permit); § 6R-3-02 (determining whether a use is reasonable).

§ 2R-2-08 DOMESTIC USE

A "domestic use" is a direct use of water for ordinary household purposes, including immediate human consumption (including sanitation and washing), the watering of animals held for personal use or consumption, and home gardens and lawns.

Commentary: The Regulated Riparian Model Water Code provides preferences to domestic use based on the fact that such uses involve a person taking water directly from a water source for uses that are immediately necessary for human health and safety and on the supposition that such uses, even in the aggregate, place relatively small demands on the waters of the State. Note that "domestic use" refers only to direct use from a water source, and does not include water that a user either buys from a delivery system or holds for sale to others. This section provides a standard definition of "domestic use" clarified to exclude general or commercial activities. As domestic uses are given a preferred status, it is inappropriate for commercial activities, such as large-scale animal husbandry, to be classified as a domestic use. In watering animals, only the water consumed by household pets or the few animals held for the personal needs of the members of the household qualify as a domestic use of water. For the common law antecedents of the concept of "domestic use," see Dellapenna, § 7.02(b)(1). For the preferences accorded domestic uses in regulated riparian codes, see Dellapenna, § 9.03(a)(3).

Cross-references: § 3R-1-03 (small water sources exempted from allocation); § 6R-1-02 (small withdrawals exempted from the permit requirement); § 6R-3-01 (standards for a permit); § 6R-3-02 (determining whether a use is reasonable); § 6R-3-04 (preferences among water rights).

Comparable statutes: ARK. CODE ANN. § 15-22-202(5); FLA. STAT. ANN. § 373.019(6); HAW. REV. STAT. § 174C-3; IND. CODE ANN. § 13-2-1-3(1); KY. REV. STAT. ANN. § 151.100(9); MISS. CODE ANN. § 51-3-3(c); S.C. CODE ANN. § 49-5-30(6).

§ 2R-2-09 DROUGHT MANAGEMENT STRATEGIES

> **"Drought management strategies" are plans devised by the State Agency pursuant to this Code for the allocation of water during periods of drought and otherwise to cope with water shortages or water emergencies and, in so far as is reasonably possible, to restore the waters of the State to their condition prior to the drought.**

Commentary: A "drought management strategy" is a specific course of conduct planned by the State Agency as a necessary or appropriate response to a water shortage or a water emergency. Generally such shortages or emergencies will arise from a drought, but they could arise from other causes as well, such as the collapse of a dam with the resulting draining of a reservoir on which a group of users depend. The strategies shall relate to possible revisions of water allocations made necessary by the shortage or emergency or to steps to conserve or restore water generally, all within a framework shaped by the pervasive goal of sustainable development. Strategies can be planned to apply either to a part of, or to all of, the State. For analysis of the drought-response patterns found in existing regulated riparian statutes, see Dellapenna, § 9.05(a), (d). *See also* SAX, ABRAMS, & THOMPSON, at 127-128.

The term "drought management strategies" reflects the focus of the Regulated Riparian Model Water Code on water allocation only. In states where the State Agency is also given responsibility for water quality, flood control, and other non-allocational issues, the term should be "water shortage and water emergency strategies," with the definition suitably revised and renumbered. The definition of "water emergency" should also be revised to reflect these broader concerns.

Cross-references: § 2R-2-24 (sustainable development); § 2R-2-29 (water emergency); § 2R-2-31 (water shortage); §§ 4R-2-01 to 4R-2-04 (planning responsibilities); §§ 7R-3-01 to 7R-3-07 (restrictions during water shortages or water emergencies).

§ 2R-2-10 INTERBASIN TRANSFER

An "interbasin transfer" is any transfer of water, for any purpose and regardless of the quantity involved, from one water basin to another.

Commentary: This definition merely makes clear that the term "interbasin transfer" is not limited in any fashion but refers to all transfers from one water basin to another. The provisions regarding interbasin transfers allow regulations to exempt certain small transfers.

Cross-references: § 1R-1-12 (recognizing local interests in the waters of the State); § 2R-1-02 (no prohibition of use based on location of use); § 2-3-28 (water basin defined); § 6R-3-01 (standards for a permit); § 6R-3-02 (determining whether a use is reasonable); § 6R-3-06 (special standard for interbasin transfers); § 7R-1-01(k) (payment into the Interbasin Compensation Fund); §§ 8R-1-01 to 8R-1-06 (multijurisdictional transfers).

Comparable statute: CONN. GEN. STAT. ANN. § 22a-367(5).

§ 2R-2-11 MODIFICATION OF A WATER RIGHT

A "modification of a water right" is any change in the terms and conditions of a permit, whether voluntary or involuntary on the part of the permit holder, including, without being limited to:

- **(a) exchanges of water rights; or**
- **(b) changes in:**
  - **(1) the holder of the permit,**
  - **(2) the type, place, or time of use,**
  - **(3) the point or means of withdrawal,**
  - **(4) the place or manner of storage or application, or**
  - **(5) the point of return flow, or**
  - **(6) any combination of such changes.**

Commentary: The term "modification of a water right" includes water reallocation as well as other changes in water rights. "Modifications" can be either voluntary or involuntary changes. In short, a modification amounts to a reallocation of the water. A voluntary modification typically involves the sale of the water right to another user. Examples of involuntary transfers include those arising on the death of a permit holder or the enforcement of creditors' rights. "Modifications" do not include involuntary losses of water rights, such as forfeitures or revocations, imposed by this Model Water Code. *See* Dellapenna, §§ 7.04, 9.03(d).

Cross-references: § 1R-1-07 (flexibility through the modification of water rights); §§ 7R-2-01 (approval required for modification of permits); § 7R-2-02 (approval of non-injurious modifications).

Comparable statute: HAW. REV. STAT. § 174C-3 ("change of use").

§ 2R-2-12 MUNICIPAL USES

> **"Municipal uses" are uses of water by a publicly or privately-owned public water supply system for the life, safety, health, and comfort of the inhabitants thereof and nonindustrial businesses serving those needs.**

Commentary: This definition indicates that the term "municipal uses" refers to all needs of inhabitants or customers of a municipal or public water supply system except for industrial uses. The Regulated Riparian Model Water Code gives a preference for municipal uses similar to the preferences for domestic uses. This preference should be limited to uses that are comparable to domestic uses. Industrial uses, however supplied, are relatively less preferred than either domestic or municipal uses as defined in this Code. The term "nonindustrial business uses" is not defined in this Code, leaving that task to regulations to be adopted by the State Agency. The point of the distinction is between the large-scale industrial users that are not so immediately tied to the life, safety, health, and comfort of the inhabitants of the municipality on the one hand, and the needs of the generally smaller scale non-industrial businesses that serve the pressing needs of the inhabitants of their communities on the other. *See* Dellapenna, §§ 7.05(c), 9.03(a)(3).

Cross-references: § 2R-2-08 (domestic use); § 2R-2-19 (public water supply system); § 6R-3-01 (standards for a permit); § 6R-3-02 (determining whether a use is reasonable); § 6R-3-04 (preferences among water rights).

Comparable statutes: HAW. REV. STAT. § 174C-3; MISS. CODE ANN. § 51-3-3(d).

§ 2R-2-13 NONCONSUMPTIVE USE

> **A "nonconsumptive use" is a use of water withdrawn from the waters of the State in such a manner that it is returned to its waters of origin at or near its point of origin without substantial diminution in quality or quantity and without resulting in or exacerbating a low flow condition.**

Commentary: Nonconsumptive uses of water do not require a permit under the Regulated Riparian Model Water Code. Such uses are defined here as including only uses that have no substantial effect on the quantity or quality of the water in the water source. The State Agency will define what constitutes a "substantial diminution" through its regulations. "Nonconsumptive uses" will include only non-polluting uses that are either instream or inground or provide a near complete return flow at or near the point of withdrawal without significant changes in quality. All other uses are considered consumptive and require a permit unless otherwise exempted under this Code. RICE & WHITE, at 176; Dellapenna, §§ 6.01(a)(3), 7.03(b).

Cross-references: §1R-1-09 (coordination of water allocation and water quality regulation); § 2R-2-06 (consumptive use): § 2R-2-20 (reasonable use); § 2R-2-21 (safe yield); § 2R-2-24 (sustainable development); §§ 6R-4-01 to 6R-4-05 (coordinating water allocation and water quality regulation).

Comparable statutes: GA. CODE ANN. § 12-5-92(7); HAW. REV. STAT. §174C-3 ("instream use"); MASS. GEN. LAWS ANN. ch 21G, § 2; N.J. STAT. ANN. § 58:1A-3(e); N.C. GEN. STAT. § 143-215.21(5); VA. CODE ANN. § 62.1-242

§ 2R-2-14 PERMIT

> **A "permit" under this Code means a written authorization issued by the State Agency to a person entitling that person to hold and exercise a water right involving the withdrawal of a specific quantity of water at a specific time and place for a specific reasonable use as described in the written authorization.**

Commentary: The introduction of the requirement of a permit for withdrawals is the central operative feature of the Regulated Riparian Model Water Code. This definition describes the concept of a "permit" in general terms that are fleshed out in detail in Chapters 6 and 7 of this Code. *See* Dellapenna, § 9.03(a). *See also* MALONEY, AUSNESS, & MORRIS, §§ 2.01-2.09; SAX, ABRAMS, & THOMPSON, at 128-34; TARLOCK, CORBRIDGE, & GETCHES, at 104-21; TRELEASE & GOULD, at 342-53; WILLIAM WALKER & PHYLLIS BRIDGEMAN, A WATER CODE FOR VIRGINIA §§ 2.01-2.08 (Va. Polytech. Inst., Va. Water Resources Res. Center Bull. No. 147, 1985). While the withdrawal of water triggers the permit requirement, the permit itself focuses on whether the withdrawal will result in the consumptive use of water. Certain small users who are in principle subject to the permit requirement are exempted by specific provisions of the Code.

Cross-references: § 1R-1-01 (protecting the public interest in the waters of the State); §§ 6R-1-01 to 6R-1-05 (the requirement of a permit); § 2R-2-06 (consumptive use); § 2R-2-34 (withdrawal or to withdraw); § 3R-2-03 (small water sources exempted from allocation); § 6R-1-06 (registration of withdrawals not subject to permits); §§ 6R-2-01 to 6R-2-08 (permit procedures); §§ 6R-3-01 to 6R-3-05 (the basis of the water right); §§ 6R-4-01 to 6R-4-05 (coordination of water allocation and water quality regulation); § 7R-1-01 (permit terms and conditions).

Comparable statutes: ALA. CODE § 9-10B-3(4) ("certificate of use"); IOWA CODE ANN. § 455B.261(10); MASS. GEN. LAWS ANN. ch. 21G, § 2; VA. CODE ANN. § 62.1-242; VA. CODE ANN. § 62.1-44.85(10).

§ 2R-2-15 PERSON

"Person" includes an individual, a partnership, a corporation, a municipality, a State (including this State), the United States, an interstate or international organization, or any other legal entity, public or private.

Commentary: The definition of "person" includes all persons known to the law, natural and artificial.

Comparable statutes: ALA. CODE § 9-10B-3(14); ARK. CODE ANN. § 15-22-202(8): CONN. GEN. STAT. ANN. § 22a-367(7); DEL. CODE ANN. tit. 7, § 6002(15); FLA. STAT. ANN. § 373.019(5); GA. CODE ANN §§ 12-5-22(7), 12-5-92(8); HAW. REV. STAT. § 174C-3: ILL. COMP. STAT. ANN. ch. 525, § 45/4(e); IND. CODE ANN. §§ 13-2-1-4(5), 13-2-2.5-2, 13-2-2.6-7, 13-2-6.1-1; KY. REV. STAT. ANN. § 151.100(13); MD. CODE ANN., NAT. RES. § 8-101(h); MASS. GEN. LAWS ANN. ch. 21G, § 2; MISS. CODE ANN. § 51-3-3(a); N.J. STAT. ANN. § 58:1A-3(f); N.Y. ENVTL. CONSERV. LAW § 15-0107(1); S.C. CODE ANN. § 49-5-30(3); VA. CODE ANN. § 62.1-44.85(11); WIS. STAT. ANN. §§ 144.01(9m), 144.026(i).

§ 2R-2-16 PHYSICAL INTEGRITY

The "physical integrity" of a water source means the volume of water necessary to:

(a) support commercial navigation of the water source as required by federal or State law or regulation;

(b) preserve natural, cultural, or historic resources as determined by or as required by federal and State law or regulation;

(c) provide adequate recreational opportunities to the people of the State; and

(d) prevent serious depletion or exhaustion of the water source.

Commentary: Water is used in-place for a range of important human uses, uses that will often be incompatible with the withdrawal of water from the water source. Sustainable development requires respect for and protection of the physical integrity of water sources. As with biological and chemical integrity, this term comes from the Clean Water Act where it is one of the three fundamental criteria for setting effluent standards, although the Clean Water Act does not express its mandate in terms of "integrity." 33 U.S.C. § 1314(b). This approach is taken in order to provide a measure of certainty to the otherwise vague standards proposed to define minimum flows or levels. The definition does not limit itself exclusively to protecting physical integrity as defined by other relevant laws and regulations, but introduces two additional restraints: the provision of adequate recreational opportunities and the prevention of serious depletion or exhaustion of the water source. These latter standards are not precisely defined but are to be informed by the policies of the Code and the limitations of the public interest as defined in this Code. This section describes those uses in general terms and defines the physical integrity of the water source in terms of the water necessary for those uses. *See generally* Hal Beecher, *Standards for Instream Flows*, 1 RIVERS 97 (1990); Dellapenna, § 9.05(b).

Cross-references: § 1R-1-09 (coordination of water allocation and water quality regulation); § 1R-1-11 (preservation of minimum flows and levels); § 2R-2-02 (biological integrity); § 2R-2-03 (chemical integrity); § 2R-2-18 (the public interest); § 2R-2-21 (safe yield); § 2R-2-24 (sustainable development); § 2R-2-33 (water source); §§ 3R-2-01 to 3R-2-05 (protection of minimum flows or levels).

Comparable statutes: ARK. CODE ANN. §§ 15-202(6)(B), 15-22-301(11); GA. CODE ANN. § 12-5-96(d)(3); IOWA CODE ANN. § 455B.267(3); MASS. GEN. LAWS ANN. ch. 21G, § 7(3), 11; MINN. STAT. ANN. § 105.417(2), (3); MISS. CODE ANN. § 51-3-7(5); VA. CODE ANN. §§ 62.1-246(1), 62.1-248(A).

§ 2R-2-17 PLAN FOR CONSERVATION

> **A "plan for conservation" is a detailed plan describing and quantifying the amount and use of water to be developed by conservation measures in the exercise of a water right.**

Commentary: A plan for conservation provides a basis for the State Agency to appraise the conservation measures that a permit applicant is committing to undertake or to determine the amount of water developed by conservation measures and the means necessary to enable the developer to use the water without unreasonable injury to other water right holders. The items to be included in the plan are intentionally left vague to allow innovative and imaginative formulations of plans for conservation. This definition is patterned after Colorado's provision of Plans for Augmentation which are intended to provide increased flexibility in the use of water rights.

Cross-references: § 1R-1-10 (water conservation); § 2R-2-05 (conservation measures); § 2R-2-21 (safe yield); § 2R-2-24 (sustainable development); § 6R-2-01 (the contents of an application for a permit); § 6R-3-01 (standards for a permit).

Comparable statute: GA. CODE ANN. §§ 12-5-31(d), 12-5-96(a)(2).

§ 2R-2-18 THE PUBLIC INTEREST

The "public interest" is any interest in the waters of the State or in water usage within the State shared by the people of the State as a whole and capable of protection or regulation by law, as informed by the policies and mandates of this Code.

Commentary: The drafters of the Regulated Riparian Model Water Code undertook to define "the public interest" with some trepidation as this phrase is invoked in innumerable contexts and with highly variable meanings. It is probably the most elastic term used by jurists, lawyers, and politicians when talking about water or any other topic. As the term is used in the Code, it is too important not to attempt some definition, yet any definition must not become a strait jacket that artificially restricts the range of concerns that a court or the State Agency can take into account when interpreting and applying this Code. We believe the foregoing definition achieves those goals.

Generally, "the public interest" will center on, but not be limited to, the pervasive goal of sustainable development. The definition of "the public interest" offered here seeks to impose only two minimal restraints on the broad range of arguments that can be marshaled regarding the public interest generally and sustainable development in particular: that the interests claimed be broadly shared by the State as a whole rather than reflecting only the narrow interests of some small segment of the community that is the State; and that the interests claimed be capable of protection or regulation by law. The Code goes on to remind potential interpreters that in seeking "the public interest" in the waters of the State, the State Agency, courts, and other interpreters are to be guided by the policies of this Code. In this regard, the overall policy of protecting "the public interest" in the waters of the State (section 1R-1-01) will often be the most important guide, but all of the policies in Chapter 1 will be relevant in suitable contexts. Nothing in these policies or in this definition of "the public interest" authorizes the disregard of an express mandate of this Code. Within these admittedly broad constraints, the interpretation and application of "the public interest" will require mature and sophisticated judgments and remain subject to considerable debate. A more specific catalogue of what concerns constitute "the public interest" is found in section 6R-3-02(c).

Cross-references: §§ 1R-1-01 to 1R-1-15 (declarations of policies); § 2R-2-24 (sustainable development); § 2R-2-32 (waters of the State); § 6R-3-02 (determining whether a use is reasonable).

§ 2R-2-19 PUBLIC WATER SUPPLY SYSTEM

(1) A "public water supply system" is a system for providing of piped water to the public for human consumption if the system has at least 15 service connections or regularly serves at least 25 individuals for their personal consumption daily for at least 60 days of the year.

(2) A "public water supply system" includes any collection, treatment, storage, and distribution facilities under control of the operator of the system and used primarily in connection with the system and any collection or pretreatment storage facilities used primarily in connection with the system regardless of who owns or controls such facilities.

Commentary: The Regulated Riparian Model Water Code provides preferences for municipal uses or other activities by public water supply systems. This definition of a "public water supply system" is taken from the federal Safe Drinking Water Act, 42 U.S.C. § 300(F)(4). The definition sets minimum standards regarding service connections or individuals served to qualify as a public water supply system, while indicating that the preferences apply to the full range of activities necessary to maintain the public supply. The definition includes privately-owned as well as publicly-owned systems. States considering enacting this Code might consider whether they would prefer to set the minimum standards lower than those expressed in subsection (1) of this section.

Any attempt to set those standards higher would prevent the State from complying with the federal standards mandated by the Safe Drinking Water Act. *See generally* Dellapenna, § 9.05(c).

Cross-references: § 2R-2-08 (domestic use); § 2R-2-12 (municipal uses); § 6R-3-01 (standards for a permit); § 6R-3-02 (determining whether a use is reasonable): § 6R-3-04 (preferences among water rights).

Comparable statutes: ALA. CODE § 9-10B-3(15); FLA. STAT. ANN. § 373.1962; MASS. GEN. LAWS ANN. ch. 21G, § 2; N.Y. ENVTL. CONSERV. LAW § 15-1301(2).

§ 2R-2-20 REASONABLE USE

> **"Reasonable use" means the use of water, whether in place or through withdrawal, in such quantity and manner as is necessary for economic and efficient utilization without waste of water, without unreasonable injury to other water right holders, and consistently with the public interest and sustainable development.**

Commentary: "Reasonable use" has long been the criterion of decision under the common law of riparian rights. In that setting, the concept was strictly relational, with the court deciding whether one use was "more reasonable" than a competing or interfering use, except in the rare case when a particular use was "unreasonable *per se*." *See generally Restatement (Second) of Torts* ch. 41 (1979; Dellapenna, §§ 7.02(d), 7.03. The Regulated Riparian Model Water Code defines "reasonable use" in rather more abstract terms relating to the manner in which water is used, but also retains the relational concept that a reasonable use is one that does not unreasonably injure other uses. See Dellapenna, § 9.03(b)(1). The framework of analysis of whether a particular use is reasonable will be dictated by the goal of sustainable development.

Generally the existing regulated riparian statutes do not attempt to define the term "reasonable use," perhaps believing that the term is incapable of definition. Several regulated riparian statutes use terms such as "equitable portion," "beneficial use," or "reasonable-beneficial use," but define those terms in language similar to the definition of "reasonable use" in this Code. Dellapenna, § 9.03(b)(2).

Cross-references: § 2R-2-18 (the public interest); § 2R-2-24 (sustainable development); § 5R-2-03 (administrative dispute resolution); § 6R-3-02 (determining whether a use is reasonable).

Comparable statutes: ALA. CODE § 9-10B-3(2) ("beneficial use"); DEL. CODE ANN. tit 7, § 6010(f)(1) ("equitable apportionment"); FLA. STAT. ANN. § 373.019(4) ("reasonable beneficial use"); HAW. REV. STAT. § 174C-3 ("reasonable-beneficial use"); ILL. COMP. STAT. ANN. ch 525, § 45/4(g); IND. CODE ANN. 13-2-6.1-1 ("reasonable-beneficial use"); IOWA CODE ANN. § 455B.261(7) ("beneficial use"); MISS. CODE ANN. § 51-3-3(e) ("beneficial use"); VA. CODE ANN. §§ 62.1-10(b), 62.1-242 ("beneficial use").

§ 2R-2-21 SAFE YIELD

(1) The "safe yield" of a water source is the amount of water available for withdrawal without impairing the long-term social utility of the water source, including the maintenance of the protected biological, chemical, and physical integrity of the source.

(2) "Safe yield" is determined by comparing the natural and artificial replenishment of the water source to existing or planned consumptive and nonconsumptive uses.

Commentary: The concept of "safe yield" is central to achieving the goal of sustainable development. The Regulated Riparian Model Water Code adopts a definition of "safe yield" that is not purely hydrologic, *i.e.*, that does not limit withdrawals under all circumstances to the average annual inflow into or recharge of the water source. Instead, the Code authorizes the

State Agency to determine the level of withdrawal that will not impair the long-term social utility of the water source, a somewhat less definite limitation, yet one that still serves to prohibit impairment of what ought to be, in the long-term, a renewable resource. As withdrawal in this Code includes controlled storage as well as actual removal from the water source, some withdrawals might actually increase the safe yield of a water source.

Often, perhaps usually, the State Agency will decide that the safe yield of a water source is no more than its natural rate of replenishment. The standard in this section, however, allows the Agency to consider human need as well as the physical characteristics of the water source and to authorize some depletion when appropriate so long as the Agency is not committed to the utter destruction of the water source. What does provide an absolute limit on the "safe yield" is the protection of the biological, chemical, and physical integrity of the water source. Analysis of the safe yield of a water source must take into account the nature of the withdrawal and use, its importance for human and other communities dependent on the water source, and the withdrawal's actual effects on the continuing yield of the water source. Some states might prefer to cast this definition simply in terms of annual inflow or recharge.

Cross-references: § 1R-1-10 (water conservation); § 2R-2-02 (biological integrity); § 2R-2-03 (chemical integrity); § 2R-2-06 (consumptive use); § 2R-2-05 (conservation measures); § 2R-2-13 (nonconsumptive use); § 2R-2-06 (consumptive use); § 2R-2-16 (physical integrity); § 2R-2-24 (sustainable development); § 2R-2-29 (water emergency): § 2R-2-31 (water shortage); § 2R-2-33 (water source); § 3R-2-01 (protected minimum flows or levels not to be allocated or withdrawn); § 3R-2-02 (standards for protected minimum flows or levels); § 3R-2-03 (effects of water shortages or water emergencies); § 4R-2-01 (the comprehensive water allocation plan); § 6R-1-03 (existing withdrawals); § 6R-3-01 (standards for a permit).

Comparable statutes: HAW. REV. STAT. § 174C-3; MASS. GEN. LAWS ANN. ch. 21G, § 2.

§ 2R-2-22 SPECIAL WATER MANAGEMENT AREA *(optional)*

A "Special Water Management Area" is a form of an administration under which the waters of the State within a hydrogeographically defined region of the State are managed by an Area Water Board responsible for the waters within that region.

Commentary: This definition is necessary only in States that opt for dividing the active management of their waters among Special Water Management Areas. While the boundaries of the Areas are to be set by the State Agency according to the hydrological and other physical features defining the interrelations among water sources, the inclusion of geographic factors enables the State Agency also to consider the proper coordination of existing or foreseeable human activities in setting the boundaries of the Areas. The State Agency is to consider underground water as well as surface water sources (usually not including diffused surface and atmospheric water) in setting the boundaries of Water Management Areas. The details of this arrangement are set forth in Part 4 of Chapter IV of this Code. *See* Dellapenna, § 9.03(a)(5)(A); Susan B. Peterson, Note, *Designation and Protection of Critical Ground Water Areas*, 1991 B.Y.U. L. Rev. 1393.

Cross-references: § 1R-1-12 (recognizing local interests in the waters of the State); §§ 4R-4-01 to 4R-4-07 (Special Water Management Areas).

Comparable statutes: ALA. CODE § 9-10B-3(3); ARK. CODE ANN. § 15-22-221; FLA. STAT. ANN. § 373.019(2); HAW. REV. STAT. § 174C-3; VA. CODE ANN. § 62.1-242.

§ 2R-2-23 STATE AGENCY

The phrase "State Agency" refers to *[the State's water resources allocation administrative agency]*. The State Agency shall serve as the central unit of

the State's government for protecting, maintaining, improving, allocating, and planning regarding the waters of the State pursuant to this Code.

Commentary: The proper name of the agency selected in each State enacting this Regulated Riparian Model Water Code could be substituted for the term "State Agency" whenever that term appears in this Code. This definition could then be omitted or modified accordingly. The State Agency is the agency responsible at the level of statewide planning and activity; Special Water Management Areas (in States using them) are defined elsewhere.

Cross-references: §§ 4-R-1-01 to 5R-5-03 (the authority and responsibility of the State Agency).

§ 2R-2-24 SUSTAINABLE DEVELOPMENT

"Sustainable development" means the integrated management of resources taking seriously the needs of future generations as well as the current generation, assuring equitable access to resources, optimizing the use of non-renewable resources, and averting the exhaustion of renewable resources.

Commentary: The concept of "sustainable development" originated in the writings of economist Kenneth Boulding. *See* Kenneth Boulding, *The Economics of the Coming Spaceship Earth,* in RESOURCES FOR THE FUTURE: ENVIRONMENTAL QUALITY IN A GROWING ECONOMY 3 (Henry Jarrett ed. 1966). A national and international consensus has emerged over the past several decades that "sustainable development" is the proper criterion for combining the exploitation of resources with the protection of the environment. *See The Rio Declaration on Environment and Development,* U.N. Doc. A/CONF.151/5/Rev. 1 (1992); MICHAEL CARLEY & IAN CHRISTIE, MANAGING SUSTAINABLE DEVELOPMENT (1993); RENE DUBOS & BARBARA WARD, ONLY ONE EARTH:

THE CARE AND MAINTENANCE OF A SMALL PLANET (1972); GREENING INTERNATIONAL LAW (Philippe Sands ed. 1994); MAKING DEVELOPMENT SUSTAINABLE: REDEFINING INSTITUTIONS, POLICY, AND ECONOMICS (John Holmberg ed. 1992); DAVID PEARCE & R. KERRY TURNER, ECONOMICS OF NATURAL RESOURCES AND THE ENVIRONMENT (1990); WORLD COMM'N ON ENVIRONMENT & DEVELOPMENT, OUR COMMON FUTURE (1987) ("The Bruntland Report"); John Batt & David Short, *The Jurisprudence of the 1992 Rio Declaration on Environment and Development: A Law, Science, and Policy Explication of Certain Aspects of the United Nations Conference on Environment and Development,* 8 J. NAT. RESOURCES & ENVTL. L. 229 (1993); Yacov Haimes, *Sustainable Development: A Holistic Approach to Natural Resources Management,* 17 WATER INT'L 187 (1992); Eric Plate, *Sustainable Development of Water Resources: A Challenge to Science and Engineering,* 18 WATER INT'L 84 (1993); Mukul Sanwal, *Sustainable Development, the Rio Declaration and Multilateral Cooperation,* 4 COLO. J. INT'L ENVTL. L.& POL'Y 45 (1994); Ismaeil Serageldin, *Water Resources Management: A New Policy for a Sustainable Future,* 20 WATER INT'L 15 (1995); Symposium, *The Promise and Challenge of Ecologically Sustainable Development,* 31 WILLAMETTE L. REV. 235 (1995); Jonathan Baert Wiener, *Review Essay: Law and the New Ecology: Evolution, Categories, and Consequences,* 22 ECOL. L.Q. 325 (1995).

No goal is more important that achieving sustainable development of the water resource. That the resource is finite and that demand is approaching or exceeding the available supply requires that sustainability become the pervasive criterion of both public and private water management. *See* Editorial, *Sustainable Development Will Foster Hydro-Solutions,* U.S. WATER NEWS, June, 1996, at 6. To achieve sustainability will require decisions regarding the conservation of water and steps to limit the use of water to uses that do not permanently impair the biological, physical, and chemical integrity of the resource. This concept was always implicit in the law of riparian rights, for the riparian right to use water has always been characterized as a "usufructory" right. The word "usufructory" combines Latin words that expressed two of the three defining characteristics of complete ownership: *usus, fructus,* and *abusus.* The right to the use of the water and to the fruits of that use simply never included the right to waste or destroy the resource. *One River Plaza Condo. Ass'n v. Mitchell,* 609 So. 2d 942, 946 (La. App.), *writ denied,* 612 So. 2d 81 (La. 1993).

The definition offered in the Regulated Riparian Model Water Code must remain a highly fact-specific analysis of the proper uses of a particular resource in a particular setting. The basic notions captured in the phrase "sustainable development" include that the needs of future generations as well as the present generation must be taken into account in resource planning and use, that all persons should have equitable access to the resources they need, that therefore resources (whether renewable or not) ought not to be exhausted, and that resource management must take place in an integrated manner. In addition to the sources already cited in this commentary, see EDITH BROWN WEISS, IN FAIRNESS TO FUTURE GENERATIONS (1988); Angela Ciccolo, Note, *Environmental Responsibility under Severe Economic Constraints: Re-Examining the Lesotho Highlands Water Project,* 4 GEO. INT'L ENVTL. L. REV. 447 (1992); Alain de Janvry, Elizabeth Sadoulet, & Blas Santos, *Project Evaluation for Sustainable Development: Plan Sierra in the Dominican Republic,* 28 J. ENVTL. ECON. & MGT. 135 (1995); Giancarlo Marini & Pasquale Sacramozzino, *Overlapping Generations and Environmental Control,* 29 J. ENVTL. ECON. & MGT. 64 (1995). These are all policies expressed and developed in this Code. The concept of "sustainable development" is closely related to the precautionary principle discussed in the commentary to section 3.04. On the need for integrated management of water resources, see RICE & WHITE, at 1-11; TARLOCK, § 2.02; Peter Davis, *Wells and Streams: Relationship at Law,* 37 MO. L. REV. 189 (1972); Peter Fontaine, *EPA's Multimedia Enforcement Strategy: The Struggle to Close the Environmental Compliance Circle,* 18 COLUM. J. ENVTL. L. 31 (1993); Samuel Wiel, *Need of Unified Law for Surface and Underground Water,* 2 S. CAL. L. REV. 358 (1929).

In a very real sense, this entire Code is a structure for fostering "sustainable development." In managing water, "sustainable development" requires the maintenance of the biological, chemical, and physical integrity of a water source, the coordination of water allocation with the protection of water quality, and steps to cope with droughts and other water emergencies. Generally, "sustainable development" will also require the integrated management of water sources on a water basin basis and the limiting of withdrawals to the safe yield of the each water source.

Cross-references: § 1R-1-01 (protecting the public interest in the waters of the State); § 1R-1-02 (assuring efficient and productive use of water); § 1R-1-03 (conformity to physical law); § 1R-1-04 (comprehensive planning); § 1R-1-05 (efficient and equitable allocation during shortfalls in supply); § 1R-1-09 (coordination of water allocation and water quality regulation); § 1R-1-10 (water conservation); § 1R-1-11 (preservation of minimum flows and levels); § 2R-1-01 (the obligation to make only reasonable use of water); § 2R-2-02 (biological integrity); § 2R-2-03 (chemical integrity); § 2R-2-04 (comprehensive water allocation plan); § 2R-2-05 (conservation measures); § 2R-2-06 (consumptive use); § 2R-2-09 (drought management strategies); § 2R-2-13 (nonconsumptive use); § 2R-2-16 (physical integrity); § 2R-2-17 (plan for conservation); § 2R-2-18 (the public interest); § 2R-2-20 (reasonable use); § 2R-2-21 (safe yield); § 2R-2-27 (waste of water); § 2R-2-29 (water emergency); § 2R-2-31 (water shortage); § 2R-2-32 (waters of the State); § 2R-2-33 (water source); §§ 3R-2-01 to 3R-2-05 (protection of minimum flows or levels); §§ 4R-2-01 to 4R-2-04 (planning responsibilities); §§ 4R-3-01 to 4R-3-05 (coordination with other branches or levels of government); §§ 6R-3-01 to 6R-3-06 (the basis of a water right); §§ 6R-4-01 to 6R-4-05 (coordination of water allocation and water quality regulation); § 7R-1-01 (permit terms and conditions); §§ 7R-3-01 to 7R-3-07 (restrictions during water shortages and water emergencies); § 8R-1-06 (regulation of uses made outside the State).

§ 2R-2-25 UNDERGROUND WATER

> **The term "underground water" means water found within zones of saturation beneath the ground, regardless of whether flowing through defined channels or percolating through the ground, and regardless of whether the result of natural or artificial recharge.**

Commentary: This definition of "underground water" includes all extractable forms of water in the ground, being equivalent to terms such as "ground water," "groundwater," or similar expressions. It excludes soil (capillary) moisture which might be drawn upon by plants but cannot practically be withdrawn by direct human activity. *See* RICE & WHITE, at 173. A somewhat more precise definition is found in the Illinois Water Use Act: water under the ground where the fluid pressure in the pore space is equal to or greater than atmospheric pressure. *See also* Dellapenna, § 6.04; Earl Finbar Murphy, *Quantitative Groundwater,* 3 WATERS AND WATER RIGHTS § 18.02.

Cross-reference: § 3R-1-01 (waters subject to allocation).

Comparable statutes: ALA. CODE § 9-10B-3(12); DEL. CODE ANN. tit. 7, § 6002(7); FLA. STAT. ANN. § 373.019(9); GA. CODE ANN. § 12-5-92(6); ILL. COMP. STAT. ANN. ch. 525, § 45/4(c); IND. CODE ANN. §§ 13-2-1-4(2), 13-2-2-1, 13-2-6.1-1; IOWA CODE ANN. § 455B.261(4); KY. REV. STAT. ANN. § 15.100(5); S.C. CODE ANN. §49-5-30(4); VA. CODE ANN. § 62.1-44.85(8).

§ 2R-2-26 UNREASONABLE INJURY

"Unreasonable injury" means an adverse material change in the quantity, quality, or timing of water available for any lawful use caused by any action taken by another person if:

(a) the social utility of the injured use is greater than the social utility of the action causing the injury; or

(b) the cost of avoiding or mitigating the injury is materially less than the costs imposed by the injury.

Commentary: Prevention of unreasonable injury to other water users is the standard by which the State Agency is to determine whether to reject, alter, or approve a modification of a water right, and how to resolve conflicts among water rights. The definition of "unreasonable injury" in the Regulated Riparian Model Water Code recapitulates the definition of unreasonable injury found in innumerable cases applying common law riparian rights. *See, e.g., Harris v. Brooks,* 283 S.W.2d 129 (Ark. 1955); *Three Lakes Ass'n v. Kessler,* 285 N.W.2d 303 (Mich. App. 1979);

Red River Rolling Mills v. Wright, 15 N.W. 167 (Minn. 1883). *See generally* RESTATEMENT (SECOND) OF TORTS § 850A (1977); Dellapenna, § 7.02(d)(2), (d)(3).

The Code incorporates the core of the common-law of riparian rights (and of some forms of the law of underground water) without necessarily accepting the particular details of the caselaw developed prior to the Code. The basic change introduced by the Code is that generally whether an injury is unreasonable will be determined by the State Agency rather than by a court. This not only means that the decision will be made by persons who better understand the hydrology of the dispute; it also means that, as the State Agency is charged with important and extensive responsibilities for gathering data and developing plans for water usage in the State, the persons making the decision are also likely to be better able to assess the competing social utilities of the two competing uses. As a result, the determination of whether an injury is unreasonable is likely to be somewhat more abstract than when the dispute is presented to a court. *See* Dellapenna, § 7.02(d)(1).

The basic notion is that an injury is unreasonable if the value or social utility of the prevailing use is less than the social value or utility of the impaired use. Another test is if the costs of avoiding or mitigating the injury through steps taken by those responsible for the action causing the injury would be less than the costs of the injury to the one responsible for the injured use. Often this second test will actually be a particular application of the first test of relative social utility, but this will not always be so. Consistent with riparian theory generally, this Code takes the position not only that a less socially valuable use of water should not interfere with a more socially valuable use, but that no injury should be caused to another lawful use of water if the costs of avoiding that injury are materially less than the losses (costs) caused by the injury.

The concept of "unreasonable injury" does not include immaterial injuries. Nor does it include injuries caused by unreasonable actions of the permit holder complaining of injury. For example, lowering of a river stage that renders withdrawal more difficult for a permit holder with an inadequate withdrawal facility is not an unreasonable injury. This definition specifically includes affects on the timing of water availability as an injury to other water rights. The maintenance of the timing of water availability to other water rights prevents, for example, a water right holder from maintaining the total volume of annual return flow while altering the temporal distribution of the return flow so that water is not available for other water rights when they are entitled to withdraw water under a permit. If no specific timing is set forth in the other permit, unreasonable injury would arise if the changes in use prevents the permit holder from withdrawing water as customary if that custom is reasonable. The application of the notion of unreasonable injury is further informed by the limited preferences among water users provided in this Code.

Cross-references: § 2R-1-03 (no unreasonable injury to other water rights); §§ 5R-2-01 to 5R-2-03 (dispute resolution); § 6R-3-01 (standards for a permit): § 6R-3-02 (determining whether a use is reasonable); § 6R-3-04 (preferences among water users); § 7R-2-01 (approval required for modification of permits).

§ 2R-2-27 WASTE OF WATER

> **"Waste of water" means causing, suffering, or permitting the consumption or use of the waters of the State for a purpose or in a manner that is not reasonable.**

Commentary: The Regulated Riparian Model Water Code adopts a broad definition of "waste of water" to enable the State Agency and the judiciary to regulate or otherwise deal with the waste of water in all of its myriad forms. "Waste of water" includes any use of water that is not reasonable. *See* Dellapenna, § 9.03(b). *See also* RICE & WHITE, at 2, 125; TARLOCK, § 5.16(3). Waste of water is one of the major impediments to assuring the sustainable development of the waters of the State.

Cross-references: § 1R-1-10 (water conservation); § 1R-1-11 (preservation of minimum flows and levels); § 2-R-2-01 (the obligation to make only reasonable use); § 2R-2-05 (conservation measures); § 2R-2-06 (consumptive use); § 2R-2-13 (nonconsumptive use); § 2R-2-17 (plan for conservation); § 2R-2-20 (reasonable use); § 2R-2-21 (safe yield); § 2R-2-24 (sustainable development); § 2R-2-29 (water emergency); § 2R-2-31 (water shortage); § 2R-2-32 (waters of the State); §§ 3R-1-01 to 3R-1-04 (waters subject to allocation); §§ 3R-2-01 to 3R-2-05 (protection of minimum flows or levels); §§ 4R-2-01 to 4R-2-04 (planning responsibilities); § 6R-3-01 (standards for a permit); § 6R-3-02 (determining whether a use is reasonable); § 7R-1-01 (permit terms and conditions); § 7R-1-03 (forfeiture of permits); § 7R-2-01 (approval required for modification of permits).

Comparable statutes: IND. CODE ANN. §§ 13-2-2-1, 13-2-2-10; IOWA CODE ANN. § 455B.261(12).

§ 2R-2-28 WATER BASIN

(1) **A "water basin" is an area of land from which all waters drain, on the surface or beneath the ground, to a common point.**

(2) **In any administrative or judicial proceeding pursuant to this Code, the water basin shall be measured at the lowest point relevant to the issue to be determined.**

Commentary: Often the most significant and most controversial withdrawals of surface or underground water are for uses outside the basin of origin. While the Regulated Riparian Model Water Code is designed to facilitate as well as to regulate such withdrawals, the importance and difficulty of the issues raised by any large-scale withdrawal out of the basin of origin has required the Code to develop special processes and standards dealing with such diversions. The Code has adopted a broad, hydrologic definition of a water basin, including underground water sources as well as water sources on the surface and limited only by the realization that the area included within a basin is not a fixed hydrologic reality but in fact varies with the scale and purpose of the analysis. For example, a proposal to withdraw water from the Mohawk River in upstate New York for use on the upper Hudson River basin is out of the basin if the complaining party would use the water lower down on the Mohawk but above its confluence with the Hudson. A complaint from someone lower down on the Hudson (below the confluence of the Mohawk), however, would not allow one to characterize the transfer as out of the basin. The Code indicates that the extent of a water basin is to be determined according to the scale necessary to resolve the specific issue under consideration. *See* Dellapenna, § 7.02(a)(2).

Cross-references: § 1R-1-03 (conformity to physical laws): § 1R-1-14 (regulating interbasin transfers); § 2R-1-02 (no prohibition of use based on location of use); § 2R-2-10 (interbasin transfer); § 4R-1-06 (regulatory authority of the State Agency); § 4R-2-01 (the comprehensive water allocation plan); § 4R-4-06 (regulatory authority of Special Water Management Areas); § 6R-3-01 (standards for a permit); § 6R-3-06 (special standard for interbasin transfers); § 7R-1-01(k) (payment into the Interbasin Compensation Fund); §§ 8R-1-01 to 8R-1-06 (multijurisdictional transfers).

Comparable statutes: FLA. STAT. ANN. § 373.403(9) ("drainage basin"), (12) ("watershed"); HAW. REV. STAT. § 174C-3 ("hydrologic unit"); IND. CODE ANN. § 13-2-1-4(6) ("watershed"); IOWA CODE ANN. § 455B.261(14) ("water basin"); KY. REV. STAT. ANN. § 151.100(8) ("watershed"); MINN. STAT. ANN. § 105.37(9) ("water basin").

§ 2R-2-29 WATER EMERGENCY

(1) A "water emergency" is a severe shortage of water relative to lawful demand such that restrictions taken under a declaration of water shortage are insufficient to protect public health, safety, and welfare in all or any part of the State.

(2) A "water emergency" is recognized in law only as declared by the State Agency.

Commentary: The authority of the State Agency to cope with water emergencies is very broad and extends to the suspension or alteration of any water right. The Regulated Riparian Model Water Code defines a "water emergency" as a severe shortage demanding the most extreme measures to protect the public health, safety, or welfare. The State Agency might properly find such a condition to exist in all or only part of the State. The procedures for planning for, declaring, and responding to a water emergency are set out in detail elsewhere in this Code. *See generally* Dellapenna, § 9.05(d). As with the term "drought management strategies," this definition reflects the exclusive focus of the Code on water allocation issues. Should the State Agency be given responsibility for water quality, flood control, and other non-allocational issues, the definition of "water emergency" should be revised to reflect these broader concerns.

Cross-references: § 1R-1-05 (equitable sharing during shortfalls in supply); § 2R-2-24 (sustainable development); § 2R-2-31 (water shortage); § 3R-2-03 (effects of water shortages or water emergencies); §§ 7R-3-01 to 7R-3-07 (restrictions during water shortages or water emergencies).

Comparable statute: HAW. REV. STAT. § 174C-3.

§ 2R-2-30 WATER RIGHT

> **A "water right" is a right to withdraw a certain portion of the waters of the State in compliance with the provisions of this Code, whether subject to a permit or otherwise.**

Commentary: This definition is adapted from COLO. REV. STAT. ANN. § 37-92-103(2). Holders of water rights have a usufructory property interest, but do not own the corpus of the water to which their right pertains. *See Tyler v. Wilkinson,* 24 F. Cas. 472 (D. R.I. 1827) (No. 14,312); *Hargrave v. Cook,* 41 P. 18 (Cal. 1895); *Clark v. Lindsey Light Co.,* 89 N.E.2d 900 (1950); *One River Place Condominium Assoc. V. Mitchell,* 609 So. 2d 942 (La. App.), *cert. denied,* 612 So.

2d 81 (La. 1993); *Pratt v. Dep't of Natural Resources,* 309 N.W.2d 767 (Minn. 1981); Dellapenna, §§ 7.02, 7.02(a). *See also* RICE & WHITE, at 1, 35-38; TARLOCK, § 3.04. Some persons will use water without withdrawing it. Examples would be commercial or recreational navigation or similar activities. Such persons do not have a water right under this Code. Their interests are to be protected by the Code's protection of minimum flows and levels.

Cross-references: §§ 3R-2-01 to 3R-2-05 (protection of minimum levels and flows); §§ 6R-1-01 to 6R-1-04 (the requirement of a permit); §§ 7R-1-01 to 7R-3-07 (scope of the water right) ; § 9R-2-05 (water rights derived from atmospheric management).

§ 2R-2-31 WATER SHORTAGE

(1) A "water shortage" is a condition, in all or any part of the State, where, because of droughts or otherwise, the available water falls so far below normally occurring quantities that substantial conflict among water users or injury to water resources are expected to occur.

(2) A "water shortage" is recognized in law only as declared by the State Agency.

Commentary: The Regulated Riparian Model Water Code adopts several strategies for coping with situations where the available water from some or all water sources within the State falls below normal levels creating a likelihood of conflict among water users who would normally be able to coexist without interference with each other, or if the shortfall otherwise injures the water resources of the State. Without such strategies, there can be no hope of achieving the sustainable development of the waters of the State. These strategies and the procedures to be followed in planning and implementing those strategies, including in declaring a water shortage in all or part of the State, are set out elsewhere in this Code. *See* Dellapenna, § 9.05(d).

Cross-references: § 1R-1-05 (efficient and equitable allocation during shortfalls in supply); § 2R-2-24 (sustainable development); § 2R-2-29 (water emergency); § 2R-2-32 (waters of the State); § 3R-2-03 (effects of water shortages or water emergencies); §§ 7R-3-01 to 7R-3-07 (restrictions during water shortages or water emergencies).

§ 2R-2-32 WATERS OF THE STATE

> **The "waters of the State" include all waters, on the surface, under the ground, and in the atmosphere, wholly within or bordering the State or within the jurisdiction of the State.**

Commentary: The Regulated Riparian Model Water Code adopts a definition of the waters of the State that includes water through all phases of the hydrologic cycle. The policy of conforming the interpretation and application of this Code to physical laws will guide the State Agency in its interpretation of the consequences of this broad definition and should preclude the Agency from attempting to regulate any aspects of the hydrologic cycle when in fact that aspect cannot be regulated practically, or cannot be regulated without infringing upon the legal rights of other States. *See* Dellapenna, § 9.03(a)(1). *See also* MALONEY, AUSNESS, & MORRIS, at 4, 88.

Cross-reference: §§ 3R-1-01 to 3R-1-03 (waters subject to allocation); § 3R-2-01 (protected minimum flows or levels not to be allocated or withdrawn).

Comparable statutes: ALA. CODE § 9-10B-3(19); CONN. GEN. STAT. ANN. § 22a-367(8); FLA. STAT. ANN. § 373.019(8); GA. CODE ANN. § 12-5-22(13); HAW. REV. STAT. § 174C-3; IND. CODE ANN. §§ 13-2-1-2, 13-2-6.1-1; IOWA CODE ANN. § 455B.264(1); KY. REV. STAT. ANN. § 151.120; MD. CODE ANN., NAT. RES. § 8-101(k); MASS. GEN. LAWS ANN. ch. 21G, § 2; MINN. STAT. ANN. § 105.37(7); MISS. CODE ANN. § 51-1-4; N.J. STAT. ANN. § 58:1A-3(g); N.Y. ENVTL. CONSERV. LAW § 15-0107(4); VA. CODE ANN. § 62.1-1-(a); WIS. STAT. ANN. § 144.01(19).

§ 2R-2-33 WATER SOURCE

A "water source" includes any lake, pond, river, stream, creek, run, spring, other water flowing or lying on or under the surface, or contained within an aquifer, or found within the atmosphere regardless of the quantity of water or its duration.

Commentary: As the Regulated Riparian Model Water Code extends the State Agency's regulatory authority to water sources within the State, this term is here defined to reach all waters found within the State regardless of the form, quantity, or duration of that water. Exemptions of some water sources from certain or all regulations are found elsewhere in this Code and might be provided by appropriate regulations made by the State Agency pursuant to this Code. *See* Robert Beck, *The Water Resources Defined and Described,* in WATERS AND WATER RIGHTS, §§ 1.02, 1.03; Dellapenna, §§ 6.02, 9.03(a)(1).

Cross-references: § 2R-2-01 (atmospheric water management or weather modification); § 2R-2-24 (sustainable development); §§ 3R-1-01 to 3R-1-04 (waters subject to allocation); § 4R-1-06 (regulatory authority of the State Agency).

Comparable statutes: HAW. REV. STAT. § 174C-3; MASS. GEN. LAWS ANN. ch. 21G, § 2.

§ 2R-2-34 WITHDRAWAL OR TO WITHDRAW

A "withdrawal" is the removal of surface or underground water from its natural course or location, or exercising physical control over surface or underground water in its natural course or location, by any means whatsoever, regardless of whether the water is returned to its waters of

origin, consumed, or discharged elsewhere. "To withdraw" is the activity of making a withdrawal.

Commentary: The "withdrawal" to which this term refers is a withdrawal of water from the course of its natural flow or percolation. Thus a dam is as much a "withdrawal" of water as a pumping station for a municipal water works. This definition also makes clear that the terms "withdrawal" and "withdraw" refer to the gross withdrawals of water from a source and not to net withdrawals. *See* Robert Beck, *The Uses and Demands for Water,* in WATERS AND WATER RIGHTS § 2.01.

Cross-references: § 3R-2-01 (protected minimum flows or levels not to be allocated or withdrawn); §§ 6R-1-01 to 6R-1-05 (the requirement of a permit).

Comparable statutes: CONN. GEN. STAT. ANN. § 22a-367(2), (3); GA. CODE ANN. § 12-5-31(b)(2), (6); HAW. REV. STAT. § 174C-3; IND. CODE ANN. § 13-2-6.1-1; KY. REV. STAT. ANN. § 151.100(11); MASS. GEN. LAWS ANN. ch. 21G, § 2; WIS. STAT. ANN. § 144.026(m).

Part 3
Transitional Provisions

This Chapter provides the usual, and basic, provisions necessary for the transition from a prior legal regime to the regime created under this Regulated Riparian Model Water Code.

§ 2R-3-01 PRIOR LAWS REPEALED

The following statutes are repealed on the effective date of the Code:

. . .

Commentary: The enactment of any law implicitly repeals, in whole or in part, all inconsistent prior laws. Which prior laws are so affected may remain unclear until there is extended litigation. This section will list the statutes to be repealed upon the enactment of this comprehensive Code. Although a listing like this will not entirely preclude later questions about implicit repeal, it should alleviate the problem.

Comparable statutes: FLA. STAT. ANN. § 373.217; MD. NAT. RESOURCES CODE ANN. § 8-801(2) (no repeal of other laws).

§ 2R-3-02 CONTINUATION OF PRIOR ORDERS, PERMITS, RULES, AND REGULATIONS

(1) Upon the effective date of this Code, all prior inconsistent orders, rules, and regulations are repealed.

(2) Prior consistent orders, rules, and regulations, even if made pursuant to any statute repealed by this Code, shall remain in effect according to their terms or until superseded by new orders, rules, or regulations made pursuant to this Code.

(3) All prior permits shall remain in effect under this Code only until replacement permits are issued, and shall remain in effect for that period even though the prior permit was issued pursuant to a statute repealed by this Code.

(4) A replacement permit issued under this Code may contain such permit terms and conditions as are consistent with this Code regardless of whether those terms or conditions are consistent with the terms or conditions of the prior permit.

Commentary: The Regulated Riparian Model Water Code seeks to provide continuity in the transition to the new body of law by preserving all prior juridical acts taken under the laws repealed by this Code until such time as the State Agency reviews the juridical act in question and takes appropriate steps to replace it by acting under the Agency's authority as conferred by this Code. The preservation of the validity of prior juridical acts does not extend to orders, rules or regulations that are inconsistent with this Code.

Subsections (3) and (4) provide prior permits remain in effect until a replacement permit is issued. These subsections also provide that the existence of an unexpired term for a prior permit does not preclude the issuance of a new permit including conditions as provided in this Code even if the new conditions are inconsistent with the terms or conditions of the prior permit. These two subsections are to be omitted in a state that has not had water use permits prior to enactment of this Code.

Cross-references: § 4R-1-06 (regulatory authority of the State Agency); §4R-4-06 (regulatory authority of Special Water Management Areas); § 6R-1-01 (withdrawals unlawful without a permit).

Comparable statutes: FLA. STAT. ANN. § 373.224, 373.249; MISS. CODE ANN. §51-3-5(2) to (5); N.J. STAT. ANN. §§ 58:1A-6(a)(1), 58:1A-17.

CHAPTER III

WATERS SUBJECT TO ALLOCATION

Scientists, economists, and legal scholars have long advocated the integrated management of all water resources within a State. After all, the hydrologic cycle is an integrated whole, and courts or administrative agencies cannot entirely segregate the parts of an ambient resource that nature integrates. As a result, water-based activities necessarily impact on each other and must be managed comprehensively if they are to be managed at all. On the other hand, activities related to various parts of the hydrologic cycle do have varying characteristics, including varying effects upon other uses related to other parts of the hydrologic cycle. *See* RICE & WHITE at 2-19; TARLOCK § 2.02; Robert Beck, *The Water Resource Defined and Described,* in 1 WATERS AND WATER RIGHTS § 1.03; Dellapenna, § 6.02. The Regulated Riparian Model Water Code deals with these realities by establishing a comprehensive management scheme animated by the goal of sustainable development. The Code makes special provision only for atmospheric water management. One of the purposes of this Chapter is to make clear the comprehensive reach of the Code.

A second problem addressed by this Chapter is the need to exempt certain waters from allocation under the system of water rights created under this Code. The Code exempts certain small water sources on the basis that the sources are too small to merit the expense of the administrative system created by this Code. *See* Dellapenna, § 9.03(a)(1). Another category of exemptions is directed at contexts in which the integrated nature of the hydrologic cycle precludes claims to exclusive management by the authorities within a single State. *See* Dellapenna, § 9.06(c). A final category is the preservation of waters necessary to protect in-place values related to the continuing existence of a water source. Properly defining and protecting minimum levels and flows in some respects will be the most important and the most difficult responsibilities of the State Agency. *See* Dellapenna, § 9.05(b).

Part 1

Waters Subject to Allocation

§ 3R-1-01 WATERS SUBJECT TO ALLOCATION

Except as expressly exempted pursuant to this Chapter, all waters of the State are subject to allocation in accordance with the provisions of this Code.

Commentary: This section declares the basic rule that all waters are subject to allocation pursuant to the Regulated Riparian Model Water Code. In general, allocation will occur by the issuing, altering, terminating, or denying of permits under Chapters VI and VII of the Code. The relevant provisions for atmospheric water resources are found in Chapter IX. For a discussion of waters traditionally subject to riparian rights, see TARLOCK, § 3.05; Dellapenna, §§ 6.02, 6.04.

Integration of the management of underground water with that in defined surface water sources is common among existing regulated riparian statutes, although not universal; generally, however, the existing statutes do not include diffused surface water or atmospheric water management. Apparently only Delaware, Florida, and Virginia include diffused surface water. DEL. CODE ANN. tit. 7, §§ 6002(22), 6003(3); FLA. STAT. ANN. §§ 373.019(8), (10), 373.023(1); VA. CODE ANN. § 62.1-242.

The allocation of water under this Code does not preclude other sorts of regulation relating to water-based activities. For example, Maryland has, separate from its comprehensive water allocation code, a statute regulating geothermal energy development. MD. CODE ANN., NAT. RES. §§ 8-8A-01 to 8-8A-09.

Cross-references: § 1R-1-01 (protecting the public interest in the waters of the State); § 1R-1-02 (assuring efficient and productive use of water); § 1R–1-03 (policy of conformity to physical laws); § 2R-2-01 (atmospheric water management or weather modification); § 2R-2-06 (consumptive use); § 2R-2-13 (nonconsumptive use); § 2R-2-14 (permit); § 2R-2-24 (sustainable development); § 2R-2-25 (underground water); § 2R-2-30 (water right); § 2R-2-32 (waters of the State); § 2R-2-33 (water source); § 2R-2-34 (withdraw or withdrawal); § 3R-1-02 (certain shared waters exempted from allocation); § 3R-1-03 (small water sources exempted from allocation); § 3R-2-01 (protected minimum flows and levels not to be allocated or withdrawn); §§ 6R-1-01 to 6R-1-05 (the requirement of a permit); §§ 6R-3-01 to 6R-3-05 (the basis of a water right); §§ 7R-1-01 to 7R-3-07 (the scope of the water right); §§ 9R-2-01 to 9R-2-05 (atmospheric water management).

Comparable statutes: ALA. CODE § 9-10B-3(19); CONN. GEN. STAT. ANN. §§ 22a-367(9), 22a-368; DEL. CODE ANN. tit. 7, §§ 6603(a)(3), (b)(4); FLA. STAT. ANN. §§ 373.019(8), 373.023(1); HAW. REV. STAT. § 174C-4(a); IOWA CODE ANN. §§ 455B.264, 455B.268(1)(a); KY. REV. STAT. ANN. §§ 151.120(1), 151.150; MD. CODE ANN., NAT. RES. §§ 8-101(K), 8-802; MASS. GEN. LAWS ANN. ch. 21G, §§ 2, 7; MINN. STAT. ANN. §§ 105.37(7), 105.41(1), 105.416; MISS. CODE ANN. §§ 51-3-1, 51-3-5; N.J. STAT. ANN. § 58-4A-2; N.C. GEN. STAT. §§ 143-215.13 to 143-215.15, 143.215.21(7).

§ 3R-1-02 CERTAIN SHARED WATERS EXEMPTED FROM ALLOCATION

Water from a transboundary water source subject to allocation by the federal government or to management under an interstate compact or an international treaty is not subject to allocation under this Code except in so far as such allocation is consistent with the federal mandate, interstate compact, or international agreement ratified by the United States.

Commentary: This section makes explicit what is implicit in the Supremacy Clause of the United States Constitution. U.S. CONST. art. VI. By that provision, any valid federal law, including any interstate compact and international agreement ratified by the United States, is supreme over and displaces any State law. See TARLOCK, § 9.05; Amy Kelley, *Federal-State Relations in Water*, in 4 WATERS AND WATER RIGHTS § 35.08. Congress has generally been careful not to displace directly the State role in allocating the use of waters within a State although such allocations can be affected indirectly by the operation of any number of federal regulations. To that extent, the State allocation system, including management under this Model Water Code, must give way. *See generally Arizona v. California,* 373 U.S. 546 (1963); RICE & WHITE, at 109-114; MALONEY, AUSNESS, & MORRIS, at 162-165; Dellapenna, § 9.06(b); Douglas Grant, *Apportionment by Congress,* in 4 WATERS AND WATER RIGHTS, ch. 47.

In one of the more direct federal preemptions of State allocational authority, Congress has enacted that no water is to be transferred out of the Great Lakes basin without the approval of the governor of every Great Lakes State. 42 U.S.C. § 1962d-20. For a Great Lakes State then, the allocational authority vested in the State Agency by this Code would apply to water withdrawals within the Great Lakes basin as within any other water basin within the State, but no interbasin transfer could be issued a permit without the approval of the governors of the other Great Lakes States. Most Great Lakes States have in fact banned such interbasin transfers in statutes that are not, however, entirely consistent with the federal statute. ILL. ANN. STAT. ch. 19, ¶ 119.2; IND. CODE ANN. § 13-2-1-9(b); MICH. COMP. LAWS ANN. §§ 323.71-323.85; MINN. STAT. ANN. §§ 105.045(4), 105.41(1a); N.Y. ENVTL. CONSERV. LAW §§ 15-1607, 15-611, 15-613; WIS. STAT. ANN. § 144.026(5)(b), (11), (d)(4). Only Ohio and Pennsylvania have not legislated on the matter. *See generally* Dellapenna, §§ 7.05(c)(2), 9.06(a).

A large number of decisions from the Supreme Court in the exercise of its original jurisdiction over suits between States have decreed equitable apportionment of their shared waters. While most of the attention given in the secondary literature has focused on such litigation in the arid states west of Kansas City, there have been a significant number of such suits in the humid east as well. *See Wisconsin v. Illinois,* 388 U.S. 426 (1967); *New Jersey v. New York,* 345 U.S. 369 (1953); *New Jersey v. New York,* 283 U.S. 336 (1931); *Connecticut v. Massachusetts,* 282 U.S. 660 (1931); *Wisconsin v. Illinois,* 281 U.S. 179 (1930); *Missouri v. Illinois,* 200 U.S. 496 (1906). As a decree from a federal court, such an apportionment overrides any inconsistent state law. This section of the Regulated Riparian Model Water Code therefore directs the State Agency to comply with any such decree. *See* Scott Anderson, Note, *Equitable Apportionment and the Supreme Court: What's So Equitable about Apportionment?,* 7 HAMLINE L. REV. 405

(1984); Douglas Grant, *Equitable Apportionment Suits between States,* in 4 WATERS AND WATER RIGHTS, ch. 45; George William Sherk, *Equitable Apportionment after* Vermejo*: The Demise of a Doctrine,* 29 NAT. RESOURCES J. 565 (1989); A. Dan Tarlock, *The Law of Equitable Apportionment Revised, Updated and Restated,* 56 U. COLO. L. REV. 381 (1985).

Interstate compacts must be approved by Congress to be effective, and thus are a type of federal law supreme over inconsistent State law. *Intake Water Co. v. Yellowstone River Compact Comm'n,* 769 F.2d 568 (9th Cir. 1985), *cert. denied,* 476 U.S. 1183 (1986). Generally, interstate compacts do not create mechanisms for actually managing water sources or for allocating water among particular users. *See* TARLOCK, § 10.05; Douglas Grant, *Water Apportionment Compacts between States,* in 4 WATERS AND WATER RIGHTS, ch. 46. The primary examples of interstate compacts which do create a multijurisdictional commission to manage water sources with authority to allocate water among particular users during times of shortage are the Delaware River Basin Compact, PUB. L. NO. 87-328, 75 Stat. 688 (1961), codified at DEL. CODE ANN. tit. 7, § 6501; N.J. STAT. ANN. §§ 32.11D-1 to -110; N.Y. ENVTL. CONSERV. LAW § 21-0701; PA. STAT. ANN. § 815.101; and the Susquehanna River Basin Compact, PUB. L. NO. 91-575, 84 Stat. 1509 (1970), codified at MD. NAT. RESOURCES CODE § 8-301; N.Y. ENVTL. CONSERV. LAW § 21-1301; PA. STAT. ANN. tit. 32, § 820.1. Both compacts create Basin Commissions that are unusual not only because of the extent of the regulatory authority conferred on them but also because the federal government is a full participant on the Commissions and is bound by most Commission decisions. The Basin Commissions are authorized to delegate their allocational authority to State Agencies if the Agencies have adequate regulatory authority to accomplish the policies adopted by the Commission. The Regulated Riparian Model Water Code is designed to enable such a delegation. *See generally* Dellapenna, § 9.06(c)(2); Joseph Dellapenna, *The Delaware and Susquehanna River Basins,* in 6 WATERS AND WATER RIGHTS 137 (1994 reissued vol.).

The ratification of the North American Free Trade Agreement (NAFTA) in 1993 highlighted for some the growing importance of international regulation of transboundary water resources. In fact, the United States entered into treaties regarding the management of its international fresh waters as far back as 1906. *See Convention Providing for the Equitable*

Distribution of the Waters of the Rio Grande for Irrigation Purposes, signed May 21, 1906, Mexico-United States, 34 Stat. 2953, T.S. No. 455; *Treaty Relating to Boundary Waters between the United States and Canada,* Jan. 11, 1909, United Kingdom-United States, 36 Stat. 2449, T.S. 548; *Treaty Respecting Utilization of Waters of the Colorado and Tijuana Rivers and of the Rio Grande,* signed Feb. 3, 1944, Mexico-United States, 59 Stat. 1219, T.S. No. 994, 3 U.N.T.S. 313; *Treaty Relating to the Uses of the Waters of the Niagara River,* signed Feb. 27, 1950, United States-Canada, 1 U.S.T. 694, T.I.A.S. No. 2130, 132 U.N.T.S. 224; *Treaty for the Co-Operative Development of the Columbia River Basin,* Jan. 17, 1961, United States-Canada, 15 U.S.T. 1555, T.I.A.S. 5638, 15 U.S.T. 1555; Albert Utton, *Canadian International Waters,* in 5 WATERS AND WATER RIGHTS, ch. 50; Albert Utton, *Mexican International Waters,* in 5 WATERS AND WATER RIGHTS, ch. 51. *See also* JOHN KRUTILLA, THE COLUMBIA RIVER TREATY: THE ECONOMICS OF AN INTERNATIONAL RIVER BASIN DEVELOPMENT (1967); THE LAW OF INTERNATIONAL DRAINAGE BASINS 167 (Albert Garretson, Robert Hayton, & Cecil Olmstead eds. 1967); DON PIPER, THE INTERNATIONAL LAW OF THE GREAT LAKES (1967); LUDWIK TECLAFF, THE RIVER BASIN IN HISTORY AND LAW (1967); Gerald Graham, *International Rivers and Lakes: The Canadian-American Regime,* in THE LEGAL REGIME OF INTERNATIONAL RIVERS AND LAKES 3 (Ralph Zacklin & Lucius Caflisch eds. 1981); Robert Hayton & Albert Utton, *Transboundary Groundwaters: The Bellagio Draft Treaty,* 29 NAT. RESOURCES J. 663 (1989); Mary Kelleher, Note, *Mexican-United States Shared Groundwater: Can It Be Managed?,* 1 GEO. INT'L ENVTL. L. REV. 113 (1988); Symposium, *U.S.-Canadian Transboundary Resource Issues,* 26 NAT. RESOURCES J. 201-376 (1986); Symposium, *U.S.-Mexican Transboundary Resource Issues,* 26 NAT. RESOURCES J. 659-850 (1986). These treaties are also part of the supreme law of the land that preempts any inconsistent state law. U.S. CONST. art. VI. This section of the Code therefore also directs the State Agency to comply with any such treaty.

Cross-references: § 1R-1-09 (coordination of water allocation and water quality regulation); § 1R-1-12 (recognizing local interests in the waters of the State); § 1R-1-13 (regulating interstate water transfers); § 1R-1-14 (regulating interbasin transfers); § 2R-2-10 (interbasin transfer); § 2R-2-32 (waters of the State); § 2R-2-33 (water source); § 3R-1-01 (waters subject to allocation); §

3R-1-03 (small water sources exempted from allocation); § 3R-2-01 (protected minimum flows not to be allocated or withdrawn); §§ 6R-4-01 to 6R-4-05 (coordination of water allocation and water quality regulation); §§ 8R-1-01 to 8R-1-06 (multijurisdictional transfers).

Comparable statutes: ARK. CODE ANN. §§ 15-202(6)(A), 15-22-217(e)(3).

§ 3R-1-03 SMALL WATER SOURCES EXEMPTED FROM ALLOCATION *(optional)*

(1) A surface water source that originates on a person's property is not subject to allocation under this Code if the total water basin down to the point the water source leaves the property in question is less than 8 acres and the water is used on the tract of land on which it originates.

(2) Exemption from allocation under this section does not preclude the application of orders or regulations adopted pursuant to this Code necessary to protect minimum flows or levels or during water emergencies.

Commentary: This provision is similar to that found in several existing regulated riparian statutes. The exemption of the uppermost riparians from regulation enables them to undertake to exploit diffused surface water in whatever manner appears to be most efficient to those landowners without entering into disputes about the precise legal category of the water at the point where it is exploited. This rule also generally serves to exempt what are usually (because of the limited nature of the water source) small-scale users of surface water sources from the expense and other burdens of the allocation process established by the Regulated Riparian Model Water Code. This preference usually will amount to a benefit to agricultural users of water, although nothing in the Code so restricts it. See Dellapenna, §§ 9.02(b), 9.03(a)(2). The provision of this section parallels the exemption of certain small withdrawals from the permit requirement.

Just because they are not subject to the requirement that the user obtain a permit for the use does not mean that those users (and uses) are exempt from all regulation pursuant to this Code. In particular, such users and their uses are subject to regulations designed to preserve the minimum flow or level in the water source and to deal with a water emergency. As with other users facing restrictions on their uses because of water emergencies, users exempted from the permit requirement might find it to their advantage to have a plan for conservation in place before the emergency in order to gain some measure of control over the steps they will have to take in response to the emergency. Under particular circumstances, a user under this section voluntarily choose to register the use or even to obtain a permit for the use under sections 6R-1-02(3) or 6R-1-06(3).

The figure of 8 acres of the maximum size of the water basin serves to restrict this privilege to genuinely small quantities of water. The few Comparable statutes express the exemption in terms of maximum flow or the maximum size of a pond rather than in terms of the size of the watershed. These approaches require greater intrusion by the State Agency to determine whether a particular stream or pond qualifies for the exemption. The Agency can easily determine whether a particular watershed has the selected size without close subsequent monitoring to determine whether the flow or size of a water source has changed, artificially or naturally. A legislature considering enacting this provision should consider carefully the size of the drainage area that will be exempted from formal allocation pursuant to this Code. If the exemption takes in too many uses of water, it will seriously impair achieving the goal of sustainable development or otherwise realizing the public interest in the waters of the State. The figure selected here is deliberately kept small to assure that any significant use of water comes within the regulatory authority of the State.

Furthermore, the exemption of small water users from the permit process according to the quantity of water withdraws (generally in gallons/per day) or the size of the impoundment does not fit easily into the concept of "waters exempt from allocation." Such exemptions are possible under this Code; they are dealt with by authorizing the exemption of small withdrawals from the permit process in section 6R-1-02. If the legislature considers these solutions to fully exhaust the question, it might omit this section on waters exempt from allocation under this Code. If this section is enacted, exemption of the waters from allocation under this Code would leave disputes concerning those waters to judicial application of the rule of reasonable use under section 2R-1-01. The difference is that waters exempt from allocation cannot be regulated by State Agency except for the purposes indicated in subsection (2), whereas water uses exempted from the permit process are subject to all regulations adopted by the State Agency except that the users do not have to acquire a permit.

One should note that as the controlling reference is to the size of the water basin, and as that applies to both surface and underground water, questions might arise whether an underground water basin stretches considerably beyond the apparent water basin looking only at the land surface. This is a potentially significant question likely to arise in areas underlain by limestone, yet as the principle goal is to limit exempt withdrawals to the small area indicated in subsection (1), it would be better to leave the question of the size of the relevant underground basin as it is expressed in that subsection. This will assure that withdrawals from waters exempted from allocation do not unduly affect withdrawals under permit from lower down in the water basin.

Cross-reference: § 1R-1-05 (efficient and equitable allocation during Shortfalls in Supply); § 1R-1-11 (preserving minimum flows and levels); § 2R-1-01 (the obligation to make only a reasonable use of water); § 2R-1-03 (no unreasonable injury to other water rights); § 2R-1-04 (protection of property rights); § 2R-2-14 (permit); § 2R-2-17 (plan for conservation); § 2R-2-23 (State Agency); § 2R-2-24 (sustainable development); § 2R-2-28 (water basin); § 2R-2-29 (water emergency); § 2R-2-32 (waters of the State); § 2R-2-33 (water source); § 2R-2-34 (withdrawal or to withdraw); § 3R-1-01 (waters subject to allocation); § 3R-1-02 (certain shared waters exempted from allocation); § 6R-1-02 (small withdrawals exempted from the permit requirement); § 6R-1-06(2) (voluntary registration); 7R-3-05 (authority to restrict withdrawals for which no allocation or permit is required).

Comparable statutes: ARK. CODE ANN. § 15-22-215(a); DEL. CODE ANN. tit. 7, § 6029(1); GA. CODE ANN. §§ 12-5-22(13), 12-5-31(b)(5), 12-5-96(a)(1); IOWA CODE ANN. § 455B.270.

See also GA. CODE ANN. §12-5-31(b)(5) (exempting farm ponds); KY. REV. STAT. ANN. § 151.120(2) (exempting natural pools left standing after a stream has ceased to flow).

Part 2

Protected Minimum Flows or Levels

One of the more important, yet more controversial, issues confronting a State in managing its waters is to devise legal protection for protecting the integrity of a water source as such. Without respect and protection for the integrity of a water source, one cannot meaningfully discuss, let alone achieve, the sustainable development of the source. While some might reject this as a goal altogether, federal law already mandates that the biological, chemical, and physical integrity of water sources be protected. Furthermore, protection of the several integrities of the waters of the State, an expression of the trust responsibilities of the State (see section 1R-1-01), are recognized by statute in nearly all States, regardless of whether the state follows appropriative rights, riparian rights, or regulated riparianism. As an expression of the trust responsibilities, such protection can seldom run afoul of the takings clauses of the state or federal constitutions, and indeed failure to protect could violate the legal obligations of the state under the public trust doctrine. *Babbitt v. Sweet Home Chapter of Communities,* 115 S. Ct. 2407 (1995); *National Audubon Soc'y v. Superior Ct.,* 658 P.2d 709 (Cal.), *cert. denied sub nom. City of Los Angeles v. National Audubon Soc'y,* 464 U.S. 977 (1983); Oliver Houck, *Why Do We Protect Endangered Species, and What Does That Say about Whether Restrictions on Private Property to Protect Them Constitute "Takings"?,* 80 IOWA L. REV. 297 (1995). *See also* Mark Sagoff, *On Preserving the Natural Environment,* 84 YALE L.J. 205 (1974); Chrisotpher Stone, *Should Trees Have Standing? Towards Legal Rights for Natural Objects,* 45 S. CAL. L. REV. 450 (1972); Laurence Tribe, *Ways Not to Think about Plastic Trees: New Foundations for Environmental Law,* 83 YALE L.J. 1315 (1974). The questions that States must address, then, are how to define the protected minimum flows (for surface sources) or levels (for underground sources) as necessary to protect these sources and how to implement the necessary protection. This part addresses those questions.

§ 3R-2-01 PROTECTED MINIMUM FLOWS OR LEVELS NOT TO BE ALLOCATED OR WITHDRAWN

(1) The State Agency shall establish by regulation the minimum flow or level in any water source that is not subject to allocation under this Code except as provided in this Part.

(2) Every person exercising a water right pursuant to this Code is required to protect the prescribed minimum flows or levels when exercising such right.

Commentary: This section sets forth the basic responsibilities of the State and of persons using water to protect the biological, chemical, and physical integrity of each water source in the State. Respect for and protection of these integrities are central to achieving the goal of sustainable development and protecting the public interest in the waters of the State. The responsibilities to protect the several integrities of the waters of the State are primarily discharged by the State Agency through the establishment of a protected minimum flow or level for each water source which is then not subject to allocation to particular water users except as provided in this Part of the Code. Additionally, the protected minimum flows or levels are to be protected from impairment by everyone using water in the State whether pursuant to a permit or otherwise.

The protection of established minimum levels or quantities usually will be through the terms and conditions attached to each permit as it is issued, or through orders or regulations adopted by the State Agency pursuant to a water shortage or water emergency. Generally this will occur through steps to define the safe yield of a water source and to limit total consumptive uses to the safe yield. The obligation of individuals to protect the minimum flows or levels of their water source will primarily be established through conditions to their permits, although that will not necessarily exhaust their obligations. The myriad of particular circumstances that could affect the protection of minimum flows or levels cannot usefully be delineated in a legal Code and cannot be fully described in conditions to a permit. *See* Dellapenna, § 9.05(b).

Cross-references: § 1R-1-01 (protecting the public interest in the waters of the State); § 1R-1-03 (conformity to physical laws); § 1R-1-05 (efficient and equitable allocation during shortfalls in supply); § 1R-1-09 (coordination of water allocation and water quality regulation); § 1R-1-11 (preservation of minimum flows and levels); § 2R-2-02 (biological integrity); § 2R-2-03 (chemical integrity); § 2R-2-06 (consumptive use); § 2R-2-13 (nonconsumptive use); § 2R-2-16 (physical integrity); § 2R-2-15 (person); § 2R-2-21 (safe yield); § 2R-2-23 (State Agency); § 2R-2-24 (sustainable development); § 2R-2-30 (water right); § 2R-2-32 (waters of the State); § 2R-2-33 (water source); § 3R-2-02 (standards for protected minimum flows or levels); § 3R-2-03 (effects of water shortages or water emergencies); § 3R-2-04 (burden of proof); § 3R-2-05 (contractual protection of additional flows or levels); § 4R-1-01 (basic responsibility and authority of the State Agency); § 4R-1-06 (regulatory authority of the State Agency); §§ 6R-1-01 to 6R-1-06 (the requirement of a permit).

Comparable statutes: ARK. CODE ANN. § 15-22-301(4), (11); DEL. CODE ANN. tit. 7, § 6029; FLA. STAT. ANN. §§ 373.042, 373.223(3) ; HAW. REV. STAT. §§ 174C-5(3), 174C-49(d), 174C-71; IND. CODE ANN. §§ 13-2-6.1-4(5), 13-2-6.1-6; IOWA CODE ANN. §§ 455B.261(15), 455B.267(1), (3), 455B.270; KY. REV. STAT. ANN. § 151.110(1); MASS. GEN. LAWS ANN. ch. 21G, §§ 4, 7(3), 11; MINN. STAT. ANN § 105.417(2) to (4); MISS. CODE ANN. § 51-3-7(2) to (6); N.J. STAT. ANN. § 58-1A-5(e); N.C. GEN. STAT. § 143-215.47; VA. CODE ANN. §§ 62.1-246, 62.1-248(A). *See also* CONN. GEN. STAT. ANN. §§ 26-141a (applicable only to streams in which the state stocks fish); N.Y. ENVTL. CONSERV. LAW § 15-2133 (applicable only to dams); WIS. STAT. ANN. §§ 31.02(1), 31.34 (applicable only to dams).

§ 3R-2-02 STANDARDS FOR PROTECTED MINIMUM FLOWS OR LEVELS

The State Agency shall establish a minimum flow or level as the larger of the amounts necessary for the biological, chemical, and physical integrity of the water source, taking into account normal seasonal variations in flow and need.

Commentary: This section establishes that the standards for minimum flows or levels are not set by this Code, but by other relevant federal and State laws. The primary laws are the Clean Water Act, , 33 U.S.C. §§ 1251-1387, the Safe Drinking Water Act, 42 U.S.C. §§ 300f to 300j-11, and the Endangered Species Act, 16 U.S.C. § 1531-1543, along with corresponding State legislation. Almost any statute dealing with protection of the environment might prove relevant to establishing the standards for a particular water source. The State Agency is to particularize the minimum flow or level for each source through a regulation adopted after suitable planning and study. The trend today is to manage withdrawals (including releases from reservoirs) so as to mimic natural seasonal variations in flow in order to preserve the biological integrity of the water source. *See, e.g.*, Jon Christensen, *River in Nevada Helps Its Own Restoration*, N.Y. TIMES, Sept. 24, 1996, at C4.

Cross-references: § 2R-2-02 (biological integrity); § 2R-2-03 (chemical integrity); § 2R-2-016 (physical integrity); § 2R-2-24 (sustainable development); § 3R-2-01 (protected minimum flows or levels not to be allocated); § 3R-2-03 (effects of water shortages or water emergencies); § 3R-2-04 (burden of proof); § 3R-2-05 (contractual protection of additional flows or levels).

Comparable statutes: ARK. CODE ANN. § 15-22-202(6); CONN. GEN. STAT. ANN. §§ 26-141b; FLA. STAT. ANN. §§ 373.042, 373.223(3); HAW. REV. STAT. § 174C-71(1)(C), (E), (2)(D), (4); IND. CODE ANN. § 13-2-6.1-6; IOWA CODE ANN. § 455B.261(15); MASS. GEN. LAWS ANN. ch. 21G, §§ 4, 7(3), 11; MINN. STAT. ANN § 105.417(3); MISS. CODE ANN. §§ 51-3-3(i), (j), 53-

3-7(4) to (6); N.Y. ENVTL. CONSERV. LAW § 15-2133; N.C. GEN. STAT. § 143-215.48; VA. CODE ANN. § 62.1-246; WIS. STAT. ANN. §§ 31.02(1), 31.34.

§ 3R-2-03 EFFECTS OF WATER SHORTAGES OR WATER EMERGENCIES

(1) Threats to impair the minimum flows or levels established by this section justify the State Agency to declare a water shortage or water emergency as appropriate.

(2) During periods of water emergency, the State Agency may allocate waters normally within protected minimum flows or levels when necessary to prevent serious injuries to water uses established before the beginning of the water emergency, but only in so far as such allocation does not permanently impair the biological, chemical, or physical integrity of the water source.

(3) To facilitate planning for water emergencies, the State Agency shall establish emergency minimum flows or levels which are not subject to allocation except to prevent grave threats to human life or health under circumstances where water is not available from other sources for coping with these needs.

Commentary: Subsection (1) provides the State Agency with authority to act to protect protected minimum flows or levels through invocation of the powers relating to water shortages or water emergencies. Subsection (2) provides the State Agency with authority to make temporarily allocations of water within the protected minimum flows or levels when strictly necessary to prevent injuries to established waters uses during a water emergency, but not during a water shortage. Such temporary allocations are authorized only if that can be done without permanent impairment of the values served by the establishment of the protected minimum flows or levels. Any lesser standard would be inconsistent with the goal of sustainable development. In order to assure this, subsection (3) requires prior planning to establish the emergency minimum flows or levels that are to be protected should the power in subsection (2) to make emergency allocations be exercised. The establishment of emergency minimum flows or levels would usually be part of the more general process of planning drought management strategies under the Code. See Dellapenna, § 9.05(b).

Cross-references: § 1R-1-01 (protecting the public interest in the waters of the State); § 1R-1-03 (conformity to physical laws); § 1R-1-04 (comprehensive planning); § 1R-1-05 (efficient and equitable allocation during shortfalls in supply); § 1R-1-06 (legal security for water rights); § 2R-1-04 (protection of property rights); § 2R-2-09 (drought management strategies); § 2R-2-24 (sustainable development); § 2R-2-29 (water emergency); § 2R-2-31 (water shortage); § 3R-2-01 (protected minimum flows or levels not to be allocated); § 3R-2-02 (standards for protected minimum flows or levels); § 3R-2-04 (burden of proof); § 3R-2-05 (contractual protection of additional flows or levels); §§ 4R-2-01 to 4R-2-04 (planning responsibilities); §§ 7R-3-01 to 7R-3-07 (restrictions during water shortages or water emergencies).

Comparable statutes: ARK. CODE ANN. §§ 15-22-217(e)(2).

§ 3R-2-04 BURDEN OF PROOF

(1) In any proceeding under this Code, the person proposing to withdraw water from a water source shall have the burden of showing by a preponderance of the evidence that the proposed withdrawal will not impair the protected minimum flows or levels as determined under this section.

(2) Nothing in this Code authorizes any person to withdraw water from a source that would impair its established protected minimum flow or

level without first securing authorization to do so from the State Agency or a court reviewing a decision by the State Agency.

Commentary: Generally, the protection of established minimum levels or quantities will be through the terms and conditions attached to each permit as it is issued, or through orders or regulations adopted by the State Agency pursuant to a water shortage or water emergency. Subsection (1) provides that in any proceeding in which a person seeks to challenge the Agency's determination in this regard, the person making the challenge has the burden of proving by a preponderance of the evidence that the person's proposed withdrawal and use will not impair the protected minimum levels or quantities. The standard of preponderance of evidence recognizes that there can be no absolute proof of a negative about the future. The person challenging the Agency's decisions regarding protected minimum levels or flows must introduce enough credible evidence that, even after rebuttal by evidence introduced by the Agency or others participating in the proceeding, it appears more likely than not that the challenger's proposed withdrawal and use will not impair the protected minimum levels and quantities. Some States might prefer to adopt a higher burden of proof in this regard to reflect the "precautionary principle." (The precautionary principle requires that in making decisions about the environment errors should be made in favor of protection as a precaution against the potentially irreversible consequences of errors that, in retrospect, turn out to have provided inadequate protection). *See generally* MICHAEL CARLEY & IAN CHRISTIE, MANAGING SUSTAINABLE DEVELOPMENT (1993); RENE DUBOS & BARBARA WARD, ONLY ONE EARTH: THE CARE AND MAINTENANCE OF A SMALL PLANET (1972); HARALD HOHMANN, PRECAUTIONARY LEGAL DUTIES AND PRINCIPLES OF MODERN INTERNATIONAL LAW (1994); WORLD COMM'N ON ENVIRONMENT & DEVELOPMENT, OUR COMMON FUTURE (1987) ("The Bruntland Report"); James Hickey, jr., & Vern Walker, *Refining the Precautionary Principle in International Environmental Law,* 14 VA. ENVTL. L.J. 423 (1995); Eric Plate, *Sustainable Development of Water Resources: A Challenge to Science and Engineering,* 18 WATER INT'L 84 (1993); Symposium, *The Promise and Challenge of Ecologically Sustainable Development,* 31 WILLAMETTE L. REV. 235 (1995).

Subsection (2) provides that when there is a dispute over whether a particular withdrawal of water would impair the legally established protected minimum flow or level, that dispute must be resolved before the withdrawal takes place. It is no defense to an enforcement proceeding that the withdrawal did not in fact impair the biological, chemical, or physical integrity of the water source. Those issues are to be fully aired and resolved through the procedures created by this Code for challenging decisions by the State Agency.

Cross-references: § 1R-1-08 (procedural protections); § 3R-2-01 (protected minimum flows or levels not to be allocated); § 3R-2-02 (standards for protected minimum flows or levels); § 3R-2-03 (effects of water shortages or water emergencies); § 3R-2-05 (contractual protection of additional flows or levels); §§ 5R-1–01 to 5R-1-05 (disputes and enforcement).

Comparable statutes: HAW. REV. STAT. § 174C-71(2).

§ 3R-2-05 CONTRACTUAL PROTECTION OF ADDITIONAL FLOWS OR LEVELS

> **The State Agency may contract with any person holding a permit to provide additional protected flows or levels of water in any water source, paying for any contract out of the State Water Fund.**

Commentary: This section authorizes the State Agency to contract with water users to protect additional flows or levels of water that are not strictly necessary for meeting the requirements established to preserve the biological, chemical, and physical integrity of a particular water source. The contracts will enable the Agency to recover water already allocated by permits prior to the expiration of the permit when the Agency determines that to be a proper means for enhancing the general environmental, ecological, and aesthetic values served by the protected minimum levels or quantities. Contracts are to be paid for out of the State Water Fund and will arise solely through the voluntary agreement of the persons who hold the affected permits. The contract provision is modeled on a provision in the laws of Indiana. A somewhat similar program is being used by the Federal government and several cities in Nevada to help restore the Truckee

River. *Novel Use of Clean-Water Loans Brightens Outlook for a River,* N.Y. TIMES, Oct. 31, 1996, at A25.

Cross-references: § 1R-1-01 (protecting the public interest in the waters of the state); § 1R-1-04 (comprehensive planning); § 1R-1-10 (water conservation); § 1R-1-11 (preservation of minimum flows and levels); § 2R-2-24 (sustainable development); § 2R-2-32 (waters of the State); § 2R-2-33 (water source); § 3R-2-01 (protected minimum flows or levels not to be allocated); § 3R-2-02 (standards for protected minimum flows or levels); § 3R-2-03 (effects of water shortages or water emergencies); § 3R-2-04 (burden of proof); § 4R-1-04 (special funds created).

Comparable statutes: IND. CODE ANN. §§ 12-2-1-7. *See also* MINN. STAT. ANN. §§ 105.392, 105.475; WIS. STAT. ANN. § 30.18(8).

CHAPTER IV

ADMINISTRATION

This and the following Chapter are designed to enable the effective implementation of the regulatory authority created in the Regulated Riparian Model Water Code in a State operating within the tradition of common law riparian rights. States that have already adopted a regulated riparian scheme will have a designated agency with some or all of the powers and responsibilities set forth in this Chapter; they might find these two Chapters useful in refining the administrative and enforcement scheme already in place. *See generally* Dellapenna, § 9.05(a)(5); WILLIAM WALKER & PHYLLIS BRIDGEMAN, A WATER CODE FOR VIRGINIA (Va. Polytech.. Inst., Va. Water Resources Res. Bull. No. 147, 1985). For a discussion of the impact of different styles on administration, see SAX, ABRAMS, & THOMPSON, at 305-07; Dellapenna, § 9.05(a)(5)(D).

This Chapter specifically addresses the State Agency's powers and responsibilities as the principal administrative organ under the Regulated Riparian Model Water Code, as well as the optional provisions on Special Water Management Areas for those States that choose to delegate the primary managerial authority to such regional arrangements. The Chapter covers both the routine administrative authority and the regulatory authority of the State Agency, its planning responsibilities, and the Agency's responsibility to coordinate with other government agencies. In this latter regard, the Chapter particularly focuses on the need to coordinate its responsibilities for water allocation with the responsibility it or another agency has for regulating water quality. The next Chapter addresses enforcement measures and dispute resolution.

Part 1

General Administrative Authority

This Part provides general provisions conferring on the State Agency the necessary administrative authority as well as certain limits on that authority. In particular, this Part confers on the State Agency the authority to adopt any necessary regulations, to create and administer special funds, and to impose appropriate fees. Other provisions confer the basic housekeeping responsibilities on the State Agency. Particular limits are found in the provisions relating to fees and in an obligation to protect confidential business information. Except as expressly provided in the Regulated Riparian Model Water Code, the State Agency is to conform to the general administrative law of the State.

§ 4R-1-01 BASIC RESPONSIBILITY AND AUTHORITY

The State Agency is responsible for general supervision and control over the development, conservation, and use of the waters of the State and is vested with all powers necessary to accomplish the purposes for which the Agency is organized in so far as those powers are delegable by the legislature.

Commentary: This section provides that the State Agency is vested with all powers necessary to accomplish its purposes. These powers include planning, the implementation of regulations and procedures, and public projects. The only limitation is any possible judicial finding that particular powers are not delegable by the legislature under the State's constitution. The following sections spell out the delegated powers and responsibilities in considerably more detail.

Cross-references: § 2R-2-23 (State Agency); § 3R-2-05 (contractual protection of additional flows or levels); § 4R-1-02 (nonimpairment of general powers); § 4R-1-03 (general administrative powers); § 4R-1-04 (special funds created); § 4R-1-05 (application of general laws to meetings, procedures, and records); § 4R-1-06 (regulatory authority of the State Agency); § 4R-1-07 (application fees); § 4R-1-09 (protection of confidential business information); §§ 4R-2-01 to 4R-2-04 (planning responsibilities); §§ 4R-3-01 to 4R-3-05 (coordination with other branches or levels of government); §§ 5R-1-01 to 5R-5-05 (disputes and enforcement); §§ 6R-4-01 to 6R-4-05 (coordination of water allocation and water quality regulation).

Comparable statutes: ALA. CODE § 9-10B-5(22); ARK. CODE ANN. § 15-22-505; FLA. STAT. ANN. § 373.026; IND. CODE ANN. § 13-2-6.1-2; IOWA CODE ANN. § 455B. 264; MD. CODE ANN., NAT. RES. § 8-203; N.J. STAT. ANN. § 58:1A-15(a); N.Y. ENVTL. CONSERV. LAW § 15-0109; VA. CODE ANN. § 62.1-44.86; WIS. STAT. ANN. § 144.025(2)(a).

§ 4R-1-02 NONIMPAIRMENT OF GENERAL POWERS

> **The enumeration of any particular powers granted shall not be construed to impair any general grant of power contained in this Code or to limit any grant of power of the same class as those enumerated.**

Commentary: Courts have often interpreted express grants of authority to an administrative agency to undertake certain activities or functions as implicit denials of authority to undertake activities or functions not expressly granted. The Regulated Riparian Model Water Code expressly rejects that approach to interpreting the provisions of the Code. While specific express limitations established in other sections of this Code are binding on the State Agency, no inference is drawn of more general limitations than those expressed in this Code.

Comparable statute: VA. CODE ANN. § 62.1-44.44.

§ 4R-1-03 GENERAL ADMINISTRATIVE POWERS

In addition to any other powers and duties, the State Agency is authorized to:

(a) administer all funds made available to the Agency for the effectuating of this Code and to disburse those funds for proper purposes, including the State Water Fund and the Interbasin Compensation Fund;

(b) accept grants, gifts, bequests, or the like of any thing to be used to carry out the purposes, powers, or duties of the State Agency;

(c) carry out data collection, surveys, research, and investigations into all aspects of waters of the State, including the availability, use, quality, and quantity of those waters;

(d) prepare, publish, and disseminate information and reports concerning its activities as the Agency deems necessary;

(e) contract and execute other instruments necessary or convenient to the exercise of its powers with any person;

(f) appoint and remove officers and employees, including specialists and consultants for the purpose of carrying out its powers and functions;

(g) acquire, hold, sell, lease as lessor or lessee, lend, transfer, or dispose of real and personal property, or interests therein, as may be necessary or convenient to the performance of its functions, including the acquisition of real property for the purpose of conserving and protecting water and related resources;

(h) hold regular and special meetings, pursuant to procedures established by regulation; and

(i) keep on file full and proper records of its work, including its proceedings, all field notes, computations, and facts made or collected, all of which shall be part of the records of its office and property of the State and, as such, open to the public during business hours with copies to be provided at the cost of reproduction, subject only to privileges of confidentiality as provided in this Code or other laws.

Commentary: This section sets forth in some detail the authority of the State Agency to undertake the usual routine steps that any governmental agency will find necessary to its own internal administration or to undertake by contract or otherwise to conduct its non-regulatory and non-planning relations with the world outside the agency. These general powers might be reshaped in any particular State to conform to the administrative law and practice of the State. In particular, if the State Agency is under a particular department in the State's government, the director of that department might be vested with staffing and budgetary needs. *See, e.g.*, VA. CODE ANN. § 62.1-44.14.

Some of the general powers specified in this section are treated in more detail elsewhere in this Regulated Riparian Model Water Code when the specified general powers intersect with regulatory or planning activities or functions, particularly those activities or functions that relate to the central policies expressed in this Code. *See* §§ 2R-1-04, 06, 08; § 4R-1-04. The responsibility of the State Agency to create and administer the State Water Fund and the Interbasin Compensation Fund, here set forth as aspects of the general authority of the Agency to administer funds, particularly exemplify this intersection of routine administration and the central policies of the Code. As already indicated, the specifics of those sections do not implicitly limit or impair the general powers granted under this section. The authority to acquire real or personal property is expressed in the most general terms. Property can be acquired by purchase or gift, or through the exercise of the power of eminent domain. A limit on the exercise of the power of eminent domain is found in section 4R-3-05.

Cross-references: § 2R-2-15 (person); § 2R-2-23 (State Agency); § 2R-2-32 (waters of the State); § 3R-2-05 (contractual protection of additional flows or levels); § 4R-1-01 (basic responsibility and authority); § 4R-1-02 (nonimpairment of general powers); § 4R-1-04 (special funds created); § 4R-1-05 (application of general laws to meetings, procedures, and records); § 4R-1-09 (protection of confidential business information); § 4R-2-03 (statewide data system); § 4R-3-02 (1) to (4) (technical assistance to other units of government); § 4R-3-05 (limitation on the power of eminent domain); § 9R-1-01 (support for voluntary conservation measures).

Comparable statutes: ALA. CODE § 9-10B-5(1) (authority to plan), (4) (to collect data), (5) to conduct studies, etc.), (6) (to consult with any person), (7) (to contract), (10) (to accept grants and other funds), (11) (to employ personnel), (14) (to undertake studies, etc.); ARK. CODE ANN. §§ 15-22-505(6) (authority to acquire water rights and related resources by gift or purchase), (7) (to invest funds for income), 15-22-508 to 15-22-211 (authority to issue or invest in bonds); FLA. STAT. ANN. §§ 373.056 (authority to receive conveyances of land), 373.079-.103 (general authority of water districts), 373.139 (authority to acquire land); GA. CODE ANN. §§ 12-5-23, 12-5-24, 12-5-93 (broad recitals of authority); HAW. REV. STAT. §§ 174C-5 (general powers and duties), 174C-14 (acquisition of real property); IND. CODE ANN. § 13-2-6.1-4 (broad recitals of authority); IOWA CODE ANN. §§ 455B.103, 455B.263 (broad recitals of authority); KY. REV. STAT. ANN. §§ 151.125, 151.220, 151.360, 151.370, 151.420 to 151.450 (broad recitals of authority); MD. CODE ANN., NAT. RES. § 8-203 (broad recitals of authority); MINN. STAT. ANN. § 105.39 (broad recitals of authority); N.J. STAT. ANN. § 58:1A-15 (broad recitals of authority); N.Y. ENVTL. CONSERV. LAW § 15-0309 (authority to sue and be sued); VA. CODE ANN. § 62.1-44.43 (broad recitals of authority); WIS. STAT. ANN. § 144.025(n) (authority to accept gifts and grants).

§ 4R-1-04 SPECIAL FUNDS CREATED

(1) The State Agency shall create and administer a State Water Fund to be used for the exclusive purpose of upgrading the environmental, ecological, or aesthetic values of the waters of the State, including, when the State Agency deems it appropriate, the repurchase of permits before the permit expires.

(2) The State Agency shall create and administer a Interbasin Compensation Fund to provide appropriate compensatory benefits, as determined by the State Agency, to the water basin of origin for which the monies in the Fund are received.

Commentary: Subsection (1) of this section requires the State Agency to create a State Water Fund to be used exclusively for the upgrading of diffused general public values in the waters of the State. This Fund is not to be used to pay general administrative expenses of the State Agency. To the extent the general administrative expenses are not covered by the fees charged by the State Agency, those expenses are a charge on the general budget. Nothing in the Regulated Riparian Model Water Code precludes a State from contributing additional monies to the Fund beyond those earmarked in this Code. Expenditures from this fund can be used for the construction of practical works that serve the general values indicated, to purchase protection for additional water, or for any other purpose that reasonably serves the public interest in the waters of the State and helps to promote the goal of sustainable development.

The section specifically authorizes the use of the State Water Fund to buy back permits prior to their expiration. *See, e.g.*, Dellapenna, § 9.03(d). This is in keeping with the emphasis of the Code on preserving flexibility by encouraging and enabling the modification of water rights. The authority for the State Agency to buy back water rights recognizes that often only a public agency will have either the incentive or the resources to enter the market on behalf of non-economic values and protect the interests of non-sellers. If the State Agency is also given responsibility for flood control or other functions not relating to water allocation as such, some of those purposes might also be included as proper uses of the Special Water Fund, although care must be taken in drafting such language to assure that the primary purpose of the Fund of enhancing highly generalized values is not neglected in favor of development projects that actually may be destructive of those purposes.

Subsection (2) of this section requires the State Agency to create a Interbasin Compensation Fund to receive compensation fees assessed for interbasin transfers. This Fund is to be used to provide benefits for the particular water basin of origin for which a special fee is assessed and received as compensation for the transfer of water out of the water basin. The Fund is not a substitute for, nor even related to, payments that a person might make to a water right holder as part of a contractual modification of a water right. Rather, the fund derives from payments intended to compensate the public generally in the basin of origin for the loss of opportunities and other costs arising from the transfer of water out of the water basin. The Fund reflects the policies of recognizing local interests in the waters of the State and of regulating interstate and interbasin transfers. The existence of this Fund does not preclude the State Agency from requiring compensation "in water" for the basin of origin rather than compensation in money. The State Agency is given considerable discretion in administering this Fund.

Cross-references: § 1R-1-01 (protecting the public interest in the waters of the State); § 1R-1-07 (encouraging flexibility through modification of water rights); § 1R-1-12 (recognizing local interests in the waters of the State); § 1R-1-13 (regulating interstate water transfers); § 1R-1-14 (regulating interbasin transfers); § 2R-2-10 (interbasin transfer); § 2R-2-11 (modification of a water right); § 2R-2-18 (the public interest); § 2R-2-23 (State Agency); § 2R-2-24 (sustainable development); § 2R-2-32 (waters of the State); § 3R-1-04(5) (contracts to protect additional levels of water to be paid for out of the State Water Fund); § 4R-1-07(3) (any surplus in the fees charged above the costs of administering permits to be paid into the State Water Fund); § 5R-4-06(3) (civil penalties to be paid to the State Water Fund); § 5R-4-07(1) (authority of the State Agency to waive claims on behalf of the State Water Fund); § 5R-4-07(3) (civil charges to be paid into the State Water Fund); § 5R-4-09(1) (claims due to the State Water Fund constitute a lien against real property); § 5R-5-01(4) (criminal fines to be paid into the State Water Fund); § 7R-1-01(k) (payments into the Interbasin Compensation Fund).

Comparable statutes: ARK. CODE ANN. § 15-22-507 (Arkansas Development Fund); DEL. CODE ANN. tit. 7, § 6005(d) (fees dedicated to the purposes of the Chapter); FLA. STAT. ANN. §§ 373.459 (Surface Water Improvement and Management Fund), 373.59 (Water Management Lands Trust Fund); KY. REV. STAT. ANN. § 151.380 (Water Resources Fund); MD. CODE ANN., NAT. RES. §§ 3-201 to 3-211 (Maryland Environmental Trust); N.J. STAT. ANN. §§ 58:1A-7.2 (Environmental Services Fund); WIS. STAT. ANN. § 144.241 (Clean Water Fund).

§ 4R-1-05 APPLICATION OF GENERAL LAWS TO MEETINGS, PROCEDURES, AND RECORDS

(1) All meetings and procedures of the State Agency shall comply with the State's Administrative Procedure Act unless different procedures are expressly prescribed by this Code.

(2) All records of the State Agency's activities and minutes of all meetings shall be maintained and made available to the public to the extent prescribed by general law unless other limits to public access are prescribed by this Code.

Commentary: This section simply recognizes that all State Agencies must comply with the State's administrative procedure and records laws except when this Code expressly provides otherwise. The Regulated Riparian Model Water Code provides special rules for certain procedures, particularly to assure participation in regulatory and planning proceedings to affected persons. A State might want to add a general requirement that meetings be open to the public and to allow public participation where appropriate if that is not already provided in the State's general Administrative Procedure Act.

Given the importance of water rights generally and in commercial settings in particular, it is essential that there be a readily accessible public record of all water rights. *See* Robert Beck, *The Uses of and Demands for Water,* in 1 WATERS AND WATER RIGHTS § 2.02. This, along with other non-confidential data collected in a statewide data system, will enable potential applicants for new or renewal permits to assess the situation of a water source in making their own plans and will enable potential buyers of land or water rights to examine the true status of both forms of property. The State Agency will maintain a public record of all permits in its publicly accessible Statewide Data System. Given the computerization of modern records, the Data System will be readily accessible to all persons interested in the use of the waters of the State. This is expected to follow from the application of the general laws of the State to the records of the Agency. If not, a section providing for public access to the statewide Data System or to the official record of permits should be added. *See, e.g.,* MD. CODE ANN., NAT. RES. § 8-808(b).

Cross-references: § 1R-1-08 (procedural protections); § 4R-1-09 (protection of confidential business information); § 4R-2-03 (the Statewide Data System); §§ 5R-1-01 to 5R-3-05 (disputes and enforcement); §§ 6R-2-01 to 6R-2-08 (permit procedures); §§ 7R-3-02, 7R-3-03 (water shortages and water emergencies).

Comparable statutes: ALA. CODE § 9-10B-30; DEL. CODE ANN. tit. 7, § 6014 (public records); HAW. REV. STAT. §§ 174C-9, 174C-60; IOWA CODE ANN. § 455B.278(2); MISS. CODE ANN. §§ 51-3-15(3), 51-3-51, 51-3-55(6); N.Y. ENVTL. CONSERV. LAW § 15-0907.

§ 4R-1-06 REGULATORY AUTHORITY OF THE STATE AGENCY

(1) The State Agency shall adopt such regulations as are necessary or convenient to administer the provisions of this Code.

(2) Regulations shall establish, without being limited to, the following:

(a) the form of an application for a permit under this Code;

(b) **procedures for hearings required under this Code;**

(c) **procedures for reviewing and acting on applications for permits under this Code;**

(d) **detailed methods for identifying and notifying persons who might be adversely affected by any action of the State Agency allocating, conserving, developing, or managing the waters of the State;**

(e) **requirements for reporting volumes and rates of withdrawal;**

(f) **methods for determining what portion of a withdrawal constitutes a consumptive use;**

(g) **procedures for developing and implementing the plans and strategies adopted under Part 2 of this Chapter; and**

(h) **a schedule of fees under section 4R-1-07.**

Commentary: This section provides a road map to the regulatory and planning functions that the Regulated Riparian Model Water Code vests in the State Agency except to the extent that some of these powers might be vested in Special Water Management Areas. Standards for various subjects of regulation are set forth in considerably greater detail throughout Chapters V, VI, VII, and VIII. *See also ASCE Policy Statement* No. 308 (revised 1993).

The authority of the State Agency to adopt regulations setting standards for activities carried out under the Code is broad. The State Agency could make regulations, for example, to set standards for the planning, design, and operation of all water withdrawal projects and facilities subject to a permit requirement under this Code or otherwise likely to have a substantial affect on the waters of the State. Such standards could include such matters as:

(1) local flood protection works;

(2) recharging operations for underground water;

(3) small water basin management programs;

(4) trunk mains for water distribution;

(5) water and waste treatment plants; and

(6) water-related recreational facilities.

Cross-references: § 4R-1-01 (basic responsibility and authority); § 4R-1-02 (nonimpairment of general powers); § 4R-1-03 (general administrative powers); § 4R-1-05 (application of general laws to meetings, procedures, and records).

Comparable statutes: ALA. CODE §§ 9-10B-5(20); 9-10B-18, 9-10B-19, 9-10B-23; ARK. CODE ANN. § 15-22-505(8); CONN. GEN. STAT. ANN. § 22a-377(c); FLA. STAT. ANN. §§ 373.043, 373.044, 373.113, 373.171; GA. CODE ANN. §§ 12-5-23(b), 12-5-94; HAW. REV. STAT. §§ 174C-8, 174C-82, 174C-86; IND. CODE ANN. § 13-2-2-12; IOWA CODE ANN. §§ 455B.105, 455B.263(8); KY. REV. STAT. ANN. §§ 151.125(3), (4), (7), 151.230; MINN. STAT. ANN. §§ 105.40, 105.535; MISS. CODE ANN. §§ 51-3-15(1), 51-3-25; N.J. STAT. ANN. §§ 58:1A-5, 58:1A-15(b); N.Y. ENVTL. CONSERV. LAW §§ 15-0901, 15-1503(4); N.C. GEN. STAT. §§ 143-215.13(d), 143.215-14; S.C. CODE ANN. § 49-5-90(A); VA. CODE ANN. § 62.1-44.92; WIS. STAT. ANN. §§ 144.025(b), (c), 144.026(10).

§ 4R-1-07 APPLICATION FEES

(1) The State Agency shall establish a schedule of application fees to be paid by every person who applies for a permit or registers a water use.

(2) Application fees shall equal the Agency's expenses for processing, monitoring, administering, and enforcing the permit and registration provisions of this Code.

Commentary: The costs of complying with the administrative requirements of the Regulated Riparian Model Water Code can become a significant burden to persons seeking to use water in various forms, and can also constitute a significant drain on the resources made available to the State Agency. The Code prevents the latter difficulty by providing that the costs of processing applications shall be born by permit applicants. This would be particularly burdensome for small users, however. The Code seeks to prevent this from becoming problematic by exempting small users from the need to apply for a permit and by exempting the smallest users even from the requirement that they register their activities. In contrast with the approach taken here, the Alabama regulatory riparian statute actually bars its regulatory agency from charging fees except as specifically authorized by the legislature. ALA. CODE § 9-10B-29.

Cross-references: § 1R-1-07 (flexibility for the transfer of water rights); § 4R-1-04 (special funds created); § 4R-01-06 (regulatory authority of the State Agency); § 4R-4-07 (funding for Special Water Management Areas); § 6R-1-01 (withdrawals unlawful without a permit); § 6R-1-06 (registration of withdrawals not subject to a permit); § 6R-2-01 (contents of an application for a permit); § 7R-2-02 (procedures for approving other modifications).

Comparable statutes: ARK. CODE ANN. §§ 15-22-219 (fees for dam permits correlated with the value of the project), 15-22-507 (fees and other cash received by the Commission to be paid into the Arkansas development fund); DEL. CODE ANN. tit. 7, §§ 6005(d) (fees dedicated to the purposes of the Chapter), 6006(5) (fee schedule to be created by the State Agency); FLA. STAT. ANN. § 373.109 (fees, not to exceed agency expenses, allocated to water management districts); HAW. REV. STAT. § 174C-61 (fees to cover administrative costs; public agencies exempted from fees); KY. REV. STAT. ANN. § 151.380(1) (all monies received to be paid into the Water Resources Fund); MASS. GEN. LAWS ANN. ch. 21G, § 18; MINN. STAT. ANN. §§ 105.41(5) (fees proportional to land irrigated or to quantity withdrawn), 105.44(10) (statutory fees for the costs of processing the application); MISS. CODE ANN. § 51-3-31 ($10 application fee); N.J. STAT. ANN. §§ 58:1A-7.2, 58:1A-11 (fees or taxes to equal the expense of processing and supervising the permit, payable to the Environmental Services Fund; actual expenses of administration to be funded from the State Treasury), 58:2-1 to 58:2-3 (public water supply systems to pay for the value of water diverted in excess of 100 gallons per person served); VA. CODE ANN. § 62.1-

44.104 (application fees of $5); WIS. STAT. ANN. §§ 30.28 (fees calibrated according to the estimated cost of the project), 144.026(10)(5) (fee set by regulation).

§ 4R-1-08 WATER USE FEES

(1) The State Agency shall, by regulation of general application after public notice and hearings, establish a schedule of reasonable water use fees as compensation for the value of water used.

(2) The State Agency shall collect water use fees from every person withdrawing water under a permit issued pursuant to this Code.

(3) Water use fees shall vary only according to the class of use as determined by the purpose or quantity of use.

(4) Such fees shall be paid into the general funds of the State.

Commentary: Water, both here and abroad, traditionally has been treated as a "free good"–*i.e.*, a good that is free of cost for the good itself, as opposed to costs for the delivery, consumption, or cleansing of the good. *See, e.g.*, 2 COUNCIL ON ENVTL. QUALITY, GLOBAL 2000 REPORT TO THE PRESIDENT 137 (1980); DIANA GIBBONS, THE ECONOMIC VALUE OF WATER (1986). Without requiring fees for the value of the water used, one cannot really hope to achieve real efficiency in the use of water and therefore of assuring sustainable development. Some States have used such fees as a means of providing significant preferences for particular uses, often as a means of assuring equitable access. The Regulated Riparian Model Water Code delegates the authority to the State Agency to set fees to recover a reasonable share of the value realized by the use of water. In general, the value of the water used would be measured by the value of the water consumed, yet in some instances that would not be the true measure of the values realized from the use of the water. For example, a person who diverts water over a waterwheel, all of which goes back to the stream without diminution or pollution, has not consumed any water but has realized considerable value from using the water. The Code contemplates charges for such uses as well as for consumptive uses. A use, such as navigation, that does not involve "withdrawals" would not be subject to water use fees.

A danger from charging water use fees is that the imposition of fees can render access to the waters of the State inequitable. The Code does not itself provide for preferences but does not precisely specify how the water use fees are to be set. The requirement that the fee allow the state to recover a reasonable share of the value of the water consumed somewhat limits the discretion of the Agency, but clearly the Agency has a broad discretion. The Agency is given the power to establish preferences consistent with the policies expressed in the Code by establishing fees by class of use. The Agency also is free to set fees in proportion to the quantity of use. *See* Dellapenna, § 9.03(a)(5)(C).

The Code does not spell out how the Agency is to set the fees. Perhaps the Agency will rely on auctioning or other market devices to set the price at or near the true economic value of the water. *See, e.g.*, LOYAL HARTMAN & DON SEASTONE, WATER TRANSFERS: ECONOMIC EFFICIENCY AND ALTERNATIVE INSTITUTIONS (1970); BONNIE SALIBA & DAVID BUSH, WATER MARKETS IN THEORY AND PRACTICE: MARKET TRANSFERS, WATER VALUES, AND PUBLIC POLICY (1987); RODNEY SMITH, TRADING WATER: AN ECONOMIC AND LEGAL FRAMEWORK FOR WATER MARKETING (1988); TRANSFERABILITY OF WATER ENTITLEMENTS (J.J. Pigram & B.P. Hooper eds. 1990); WATER TRANSFERS IN THE WEST: EFFICIENCY, EQUITY, AND THE ENVIRONMENT (A. Dan Tarlock ed. 1992). However the Agency sets the fees, the cost should be phased in over a transition period rather than imposed immediately at the introduction of the first fee schedule under the Code. A phase-in is necessary to cushion possible dislocation to the State's economy from charging for what heretofore had been a free good.

The broad discretion accorded to the State Agency in this section might be unacceptable to some States. A legislature with such qualms might prefer to set the fees by statute or to specify more precisely how fees are to be set, as well as to provide specific guidelines to govern the phase-in period. *See, e.g.*, ALA. CODE § 9-10B-29 (no fees to be charged except as specifically set by the legislature). In either event, it is important that water users cease to consider water a "free good" if we are to achieve a higher measure of efficiency in the use of water and to see the application of water to its higher valued uses.

The income from water use fees is to be paid into the treasury of the State to become part of the general revenues of the State. In this fashion, the allocation of a public resource to particular private uses would benefit of the entire community, leaving it to the people's elected representatives to decide how best to expend the resulting income. An alternative would be designate water use fees for payment into the State Water Fund created by section 4R-1-04. That fund is to be used exclusively for upgrading the environmental, ecological, and aesthetic values which are among the core values that this Code is designed to foster. A final possibility would be to use the monies generated by the water use fee to defray the general expenses of the Administering Agency, although this last option risks freeing the Agency too greatly from political review of their operations.

Cross-references: § 1R-1-07 (policy of flexibility for the transfer of water rights); § 2R-2-24 (sustainable development); § 2R-2-32 (waters of the State); §§ 4R-1-04 (special funds created); § 4R-01-06 (regulatory authority of the State Agency); § 4R-1-07 (application fees); § 4R-4-07 (funding for Special Water Management Areas); §§§ 5R-1-01 to 5R-1-05 (hearings); §§ 5R-3-01 to 5R-3-03 (judicial review); § 6R-3-04 (preferences among water rights); §§ 7R-2-01 to 7R-2-04 (modification of water rights).

Comparable statutes: ARK. CODE ANN. §§ 15-22-219 (fees for dam permits correlated with the value of the project), 15-22-507 (fees and other cash received by the Commission to be paid into the Arkansas development fund); DEL. CODE ANN. tit. 7, §§ 6005(d) (fees dedicated to the purposes of the Chapter), 6006(5) (fee schedule to be created by the State Agency); KY. REV. STAT. ANN. § 151.380(1) (all monies received to be paid into the Water Resources Fund); MINN. STAT. ANN. §105.41(5) (fees proportional to land irrigated or to quantity withdrawn); N.J. STAT. ANN. § 58:A-7.2 (no fee for agricultural or horticultural uses), 58:A–11 (fees or taxes to equal the expense of processing and supervising the permit, payable to the Environmental Services Fund; actual expenses of administration to be funded from the State treasury), 58:2-1 to 58:2-3 (public water supply systems to pay for the value of water diverted in excess of 100 gallons per person served); WIS. STAT. ANN. § 30.28 (fees calibrated according to the estimated cost of the project), 144.026(10)(5) (fee set by regulation).

§ 4R-1-09 PROTECTION OF CONFIDENTIAL BUSINESS INFORMATION

(1) Any confidential business information in any information provided by any person to the State Agency or obtained by the Agency through its investigatory powers, under this Code or under any order, permit term or condition, or regulation made pursuant to this Code, shall be kept confidential by the Agency.

(2) A person claiming the privilege of confidential business information must identify the information allegedly embodying the confidential business information which thereafter will be kept in a separate place from the general records pertaining to that applicant.

(3) No person shall be able to claim as confidential business information data reporting the amount of water withdrawn or consumed pursuant to that person's permit.

(4) Presumptively confidential information will be made available only to employees of the State Agency in so far as is necessary to fulfill their duties pending a final determination of the validity of the claimed privilege.

(5) The State Agency will from time to time review claims of privilege for confidential business information and, after affording the person claiming the privilege a confidential hearing upon that person's request, shall release to the general records any information

determined by the Agency not to embody confidential business information.

(6) The disclosure or use of any information regarding confidential business information privileged under this section in any administrative or judicial proceeding shall be determined by the rules of evidence.

(7) A person claiming the privilege shall be provided notice 10 business days before any disclosure or use in any administrative or judicial proceeding

(8) The State Agency will not oppose any motion by the person claiming the privilege to intervene as a party to the administrative or judicial proceeding in which the disclosure or use is planned.

Commentary: Applicants and others will from time to time be required under the Regulated Riparian Model Water Code to disclose information that the person considers to be confidential business information. This section of the Code establish the obligation of the State Agency to protect confidential business information under most circumstances. The section also establishes procedures to determine whether a claim of confidential business information was properly made and for disclosing confidential business information in the course of administrative or judicial proceedings.

If confidential business information is to be used in a legal proceeding, the Code requires that the person claiming confidentiality be given notice of the intent to do so at least 10 business days before the attempt to admit the information and that the person claiming confidentiality not be opposed by the State Agency when that person seeks to enter the case to litigate the question of confidentiality. A legislature might select some notice period other than 10 business days specified in this section, but the principle that the person claiming confidentiality be heard before the evidence is admitted into open court or an administrative proceeding is an important principle that no State should ignore.

This Code rejects, however, the common practice of claiming simple data of how much water is withdrawn or consumed as confidential business information. If the public is to be in a position to evaluate the performance of the Agency, this information must be a matter of public record.

Cross-references: § 1R-1-08 (procedural protections); §§ 5R-1-01 to 5R-3-05 (disputes and enforcement); §§ 5R-3-01 to 5R-3-03 (judicial review).

Comparable statutes: GA. CODE ANN. § 12-5-98(a); MASS. GEN. LAWS ANN. ch. 21G, § 13; N.C. GEN. STAT. § 143-215.19(c).

Part 2
Planning Responsibilities

The Regulated Riparian Model Water code vests the State Agency with responsibility for intermediate- and long-term planning both for periods of normal water availability and for the management of droughts. Only if such planning is done properly can the State hope to achieve the sustainable development of the waters of the State and the realization of the public interest. This Part sets out the obligation to undertake planning, and also creates a Statewide Data System and Planning Advisory Committees. The Data System, in particular, could well be the most useful planning tool created by the code, a tool useful both for state activities and for private actors. If the State gives the State Agency responsibility for maintaining water quality, flood control, and similar issues, the planning responsibilities of the State Agency should be correspondingly enlarged.

§ 4R-2-01 THE COMPREHENSIVE WATER ALLOCATION PLAN

(1) The State Agency shall develop and adopt a comprehensive water allocation plan within five (5) years of the effective date of this Code, and shall review and revise the plan from time to time thereafter.

(2) The plan shall collect data and devise strategies for achieving sustainable development of the waters of the State. The plan shall include, but need not be limited to:

(a) identification of existing uses of the waters of the State;

(b) estimates of future trends in uses of the waters of the State, including the current and future capabilities of public water supply systems to provide an adequate quantity and quality of water to their service areas and the developmental choices necessary to attain the optimum reasonable use of water;

(c) identification of the boundaries of the water basins of the major water sources within the State;

(d) an estimate of the safe yield for each major water source and, where applicable:

(1) the minimum flows and levels necessary, during normal and drought conditions, to preserve the protected biological, chemical, and physical integrity of the water source; and

(2) the prime recharge areas for underground water;

(e) an evaluation of the reasonableness of various classes of use;

(f) a description of systems for allocating the waters of the State during a water shortage or emergency; and

(g) **a set of recommended goals for the use, management, and protection of the waters of the State and related land resources, with evaluations of alternative recommendations according to economic, environmental, hydrologic, jurisdictional, legal, social, and other relevant factors.**

(3) **The State Agency shall provide reasonable opportunities for all interested persons to comment on the plan while it is being formulated, including, where appropriate, one or more public hearings on the proposed plan.**

Commentary: Planning obligations are usually included in existing regulated riparian statutes. *See generally* Dellapenna, § 9.05. In fact, some commentators have concluded that the existing regulated riparian statutes require permits more to assure data for the State's planning processes than for actually controlling how water is used. *See* TARLOCK, § 3.20(4). While the Regulated Riparian Model Water Code does not subscribe to the latter view, it does place planning at the center of the State Agency's responsibility. The Comprehensive Water Allocation Plan is to guide the State Agency in all of its activities and other persons whose activities are subject to regulation by the Agency. This section sets forth the obligations and limits of the Agency's intermediate- and long-term planning authority, spelling out in some detail the matters that must be considered and the conclusions that must be included in the State's Comprehensive Water Allocation Plan.

Subsection (1) establishes the obligation to complete development of the comprehensive water allocation plan within five years of the effective date of this Code. The plan is defined in section 2R-2-04 as a plan for the intermediate and long-term management of the waters of the State with a view toward the sustainable development and reasonable use of the waters of the State. After completing the initial plan, the State Agency is to update the plan as needed, being given the discretion to decide when and how often to do so.

Subsection (2) establishes sustainable development as the legal goal of the planning process. The goal of achieving sustainable development is pervasive throughout the Code, but it comes to the fore in the planning process. As consistency with the comprehensive water allocation plan is a prerequisite for obtaining a permit, sustainable development also serves as a legal standard for use of the waters of the State. Furthermore, although the plan will probably never be the exclusive consideration in determining whether a use is reasonable, the plan will go a long way toward resolving that question, including an evaluation of the reasonableness of particular classes of use from a particular water source. Subsection (2) specifies the minimum contents of any Comprehensive Water Allocation Plan.

Subsection (3) assures a reasonable opportunity for all interested persons to have input on the plan while it is being formulated. The procedures for providing such access presumably would include hearings as provided in part 1 of Chapter V. Because of the extensive reach of this section, States may consider inviting the federal government or pertinent international institutions to join in formulating the plan.

Cross-references: § 1R-1-01 (protecting the public interest in the waters of the State); § 1R-1-04 (comprehensive planning); § 2R-2-04 (comprehensive water allocation plan); § 2R-2-09 (drought management strategies); § 2R-2-21 (safe yield); § 2R-2-24 (sustainable development); § 2R-2-28 (water basin); § 2R-2-32 (waters of the State); § 2R-2-33 (water source); § 4R-2-02 (drought management strategies); § 4R-2-03 (the statewide data system); § 4R-2-04 (planning advisory committees); § 4R-3-01 (cooperation with the federal government); § 4R-3-02 (cooperation with other units of state and local government); §§ 5R-1-01 to 5R-1-05 (hearings); § 6R-3-01 (standards for a permit); § 6R-3-02 (determining whether a use is reasonable); §§ 7R-3-01 to 7R-3-07 (restrictions during water shortages or water emergencies).

Comparable statutes: ALA. CODE § 9-10B-5(1), (5), (14); ARK. CODE ANN. §§ 15-22-301, 15-22-503, 15-22-504; CONN. GEN. STAT. ANN. § 22a-352; DEL. CODE ANN. tit. 7, §§ 6010(a), 6014; FLA. STAT. ANN. §§ 373.036, 373.039, 373.0395; GA. CODE ANN. §§ 12-5-443, 12-5-521, 12-5-522 (river basin management plans); HAW. REV. STAT. § 174C-31; IND. CODE ANN. §§ 13-2-6.1-3, 13-2-6.1-5, 13-2-7-1 to 13-2-8-2; IOWA CODE ANN. §§ 455B.262, 455B.263(1); KY. REV. STAT. ANN. §§ 151.112, 151.220, 151.240; MASS. GEN. LAWS ANN. ch. 21G, § 3; MINN.

STAT. ANN. §§ 105.391, 105.403, 105.405; MISS. CODE ANN. § 51-3-21; N.J. STAT. ANN. § 58:1A-13; N.Y. ENVTL. CONSERV. LAW §§ 15-503(3), 15-2901 to 15-2913; N.C. GEN. STAT. §§ 143-354(a), 143-355; S.C. CODE ANN. §§ 49-3-40, 49-3-50; VA. CODE ANN. § 62.1-44.38; WIS. STAT. ANN. § 144.026(8).

§ 4R-2-02 DROUGHT MANAGEMENT STRATEGIES

(1) The State Agency shall devise and publish a set of drought management strategies in anticipation of reasonably foreseeable water shortages and water emergencies.

(2) The drought management strategies for each major water source within the State shall include, but not be limited to:

- **(a) criteria for identifying the onset and severity of a water shortage or water emergency;**
- **(b) a specification of the classes of uses and their priorities, based on their relationship to the public interest as determined according the policies, standards, and grounds established in this Code;**
- **(c) measures for auditing water use and detecting leaks;**
- **(d) measures for overall system rehabilitation;**
- **(e) a registry of conservation measures for public and private buildings, including, under appropriate conditions, a moratorium on new construction;**
- **(f) registered private agreements to curtail use in times of water shortage or water emergency;**
- **(g) possible bans or restrictions on certain water uses; and**
- **(h) other necessary contingency plans.**

Commentary: Responding to water shortages and water emergencies will often be the most controversial steps that the State Agency will undertake. *See* Dellapenna, § 9.05(d). To assure both that the State Agency responds in a careful manner to any shortfall in available water and that water users have ample notice of the risks they run in the event of a serious shortfall in the water available in the water source on which they rely, the Regulated Riparian Model Water Code requires the State Agency to undertake advance planning of drought management strategies and to keep abreast of conservation measures and plans of conservation by permit holders. The resulting published drought management strategies will serve to guide the drought responses both of the State Agency and of persons using water. The planning of drought management strategies cuts across comprehensive water planning otherwise required by this Code. *See id.* § 9.05(a).

Drought management strategies will indicate the sort of shortfalls that will cause the State Agency to invoke its powers relating to water shortages and water emergencies. The strategies will also specify the priorities to be given to different classes of use. In general, the priorities will reflect the protection of minimum levels in water sources and the preferences applicable to competing applications. Priority will also have to be given to water uses mandated by the federal government or under interstate obligations binding on this State. Additional priorities might be found in the Comprehensive Water Allocation Plan or in Area Water Management Plans created by Special Water Management Areas.

The drought management strategies will contain an inventory of steps to curtail use and otherwise to protect the biological, chemical, and physical integrity of the affected water sources and to assure water to the most essential uses, redefining the safe yield of the affected water source under the drought conditions. The drought management strategies will also outline means for assuring compliance with such measures, and proposed means for, in so far as possible, restoring ("rehabilitating") the water sources to their normal or usual physical state under conditions of sustainable development. If it becomes necessary to compromise these several goals (protection, assurance, and rehabilitation), the drought management strategies will include the indicia of, and the steps for responding to, the water emergency conditions that alone justify such compromises.

In keeping with the emphasis of this Code on encouraging and enabling persons to respond through their own arrangements to the needs and problems, the Code, in section 7R-3-05, provides for conservation credits for persons who undertake voluntarily to curtail their usage during periods of shortage or emergency. The same section of the Code also encourages water right holders to agree among themselves how to curtail use during water shortages or water emergencies. To take such agreements into account in planning for the water shortages and water emergencies, the Code requires such agreements to be registered in advance and reserves the authority to the State Agency to disallow the agreements on the same basis as the Agency might disapprove a transfer or other modification of a water right.

The focus on drought management strategies in this Code reflects its focus on water allocation issues. In some states, the State Agency will also be given responsibility for water quality, flood control, and other non-allocational issues. In those States, this section should be expanded to cover these broader responsibilities in the form of general water shortage and water emergency strategies rather than just drought management strategies..

Cross-references: § 1R-1-01 (protecting the public interest in the waters of the State); § 1R-1-04 (comprehensive planning); § 1R-1-05 (efficient and equitable allocation during shortfalls in supply); § 1R-1-10 (water conservation); § 1R-1-11 (preservation of minimum flows and levels); § 1R-1-12 (recognizing local interests in the waters of the State); § 1R-1-13 (regulating interstate water transfers); § 2R-2-02 (biological integrity); § 2R-2-03 (chemical integrity); § 2R-2-04 (comprehensive water allocation plan); § 2R-2-05 (conservation measures); § 2R-2-09 (drought management strategies); § 2R-2-16 (physical integrity); § 2R-2-17 (plan for conservation); § 2R-2-21 (safe yield); § 2R-2-24 (sustainable development); § 2R-2-27 (waste of water); § 2R-2-29 (water emergency); § 2R-2-31 (water shortage) § 2R-2-32 (waters of the State); § 2R-2-33 (water source); § 3R-1-02 (certain shared waters exempted from allocation); §§ 3R-2-01 to 3R-2-05 (protection of minimum flows or levels); § 4R-2-01 (the comprehensive water allocation plan); § 4R-2-03 (the statewide data system); § 4R-2-04 (planning advisory committees); § 4R-3-01 (cooperation with the federal government); § 4R-4-05 (Area Water Management Plans); § 6R-3-04 (preferences among water rights); §§ 7R-3-01 to 7R-3-07 (restrictions during water shortages or water emergencies); §§ 8R-1-01 to 8R-1-07 (multijurisdictional transfers).

Comparable statutes: ALA. CODE § 9-10B-5(13); HAW. REV. STAT. § 174C-62(a).

§ 4R-2-03 THE STATEWIDE DATA SYSTEM

(1) In cooperation with the political subdivisions of the State, of county or local governmental organizations, and of agencies created for the purpose of utilizing or conserving the waters of this State, the State Agency shall establish and maintain a statewide system to gather, process, and distribute information on the availability, distribution, quality, and use of the waters of the State, including data on all permits issued under this Code.

(2) The State Agency shall invite interested agencies of the federal government and interstate and international agencies with responsibility for waters of the State to join the statewide data system and shall cooperate with any such agency choosing to join the system.

(3) Information gathered in the statewide data system, subject to the protection provided to confidential business information under section 4R-1-09, shall be made available to any person on payment of a reasonable fee to cover the expenses of making the information available to that person.

Commentary: The State Agency, and other persons within the State, need accurate and complete information in order to fulfill their responsibilities relating to water. In particular, without accurate data, the sort of comprehensive planning that the Regulated Riparian Model Water Code contemplates is impossible. The Code creates a statewide data system to be administered by the State Agency and accessible to public and private persons upon the payment of a reasonable fee to recover the expenses of making the data available to that person–not the expenses of gathering and maintaining the data. The availability of the data to the public is limited by the protection required for confidential business information.

The Code also imposes an express duty on all other agencies and branches under the State's authority to provide relevant data to the System. The State cannot require the agencies or branches of the federal government or of interstate or international organizations to cooperate with the statewide data system, yet their cooperation could be vital to the success of the system. The Code requires the State Agency to invite the participation of these agencies or branches and authorizes the State Agency to cooperate with them. The terms of cooperation, including cost sharing and assured access, would need to be negotiated in each instance.

ASCE has long recognized the importance of data collection. Therefore, ASCE supports broad funding for United States Geological Survey and State data collection efforts. *See ASCE Policy Statement* No. 275 (1988).

Cross-references: § 2R-2-15 (person); § 2R-2-32 (waters of the State); § 4R-2-01 (the comprehensive water allocation plan); § 4R-2-02 (drought management strategies); § 4R-2-04 (planning advisory committees); § 4R-3-01 (cooperation with the federal government); § 4R-3-02 (cooperation with other units of state and local government); § 4R-3-03 (duty to cooperate); § 6R-4-02(3) (duty of water quality agency to provide relevant data to the statewide data system).

Comparable statutes: ALA. CODE § 9-10B-5(4); FLA. STAT. ANN. § 373.026(2); HAW. REV. STAT. § 174C-5(13); KY. REV. STAT. ANN. §§ 151.035, 151.112(e); MINN. STAT. ANN. § 105.39(6).

§ 4R-2-04 PLANNING ADVISORY COMMITTEES

(1) The State Agency shall establish planning advisory committees to assist in the formulation of its plans, programs, and strategies, providing by regulation for the constitution and functioning of the committees.

(2) Advisory committees may include representatives from agencies or branches of the United States, agencies or branches of interstate or international organizations with responsibility for water of the State, other agencies or branches of the State, other States sharing the water basin under study, the political subdivisions of the State, and all persons or groups interested in or directly affected by any proposed or existing plan or strategies.

Commentary: The Regulated Riparian Model Water Code seeks to assure the participation of affected persons in activities undertaken by the State Agency. For the planning functions, the numbers of people affected are generally too large to enable all to participate in person. Some regulated riparian statutes provide in detail for separate planning bodies, often with elaborate provisions as to the constitution and functioning of those bodies. This section Code provides for representative participation by the inclusion of representatives in planning advisory committees to work with the State Agency in formulating the comprehensive water allocation plans and drought management strategies required under this Part. The Code leaves it to the State Agency to define by regulation how such committees are to be established and function. Such regulations are subject to judicial review on the same basis as any other regulation adopted by the State Agency pursuant to this Code.

Cross-references: § 1R-1-04 (comprehensive planning); § 2R-2-04 (comprehensive water allocation plan); § 2R-2-09 (drought management strategies); § 2R-2-15 (person); § 4R-2-01 (the comprehensive water allocation plan); § 4R-2-02 (drought management strategies); § 4R-2-03 (the statewide data system); § 5R-3-01 (judicial review of regulations).

Comparable statutes: ALA. CODE § 9-10B-24 (water resource council); GA. CODE ANN. § 12-5-523; MASS. GEN. LAWS ANN. ch. 21G, § 3; N.Y. ENVTL. CONSERV. LAW § 15-2901 (water resources planning council); VA. CODE ANN. §§ 62.1-44.38(D), 62.1-44.98.

Part 3

Coordination with Other Branches or Levels of Government

The ambient nature of water assures that no level or agency of government can operate without affecting other levels and agencies of government, just as no user of water can withdraw water without affecting other users. This Part sets forth a comprehensive set of provisions for the cooperation and coordination of the State Agency with other levels and agencies of government. To the extent it is within the authority of the State to do so, this Part also imposes an obligation on other agencies of government to cooperate and coordinate with the State Agency. Where, as with federal, interstate, and international units of government, the State cannot impose the duty, the Code authorizes the State Agency to cooperate with those units on a voluntary basis. Finally, this Part provides for certain protections of persons subject to regulation or condemnation from difficulties they might confront from incomplete coordination. The specific problems of coordinating water allocation with water quality issues, if responsibility for those issues are vested in different agencies of the State, are further addressed in part 4 of the Chapter VI.

§ 4R-3-01 COOPERATION WITH THE FEDERAL GOVERNMENT AND INTERSTATE AND INTERNATIONAL ORGANIZATIONS

The State Agency shall cooperate with any appropriate agency or officer of the United States or any agency, officer, or body acting under the authority of an interstate compact or international treaty ratified by the United States

when such agency, officer, or body's responsibilities relate to the management, conservation, or development of the waters of the State and the State Agency determines that cooperation is consistent with this Code.

Commentary: As the federal government becomes an ever more important player in the conservation, development, and use of water, it becomes ever more important that the State Agency have clear authority to coordinate its activities with those of federal agencies. The Regulated Riparian Model Water Code authorizes such cooperation, but only when the State Agency determines that to do so would be consistent with the policies and provisions of the Code. In case of conflict between the policies and provisions of this Code and federal law or programs, federal law (including interstate compacts and international treaties ratified by the United States), of course, prevails, but such problems must be addressed by the legislature or other responsible organs of State government and not by the State Agency. *See* JOHN MATHER, WATER RESOURCES, DISTRIBUTION, USE, AND MANAGEMENT 294-305 (1984); SAX, ABRAMS, & THOMPSON, at 644-74, 804-916; TARLOCK, CORBRIDGE, & GETCHES, at 664-830; TRELEASE & GOULD, at 635-808; Dellapenna, § 9.06(b); Amy Kelley, *Constitutional Foundations of Federal Water Law,* in 4 WATERS AND WATER RIGHTS § 35.08; Amy Kelly, *Federal-State Relations in Water,* in 4 WATERS AND WATER RIGHTS § 36.01. The Code deals similarly with the coordination of the State Agency's activities with the activities of interstate or international commissions or other bodies created by interstate compact or international treaty to manage, develop, or conserve waters shared across state or national boundaries.

Most interstate compacts in States likely to adopt regulated riparian statutes merely call for the States to share information and to consult in formulating individual state plans and policies. Two eastern compacts, however, go far beyond such a limited arrangement: the Delaware River Basin Compact, Pub. L. No. 87-328, 75 Stat. 688 (1961), codified at DEL. CODE ANN. tit. 7, § 6501; N.J. STAT. ANN. §§ 32.11D-1 to -110; N.Y. ENVTL. CONSERV. LAW § 21-0701; PA. STAT. ANN. § 815.101; and the Susquehanna River Basin Compact, Pub. L. No. 91-575, 84 Stat. 1509 (1970) , codified at MD. NAT. RESOURCES CODE § 8-301; N.Y. ENVTL. CONSERV. LAW § 21-1301; PA. STAT. ANN. tit. 32, § 820.1. The Delaware and Susquehanna Compacts together form a unique package found nowhere else in the United States. Both compacts provide that the governing commission can regulate individual direct water users (of either surface water or "tributary" underground water) within the basin, and under both compacts the federal government is a full participant, with both a single vote on the commissions (along with each state in the basin) and the obligation to follow most decisions made by simple majority vote. The regulatory authority of the commissions largely has been delegated to the regulated riparian authorities found in the States within the basin. While Delaware and Maryland had enacted regulated riparian statutes before the relevant compacts were ratified, New Jersey and New York did so only after the compacts were ratified and apparently to some considerable extent in order to enable the delegation of authority to occur. Only Pennsylvania thus far has not enacted a regulated riparian statute, although one has been under consideration there for some years. On the Delaware and Susquehanna Compacts, see SAX, ABRAMS, & THOMPSON, at 742-46; Dellapenna, § 9.06(c)(2); Joseph Dellapenna, *The Delaware and Susquehanna River Basins,* in 6 WATERS AND WATER RIGHTS 137 (1994 reissued vol.). On compacts generally, see SAX, ABRAMS, & THOMPSON, at 700-15, 733-42; TARLOCK, CORBRIDGE, & GETCHES, at 863-80; TRELEASE & GOULD, at 616-22; Douglas Grant, *Water Apportionment Compacts between States,* in 4 WATERS AND WATER RIGHTS, ch. 46.

Important international bodies that have responsibility for waters shared by the United States include the International Joint Commission between the United States and Canada, created in 1909, and the International Boundary and Water Commission, between the United States and Mexico. *Treaty Relating to Boundary Waters and Questions Arising between the United States and Canada,* signed Jan. 11, 1909, United Kingdom-United States, 36 Stat. 2449, T.S. 548; *Treaty Respecting Utilization of Waters of the Colorado and Tijuana Rivers and of the Rio Grande,* signed Feb. 3, 1944, Mexico-United States, 59 Stat. 1219, T.S. No. 994, 3 U.N.T.S. 313. *See generally* F.J. BERBER, RIVERS IN INTERNATIONAL LAW 110-15 (R.K. Batstone trans. 1959); DON PIPER, THE INTERNATIONAL LAW OF THE GREAT LAKES (1967); SAX, ABRAMS, & THOMPSON, at 790-803; LUDWIK TECLAFF, WATER LAW IN HISTORICAL PERSPECTIVE 428-33, 438-43, 458-61 (1985); Gerald Graham, *International Rivers and Lakes: The Canadian-American Regime,* in THE LEGAL REGIME OF INTERNATIONAL RIVERS AND LAKES 3 (Ralph Zacklin & Lucius Caflisch eds. 1981);

Symposium, *U.S.-Canadian Transboundary Resource Issues,* 26 NAT. RESOURCES J. 201-376 (1986); Symposium, *U.S.-Mexican Transboundary Resource Issues,* 26 NAT. RESOURCES J. 659-850 (1986); Albert Utton, *Canadian International Waters,* in 5 WATERS AND WATER RIGHTS, ch. 50; Albert Utton, *Mexican International Waters,* in 5 WATERS AND WATER RIGHTS, ch. 51. Numerous other treaties dealing with more localized issues have been ratified over the years. *See, e.g., Convention Providing for the Equitable Distribution of the Waters of the Rio Grande for Irrigation Purposes,* signed May 21, 1906, Mexico-United States, 34 Stat. 2953, 34 Stat. 2953, T.S. No. 455; *Treaty for the Co-Operative Development of the Columbia River Basin,* signed Jan. 17, 1961, Canada-United States, 15 U.S.T. 1555, T.I.A.S. 5638, 542 U.N.T.S. 244; *Treaty Relating to the Uses of the Waters of the Niagara River,* signed Feb. 27, 1950, United States-Canada, 1 U.S.T. 694, T.I.A.S. No. 2130, 132 U.N.T.S. 224; JOHN KRUTILLA, THE COLUMBIA RIVER TREATY: THE ECONOMICS OF AN INTERNATIONAL RIVER BASIN DEVELOPMENT (1967); Ralph Johnson, *Columbia Basin,* in THE LAW OF INTERNATIONAL DRAINAGE BASINS 167 (Albert Garretson, Robert Hayton, & Cecil Olmstead eds. 1967). The North American Free Trade Agreement of 1993 (NAFTA) also contained important and extensive provisions relating to transboundary water management. *Agreement Concerning the Establishment of the Border Environment Cooperation Agreement and a North American Development Bank,* signed Nov. 18, 1993, Canada-Mexico-United States, reprinted in 32 INT'L LEG. MAT'LS 1545; Joseph Block, *The Environmental Aspects of NAFTA and their Relevance to Possible Free Trade Agreements between the United States and Caribbean Nations,* 14 VA. J. ENVTL. L. 1; Jan Gilbreath, *Financing Environment and Infrastructure Needs on the Texas-Mexican Border: Will the Mexican-U.S. Border Plan Help,* 1 J. ENVT. & DEV. 151 (1992); Nick Johnstone, *International Trade, Transfrontier Pollution, and Environmental Cooperation: A Case Study of the Mexican-American Border Region,* 35 NAT. RESOURCES J. 33 (1995); Lawrence Rowe, *NAFTA, the Border Area Environmental Program, and Mexico's Border Area: Prescription for Sustainable Development?,* 18 SUFFOLK TRANSNAT'L L. REV. 197 (1995).

Cross-references: § 1R-1-04 (comprehensive planning); § 1R-1-13 (regulating interstate water transfers); § 2R-2-10 (interbasin transfers); § 3R-1-02 (certain shared waters exempt from allocation); §§ 4R-2-01 to 4R-2-04 (planning responsibilities); § 6R-3-06 (special standard for interbasin transfers); §§ 8R-1-01 to 8R-1-07 (multijurisdictional transfers).

Comparable statutes: ALA. CODE §§ 9-10B-5(6), (7), (14), 9-10B-6, 9-10B-26; ARK. CODE ANN. § 15-22-506; DEL. CODE ANN. tit. 7, §§ 6001(c)(5), 6021; FLA. STAT. ANN. §§ 373.012, 373.026(8); GA. CODE ANN. §§ 12-5-32 to 12-5-34, 12-5-38, 12-5-50; HAW. REV. STAT. §§ 174C-5(4), (6), (11), (12), 174C-31(l), 174C-71; IND. CODE ANN. §§ 13-2-2-3, 13-2-6.1-4(7); IOWA CODE ANN. § 455B.263(2) to (5); KY. REV. STAT. ANN. §§ 151.112(b), 151.220(4), 151.360(a), 151.580, 105.49; MISS. CODE ANN. § 51-3-21(3); N.J. STAT. ANN. § 58:1A-15(g) to (i); S.C. CODE ANN. §§ 49-3-40(g), 49-5-90(B), 49-5-130; VA. CODE ANN. § 62.1-44.38(E), (F).

4R-3-02 COOPERATION WITH OTHER UNITS OF STATE AND LOCAL GOVERNMENT

(1) The State Agency shall cooperate with political subdivisions of this State, with county or local governmental organizations, and with agencies created for the purpose of utilizing or conserving the waters of this State, assisting such entities to coordinate facilities and participating in the exchange of ideas, knowledge, and data with such other units of government.

(2) Upon the written request of any other unit of government within the State, the State Agency is authorized to provide water supply planning assistance to that unit of government in so far as Agency resources permit.

(3) Water supply planning assistance as authorized in subsection (2) of this section shall relate to:

(a) applications for federal grants or permits;

(b) drought management strategies;

(c) evaluation of alternative water sources;

(d) the necessity for new enabling legislation;

(e) steps for conserving water; or

(f) such other planning activities as the Agency determines to be appropriate.

(4) The State Agency shall maintain an advisory staff of experts for the purposes set forth in this section.

Commentary: All States have local units of government and many States also have special purpose units of government directed at conserving or managing local water supplies to meet particular needs. *See* SAX, ABRAMS, & THOMPSON, at 628-644, 674-99; SPECIAL WATER DISTRICTS: CHALLENGE FOR THE FUTURE (James Corbridge, jr., ed. 1983); TRELEASE & GOULD, at 511-45. The Regulated Riparian Model Water Code does not usually displace the responsibilities of these other units of State and local government. Although the responsibility and authority to implement the policies and provisions of this Code remain vested in the State Agency and are not delegated to other units of government except as might be specifically authorized in this Code, the Code seeks to foster a cooperative rather than a competitive attitude among these various units of government. This section goes beyond merely requiring the cooperation of different units of State government; it authorizes to the State Agency to provide active support to the activities and functions of other units of State and local government relating to water in so far as the resources available to the Agency enable it to do so.

The section specifically authorizes the State Agency to assist other units of government in their planning activities related to water and to maintain the necessary staff to aid those units in both achieving their own purposes and in conforming their activities and functions to the requirements of the State Agency pursuant to this Code. Support will better enable the other units of State and local government to comply with the policies and provisions of this Code and also to take best advantage of the opportunities provided by federal grants and other programs. The

Agency is also authorized to assist the other units of State and local government in their relations with the State legislature in so far as those relations concern the waters of the State.

Cross-references: § 1R-1-04 (comprehensive planning); § 1R-1-12 (recognizing local interests in the waters of the State); § 1R-1-14 (regulating interbasin transfers); § 2R-2-09 (drought management strategies); § 2R-2-12 (municipal uses); § 2R-2-19 (public water supply system); § 2R-2-33 (water source); §§ 4R-2-01 to 4R-2-04 (planning responsibilities); § 4R-3-04 (combined permits); § 4R-3-05 (limitation on the power of eminent domain); § 6R-3-01 (standards for a permit); § 6R-3-02 (determining whether a use is reasonable); § 6R-3-04 (preferences among water rights); §§ 6R-4-01 to 6R-4-05 (coordination of water allocation and water quality regulation).

Comparable statutes: ARK. CODE ANN. § 15-22-505(5); DEL. CODE ANN. tit. 7, §§ 6001(c)(5), 6003(c); FLA. STAT. ANN. §§ 373.026(3), 373.046, 373.0391, 373.1961; GA. CODE ANN. §§ 12-5-33 to 12-5-41; HAW. REV. STAT. §§ 174C-5(6), (12), 174C-31(l); IND. CODE ANN. § 13-2-6.1-4(7); IOWA CODE ANN. §§ 455B.105(2), 455B.263(2); KY. REV. STAT. ANN. §§ 151.112(b), 151.220(4), 151.390 to 151.410; MASS. GEN. LAWS ANN. ch. 21G, § 10; MINN. STAT. ANN. §§ 105.416(3), 105.44, 105.49; MISS. CODE ANN. §§ 51-3-16, 51-3-18, 51-3-21; N.J. STAT. ANN. § 58:1A-15(g); N.Y. ENVTL. CONSERV. LAW § 15-13-3; S.C. CODE ANN. §§ 49-3-40(d), 49-6-90(B); VA. CODE ANN. §§ 62.1-243(b), 62.1-250.

§ 4R-3-03 DUTY TO COOPERATE

(1) All local, regional, special purpose, and State governmental units within this State shall cooperate with the State Agency in its carrying out of its responsibilities under this Code.

(2) Every official of the State or of any county or local government, including agencies created for the purpose of utilizing or conserving

the water of this State, is under a duty, upon request, to assist the State Agency or its duly authorized employees in the enforcement of the provisions of this Code or of any order, permit term or condition, or regulation made pursuant to this Code.

Commentary: Similarly to the charge to the State Agency to cooperate with other units of State and local government, the Regulated Riparian Model Water Code requires all other governmental units within the State to cooperate with the State Agency in the fulfillment of its duties under the Code. This requirement relieves the other units of government from any objections they might make to cooperating based on lack of authority under State or local law. The only surviving legal impediments to cooperation, if any, must be found in the State constitution.

Ordinary law enforcement officers throughout the State are placed under a duty to cooperate with the officers or employees of the Agency in the enforcement of the provisions and requirements of the Code. The duty is generalized to a duty of all officials of State and local government to cooperate within the limits of their offices. Such a general duty is justified by the importance attached to the proper planning, management, and regulation of the waters of the State. As a corollary to this duty, duly authorized employees of the State Agency are required to turn persons they arrest over to the ordinary law enforcement officers promptly.

Cross-references: § 1R-1-14 (regulating interbasin transfers); § 2R-2-12 (municipal uses); § 2R-2-20 (public water supply system); §§ 4R-2-01 to 4R-2-04 (planning responsibilities); § 4R-3-02 (cooperation with other units of state and local government); § 4R-3-04 (combined permits); § 4R-3-05 (limitations on the power of eminent domain); § 5R-5-01 (crimes); § 5R-5-03 (temporary arrest power); § 6R-3-01 (standards for a permit); § 6R-3-02 (determining whether a use is reasonable); § 6R-3-04 (preferences among water rights); §§ 6R-4-01 to 6R-4-05 (coordination of water allocation and water quality regulation).

Comparable statutes: ARK. CODE ANN. § 15-22-503 (d), (e) (generalized duty to cooperate); FLA. STAT. ANN. §§ 373.026(9), 373.196 (generalized duty to cooperate); HAW. REV. STAT. § 174C-4(b) (duty not to enforce contrary laws); MINN. STAT. ANN. § 105.49 (criminal enforcement); MISS. CODE ANN. § 51-3-21(4) (generalized duty to cooperate); VA. CODE ANN. § 62.1-44.42(3) (generalized duty to cooperate).

§ 4R-3-04 COMBINED PERMITS

> **The State Agency and other interested units of the government of the State shall combine a permit issued under this Code with a permit issued under authority of any law of the State when that combination would improve the administration of both laws.**

Commentary: The Regulated Riparian Model Water Code recognizes the close relationship between water allocation and water quality. Although the focus of the Code is on water allocation issues, the Code cannot avoid addressing at least some water quality issues. States that already combine the decision-making processes relating to water allocation, water quality, and other water management issues in a single agency will have a much easier time coordinating the two policies. For States that assign the regulation of these different water management issues to different agencies, statutory coordination is necessary. To assure that persons subject to these separate processes are bound by a single, consistent set of requirements and are not unduly burdened by the costs of security duplicative permits, the two agencies are charged to combine their permits when permits from different levels of government are necessary regardless of whether the differing permits serve quantity, quality, or other purposes.

Cross-references: § 1R-1-09 (coordination of water allocation and water quality regulation); § 4R-2-03 (the statewide data system); § 4R-3-02 (cooperation with other units of state and local government); § 4R-3-03 (duty to cooperate); §§ 6R-4-01 to 6R-4-05 (coordination of water allocation and water quality regulation).

§ 4R-3-05 LIMITATION ON THE POWER OF EMINENT DOMAIN

No person possessing the power of eminent domain over lands, waters, or water rights within the State shall exercise that power to acquire a new or additional water source, or access to such a water source, until that person has first received a permit to withdraw the water pursuant to this Code.

Commentary: The Regulated Riparian Model Water Code is explicit that no investment in land or other costs with a view to a possible water right to be obtained in the future shall create any equity in the permit application process. This section is designed to further that provision by preventing any person vested with the eminent domain power from exercising that power with a view of acquiring a new or additional water source, or access to such water source, before obtaining the necessary permit. The section reflects a concern that despite the rule against equities acquired through anticipatory investment, the State Agency might still be influenced by such investments when made by a public authority or other person entitled to exercise eminent domain. The section also seeks to prevent the mere application for a permit from being used as a subterfuge to condemn property for some other purpose. The usual rule that property to be condemned is to be valued as of the announcement of the project, *i.e.*, without any enhancement to its value because of the project for which it is condemned, should be adequate to protect the person exercising the eminent domain power from suffering financial loss from a delay in condemning the property.

Cross-references: § 2R-2-15 (person); § 6R-3-05 (prior investment in withdrawal or use facilities).

Comparable statutes: HAW. REV. STAT. § 174C-4(c); N.J. STAT. ANN. § 58:1A-12.

Part 4

Special Water Management Areas (*optional*)

About one-third of the States that have already enacted regulated riparian statutes do not have statewide water withdrawal permit requirements. In the absence of specific water allocations, however, conflict often arises over interference between uses after overall demand approaches the available supply. Often the conflicts are not statewide, but rather are limited to localized areas of limited supply or intensive use. States which are reluctant to impose statewide permit requirements address such localized conflicts through Special Water Management Areas created to include areas with severe or recurring water supply or water pollution problems. In fact, resolving such conflicts without unnecessary statewide regulation frequently is the reason a State opts for Special Water Management Areas, although other States have found that localized needs are best served in hydrologically diverse settings through resort to that option even when implementing a statewide requirement of water withdrawal permits.

The concept of Special Water Management Areas has proven sufficiently flexible that it has been adopted for both prior appropriation and regulated riparian systems. In some States, the administering agency has been given broad discretion to create Special Water Management Areas and to determine what authority to delegate to the Areas, while in other States the legislature has taken responsibility for defining the Areas and their authority. Even in such a State, the legislature is likely to delegate considerable discretion to the State Agency or to the Special Water Management Areas to decide when or how to implement the Area program. *See generally* Dellapenna, § 9.03(a)(5)(A). For Special Water Management Areas in appropriative rights states, see John Davidson, *Public Water Districts,* in 3 WATERS AND WATER RIGHTS §§ 27.01-27.03; C. Peter Goplerud III, *Protection and Termination of Water Rights,* in 2 WATERS AND WATER RIGHTS § 17.04. *See generally* RICE & WHITE, at 131; TARLOCK, §§ 2.05(1), 5.19(5); J.W. Looney, *Enhancing the Role of Water Districts in Groundwater Management and Surface Water Utliization in Arkansas,* 48 ARK. L. REV. 643 (1995); Susan Peterson, Note, *Designation and Protection of Critical Ground Water Areas,* 1991 B.Y.U. L. REV. 1393. *See generally* SAX, ABRAMS, & THOMPSON, at 628-44; SPECIAL WATER DISTRICTS: CHALLENGE FOR THE FUTURE (James

Corbridge, jr., ed. 1983); TARLOCK, CORBRIDGE, & GETCHES, at 617-63; TRELEASE & GOULD, at 511-45.

Florida provides one of the better illustrations of the discretion typical in the implementation of Special Water Management Areas. Florida's Water Management Districts are mandated in detailed and lengthy legislation that constitute one of the nation's most elaborately developed systems of Special Management Areas, and these are in turn subdivided by delegations of authority to "Basin Boards." Even in Florida, however, the legislature left it to the discretion of the District governing boards to decide whether or when to implement the permit requirement, a process that took about 18 years before the entire State became subject to the permit process. Usually, Special Water Management Areas are defined in terms of water basins, so that an Area typically will consist of a single important water basin within a State. Occasionally, a large water basin might be divided into two or more Areas. Florida again presents a different picture. The Florida legislature defined the State's Water Management Districts only vaguely in terms of water basin boundaries, reflecting communities of use as much as natural hydrologic divisions. The Florida system has worked well up to now, but it has begun to show strains primarily from the lack of adequate statewide regulatory authority: Too much authority has been delegated to the water districts, preventing effect responses to problems and needs that transcend district boundaries. *See* Ronald Christaldi, *Sharing the Cup: A Proposal for the Allocation of Florida's Water Resources,* 23 FLA. ST. UNIV. L. REV. 1063 (1996).

Not all States use Special Water Management Areas. Some smaller regulated riparian States which are more or less homogenous in hydrologic terms rely on a permit system operated on a statewide basis only. Examples include Connecticut, Delaware, and Maryland. On the other hand, some large States use similarly integrated statewide permit systems despite a size that alone can create a considerable staffing burden on a single agency. Some would also question the suitability of a statewide system to the diverse hydrologic conditions found in larger States. Examples of large, hydrologically diverse States with integrated statewide systems include Georgia, Hawaii, Iowa, Kentucky, Minnesota, Mississippi, and Wisconsin. Other large States have understandably opted for reliance on Special Water Management Areas. Besides Florida, examples include Alabama, Arkansas, Illinois, Indiana, New York, North Carolina, South

Carolina (underground water only), and Virginia. At the other extreme, at least one rather small state (Massachusetts) relies on Special Water Management Areas. New Jersey uses a single statewide system for surface water sources, but regional management for underground water sources.

The choice whether to use Special Water Management Areas depends on such variables as the political and economic diversity of the State as well as the hydrologic diversity of the State. Altogether, whether in large or small States, a small majority half of the regulated riparian States do not rely on Special Water Management Areas. As the foregoing catalogue of States suggests, the decision to use Special Water Management Areas is as much a political decision as it is a managerial decision. Because of these realities, this entire Part is described as optional, unlike most of the rest of the Code. This Part has been designed with five options in mind.

First, a State could omit the Part entirely, along with references to Special Water Management Areas elsewhere in the Code. As just noted, this approach has been adopted by a bit more than half of the States which have already enacted regulated riparian statutes. The only other such references in the actually statutory language is found in section 2R-2-24, although there are numerous references scattered throughout the commentary and cross-references. One would also have to be wary of cross-references to Area Water Management Plans that are provided for in this Part and referred to in connection with other Chapters and Parts of this Code.

Second, a State could adopt the approach of relying on Special Water Management Areas much as outlined in this Code, except with the legislature determining that there shall be such Areas and what their dimensions shall be. This option is provided in the alternative version of section 4R-4-03. In such a case, it would be unnecessary to undertake a Special Water Management Area study, and section 4R-4-02 (dealing with such studies) would be omitted and the following sections would be renumbered appropriately.

Third, a State could opt for the creation and implementation of Special Water Management Areas only when circumstances in particular region require it. This saves the costs of such a bureaucracy for regions where it is not necessary. To work effectively, the decision must be vested in the State Agency, as has been done in most of the States operating under the Special

Water Management Area model. This approach, which requires the enactment of the first version of section 4R-4-03, is fully worked out in this Part of the Code.

The final two options cuts across the second and third. Either of these following options could be chosen regardless of which version of the creation of Special Water Management Areas (section 4R-4-03) is selected. The Code proceeds on the premise that permit issuing authority should remain vested in the State Agency. Some regulated riparian statutes, however, devolve this power to the Special Water Management Area. Under the Code, the Area is given important planning, regulatory, and dispute resolution functions. The Area is not given the authority to issue permits. Some States might prefer to have permits issued by the Area and an option to this effect is provided in the alternative version of section 4R-4-06. This Code also adopts the plan of having the Area Water Board that exercises the powers of the Special Water Management Area appointed by the governor with the advice and consent of the Senate. Some States might prefer to have the Area Water Board appointed by affected units of local government, or elected by the population generally, or by water users within the Area. The Code does not attempt to work out these infinitely variable possibilities, only noting that should some such scheme be adopted section 4R-4-04 would have to be rewritten.

§ 4R-4-01 PURPOSES FOR SPECIAL WATER MANAGEMENT AREAS

Special Water Management Areas shall address specific local water management problems, including:

- **(a) the prevention of the unreasonable depletion or contamination of the Area's water resources for the benefit of all authorized nonconsumptive and consumptive uses;**
- **(b) the limitation of withdrawals to the safe yield and the protection of minimum flows and levels as provided by this Code;**

(c) the sustainable development of total regional water resources in the public interest, including but not limited to surface water, underground water, return flows, and atmospheric water;

(d) the resolution of conflicts among water users within the boundaries of the Area; and

(e) the implementation of regulations to address such specific water management problems.

Commentary: The present examples of Special Water Management Areas include Areas addressing problems with surface water and underground water, surface water exclusively, underground water exclusively, water allocation and quality, water allocation exclusively, and water quality exclusively. In this section, the Regulated Riparian Model Water Code attempts to define a discrete set of purposes of Special Water Management Areas under the Code, including the protection of the waters of the State in both quantitative and qualitative terms, the development of plans and regulations appropriate to the particular needs of the Area, and the resolution of conflicts among users. This is a somewhat broader schedule of purposes than is found in some regulated riparian statutes, which often provide only for the resolution of disputes, but is also narrower than other regulated riparian statutes under which Special Water Management Areas (variously titled) served as the primary water management and regulatory authorities. As the remaining sections of this Part will make clear, Special Water Management Areas under the Code are supplemental to the State Agency even when fulfilling the purposes for which the Areas were created.

Cross-references: § 1R-1-01 (protecting the public interest in the waters of the State); § 1R-1-02 (assuring efficient and productive use of water); § 1R-1-03 (conformity to the policies of the Code and to physical laws); § 1R-1-05 (efficient and equitable allocation during shortfalls in supply); § 1R-1-06 (legal security for water rights); § 1R-1-09 (coordination of water allocation and water quality regulation); § 1R-1-10 (water conservation); § 1R-1-11 (preservation of minimum flows and levels); § 1R-1-12 (recognizing local interests in the waters of the State); § 1R-

1-15 (atmospheric water management); § 2R-1-03 (no unreasonable injury to other water rights); § 2R-2-01 (atmospheric water management); § 2R-2-06 (consumptive use); § 2R-2-09 (drought management strategies); § 2R-2-13 (nonconsumptive use); § 2R-2-18 (the public interest); § 2R-2-21 (safe yield); § 2R-2-22 (Special Water Management Areas); § 2R-2-24 (sustainable development); § 2R-2-25 (underground water); § 2R-2-26 (unreasonable injury); § 2R-2-28 (water basin); § 2R-2-30 (water right); § 2R-2-31 (water shortage); §§ 3R-2-01 to 3R-2-05 (protection of minimum flows or levels); § 4R-4-02 (Special Water Management Area studies); § 4R-2-03 (creation of Special Water Management Areas); § 4R-4-04 (Area Water Boards); § 4R-4-05 (Area Water Management Plans); § 4R-4-06 (regulatory authority of Special Water Management Areas); § 4R-4-07 (conflict resolution within Special Water Management Areas); § 4R-4-08 (funding Special Water Management Areas).

Comparable statutes: GA. CODE ANN. § 12-5-96(e); HAW. REV. STAT. § 174C-41(a); ILL. CON. STAT. ch. 525, § 45/3; MISS. CODE ANN. § 51-8-3; S.C. CODE ANN. § 49-5-40(B).

§ 4R-4-02 SPECIAL WATER MANAGEMENT AREA STUDIES (optional)

(1) The State Agency, upon its own determination that a specific localized water resource problem or combination of problems exists or are likely to exist, shall initiate a Special Water Management Area study to determine whether to create such an Area.

(2) (a) The State Agency shall initiate a Special Water Management Area study upon receipt of a petition from any interested person alleging that such a problem exists or is likely to exist if the Agency determines upon a summary review that the allegations are substantially true.

(b) A decision not to undertake such a study pursuant to this subsection is subject to judicial review under section 5R-3-02.

(3) A Special Water Management study shall:

(a) determine the exact nature and extent of the water problems in light of the public interest in sustainable development, including (in so far as possible) quantification of the availability of the water resource and the past, present, projected future water demand; and

(b) determine whether those problems warrant special regulatory attention through a Special Water Management Area.

(4) Upon undertaking to a Special Water Management Area study, the State Agency may declare that Area to be a Temporary Special Water Management Area and shall issue an order creating the procedures necessary to protect the water resources in the Area pending a final determination whether to designate the area permanently as a Special Water Management Area.

(5) Any decision to undertake a Special Water Management study, the conclusion of such a study, and any decision to create a temporary Special Water Management Area are subject to judicial review under section 5R-3-01.

Commentary: Most States with Special Water Management Areas (variously titled) delegate considerable responsibility for identifying problems that are best addressed by such Areas to the administrative agency with the greatest authority over water within the State. This section requires the State Agency to undertake appropriate studies to determine whether and where to establish a Special Water Management Area whenever the State Agency determines there is need for such a study. The State Agency's determination that a study is needed can occur on the Agency's initiative or because of a petition filed by any interested person. The sort of water problems calling for State Agency study include:

(1) water withdrawals consistently and considerably in excess of runoff or recharge, either currently or in the foreseeable future;

(2) a water source that has lost substantial value derived from existing flows or levels as evidenced by interference with lawful nonconsumptive and consumptive uses or of generalized public values such as recreation, habitat, cultural, or aesthetic attributes;

(3) recurring significant disputes regarding rights, amounts, and priority of water uses;

(4) threats of contamination or diminishment to an area of origin of recharge or runoff;

(5) existing or potential serious soil subsidence from the withdrawal of underground water;

(6) existing or potential contamination of drinking water supplies;

(7) degradation of the quality or quantity of water available for nonconsumptive uses;

(8) underground water levels or pressures that are declining significantly or have declined significantly; and

(9) any other serious threat to the biological, chemical, or physical integrity of a regional water source.

The values of preserving water in place have already been addressed in the Commentary to Chapter 3, and need not be repeated here. The list of problems described here, as indicated more generally in the text of subsection (3) of this section, is broader, however, than just the protection of minimum flows and levels. As section 4R-4-01 also indicates, the problems that justify the creation of a Special Water Management Area include any localized problem affecting the availability and the quality of the waters of the State and conflicts between lawful uses that cannot be dealt with adequately on a case-by-case basis.

Some existing Special Water Management Area provisions in regulated riparian statutes allow for local initiative in the determination of need for the Areas. Examples include Arizona (for underground water), Hawaii, Mississippi, New York, and South Carolina (for underground water). Similar provisions are found under appropriative rights in Colorado, Kansas, Nebraska, and Texas. The Regulated Riparian Model Water Code does not allow local initiative to determine the question, but enables any interested person (which would include individuals, corporations, local units of government, or other units of state government) to petition the State Agency to undertake a Special Water Management Area study. The State Agency's response to such a petition is subject to the general public hearing requirement of the State's Administrative Procedure Act and would be reviewable in the same fashion as any other final decision by the Agency.

The State Agency is given the authority in subsection (4) to implement a temporary Special Water Management Area pending the study required in this section. The necessary study might take considerable time, and during this time a serious problem could become a true crisis. The temporary imposition of a Special Water Management Area when serious problems have already arisen or are imminent, particularly if the State does not have any other active water allocation system in place, will permit appropriate flexibility in the responses available to the Agency to assure the necessary steps are taken to prevent any serious worsening of the situation giving rise to the study in question. Subsection (5) indicates that all decisions under this section, other than a decision not to undertake a Special Water Management Area study in response to a petition from an interested person, are subject to judicial review in the manner of a challenge to a regulation rather than as review of a final order or decision.

This section is described as optional within an overall Part that is optional because it would be unnecessary if the legislature takes it upon itself to create and define Special Water Management Areas by statutory enactment. *See* section 4R-4-03 (alternative version). In such a case, the decision having already been made by the legislature, there would simply be nothing for the State Agency to Study.

Cross-references: § 1R-1-01 (protecting the public interest in the waters of the State); § 1R-1-02 (assuring efficient and productive use of water); § 1R-1-03 (conformity to the policies of the Code and to physical laws); § 1R-1-05 (efficient and equitable allocation during shortfalls in supply); § 1R-1-06 (legal security for water rights); § 1R-1-09 (coordination of water allocation and water quality regulation); § 1R-1-10 (water conservation); § 1R-1-11 (preservation of minimum flows and levels); § 1R-1-12 (recognizing local interests in the waters of the State); § 1R-1-15 (atmospheric water management); § 2R-2-02 (biological integrity); § 2R-2-03 (chemical integrity); § 2R-2-06 (consumptive use); § 2R-2-07 (cost); § 2R-2-13 (nonconsumptive use); § 2R-2-15 (person); § 2R-2-16 (physical integrity); § 2R-2-18 (the public interest); § 2R-2-21 (safe yield); § 2R-2-22 (Special Water Management Area); § 2R-2-23 (State Agency); § 2R-2-24 (sustainable development); § 2R-2-28 (water basin); § 2R-2-31 (water shortage); § 2R-2-33 (water source); § 2R-2-34 (withdrawal or to withdraw); §§ 3R-2-01 to 3R-2-05 (protection of minimum flows and levels); § 4R-1-05 (application of general laws to meetings, procedures, and records); § 4R-4-01 (purposes for Special Water Management Areas); § 4R-4-04 (Area Water Boards); § 4R-4-05 (Area Water Management Plans); § 4R-4-06 (regulatory authority of Special Water Management Areas); § 4R-4-07 (conflict resolution within Special Water Management Areas); § 4R-4-08 (funding Special Water Management Areas); § 5R-1-01 (right to a hearing); § 5R-3-01 (judicial review of regulations); § 5R-3-02 (judicial review of orders or decisions of the State Agency).

Comparable statutes: ALA. CODE §§ 9-10B-3(7), 9-10B-5(5), (14), 9-10B-21, 9-10B-25; HAW. REV. STAT. § 174C-43; IND. CODE ANN. § 13-2-2-3, -4; MISS. CODE ANN. § 58-1-5 to -11; N.C. GEN. STAT. ANN. § 143-215.13(c), (d); S.C. CODE ANN. § 49-5-40(c); VA. CODE ANN. §§ 62.1-44.95, 62.1-246(A).

§ 4R-4-03 CREATION OF SPECIAL WATER MANAGEMENT AREAS

(1) The State Agency shall create such Special Water Management Areas as it determines are necessary to address particular localized

hydrologic conditions producing water allocation problems that do or might require special attention.

(2) The State Agency shall designate the boundaries of each Special Water Management Area it shall create.

§ 4R-4-03 CREATION OF SPECIAL WATER MANAGEMENT AREAS *(alternate version)*

The State is hereby divided into the following Special Water Management Areas: *[here follow the boundaries or descriptions of the several Areas]*.

Commentary: While the specifics of Special Water Management Area statutes vary highly from State to State, and sometimes even within a State, most Special Water Management Area programs depend on specific legislation authorizing the State Agency to designate the Areas upon the happening of certain events or as the State Agency deems necessary. This is the first alternative offered in subsection (1) of the primary version of this section, with subsection (2) authorizing the State Agency to designate the boundaries of the Areas that it creates. The Agency's discretion is bounded by the requirement that it study the need for a Special Water Management Area, with decisions made in the course of that process being made expressly subject to judicial review.

The alternative proposed here is for the legislature itself to designate the boundaries of the Special Water Management Areas, following the approach adopted in Florida. If this approach is taken, section 4R-4-02 (requiring the State Agency to study the need for a Special Water Management Area) would be unnecessary and should be omitted. The remainder of this Part could be adopted without change regardless of the method used to create the Areas. Nonetheless, if the legislature takes upon itself the task of defining the Areas, it might also want to reconsider the relationship between the Areas and the State Agency generally. Such reconsideration could extend as well to the first alternative's criteria for the State Agency's determination to create a Special Water Management Area.

The first alternative limits the State Agency to considering only water allocation problems in defining a Special Water Management Area. This reflects the almost exclusive focus of this Code on water allocation, as discussed in the preface. In a state where the allocation responsibilities of the State Agency under this Code are combined with other water management responsibilities, such as pollution regulation or flood control, the criteria might be fruitfully broadened to include some or all of these other responsibilities as well as allocational concerns.

Cross-references: § 1R-1-12 (policy of recognizing local interests in the waters of the State); § 2R-2-22 (Special Water Management Area); § 2R-2-23 (State Agency); § 2R-2-28 (water basin); § 4R-1-05 (application of general laws to meetings, procedures, and regulations); § 4R-4-01 (purposes of Special Water management Areas); § 4R-4-02 (Special Water Management Area studies); § 4R-4-04 (Area Water Boards); § 4R-4-05 (Area Water Management Plans); § 4R-4-06 (regulatory authority of Special Water Management Areas); § 4R-4-07 (conflict resolution within Special Water Management Areas); § 4R-4-08 (funding Special Water Management Areas); § 5R-1-01 (right to a hearing); § 5R-3-02 (judicial review of orders or decisions of the State Agency).

Comparable statutes: ALA. CODE §§ 9-10B-3(3), 9-10B-21; FLA. STAT. ANN. § 373.069 (precise statutory definition of water districts); GA. CODE ANN. § 12-5-96(e); HAW. REV. STAT. § 174C-41; IND. CODE ANN. §§ 13-2-2-3, -4; MASS. GEN. LAWS ANN. ch. 21G, § 4; MISS. CODE ANN. §§ 51-3-15(2)(f), 51-8-13; N.C. GEN. STAT. ANN. § 143-215.13; S.C. CODE ANN. § 49-5-40(a); VA. CODE ANN. §§ 62.1-44.94, -44.96, 62.1246(B).

§ 4R-4-04 AREA WATER BOARDS

(1) The powers and authority of each Special Management Area shall be vested in an Area Water Board consisting of five (5) members appointed by the Governor with the advice and consent of the Senate.

(2) Members of an Area Water Board shall reside in the designated Special Water Management Area and shall serve five (5) year terms staggered so that one term expires each year.

(3) In the case of a vacancy before the expiration of the term of a member of an Area Water Board, the Governor shall fill the vacancy, with the advice and consent of the Senate, with an appointment for the remainder of the unexpired term.

(4) Unless displaced by specific provisions of this Part, each Area Water Board is vested with all powers necessary to accomplish the purposes for which it is organized in so far as those powers are delegable by the legislature, subject to the general procedural provisions of this Code governing the discharge of the State Agency's responsibilities.

Commentary: This section deals with what are perhaps the most sensitive issues in creating Special Water Management Areas, namely whether to have a local governing board and, if so, how to staff that board. A number of States with Special Water Management Areas (for example, Massachusetts, North Carolina, and Virginia) do not create local boards, using the device simply as an administrative tool for the State Agency. This approach generally reflects a decision to limit the regulatory effect of the controlling statute to those regions of the State which face immediate water crisis. If the permit system and other regulatory innovations are to apply generally in the State, to have all decisions made on a statewide basis ignores the diverse hydrological concerns of different water basins and the different ecological, economic, and social concerns of different regions of the State. These concerns suggest that local governing boards are desirable, at least in the larger States.

Those States which have created such local boards, have each used a distinct method for creating the board that reflects the local political and legal traditions of that State. The members of an Area Water Board could be elected by the general electorate within the Area or perhaps in some manner designed to represent water users within the Area, or appointed by local units of government within the Special Water Management Area, or even appointed by various departments of the State government. The Regulated Riparian Model Water Code rejects these alternatives because it makes it too likely that the Area Water Board would see its function as serving the short-term needs of those who elect or appoint it rather than as implementing the State's regulatory policies relative to the waters of the State. Similarly, the Code rejects the possibility of selecting the members of these Boards through appointment by the State Agency to serve for short terms or at the pleasure of the Agency. This would create too great a risk of the Boards being simply a more expensive means of staffing what would function as a single, statewide agency. Eliminating these options, what is left is having the members of an Area Water Board appointed by the Governor to staggered five-year terms. A State that would prefer one of the other approaches to creating or staffing Area Water Boards would need to rewrite this section accordingly.

Although there is an obvious advantage to having an odd number of members on the Board, there is no magic in the number five. The staggered terms provided in this section guarantees a measure of continuity in each Board's activities yet allows a Governor to influence the Boards annually and to reshape them in only three years if the Governor is intent on doing so. Such continuity itself provides a measure of legal security to water right holders. The appointment (or reappointment) of one member of the board each year, on the other hand, assures a measure of accountability that prevents a Board from becoming an irresponsible power unto itself. Continuity and responsibility are further assured through the regulatory authority of the State Agency–the primary means for the State to supervise the activities of the Area Water Boards. Should any particular Board prove inadequately responsive to situations as they arise, the Agency's power to intervene in any water shortage or water emergency serves as a backup means for protecting vital public interests. *See* sections 2R-2-29, 7R-3-01 to 7R-3-07.

States not only will want to consider the number of Board members appropriate for their traditions and other circumstances, but also to consider whether to spell out some formula requiring balanced representation of varied interests on each Area Water Board. The more such interests the legislature requires to be represented on the Boards, the larger each Board will have to be. The Code does not include such a requirement here not only because the interests meriting inclusion on such a list will vary from State to State, but also because the Code prefers the model of Board members conceiving of themselves as responsible for the public interest rather than as representing the particular interests of particular persons placing demands on the waters of the State.

There are no detailed provisions on general administrative practices or on coordination with other branches of government. For these purposes, Special Water Management Areas and Area Water Boards are considered as branches of the State Agency even though at times they will have adversarial relationships to the State Agency. Similarly, the provisions regarding hearings and review of State Agency regulations and actions apply to the Area Water Boards. See sections 5R-1-01 to 5R-1-05, 5R-3-01 to 5R-3-03. If there is a direct conflict between such general provisions and the specific provisions of this Part of the Code, the specific provisions control. A State's legislature might want to spell out in more detail the relation between these powers and responsibilities of the State Agency and the corresponding powers and responsibilities of the Area Water Boards.

Cross-references: § 1R-1-06 (legal security for the right to use water); § 1R-1-12 (recognizing local interests in the waters of the State); § 2R-2-22 (Special Water Management Area); § 2R-2-23 (State Agency); § 2R-2-32 (waters of the State); § 4R-1-02 (nonimpairment of general powers); § 4R-1-03 (general administrative powers); § 4R-1-05 (application of general laws to meetings, procedures, and records); § 4R-1-09 (protection of confidential business information); §§ 4R-3-01 to 4R-3-05 (cooperation with other branches or levels of government); § 4R-4-01 (purposes of Special Water Management Areas); § 4R-4-02 (Special Water Management Area studies); § 4R-4-05 (Area Water Management Plans); § 4R-4-06 (regulatory authority of Special Water Management Areas); § 4R-4-07 (conflict resolution within Special Water Management Areas); § 4R-4-08 (funding Special Water Management Areas); §§ 5R-1-01 to 5R-1-05 (hearings); §§ 5R-3-01 to 5R-3-03 (judicial review); §§ 5R-4-01 to 5R-5-03 (civil and criminal enforcement); §§ 7R-3-01 to 7R-3-07 (restrictions during water shortages or water emergencies).

Comparable statutes: FLA. STAT. ANN. §§ 373.0695(1)(e), (2)(d) to (g), (4); 373.0698, 373.073 to 373.083, 373.103(6); MISS. CODE ANN. §§ 51-8-21 to 25, 51-8-29 to 51-8-35; VA. CODE ANN. § 62.1-44.98 (advisory committee of residents within underground water management areas).

§ 4R-4-05 AREA WATER MANAGEMENT PLANS

(1) Each Area Water Board shall develop an Area Water Management Plan to address any water problems that exist or are foreseen within the Special Water Management Area for which the Board is responsible.

(2) The Area Water Board shall provide reasonable opportunities for public participation in the process of creating the Area Water Management Plan.

(3) An Area Water Management Plan becomes final upon approval by the State Agency after review for conformity with this Code, other laws of the State, laws and regulations of the federal government, and the orders, regulations, plans, and strategies adopted by the Agency.

(4) The preparation of the Area Water Management Plan shall not exceed 1 year from the designation of a Special Water Management Area; the Area Management Plan shall be revised at least every five years after its previous approval, remaining in effect until the revision is completed.

Commentary: Most existing Special Water Management Areas statutes require some form of planning by the governing board of the Area. *See* Dellapenna, § 9.05(a). As with the activities of the State Agency, such planning is necessary if the administrative system is to achieve the benefits of rational, expert decision-making that justify its existence. Care is taken to assure that any Area Water Management Plan adopted by an Area Water Board is consistent with the relevant statewide laws and programs, as well as with federal law, by requiring, in subsection (3), the approval of the State Agency before any Area Water Management Plan becomes final.

The public nature of the process provided in subsection (2) assures both that the public is involved in the planning process and serves as some check on the discretion of the State Agency to overrule Area Water Management Plans adopted with broad public participation and support. That a Special Water Management Area was created to respond to pressing needs justifies the requirement that a plan be in place within one year of the creation of the Area, although some States might prefer to set a different time limit for preparation of the Plan. The requirement that Plans be revised at least every five years assures that Plans will be kept up to date and that, upon complete renewal of every Area Water Board, the new Board (or at least a majority of the members of the new Board) will have had a hand in creating the Plan which shall guide and control the Board's actions.

Cross-references: § 1R-1-12 (recognizing local interests in the waters of the State); § 2R-2-18 (the public interest); § 4R-1-05 (application of general laws to meetings, procedures, and records); § 4R-1-09 (protection of confidential business information); §§ 4R-2-01 to 4R-2-04 (planning responsibilities); § 4R-4-01 (purposes for Special Water Management Areas); § 4R-4-02 (Special Water Management Area studies); § 4R-4-03 (creation of Special Water Management Areas); § 4R-4-04 (Area Water Boards); § 4R-4-06 (regulatory authority of Special Water Management Areas); § 4R-4-07 (conflict resolution within Special Water Management Areas); § 4R-4-08 (funding Special Water Management Areas); §§ 5R-1-01 to 5R-1-05 (hearings); §§ 5R-3-01 to 5R-3-03 (judicial review).

Comparable statutes: FLA. STAT. ANN. §§ 373.0695(1)(a), (b), (f), (2)(a), (b), 373.103(7); GA. CODE ANN. § 12-5-96(e); ILL. COMP. STAT. ANN. ch. 525, § 45/5.1.

§ 4R-4-06 REGULATORY AUTHORITY OF SPECIAL WATER MANAGEMENT AREAS

(1) Each Area Water Board shall adopt its own regulations relating to waters within the Area and based upon the Area Water Management Plan so long as the regulations serve the public interest and are consistent with the provisions of this Code, other laws of the State, laws and regulations of the federal government, and the orders, regulations, plans, and strategies adopted by the State Agency.

(2) Special Water Management Areas shall coordinate their regulations with the State's water quality regulations in the same manner as the State Agency is required to coordinate its water allocation authority with the State's water quality regulations.

(3) The regulations adopted by an Area Water Board may have provisions regarding:

(a) closing part or all of the Special Water Management Area to further withdrawals or development of the Area's water resources;

(b) the permissible total withdrawal and use of water during a given time period and means to apportion the total among holders of existing water rights;

(c) drought management strategies particular to the needs of the - Special Water Management Area;

(d) proposals to limit land use practices that have an impact on the quantity or quality of water available from a particular water source within the Special Water Management Area;

(e) dissolution of the Special Water Management Area if and when there is no longer need for the Area; and

(f) any other step necessary to protect existing water sources from depletion and contamination, and to ensure a supply for future needs, both in-place and by withdrawal.

(4) *(optional, but not recommended, subsection)* **Upon approval of the Area Water Management Plan and the Special Water Management Area's regulations by the State Agency, the Area Water Board shall be responsible for issuing, administering, and enforcing permits pursuant to Chapters 5-7 under the supervision of the ongoing State Agency. If the State Agency determines that an Area Water Board is not fulfilling its responsibilities under this subsection, the State Agency shall revoke the delegation of authority over permits to the Area Water Board and resume direct responsibility for issuing, administering, and enforcing permits.**

(5) Regulations proposed or adopted by an Area Water Board shall be subject to judicial review in the manner as provided in section 5R-3-01 in a court of competent jurisdiction in the county in which the Area Water Board's executive office is located. The Area Water Board shall conform its regulations to the orders or judgments of the reviewing court as provided in section 5R-3-03.

Commentary: Most existing Special Water Management Area statutes include provisions similar to those set forth in this section. Often the provisions empowering the governing board for a Special Water Management Area are considerably more specific than the more general provisions used in the Regulated Riparian Model Water Code. Not all such specific provisions are applied uniformly in separate management areas even within single States, however.

Most States with Special Water Management Areas allow the Areas to adopt special regulation of water withdrawals as well, perhaps, as effluent discharge, well-head protection, and other activities related to water resource management and protection. These special regulations are typically more stringent than those applied to the rest of the State, although such restrictions still must coordinate with broader statewide water regulatory schemes. This Code authorizes such regulations by Special Water Management Areas, but requires that the Areas' regulations be consistent with the public interest, the Code, other relevant laws, and the plans and regulations adopted by the State Agency. Implicit in this is the requirement that the Special Water Management Area's regulations will serve the goal of sustainable development. The State Agency will from time to time adopt regulations specifically directed at coordinating the varying regulations of the Special Water Management Areas and otherwise guiding the actions of the Areas.

The regulations adopted by an Area Water Board can include such specific management mechanisms as well spacing, water pricing, special water rights transfer programs, special water reporting and metering, rotation of allowed water use days, programs of river basin management, and so on. These regulations might be quite different in different Special Water Management Areas of the State, reflecting the different problems and different needs of the several Areas. These differences could be as basic as one Special Water Management Area stressing the privatization of water usage with another, perhaps adjacent Special Water Management Area stressing public decision-making about water usage. The problems and questions to be resolved are simply too varied to be resolved in the abstract or by general prescription. Any regulations proposed or adopted under this section are subject to judicial review in the same manner as provided in section 5R-3-01 for regulations proposed or adopted by the State Agency. By also incorporating section 5R-3-03 into subsection (5) of this section, the section not only assures that the Area Water Board shall conform its regulations to the orders and decisions of the Court, but also that a judgment for the expenses of another person's litigation will not be entered against the Area Water Board.

Some States, such as Florida, delegate the primary responsibility for issuing permits for water rights to the Special Water Management Areas. FLA. STAT. ANN. §§ 373.203-373.249. An optional subsection (4) is provided to cover this possibility. This Code, however, prefers to keep the permit issuing function vested in the State Agency. As the Agency is necessarily charged with issuing permits both to obviate the need for an elaborate statewide permit process to deal with interbasin or trans-Area transfers and to assure consistent application of the relevant criteria throughout the Area and the State, the keeping of the entire permitting process vested in the State Agency reduces the risks of conflicts over what is the proper source of a particular permit or the possibility of conflicting permits from different sources. If subsection (4) is omitted as recommended in this Code, subsection (5) will be renumbered as (4).

The Area Water Boards are to consider water quality concerns as well as water allocation in formulating their Area Water Management Plans and regulations. Still, as is generally true with this Code, the focus is primarily on water allocation rather than other issues. Therefore, this section speaks in terms of Drought Management Strategies and the obligation to coordinate with agencies responsible for water quality. If, as is currently true in several regulated riparian States, a single agency is responsible for water allocation, water quality, flood control, and other issues relating to water management, with the whole package being delegated to Special Water Management Areas, the language of this section would need to be revised. "Drought Management Strategies" would need to become "Water Shortage and Water Emergency Strategies." Subsection (2) on coordination with other agencies would simply be omitted.

Florida is unusual in mandating that Water Management Districts cooperate with each other. FLA. STAT. ANN. § 373.047. This legislative mandate goes so far as to direct two Districts to enter into a specific agreement allowing one District to issue permits for water withdrawals within a county in the other District. One naturally ponders why the Florida legislature did not just transfer the county to the other District. *Id.*, § 373.046(2). *See also id.*, § 373.0691 (transfer of areas). This Code does not directly address conflicts between Special Water Management Areas, in part because the permit issuing authority remains with the State Agency. Should such a conflict arise, the duty to cooperate is found in the general administrative provisions of the Code. *See* sections 4R-3-01 to 4R-3-05. *Compare* FLA. STAT. ANN. § 373.103(2) (water management districts to cooperate with the federal government).

Often existing Special Water Management Areas are charged with responsibility for constructing and managing water use facilities within the Area as well as (or in place of) regulatory authority. This Code does not provide for such responsibilities given the Code's focus on the regulation of water allocation rather than other sorts of activities relevant to the development and preservation of water sources. Appropriate provision for such additional duties should be added if the State so desires.

Cross-references: § 1R-1-01 (protecting the public interest in the waters of the State); § 1R-1-02 (assuring efficient and productive use of water); § 1R-1-03 (conformity to the policies of the Code and to physical laws); § 1R-1-05 (efficient and equitable allocation during shortfalls in supply); § 1R-1-06 (legal security for water rights); § 1R-1-09 (coordination of water allocation and water quality regulation); § 1R-1-10 (water conservation); § 1R-1-11 (preservation of minimum flows and levels); § 1R-1-12 (recognizing local interests in the waters of the State); § 1R-1-13 (regulating interstate water transfers); § 1R-1-14 (regulating interbasin transfers); § 1R-1-15 (atmospheric water management); § 2R-2-02 (biological integrity); § 2R-2-03 (chemical integrity); § 2R-2-06 (consumptive use); § 2R-2-07 (cost); § 2R-2-13 (nonconsumptive use); § 2R-2-15 (person); § 2R-2-16 (physical integrity); § 2R-2-18 (the public interest); § 2R-2-21 (safe yield); § 2R-2-22 (Special Water Management Area); § 2R-2-23 (State Agency); § 2R-2-24 (sustainable development); § 2R-2-28 (water basin); § 2R-2-29 (water emergency); § 2R-2-30 (water right); § 2R-2-31 (water shortage); § 2R-2-33 (water source); § 2R-2-34 (withdraw or withdrawal); § 4R-1-06 (regulatory authority of the State Agency); § 4R-3-02 (cooperation with other units of State and local government); § 4R-3-03 (duty of other units of government to cooperate with the State Agency); § 4R-4-01 (purposes for Special Water Management Areas); § 4R-4-02 (Special Water Management Area studies); § 4R-4-04 (Area Water Boards) § 4R-4-05 (Area Water Management Plans); § 4R-4-07 (conflict resolution within Special Water Management Areas); § 4R-4-08 (funding Special Water Management Areas); §§ 6R-3-01 to 6R-3-06 (the basis of a water right); §§ 7R-1-01 to 7R-3-07 (the scope of the water right); §§ 8R-1-01 to 8R-1-07 (multijurisdictional transfers).

Comparable statutes: ALA. CODE § 9-10B-22 (regulations for capacity stress areas issued by statewide authority); FLA. STAT. ANN. §§ 373.0695(1)(d), (2)(e), 373.083(2), 373.103(1), (4), 373.106, 373.113, 373.146, 373.161; HAW. REV. STAT. § 174C-48; ILL. CON. STAT. ch. 525, § 45/5.1; IND. CODE ANN. § 13-2-2-5(a) (permits in restricted use areas issued by statewide authority); MASS. GEN. LAWS ANN. ch. 21G, § 4 (same); MISS. CODE ANN. §§ 51-3-15, 51-8-27; N.C. GEN. STAT. §§ 143-215.14 to 143-215.16 (permits for capacity use areas, issued by statewide authority); S.C. CODE ANN. § 49-5-50 (same, underground water); VA. CODE ANN. §§ 62.1-44.97, 62.1-44.100 (same, underground water), 62.1-247 to 62.1-249 (same, surface water sources).

§ 4R-4-07 CONFLICT RESOLUTION WITHIN SPECIAL WATER MANAGEMENT AREAS

(1) Each Area Water Board shall provide by specific regulation for the resolution of conflict among water users within the boundaries of the Special Water Management Area.

(2) The State Agency may refer proceedings under administrative dispute resolution to an appropriate Area Water Board when the State Agency determines that appropriate procedures exist in that Special Water Management Area and that the Area Water Board provides an appropriate forum for resolving the dispute.

(3) Nothing in this Part shall impair any remedy provided to any person under the provisions of this Code or under any applicable general rule of law except to the extent that a regulation creates an

administrative procedure that must be exhausted before a person is entitled to resort to a court.

Commentary: As the resolution of conflicts that are more intense in some part of the State than in others will often be the primary reason for creating Special Water Management Areas, the Area Water Boards are required to devise special procedures for dealing with those conflicts. This section makes clear that any such procedure does not preempt the legal rights of any person, although the regulation can enforce reasonable delays necessary to give the prescribed procedure an opportunity to work before a person can disregard the procedure and resort to some other remedy. The State Agency is authorized, in appropriate cases, to refer a proceeding brought under section 5R-2-03 (administrative resolution) to a proceeding under the appropriate Area Water Board's procedure. This section is supplemented by, but not preempted by, the provisions on dispute resolution found elsewhere in this Code.

Disputes could be brought to the Area Water Board by the persons involved in the dispute. Or those persons might initiate a proceeding before the State Agency or in a court. Either the State Agency, under subsection (2), or the court, under subsection (3), would refer the decision to the Area Water Board whenever that would be the best method for making an initial attempt to resolve the dispute. As a result, each Area Water Board could be said to exercise primary jurisdiction over disputes relating to water within its Special Water Management Area. Vesting primary jurisdiction in the Area Water Board is appropriate as the members are likely to more familiar with local conditions and needs than the State Agency with its broader focus and limited resources. Having primary jurisdiction in the Area Water Board might be even more appropriate if the governor's appointment power under section 4R-4-04 is exercised to make the Board broadly representative of the different major interests in the use and protection of water in the Special Water Management Area. If the dispute is transferred from the State Agency, the Area Water Board can exercise functions equivalent to an administrative hearing under the State Agency. The Area Water Board is not authorized to function as the equivalent of a court, and if a dispute is transferred from a court to the Board, the Board will function more akin to mediation and conciliation than to a formal administrative adjudicatory hearing. The State Agency could also refer a dispute to an Area Water Board as a step in alternative dispute resolution, when the Board could function as a mediation or conciliation service or (as provided in section 5R-2-03) as an arbitral proceeding. In any event, the Area Water Board's responsibility is to pursue the public interest in its dispute resolution processes. The problem is to reconcile individual water rights and other legally protected interests with the preeminent goal of sustainable development.

If a conflict resolution proceeding before an Area Water Board produces, or is expected to produce, a binding order or decision, any resulting order or decision is reviewable in the manner provided in section 5R-3-02 for an order or decision of the State Agency. That section provides for review under the State's Administrative Procedure Act for final orders or decisions, and also for preliminary, procedural, and intermediate orders or decisions when awaiting a final order or decision before review is allowed would not afford an aggrieved party an adequate remedy. By also incorporating section 5R-3-03 into subsection (5) of this section, the section not only assures that the Area Water Board shall conform its orders and decisions to the orders and decisions of the Court, but also that a judgment for the expenses of another person's litigation will not be entered against the Area Water Board.

Cross-references: § 1R-1-05 (efficient and equitable allocation during shortfalls in water supply); § 1R-1-06 (legal security for water rights); § 1R-1-08 (procedural protections); § 2R-1-04 (protection of property rights); § 2R-2-15 (person); § 2R-2-18 (the public interest); § 2R-2–22 (State Agency); § 2R-2-24 (sustainable development); § 4R-3-02 (cooperation with other units of State and local government); § 4R-3-03 (duty of other units of government to cooperate with the State Agency); § 4R-4-01 (purposes for Special Water Management Areas); § 4R-4-04 (Area Water Boards) § 4R-4-06 (regulatory authority of Special Water Management Areas); §§ 5R-2-01 to § 5R-2-03 (dispute resolution); § 6R-4-05 (preservation of private rights of action).

Comparable statute: FLA. STAT. ANN. §§ 373.119; ILL. CON. STAT. ch. 525, § 45/5.

§ 4R-4-08 FUNDING SPECIAL WATER MANAGEMENT AREAS

The activities of Special Water Management Areas through their Area Water Boards shall be funded by a special surcharge on the fees paid for permits to withdraw water from water sources within the Area.

Commentary: All Special Water Management Areas require some level of operational funding to support administrative and other expenses necessary to fulfill their water planning and management activities. *See generally* Dellapenna, § 9.03(a)(5)(A). In most States with existing Special Water Management Area programs, this funding comes from a combination of sources such as general State revenues, locally levied property taxes, special resource management funds, and general water use fees. *Id.*, § 9.03(a)(5)(C). A State might well consider whether to substitute such a source for the surcharge on permit fees indicated here. One reason for again burdening the permit fees is that as Special Water Management Areas, almost by definition, are areas of sustained overuse and conflict over water. Reliance on additional revenues to be generated by surcharges on the permit fees will provide an incentive for those water users who are making low-valued uses to curtail use or to stop using the water altogether, thereby reducing the stress on water sources within the Area.

Permit procedures are designed, in part, to prevent the issuance of permits for water use with the intention of creating water shortages or conflicts among permit holders. If those procedures are followed correctly by the State Agency, or enforced properly by the courts, the various incentives for low-valued users to discontinue use will come into play solely in times of true shortfalls in water supply, and not as a back-door way of compelling the shift of water to higher valued uses. The promotion of such shifts is provided for elsewhere in the Regulated Riparian Model Water Code through provisions regarding the duration and modification of permits.

Cross-references: § 4R-1-07 (application fees); § 4R-4-01 (purposes for Special Water Management Areas); § 4R-4-03 (creation of Special Water Management Area); § 4R-4-04 (Area Water Boards) § 4R-4-05 (Area Water Management Plans); § 4R-4-06 (regulatory authority of

Special Water Management Areas); § 4R-4-07 (conflict resolution within Special Water Management Areas); §§ 6R-3-01 to 6R-3-06 (the basis of a water right); § 7R-1-02 (duration of permits); § 7R-1-03 (forfeiture of permits); §§ 7R-2-01 to 7R-2-04 (modification of water rights); §§ 7R-3-01 to 7R-3-07 (restrictions during water shortages or water emergencies).

Comparable statutes: FLA. STAT. ANN. §§ 373.0695(1)(c), 373.0697, 373.088 to 373.93, 373.109; MISS. CODE ANN. §§ 51-8-35 to 51-8-49.

CHAPTER V

ENFORCEMENT AND DISPUTE RESOLUTION

Inevitably, there will be disputes between the State Agency and those subject to its regulatory authority, as well as disputes between holders of water rights. The Regulated Riparian Model Water Code seeks to provide a complete and effective range of remedies for these several kinds of dispute. The Code relies on general law for most of the details of these remedies, but does spell out the essential terms of the rights of persons and of the Agency to basic remedies and some of the means of proving their claims.

The Code does not automatically require a hearing before any order or decision by the State Agency, but does provide full opportunity for a contested hearing by any person affected by an order or decision. These provisions apply both to specific decisions such as the issuance or denial of a permit or a decision to undertake a Special Water Management Area study, but also apply to decisions of a more general nature, such as the adoption of a regulation. These same provisions generally apply to Area Water Boards and Special Water Management Areas in comparable circumstances. *See* Part 4 of Chapter IV. The provisions in the first Part of this Chapter spell out the most central features of the right to a hearing. These provisions will apply to any hearing held pursuant to the Code, whether under this Chapter or otherwise.

The Code seeks to emphasize alternate dispute resolution, both between the Agency and the persons it regulates and between water right holders. This can include recourse to the dispute resolution facilities of the Area Water Board of the appropriate Special Water Management Area. In the event such devices fail, this Chapter also provides a full panoply of formal dispute resolution methods, including administrative hearings to resolve disputes between holders of water rights. The Code also provides enforcement measures for the Agency of both a civil nature and of a criminal nature. For a general discussion on the enforcement of permits, see Dellapenna, § 9.03(a)(5)(B).

Part 1

Hearings

The essence of due process of law is fair procedures to assure that any person affected by a government decision has an appropriate opportunity to be heard in the matter during the decision-making process. This Part provides for hearing generally, and provides the State Agency with authority to compel the production of necessary evidence. The Agency is also empowered to decline to provide a hearing if there is no material question in dispute.

§ 5R-1-01 RIGHT TO A HEARING

(1) Any person aggrieved by an order or decision of the State Agency, or whose interests in fact are likely to be affected adversely by a regulation proposed or adopted by the State Agency, must submit a written request for a hearing within 30 days of that person's receipt of notice of the order or decision or within 60 days of the publication of the proposed or adopted regulation.

(2) The State Agency shall provide a hearing within 30 days of the receipt of a written request for a hearing pursuant to subsection (1) unless the requesting person has been heard previously on the same matter.

(3) The person requesting a hearing must indicate in the written request the reasons why that person believes the order or decision in question should be changed.

Commentary: This section provides for an administrative hearing before the State Agency at the request of any person aggrieved by an order or decision of the Agency or likely to be adversely affect by a regulation adopted by the State Agency. The Regulated Riparian Model

Water Code rejects always requiring a mandatory hearing (whether informational or adjudicatory) before the Agency acts. Such a requirement is found in the law of some regulated riparian States. Still, the Code recognizes that fundamental fairness requires that any person aggrieved by an order or decision or likely to be affected by a proposed or adopted regulation should be heard if that person deems it worth the effort to request the hearing and to undertake to make a presentation, whether in person or through counsel.

The requirements to qualify to request a hearing are that the person be "aggrieved" by a decision focusing on specific interests or rights or "interested in fact" in a regulation cast in general terms. These are the usual requirements for "standing" before federal courts, and are often the law in the states as well. A person is "aggrieved" by an order or decision if her, his, or its legal rights actually are affected by the order or decision. *Sierra Club v. Morton,* 405 U.S. 727 (1972). A person has an "interest in fact" if their property or activities are likely to be affected adversely by the regulation in question even if no specific legal right is involved. *Lujan v. Defenders of Wildlife,* 504 U.S. 555 (1992). The person requesting the hearing must indicate the grounds for the requested hearing in the request for the hearing and shall have the right, so long as the grounds alleged are not frivolous (according to the next section).

Hawaii provides a considerably more restrictive model. Hawaii limits the right to a hearing to persons who own land within the water basin in which the withdrawal is to occur or who will be "directly and immediately affected" by the proposed water use. HAW. REV. STAT. § 174C-53(b). This Code is more forthcoming regarding the right to request a hearing, but requires the adversely affected person to act promptly in order to obtain the hearing, within 30 days of receiving written notice of an Agency order or decision. A longer period of 60 days is allowed for persons seeking a hearing after the Agency publishes a regulation as the regulation might not come to the attention of adversely affected persons as quickly as an order or decision communicated directly to those affected by the order or decision. If the right to a hearing is invoked by a non-frivolous written request, the hearing must be held within 30 days. Such relatively short time limits both assure fairness to the affected individuals and ensures that the State Agency will be able to implement its orders, decisions, and regulations promptly. A State legislature may choose some other time limit for the holding of the hearing depending on local traditions, anticipated demand for hearings, or other relevant considerations.

Cross-references: § 1R-1-08 (procedural protections); § 2R-2-15 (person); § 2R-2-23 (State Agency); § 5R-1-02 (hearing not required for a frivolous claim); § 5R-1-03 (hearing participation); § 5R-1-04 (authority to compel evidence); § 5R-1-05 (hearings not to delay the effectiveness of permits); §§ 5R-2-01 to 5R-2-03 (dispute resolution); §§ 5R-3-01 to 5R-3-03 (judicial review); § 6R-2-02 (notice and opportunity to be heard); § 6R-2-04 (contesting an application); § 6R-2-05 (public right of comment); § 7R-2-02 (procedures for approving other modifications); § 7R-3-02 (declaration of a water shortage); § 7R-3-03 (declaration of a water emergency).

Comparable statutes: ALA. CODE §§ 9-10B-5(9), 9-10B-30; ARK. CODE ANN. § 15-22-206(a), (b) (mandatory hearing); CONN. GEN. STAT. ANN. §§ 22a-371, 22a-372; DEL. CODE ANN. tit. 7, § 6004, 6006; FLA. STAT. ANN. § 373.229(3) (hearings required if the withdrawal is over 100,000 gallons per day); GA. CODE ANN. §§ 12-5-31(o), 12-5-43, 12-5-95(b), 12-5-96(g), 12-5-99(2), 12-5-106(b); HAW. REV. STAT. §§ 174C-11, 174C-13, 174C-27(b), 174C-31(m), 174C-42, 174C-50(b), 174C-53, 174C-71(1)(F); KY. REV. STAT. ANN. § 151.184; MD. CODE ANN., NAT. RES. § 8-806(f), (i) to (k); MASS. GEN. LAWS ANN. ch. 21G, § 12; MINN. STAT. ANN. § 105.44(3)-(6); N.Y. ENVTL. CONSERV. LAW § 15-0903(1); S.C. CODE ANN. § 49-5-60(D), (E).

§ 5R-1-02 A HEARING NOT REQUIRED FOR A FRIVOLOUS CLAIM

> **The State Agency may disallow a hearing if the State Agency determines that the proposed grounds for questioning the State Agency's action are frivolous, serving notice of that determination on the person requesting the hearing and allowing that person a reasonable opportunity to demonstrate a non-frivolous basis for convening a hearing.**

Commentary: Recognizing that some requests for hearings under section 5R-1-01 are made for purposes of delay rather than because of any actual belief that the order or decision is wrong, the Regulated Riparian Model Water Code authorizes the State Agency, upon proper notice and an opportunity to contest the Agency's conclusion, to disallow the hearing when the Agency determines that the hearing request is based upon frivolous grounds or otherwise fails to present a material issue.

Cross-reference: § 5R-1-01 (right to a hearing).

Comparable Statutes: MD. CODE ANN., NAT. RES. § 8-806(k).

§ 5R-1-03 HEARING PARTICIPATION

(1) Any hearing shall be held in any county in which the withdrawal or use in question is or would be made and shall, except when required to protect confidential business information as provided in § 4R-1-09, be open to the public.

(2) Any person shall be allowed to participate in any hearing in which that person has an interest in fact.

(3) Any person participating in a hearing pursuant to this Code may be represented by counsel, make written or oral arguments, introduce any relevant testimony or evidence, cross-examine witnesses, or take any combination of such actions.

Commentary: This section sets forth certain limited procedures to be followed in holding a hearing under the Regulated Riparian Model Water Code. The State Agency has the authority to adopt regulations to define in more detail the procedures pertaining to hearings.

Subsection (1) provides that hearings are to be held in any county in which the withdrawal or use is to be made, and is to be open to the public. If withdrawals or uses are to occur in several counties, the State Agency has discretion to select the county in which the hearing. If only one person is to be heard, the hearing normally would be held in the county that is the most convenient for that person. When numerous people are to be heard, the State Agency would schedule the hearing the optimize the convenience of all concerned, and might even hold the hearing in a number of sessions in several authorized counties.

The major limitation on the openness requirement is the preservation of confidential business information. That protection is not absolute. Confidential business information shall be made public when relevant to an administrative process. This clause merely provides that no such disclosure shall occur without the notice to the person entitled to confidentiality provided in section 4R-1-09, and then only after a hearing to determine its relevancy to the proceeding.

Subsection (2) allows any person to participate in the hearings, *i.e.*, to be heard, so long as that person is "interested in fact." *See Lujan v. Defenders of Wildlife,* 504 U.S. 555 (1992). This is a broader right to be heard than is necessary to qualify to request a hearing under section 5R-1-01(1). To request a hearing, one's interests must be adversely affected in some fashion. To be heard at a hearing, one need only have an interest in fact, even if that interest would not be adversely affected by the order, decision, or regulation that is the subject matter of the hearing.

Subsection (3) provides that any participant in a hearing has a legal right to be represented by counsel, to present evidence or witnesses, and to cross-examine adverse witnesses.

Cross-references: § 1R-1-08 (procedural protections); § 2R-2-15 (person); § 2R-2-23 (State Agency); § 4R-1-06 (regulatory authority of the State Agency); § 5R-1-01 (right to a hearing); § 5R-1-02 (hearing not required for a frivolous claim); § 5R-1-04 (authority to compel evidence); § 5R-1-05 (hearings not to delay effectiveness of permits); §§ 5R-2-01 to 5R-2-03 (dispute resolution); §§ 5R-3-01 to 5R-3-03 (judicial review); § 6R-2-02 (notice and opportunity to be heard); § 6R-2-04 (contesting an application); § 6R-2-05 (public right of comment); § 7R-2-02 (procedures for approving other modifications); § 7R-3-02 (declaration of a water shortage); § 7R-3-03 (declaration of a water emergency).

Comparable statutes: ARK. CODE ANN. § 15-22-206(a); CONN. GEN. STAT. ANN. §§ 22a-371(c), (d), (g), 22a-372; DEL. CODE ANN. tit. 7, § 6004, 6006; GA. CODE ANN. §§ 12-5-43, 12-5-96(h)(2); HAW. REV. STAT. §§ 174C-11, 174C-13, 174C-27(b), 174C-31(m), 174C-42, 174C-50(b), 174C-53, 174C-71(1)(F); KY. REV. STAT. ANN. § 151.184; MD. CODE ANN., NAT. RES. § 8-806(f), (i), (j); MASS. GEN. LAWS ANN. ch. 21G, § 12; MINN. STAT. ANN. § 105.44(3)-(5) ; N.Y. ENVTL. CONSERV. LAW § 15-0903; S.C. CODE ANN. § 49-5-60(D) to (F).

§ 5R-1-04 AUTHORITY TO COMPEL EVIDENCE

(1) The State Agency is authorized for all purposes falling within the State Agency's jurisdiction to administer oaths, issue subpoenas, and to compel the attendance of witnesses and the production of necessary or relevant data, including witnesses or evidence that appear necessary to evaluate the arguments of any party.

(2) Any person who defies a proper subpoena or other order to attend a proceeding or to produce evidence without lawful excuse is guilty of criminal contempt, and may be prosecuted in any court of competent jurisdiction.

Commentary: The Regulated Riparian Model Water Code provides full authority to the State Agency to compel the attendance of relevant witnesses and the production of any relevant evidence at any hearing. Evidence is relevant whether it is necessary to evaluate the Agency's position or is necessary to evaluate any other person's position at the hearing. This power, then, is to be exercised to compel the attendance of witnesses and the production of evidence on behalf of someone challenging the Agency's orders or decisions as well as in support of those orders or decisions. Failure to obey an order to attend or produce evidence without lawful excuse, or providing false witness or evidence, is treated as a contempt of court upon conviction before any competent court. While the authority to order appearance or production of evidence applies to any party, it is defeated by a valid claim of privilege (such as the attorney-client privilege or as otherwise provided by the applicable general law of evidence), or a valid claim of immunity (as of the federal government or its agencies or instrumentalities to immunity from state process).

Cross-references: § 2R-2-15 (person); § 2R-2-23 (State Agency); § 5R-1-01 (right to a hearing); § 5R-1-03 (hearing participation).

Comparable statutes: ARK. CODE ANN. §§ 15-22-207, 15-22-208; DEL. CODE ANN. tit. 7, § 6006(3); ; KY. REV. STAT. ANN. § 151.184(3)MINN. STAT. ANN. § 105.44(7); N.J. STAT. ANN. § 58:1A-15(d); N.Y. ENVTL. CONSERV. LAW § 15-0903(3)(c).

§ 5R-1-05 HEARINGS NOT TO DELAY THE EFFECTIVENESS OF A PERMIT

Pending the outcome of a hearing or ensuing litigation concerning the terms and conditions of a permit, the person holding the permit must comply with the contested terms or conditions.

Commentary: A request for a hearing is not allowed to delay the implementation of the State Agency's decisions regarding the terms and conditions of permits. Persons contesting the terms or conditions of a permit must abide by the contested terms or conditions pending the outcome of the hearing or subsequent litigation. This is necessary in order to prevent a person from using the hearing process and judicial review to delay necessary steps to manage, conserve, and develop the waters of the State.

Cross-references: § 1R-1-08 (procedural protections); § 2R-2-15 (person); § 2R-2-23 (State Agency); § 5R-1-01 (right to a hearing); § 5R-1-02 (hearing not required for a frivolous claim); § 5R-1-03 (hearing participation); § 5R-1-04 (authority to compel evidence); §§ 5R-2-01 to 5R-2-03 (dispute resolution); §§ 5R-3-01 to 5R-3-03 (judicial review); § 6R-2-04 (contesting an application for a permit); § 6R-2-05 (public right of comment); § 7R-1-01 (permit terms and conditions).

Part 2

Dispute Resolution

Disputes over the allocation of water or the modification of water rights should be resolved as expeditiously, inexpensively, and fairly as possible. *See ASCE Resolution* No. 256 (1989). Once a dispute arises, the persons involved generally discuss their differences and try to settle the misunderstanding or disagreement through the informal process of negotiation. Negotiation offers the advantage of allowing the persons themselves to control the process and the solution, and thus offers the greatest assurance of achieving a mutually satisfactory outcome that they will honor rather than seek to evade. As a result, the majority of disputes will never enter any formal dispute resolution process; most will be settled through negotiation. *See* ROGER FISHER & WILLIAM URY, GETTING TO YES: NEGOTIATING AGREEMENT WITHOUT GIVING IN (1981).

If direct negotiations between the parties to a dispute fail, various forms of alternate dispute resolution have been developed to combine the advantages of greater party control than is possible for litigation and third-party intervention designed to facilitate (mediation) or mildly compel a resolution to the dispute (arbitration). The four goals of alternative dispute resolution include:

(1) to relieve more formal dispute resolution mechanisms of congestion and the parties to the dispute of undue cost and delay;

(2) to enhance the community involvement in the dispute resolution process;

(3) to facilitate access to justice; and

(4) to provide more "effective" dispute resolution.

See generally John Cooley, *Arbitration v. Mediation–Explaining the Differences,* 69 JUDICATURE 263 (1986); Judge Irving Kaufman, *Reform for a System in Crisis: Alternative Dispute Resolution in the Federal Courts,* 59 FORDHAM L. REV. 1 (1990); J. Stewart McLendon, *Alternative Methods of Dispute Settlement,* 17 HOUS. L. REV. 979 (1976); Frank Sander, *Alternative Methods of Dispute Resolution: An Overview,* 37 U. FLA. L. REV. 1 (1985).

Most regulated riparian statutes already in place say little or nothing about resolving disputes between holders of water rights. See Dellapenna, § 9.03(c). This silence relegates the parties to any such dispute, once they have exhausted their own efforts to negotiate their differences, to the law courts. This Part of the Regulated Riparian Model Water Code encourages a wider range of informal dispute resolution for all disputes involving the waters of the State and requires arbitration for disputes between permit holders.

§ 5R-2-01 SUPPORT FOR INFORMAL DISPUTE RESOLUTION

When the State Agency determines that an agreement, executed in writing by all persons having an interest in a dispute regarding the waters of the State and filed with the State Agency, is consistent with the policies and requirements of this Code, the State Agency shall approve the agreement and the agreement shall thereafter control in place of a formal order or regulation of the State Agency until terminated by agreement of the persons bound by the agreement or terminated by the State Agency because the agreement or its effects have become inconsistent with the policies or requirements of this Code.

Commentary: The Regulated Riparian Model Water Code facilitates the settlement of disputes by negotiation between the parties, whether through mediation or otherwise, by providing that the State Agency will be bound by the terms of the resulting agreement once it is filed by the Agency, unless the Agency determines that the agreement or its effects are inconsistent with the policies or requirements of the Code. Any person aggrieved by the Agency's determination to recognize such an agreement is entitled to judicial review on the same terms as any person aggrieved by any final order or decision by the Agency. *See* § 5R-3-02. No existing water allocation law includes such a provision. The Agency itself has the authority to resolve its disputes through negotiations with the parties rather than solely through formal proceedings. *See* section 5R-2-02.

Cross-references: § 2R-2-15 (person); § 2R-2-23 (State Agency); § 5R-2-02 (conciliation or mediation); § 5R-2-03 (administrative resolution); § 5R-3-02 (judicial review for orders or decisions of the State Agency); § 5R-4-07 (civil charges).

Comparable statutes: GA. CODE ANN. § 12-5-23 (b)(3); OR. REV. STAT. § 537.745.

§ 5R-2-02 CONCILIATION OR MEDIATION

(1) With the consent of persons involved in disputes over water or the allocation thereof, the State Agency may conduct informal negotiations to encourage and assist the conciliation, mediation, or other informal resolutions of the dispute.

(2) The State Agency shall recover from the parties the expenses of its activities in encouraging and assisting the conciliation or mediation of disputes, allocating the expenses to the parties in the same proportions as their water use fees bear to each other.

Commentary: If negotiations directly between the parties fail, this section authorizes the State Agency to facilitate the negotiations in an effort to achieve the sort of informal outcome that offers the best chance of long-term success. Two techniques are available for this intervention and both are authorized. The least intrusive role possible for a representative of the State in helping to resolve a dispute not involving the State is conciliation in which the State Agency merely functions as a conduit for information and encourages the parties to devise their own solutions. The State Agency takes on a slightly greater role in the process of mediation; in that process, the mediator suggests solutions to the dispute, although the Agency refrains from attempting to impose any solution it suggests to the parties. Jerry Murase & Kanon Alpert, *Mediation: An Alternative to the Litigation Wars*, 10 L.A. LAW. 44 (1987); Leonard Riskin, *The Special Place of Mediation in Alternative Dispute Resolution*, 37 U. FLA. L. REV. 19 (1985). This express recognition is not to foreclose other modes of intervention that could also facilitate the informal resolution of a dispute. Illinois, for example, prescribes a somewhat different role for its administering agency, that of "fact finder." Any informal techniques that are mutually agreeable to the parties to the dispute and that the Agency finds it can usefully perform, are authorized by this section.

Some will consider this to be the most important function of the State Agency. Still, the Agency cannot undertake to conciliate or mediate every dispute between water right holders if only because of budget limitations, for conciliation and mediation can become a time-consuming and expensive process. Therefore, the section merely authorizes the Agency to become involved. The Agency retains discretion on how often and how extensively it will become involved in conciliation or mediation. The exercise of this discretion will necessarily be strongly influenced by the appropriations by the State legislature authorized for this purpose or for the State Agency generally. In a proper case, the State Agency can refer the interested persons to an Area Water Board for conciliation or mediation, which could somewhat ameliorate the burdens of conciliating or mediating a large number of disputes.

Subsection (2) requires the State Agency to recover the costs of its services from the parties. As the process is non-adversarial, there is not, strictly speaking, a "winner" or a "loser" when the process is concluded. Therefore, one cannot allocate the costs to the loser, as might be done after litigation. To allocate the costs equally between the parties would often impose an impossible financial burden on the smaller participants in the process. The Regulated Riparian Model Water Code allocates the costs in proportion to the water use fees paid by the participants. Such an approach is consistent with the nonadversarial nature of the process and generally will be consistent with the ability of the participants to pay for the process. In short, the formula will usually be fair or equitable.

Cross-references: § 2R-2-15 (person); § 2R-2-23 (State Agency); § 4R-4-04 (Area Water Boards); § 4R-4-06 (conflict resolution within Special Water Management Areas); § 5R-2-01 (support for informal dispute resolution); § 5R-2-03 (administrative resolution).

Comparable Statute: GA. CODE ANN. § 12-5-99(1).

§ 5R-2-03 ADMINISTRATIVE RESOLUTION OF DISPUTES AMONG HOLDERS OF PERMITS TO WITHDRAW WATER

(1) If the State Agency determines that the more informal procedures contained in sections 5R-2-01 and 5R-2-02 will not succeed in resolving a dispute among holders of water rights evidenced by a permit or upon the request of any person interested in such a dispute, the State Agency shall convene a hearing to arbitrate the dispute administratively.

(2) The State Agency shall provide at least 21 days notice of the proposed hearing to any holder of a water right involved in the dispute prior to convening the arbitral hearing, sending the notice by any form of mail requiring return receipt to the last address reported to the State Agency for any reason by the holder in question.

(3) Upon the conclusion of the arbitral hearing, the State Agency shall issue an order determining whether there has been an unreasonable injury to any holder of a water right invited to participate in the arbitral hearing or to the public interest, and ordering as appropriate:

(a) steps to be taken by those parties best able to avoid or abate the injury at the least cost;

(b) compensation to the injured person by the person responsible;

(c) the modification or revocation of the permit of the offending person as necessary to prevent the unreasonable injury.

(4) The only recourse for any party to the arbitral hearing who is aggrieved by the result shall be judicial review of the State Agency's decision after it becomes final.

(5) If the State Agency fails within six months to conclude the proceedings under this section, or fails with reasonable diligence to effectuate or enforce the decision rendered through the hearing, any aggrieved party to the arbitral hearing may initiate a proceeding in any court of competent jurisdiction to resolve the dispute according to the provisions of this Code and other relevant laws.

Commentary: The Regulated Riparian Model Water Code preempts most litigation between holders of water rights held pursuant to a permit by providing a formal administrative process before the State Agency to resolve the dispute. While the compulsory aspects of this administrative process make it resemble full-blown litigation, the Code intends that the process generally remain more informal, less costly, and faster than litigation. *See* Herbert Kritzer & Jill Anderson, *The Arbitration Alternative: A Comparative Analysis of Case Processing Time, Disposition Mode, and Cost in the American Arbitration Association and the Courts*, 8 JUS. SYS. J. 6 (1983).

The United States Supreme Court long ago upheld the constitutionality of removing disputes over water from courts to an administrative proceeding, so long as there is judicial review of the outcome of the administrative proceeding. *Pacific Live Stock Co. v. Oregon Water Board*, 241 U.S. 440 (1916). *See also United States v. Idaho*, 113 S. Ct. 1983 (1993). This

Code provides for judicial review, so there seems to be no credible basis for challenging this provision as a denial of due process.

While certain features of this administrative process are found in some of the existing regulated riparian statutes, none of them contains a provision as extensive or complete as the one set out in this Code. This procedure is designed to enable the Agency to retain its managerial control of the waters of the State without fear of confronting, for example, inconsistent judicial decrees entered in several separate private proceedings or that would somehow give third persons veto power over particular water sources or uses. The process is not available for all disputes as it does not reach disputes regarding water rights for which a permit is not required as well as disputes involving nonconsumptive uses.

The State Agency and the participants in the dispute remain bound to attempt informal dispute resolution before resorting to the arbitration hearing. Once the Agency or one of the participants determine that such informal steps will not succeed, the Agency is to convene a formal hearing, giving written notice to the interested parties. The Agency will conduct the hearing under the general rules in this Code supplemented by the State's Administrative Procedure Act. The only recourse for someone disappointed in the outcome to the hearing is through judicial review–an approach that makes the Agency a party to any litigation and gives a strong presumption of validity to its decision in the hearing.

The Agency is to order a remedy only against a person found to have unreasonably injured another permit holder or the public interest. The remedies are to be sculpted by the Agency to provide the least cost avoidance or abatement of the injury, and can include physical solutions, compensation, and even modification or cancellation of the permit of the offending holder. In determining whether an injury is unreasonable, the Agency may consider the age and condition of the facilities of the several parties and the consequent reasonableness of continuing to insist on relying on each system without interference from the activities of another holder of a water right. The Agency might also require the parties to submit estimates of their costs to take various remedial steps such as repairs or improvements in one party's water delivery system. If the remedy ordered requires the construction or reconstruction of a water withdrawal or use facility, the Agency shall supervise the design, construction, and testing of the resulting facility to assure that it meets any general standards for such facility adopted by regulation by the Agency and the particular standards set by the Agency in this proceeding as necessary to prevent further unreasonable injury.

Once the Agency renders its decision, the Agency is free to invoke any relevant civil enforcement measure to compel compliance with the decision. If noncompliance involves the knowing reporting of false information or the like, criminal sanctions become a possibility as well. The Agency might also refer a particular dispute in a proper case to an Area Water Board for arbitration pursuant to this section.

This section provides a rather lengthy maximum period for the proceedings to be concluded in an effort to assure that the Agency has adequate time to complete the proceedings. If the Agency fails to render a decision within the period indicated, or fails to effectuate or enforce its decision with reasonable dispatch, an aggrieved party is then free to go to court and seek any appropriate relief in any court of competent jurisdiction. A State would want to consider whether, given budgetary and other constraints, this period should be longer or shorter than the period provided in this section.

Cross-references: § 1R-1-01 (protecting the public interest in the waters of the State); § 1R-1-06 (legal security for the right to use water); § 1R-1-08 (procedural protections); § 2R-1-01 (the obligation to make only reasonable use of water); § 2R-1-03 (no unreasonable injury to other water rights); § 2R-1-04 (protection of property rights); § 2R-2-07 (cost); § 2R-2-15 (person); § 2R-2-18 (the public interest); § 2R-2-20 (reasonable use); § 2R-2-23 (State Agency); § 2R-2-26 (unreasonable injury); § 2R-2-30 (water right); § 4R-4-04 (Area Water Boards); § 4R-4-06 (conflict resolution within Special Water Management Areas); § 5R-1-01 (right to a hearing); § 5R-1-03 (hearing participation); § 5R-1-04 (authority to compel evidence); § 5R-2-01 (support for informal dispute resolution); § 5R-2-02 (conciliation or mediation); § 5R-3-02 (judicial review for orders or decisions of the State Agency); §§ 5R-4-01 to 5R-4-09 (civil enforcement); § 5R-5-01 (crimes); § 5R-5-02 (revocation of permits); § 6R-3-02 (determining whether a use is reasonable); §§ 7R-2-01 to 7R-2-04 (modification of water rights).

Comparable statutes: DEL. CODE ANN. tit. 7, § 6031; HAW. REV. STAT. § 174C-10; ILL. CONS. STAT. ANN. ch. 525, § 45/5; IND. CODE ANN. § 13-2-1-6(2); IOWA CODE ANN. §§ 455B.271(2)(d), 455B.281; VA. CODE ANN. § 62.1-44.37.

Part 3
Judicial Review

Judicial review of regulations and decisions or orders is an essential element of due process. This Part provides for generous review of either sort of action by the State Agency, but leaves to the general administrative law of the State questions of standards of review and of the procedural details of such judicial review.

§ 5R-3-01 JUDICIAL REVIEW OF REGULATIONS

Any person likely to be affected by a regulation adopted or proposed by the State Agency may obtain a judicial declaration of the validity, meaning, or application of the regulation by bringing an action for a declaratory judgment in a court of competent jurisdiction in the county in which the executive offices of the State Agency are maintained.

Commentary: This section provides for definitive judicial review and interpretation of the regulations made by the State Agency under this Code by means of a declaratory judgment. The section removes any limitations to such review that might be found in the State's Administrative Procedure Act and provides the exclusive basis for challenging a regulation before the regulation is applied individually through an order or decision of the Agency. This section precludes a proceeding (such as for the extraordinary writs of mandamus or prohibition) under the general provisions of the State's Administrative Procedure Act as such, but the general legal standards of the Administrative Procedure Act (such as the legal bases for review and the standards that determine whether the Agency's action is valid) apply as those questions are neither addressed nor displaced by this section. *See generally* MALONEY, AUSNESS, & MORRIS, at 115, 116; WILLIAM WALKER & PHYLLIS BRIDGEMAN, A WATER CODE FOR VIRGINIA 75 (Va. Polytech.. Inst., Va. Water Resources Res. Center Bull. No. 147, 1985).

An alternative model would be to establish a mechanism for appeal and review within the administrative structure. Thus, for example, Florida vests "exclusive" authority to review the validity of regulations in the "Land and Water Adjudicatory Commission," composed of the governor and the cabinet. FLA. STAT. ANN. § 373.114. Delaware has an "Environmental Appeals Board" with primary authority to review both regulations and final decisions by the Secretary of Natural Resources and Environmental Control, the officer vested with the permit issuing authority. Appeal from these boards then brings the issues before the courts. The Regulated Riparian Model Water Code expedites this process by taking appeals directly from the State Agency to the courts.

Cross-references: § 4R-1-05 (application of general laws to meetings, procedures, and records); § 4R-1-06 (regulatory authority of the State Agency); § 4R-4-02 (Special Water Management Area studies); § 4R-4-07 (conflict resolution within Special Water Management Areas); § 5R-1-01 (right to a hearing); § 5R-3-02 (judicial review of orders or decisions of the State Agency); § 5R-3-03 (compliance with competent judicial orders or judgments); § 5R-4-09 (citizen suits).

Comparable statutes: ARK. CODE ANN. § 15-22-209; DEL. CODE ANN. tit. 7, § 6006(2); GA. CODE ANN. § 12-5-95(c); HAW. REV. STAT. § 174C-12; MINN. STAT. ANN. § 105.471.

§ 5R-3-02 JUDICIAL REVIEW OF ORDERS OR DECISIONS OF THE STATE AGENCY

(1) **Any person who has exhausted all administrative remedies available within the State Agency and who is aggrieved by any final order or decision of the Agency is entitled to judicial review of the order or decision under the State's Administrative Procedure Act.**

(2) A preliminary, procedural, or intermediate decision is reviewable if review of the final decision would not afford an adequate remedy.

Commentary: This section allows any person aggrieved by any final order or decision of the State Agency to appeal the Agency's order or decision to a court of competent jurisdiction. No special provisions are provided for the judicial review of other orders or decisions except to indicate that non-final orders are reviewable if awaiting a final order or decision would not afford the aggrieved party an adequate remedy. *See Hermiston Irrig. Dist. v. Water Resources Dep't*, 886 P.2d 1093 (Or. 1994). As noted in the introduction to this Part, the standards of review are left to the general administrative law of the State. An alternative model is found in Delaware which makes review by an independent "Environmental Appeals Board" a precondition to judicial review of agency decisions. DEL. CODE ANN. tit. 7, §§ 6007-9.

Subsections 5R-2-03(4) and 5R-2-03(5) together provide a limit on this possibility of interlocutory judicial review. They provide that recourse through judicial review is available only after the entry of a final decision by the hearing officer or board. Failure of the Agency to render a decision within a reasonable period releases the aggrieved person to litigate the dispute in ordinary courts, but not as a form of interlocutory review. Instead, the Agency, by its failure to act within the specified time limits, loses its rather large control over the dispute resolution process to a competent court which shall proceed to provide a proper remedy on the merits of the dispute.

Cross-references: § 4R-1-05 (application of general laws to meetings, procedures, and records); § 5R-1-01 (right to a hearing); § 4R-4-02 (Special Water Management Area studies); § 4R-4-06 (regulatory authority of Special Water Management Areas); § 5R-3-01 (judicial review of regulations); § 5R-3-03 (compliance with competent judicial orders or judgments); § 5R-4-09 (citizen suits).

Comparable statutes: ARK. CODE ANN. § 15-22-209; CONN. GEN. STAT. ANN. § 22a-374; DEL. CODE ANN. tit. 7, § 6006(1); GA. CODE ANN. §§ 12-5-44, 12-5-96(h)(1), 12-5-99(c), 12-5-106(b); HAW. REV. STAT. § 174C-12; KY. REV. STAT. ANN. § 151.186; MASS. GEN. LAWS ANN. ch.

21G, § 12; MISS. CODE ANN. §§ 51-3-49, 51-3-55(4); N.Y. ENVTL. CONSERV. LAW § 15-0905; WIS. STAT. ANN. § 30.18(9).

§ 5R-3-03 COMPLIANCE WITH COMPETENT JUDICIAL ORDERS OR JUDGMENTS

(1) The State Agency shall comply with all orders or judgments of a court of competent jurisdiction relating to the waters of the State, conforming its regulations, orders, and decisions to the directions of the reviewing court.

(2) If a reviewing court finds that an order or decision under review is unlawful or constitutes a taking without just compensation, the court shall remand the matter to the State Agency which shall, within a reasonable time, as appropriate:

- **(a) issue any necessary permit;**
- **(b) pay just compensation; or**
- **(c) modify its order or decision to remedy the unlawful aspects of its prior decision.**

(3) No judgment for the expenses of any litigation may be entered against the State Agency.

Commentary: Because of the nature of the activities and functions of the State Agency, the Agency will often find its orders, permits, and regulations challenged in litigation. The Regulated Riparian Model Water Code not only requires the Agency to comply with any valid judgment of a competent court, but it also authorizes the Agency to take any necessary steps to comply. This authorization eliminates as a defense any claim that the Agency is not authorized to undertake the action required by the court. The only proper response of the Agency to a judicial order that allegedly violates the provisions of this Code is to appeal to a higher court, or to the legislature should the objectionable order issue from the State's highest court.

The State Agency must then, as appropriate, either issue any necessary permit, pay just compensation, or modify its order or decision, or some combination of the above actions, although the Agency is not made liable for any expenses of litigation other than its own. In general, the court should allow the Agency to select the mode of compliance so long as the mode chosen by the Agency will in fact remedy the illegality the court has found. If the court directs a particular response, however, the Agency must comply unless it can obtain a reversal of the order on appeal.

Cross-references: § 4R-4-02 (Special Water Management Area studies); § 4R-4-06 (regulatory authority of Special Water Management Areas); § 4R-4-07 (conflict resolution within Special Water Management Areas); § 5R-1-01 (right to a hearing); § 5R-3-01 (judicial review of regulations); § 5R-3-02 (judicial review of orders or decisions or decisions); § 5R-4-09 (citizen suits); § 7R-1-01 (permit terms and conditions).

Comparable statute: MISS. CODE ANN. § 51-3-47.

Part 4
Civil Enforcement

Achieving the purposes and requirements of the Regulated Riparian Model Water Code are impossible without effective enforcement. The Code includes a detailed plan for the State Agency to enforce the provisions of the Code. The following measures should be read as a series of discreet steps following, when necessary, in succession until compliance is achieved. In a particular case, however, the sequence might be inverted or abbreviated.

The measures set forth in this Part would be available to enforce the outcome of an arbitration proceeding as well as the requirements of this Code and regulations, orders, or decisions of the State Agency. Each of these measures includes some degree of actual or threatened punishment as well as (often) means for compensating the State Agency or others for the effects of the violation. The more strictly punitive sanctions are set off in a separate Part of this Chapter, denominated criminal enforcement. For a summary of the various enforcement measures found in existing regulated riparian statutes, see Dellapenna, § 9.03(a)(5)(B).

§ 5R-4-01 INSPECTIONS AND OTHER INVESTIGATIONS

(1) Any duly authorized employee of the State Agency may, pursuant to a valid administrative inspection warrant, enter at reasonable times upon any property, other than a building used as a dwelling place, in which that employee reasonably believes that water is withdrawn from the waters of the State, to inspect, investigate, study, or enforce this Code, or any order, term or condition of a permit, or regulation made pursuant to this Code.

(2) An employee acting pursuant to subsection (1) of this section remains liable for any actual damage caused in the course of an inspection by unlawful conduct.

(3) Duly authorized employees are authorized to undertake, with reasonable frequency, any investigations reasonably pertinent to any matter relevant to the administration or enforcement of this Code, including making tests, reviews, studies, monitorings, or samplings, or examining books, papers, and records, as the responsible employee present at the scene deems necessary.

Commentary: The first step of effective enforcement is the power to inspect or otherwise investigate whether users of water are complying with the provisions of the Regulated Riparian Model Water Code. The Code empowers duly authorized employees of the State Agency to carry out administrative inspections as necessary to enforce the Code. *See* Dellapenna, § 9.03(a)(5)(B); *V-1 Oil Company v. State of Wyoming, Dep't. of Envtl. Quality* 696 F. Supp. 578 (D. Wyo, 1988).

The power to conduct an administrative inspection is defined quite broadly in the Code and does not require a criminal search warrant. The constitution of the United States permits a State to conduct administrative inspections without any warrant at all for highly regulated industries or under certain exigent circumstances, or subject to an administrative search warrant for other inspections. *Michigan v. Clifford*, 464 U.S. 287 (1984); *Michigan v. Tyler*, 436 U.S. 499 (1978); *Marshall v. Barlow's, Inc.* 436 U.S. 307 (1978). Administrative searches or inspections and administrative inspection warrants do not require a showing of "probable cause" in the technical legal sense, but only "reasonable grounds"–grounds that can include a regular pattern of inspections as well as some particularized reason for a given inspection. *New York v. Burger*, 482 U.S. 691 (1987); *Camara v. Municipal Court*, 387 U.S. 523 (1967). The power to inspect and investigate under this Code is so broad that administrative inspection warrants are required to avoid successful challenges under the U.S. Constitution. This Code does not spell out in detail the requirements for such administrative inspection warrants, leaving that to the general laws of the State and to regulations adopted under the Code. If the State does not have a statute regulating administrative search warrants, it might consider adopting one rather than leaving the question entirely to the regulations to be developed by the State Agency. Any evidence found through an administrative inspection can be used even in the criminal proceeding as long as the inspection was not merely a subterfuge for an unwarranted criminal search. *Michigan v. Clifford, supra; Michigan v. Tyler, supra; Abel v. United States*, 362 U.S. 217 (1960).

One concern with inspections and investigations is that the State Agency, or one of its duly authorized employees, shall exploit the authority to harass a particular water user or class of users. The Code seeks to prevent this by limiting inspections to "reasonable times," and by limiting investigations to "reasonable frequency." Hearings and judicial review are available to redress violations of these limits. Furthermore, while poking around in the yard is clearly authorized by this section, it specifically excludes actual dwelling places (as opposed to the yard, garage, and other outbuildings) from the searches and inspections authorized by this section. Furthermore, subsection (2) makes the employee personally liable for unlawful conduct in carrying out a search or inspection under this section.

Subsection (3) makes explicit that the search or inspection includes the records of the permit holder, including the records of any self-monitoring required by the terms and conditions of a relevant permit. Such searching or inspection of records are subject to the obligation to protect confidential business information from unauthorized disclosure. The search or inspection also includes the power to conduct such tests and similar investigations as, in the judgment of the duly authorized employee, are necessary to determine whether the permit holder is complying with the terms and conditions of the permit and of the Code generally.

Cross-references: § 1R-1-08 (procedural protections); § 2R-2-23 (State Agency); § 4R-1-06 (regulatory authority of the State Agency); § 4R-1-09 (protection of confidential business information); §§ 5R-1-01 to 5R-1-05 (hearings); §§ 5R-3-01 to 5R-3-03 (judicial review); § 7R-1-01 (permit terms and conditions).

Comparable statutes: CONN. GEN. STAT. ANN. § 22a-375; DEL. CODE ANN. tit. 7, §§ 6016, 6024; GA. CODE ANN. §§ 12-5-23(b)(11), 12-5-25, 12-5-26, 12-5-97; HAW. REV. STAT. § 174C-5(5); ILL. COMP. STAT. ANN. ch. 525, § 45/5.2; IND. CODE ANN. § 13-2-6.1-4(3), (4); MASS. GEN. LAWS ANN. ch. 21G, § 13; MINN. STAT. ANN. §§ 105.41(3), 105.462; MISS. CODE ANN. § 51-3-43; N.J. STAT. ANN. § 58:1A-15(c); N.Y. ENVTL. CONSERV. LAW §§ 15-0303 to 15-0307; N.C. GEN. STAT. § 143-215.19; S.C. CODE ANN. § 49-5-80; WIS. STAT. ANN. §§ 144.025(f), 144.03.

§ 5R-4-02 NOTICE OF VIOLATION

(1) Whenever a duly authorized employee of the State Agency has reason to believe that any person has violated any provision of this Code, or any order, permit term or condition, or regulation made pursuant to this Code, the employee shall issue and serve upon the person or persons so suspected a written notice of violation indicating

the provision(s), order(s), permit term(s) or condition(s), or regulation(s) allegedly violated and the facts alleged to constitute the violation.

(2) The notice of violation shall require the person or persons served to answer the charges set out in the notice at a hearing before the State Agency not less than 30 days after the date the notice was served unless the person or persons served waive in writing the minimum period before the hearing can be held.

Commentary: The simplest response to any finding that a person is violating the provisions and requirements of the Regulated Riparian Model Water Code is a notice of violation to be issued by the employee of the State Agency who is making the investigation or inspection. The notice, which serves a function similar to a traffic citation, simply sets in motion a process consisting of further inspection and investigation and a hearing. Based on that process, the State Agency will determine the appropriate legal response to the violation.

Cross-references: § 1R-1-08 (procedural protections); § 2R-2-15 (person); § 2R-2-23 (State Agency); § 4R-1-06 (regulatory authority of the State Agency); § 4R-4-05 (regulatory authority of Special Water Management Areas); §§ 5R-1-01 to 5R-1-05 (hearings); §§ 5R-3-01 to 5R-3-03 (judicial review); § 5R-4-01 (inspections or other investigations); § 7R-1-01 (permit terms and conditions).

Comparable statutes: DEL. CODE ANN. tit. 7, § 6019; KY. REV. STAT. ANN. § 151.182.

§ 5R-4-03 ORDERS TO CEASE OR RESTORE

(1) The State Agency has full authority, after a hearing, to order any person to cease violations or to restore the condition of the waters of

the State and related land resources to their condition prior to the violation, or both, as is reasonably necessary to the enforcement of this Code and any order, permit term or condition, or regulation made pursuant to this Code.

(2) If the State Agency determines that an emergency exists requiring immediate correction of the violation, the State Agency shall, without a hearing, issue an order with immediate effect with a hearing to follow within 10 days of the issuance of the order.

Commentary: Orders to "cease and desist" are one of the most common techniques available to administrative agencies to put an end to continuing violations of laws or regulations. *See* Dellapenna, § 9.03(a)(5)(B). Such orders are the administrative equivalent of injunctions in that the orders as such impose no liability or penalty for past conduct, instead focusing on directing what conduct is to be undertaken or authorized in the future. Should a person subject to such an order nonetheless persist in the prohibited conduct, penalties are attached to the violation of the order without reference to whether the original decision to issue the order was correct. Should the person under the order believe it was improvidently or improperly issued, that person's proper remedy is to seek judicial review of the order, not simply to defy it. *See* sections 5R-3-01 to 5R-3-03.

The Regulated Riparian Model Water Code adapts this traditional remedy to the context of managing the waters of the State. Rather than a "cease and desist" order (which, after all, is a mere redundancy), the State Agency is to issue an order to "cease," or an order to "restore," or an order to "cease and restore." A similar approach is found in the power of the Environmental Protection Agency to issue an administrative cleanup order under the Comprehensive Environmental Response, Compensation, and Liability Act (CERCLA). *See* 42 U.S.C. § 9606(a). Under this Code, the Agency can expand on this concept to make any order reasonably necessary to achieve the enforcement of the Code. The Agency can then recover for civil liability or civil penalties, or negotiate civil charges, should the person(s) subject to the order defy it. In those cases when the noncompliance involves the knowing reporting of false information or the like, criminal prosecution also becomes a possibility.

Generally such orders will be issued only after giving a hearing to the person accused of a violation and will allow a reasonable time to comply before sanctions come into play. In emergencies, the Agency can issue an order before the hearing and give that order immediate effect. In such a case, the Agency is to expedite its procedures, holding the hearing within a brief period of days to be determined by the legislative. The Code adopts a period of ten days, probably the outermost period that would withstand constitutional challenge. *See, e.g., Mitchell v. W.T. Grant Co.*, 416 U.S. 600 (1974); *Fuentes v. Shevin*, 407 U.S. 67 (1972); *Sniadach v. Family Finance Corp.*, 395 U.S. 337 (1969). A State legislature might consider whether a shorter period might be administratively feasible.

Cross-references: § 1R0–08 (procedural protections); § 2R-2-15 (person); § 2R-2-23 (State Agency); § 4R-1-06 (regulatory authority of the State Agency); § 4R-4-05 (regulatory authority of Special Water Management Areas); §§ 5R-1-01 to 5R-1-05 (hearings); §§ 5R-3-01 to 5R-3-03 (judicial review); § 5R-4-05 (civil liability); § 5R-4-06 (civil penalties); § 5R-4-07 (civil charges); § 5R-5-01 (crimes); § 5R-5-02 (revocation of permits); § 7R-1-01 (permit terms and conditions).

Comparable statutes: CONN. GEN. STAT. ANN. § 22a-378; DEL. CODE ANN. tit. 7, § 6018; FLA. STAT. ANN. § 373.119(1); GA. CODE ANN. §§ 12-5-23(b)(12), 12-5-45, 12-5-99(b); IOWA CODE ANN. § 455B.279(1); KY. REV. STAT. ANN. § 151.125(5), (10); MD. CODE ANN., NAT. RES. § 8-203(g); MASS. GEN. LAWS ANN. ch. 21G, § 14; MINN. STAT. ANN. § 105.462; N.J. STAT. ANN. § 58:1A-15(f); WIS. STAT. ANN. § 144.025(k).

§ 5R-4-04 INJUNCTIONS

(1) The State Agency has full authority to initiate and maintain suits in courts of competent jurisdiction to enjoin any unlawful withdrawal and use of the waters of the State, or the waste, loss, or pollution of

the waters of the State, and as otherwise necessary to carry out its duties.

(2) The Agency need not prove irreparable damage from the violation or that there is no adequate remedy at law, nor need the Agency prove either prior notice or negotiations about the violation before the filing of the complaint.

(3) The initiation of a proceeding for an injunction or its issuance shall not relieve any person of any duty, sanction, or penalty otherwise applicable under this Code.

Commentary: Injunctions are orders from a court requiring a person to do something or to refrain from doing something. Injunctions are functionally similar to a "cease and restore" order. Injunctions carry greater force than orders to cease and restore in that persons who violate an injunction faces imprisonment for contempt of court until they purge themselves of the contempt by complying with the injunction. Injunctions are one of the more commonly authorized methods for enforcing existing regulated riparian statutes. CERCLA provides an example of a statute that also authorizes injunctions even though the Environmental Protection Agency itself is empowered to issue administrative cleanup orders. 42 U.S.C. § 9606(a).

Because injunctions receive judicial scrutiny before they are issued, the Regulated Riparian Model Water Code authorizes the availability of an injunction in somewhat more broad terms than it authorizes orders to cease and restore. The Code also removes certain traditional restrictions on the availability of injunctions, including the requirements of irreparable injury and that there is no adequate remedy at law. *See* Dellapenna, § 9.03(a)(5)(B). In effect, the Code presumes that both conditions exist whenever there is a violation of the law, permits, or regulations relating to the waters of the State. Nor need the Agency attempt to seek a resolution of any problem through negotiations as a precondition to seeking an injunction. On the other hand, the initiation of a suit for an injunction does not relieve anyone of any other possible enforcement measure available under the Code.

Cross-references: § 1R-1-02 (assuring efficient and productive use of water); § 1R-1-08 (procedural protections); § 1R-1-10 (water conservation); § 2R-215 (person); § 2R-2-23 (State Agency); § 2R-2-27 (waste of water); § 2R-2-32 (waters of the State); § 2R-2-34 (withdraw or withdrawal); § 5R-4-03 (orders to cease or restore); § 5R-5-02 (revocation of permits); § 7R-1-01 (permit terms and conditions); § 7R-3-01 (authority to restrict permit exercise).

Comparable statutes: ARK. CODE ANN. § 15-22-204(b)(3); CONN. GEN. STAT. ANN. § 22a-376(a); DEL. CODE ANN. tit. 7, § 6005(b)(2); FLA. STAT. ANN. §§ 373.129(1) to (4), 373.136(1); GA. CODE ANN. §§ 12-5-48, 12-5-101; HAW. REV. STAT. § 174C-15(a), (c); IND. CODE ANN. §§ 13-2-2.5.-9(b) (emergencies relating to underground water), 13-2-2.6-17(b) (emergencies relating to lakes); IOWA CODE ANN. §§ 455B.112, 455B.275; KY. REV. STAT. ANN. §§ 151.125(11), 151.460; MD. CODE ANN., NAT. RES. § 8-813; MASS. GEN. LAWS ANN. ch. 21G, § 14; MINN. STAT. ANN. § 105.55; MISS. CODE ANN. § 51-3-55(5); N.J. STAT. ANN. § 58:1A-16; N.C. GEN. STAT. § 143-215.17(c); S.C. CODE ANN. § 49-5-100(B); VA. CODE ANN. §§ 62.1-44.105 62.1-252(C); WIS. STAT. ANN. § 30.294.

§ 5R-4-05 CIVIL LIABILITY

> **Every person who shall violate any provision of this Code, or any order, permit term or condition, or regulation made pursuant to this Code, shall be liable in a proceeding before any court of competent jurisdiction for the expenses incurred by the State Agency to investigate and resolve the violation and to correct its effects, and also to any person injured by the violation when no other private remedy is provided in this Code.**

Commentary: The Regulated Riparian Model Water Code recognizes that any person injured by a violation of any aspect of the law created by or pursuant to this Code is entitled to compensation for their damages caused by the violation. The Code makes explicit that this includes the expenses of investigating and resolving the violation incurred by the State Agency as well as the more usual damages (such as restoration expenses) that the State Agency or an injured private party might recover. *See* Dellapenna, § 9.03(a)(5)(B). This section does not address whether the Agency can recover damages for the generalized degradation of the environment or ecosystems, in part because those concerns are at least partially covered by other sections of the Code, such as the provision of civil penalties. *See* section 5R-4-06. This again resembles the arrangement of remedies under CERCLA in adding civil liability to the possibilities of injunctions and administrative cleanup orders. 42 U.S.C. § 9604(a), 9606(a), 9607(a). Courts will need to work out the interrelation of these several enforcement measures as experience demonstrates their interaction.

Generally, disputes between permit holders are to be resolved through the mechanisms provided in this Code. The Code encourages alternative dispute resolution, including arbitration of disputes between the holders of permits to withdraw water. *See* § 5R-2-03. Those procedures will include provision of appropriate compensation with the possibility of judicial review. The section indicates, however, that private parties without a remedy under this Code can sue for damages.

Cross-references: § 1R-1-08 (procedural protections); § 2R-2-15 (person); § 2R-2-23 (State Agency); § 4R-1-06 (regulatory authority of the State Agency); § 4R-4-05 (regulatory authority of Special Water Management Areas); §§ 5R-2-01 to 5R-2-03 (dispute resolution); § 5R-4-01 (inspections and other investigations); § 5R-4-03 (orders to cease or restore); § 5R-4-04 (injunctions); § 5R-4-06 (civil penalties); § 5R-4-07 (civil charges); § 5R-4-08 (liens for liquidated monetary claims).

Comparable statutes: ALA. CODE § 9-10B-5(18); ARK. CODE ANN. § 15-22-204(b)(2); DEL. CODE ANN. tit. 7, § 6005(c); FLA. STAT. ANN. §§ 373.129(6), 373.245; GA. CODE ANN. § 12-5-51; HAW. REV. STAT. § 174C-15(a).

§ 5R-4-06 CIVIL PENALTIES

(1) A court may assess a civil penalty, not to exceed $10,000 for each violation, against any person found to have violated any provision of this Code or any order, permit term or condition, or regulation made pursuant to this Code.

(2) The court shall assess a civil penalty at least equal the monetary benefits obtained by the violator if that sum is less than the maximum lawful penalty.

(3) The court may assess a civil penalty that is higher than the monetary benefits obtained by the violator to reflect the nature of the violation, non-monetary benefits obtained by the violator, and the harm to others or to the public generally, so long as the maximum penalty is not exceeded.

(4) Each day of a continuing violation counts as a separate violation for purposes of this section.

(5) Civil penalties shall be paid into the State Water Fund.

Commentary: The Regulated Riparian Model Water Code authorizes the State Agency to sue for civil penalties for any violation of the law created by or pursuant to the Code. The figure of $10,000 is used in several states for a similar form of liability, although that figure is not universal. The figure selected needs to be high enough to discourage violations without being so high that a court would be reluctant to enforce it. The following compilation of provisions from comparable statutes suggests the range currently used in similar provisions in existing regulated riparian statutes. In part, the problem of judicial reluctance is resolved by according the court discretion to assess the penalty (up to the limit expressed in the section) depending on the seriousness of the violation and other relevant factors. Normally, the civil penalty shall be at least equal to the monetary benefits to the violator, so long as that figure is not more than the maximum penalty provided for in the section. *See* Dellapenna, § 9.03(a)(5)(B).

Civil penalties are to be paid into the State Water Fund. Thus, civil penalties shall be used to restore or enhance the diffused non-economic values that are one of the purposes of this Code to promote. The payment of monies collected as civil penalties into the State Water Fund is taken from the Arkansas and Kentucky regulated riparian statutes.

The threat of civil penalties is a powerful tool to compel compliance with the Code, or any order, permit, or regulation under the Code. As the penalty is civil, the various procedural limitations applicable to crimes do not apply. *United States v. Ward*, 448 U.S. 242 (1980). The State Agency can act quickly as assessing the penalty does not depend upon the completion of all related judicial proceedings. Even modest penalties will mount quickly to a sizable sum if the violation persists through any significant amount of time because of the policy of counting each day as a separate violation. Finally, the order assessing penalties creates a lien enforceable by a summary proceeding. *See* section 5R-4-08. On the other hand, if the court assesses an excessive remedy, the State Agency can negotiate a settlement for a lesser amount, or the amount of the penalty can be challenged on appeal.

Cross-references: § 1R-1-08 (procedural protections); § 2R-2-15 (person); § 2R-2-23 (State Agency); § 4R-1-04 (special funds created); § 4R-1-06 (regulatory authority of the State Agency); § 4R-4-05 (regulatory authority of Special Water Management Areas); §§ 5R-3-01 to 5R-3-03 (judicial review); § 5R-4-01 (inspections and other investigations); § 5R-4-03 (orders to cease or restore); § 5R-4-05 (civil liability); § 5R-4-07 (civil charges); § 5R-4-08 (liens for liquidated monetary claims); § 5R-4-09 (citizen suits).

Comparable statutes: ALA. CODE § 9-10B-5(19) (judicially assessed civil penalties not to exceed $1,000 per offense or $25,000 per year); ARK. CODE ANN. § 15-22-204(b)(3) (judicially assessed civil penalties of not more than $10,000 per offense), 15-22-507 (fees and other cash received by the Commission to be paid into the Arkansas development fund); DEL. CODE ANN. tit. 7, § 6005(b)(1) (judicially assessed civil penalties between $1,000 and $10,000 per offense), (d) (civil penalties dedicated to carrying out the purposes of the Chapter); FLA. STAT. ANN. § 373.129(5) (judicially assessed civil penalty not to exceed $10,000 and deposited in fund dedicated to purposes of water code); GA. CODE ANN. §§ 12-5-52 (administratively imposed civil penalties of not more than $25,000 per day for violations regarding withdrawals from surface water sources), 12-5-106 (administratively imposed penalties of not more than $1,000 + $500 per day for duration of violation regarding underground water sources); HAW. REV. STAT. § 174C-15(b) (administratively imposed fine of not more than $1,000); IOWA CODE ANN. § 455B.109 (administratively imposed civil fines of not more than $1,000); KY. REV. STAT. ANN. §§ 151.380(1) (all monies received to be paid into the Water Resources Fund), 151.460, 151.990 (judicially assessed civil penalties of not more than $1,000 per day); MASS. GEN. LAWS ANN. ch. 21G, § 14 (administratively imposed penalties not to exceed $25,000 per day); MISS. CODE ANN. § 51-3-55(3) (administratively imposed civil penalties of not more than $25,000); N.J. STAT. ANN. § 58:1A-16 (administratively imposed penalties of not more than $5,000 per day); N.C. GEN. STAT. § 143-215.17(b) (administratively imposed civil penalty between $100 and $250, accruing daily for willful violations); S.C. CODE ANN. § 49-5-100(C) (administratively assessed civil penalties between $50 and $1,000 per day of violation); VA. CODE ANN. §§ 62.1-44.105, 62.1-252(A) (judicially assessed civil penalty of not more than $1,000 per day).

§ 5R-4-07 CIVIL CHARGES

(1) The State Agency may waive any civil liability or civil penalty provided in this Chapter against any person and payable to the State Agency or the State Water Fund if that person undertakes to pay the costs of restoring or repairing any damage caused by the violation and agrees to pay an additional civil charge assessed by order of the State Agency, not to exceed $5,000 for each violation.

(2) **Each day of a continuing violation counts as a separate violation for purposes of this subsection.**

(3) **Civil charges shall be paid into State Water Fund.**

Commentary: The Regulated Riparian Model Water Code recognizes that for various reasons the State Agency might find it more effective to waive other possible liabilities or penalties payable to the Agency as a means of obtaining voluntary compliance from the offender. This approach is consistent with the Code's general approach of supporting informal and administrative dispute resolution whenever possible. This section authorizes the Agency to compromise its claims in just such an agreement, but only if the offender agrees to pay a negotiated civil charge payable into the same State Water Fund as are civil penalties, an approach consistent with the Code's encouragement of alternate dispute resolution. *See* sections 5R-2-01 to 5R-2-03. The figure is set at one-half the amount of civil penalties in order to provide some incentive for the Agency to use that more procedurally constrained enforcement tool.

The Code does not expressly provide for enforcement of the agreement to pay civil charges. Under ordinary rules of contract law, the Agency can rescind the agreement if there is a material breach of the agreement. If the Agency rescinds the agreement, the usual liabilities and penalties become available once again to the Agency.

Cross-references: § 1R-1-08 (procedural protections); § 2R-2-15 (person); § 2R-2-23 (State Agency); § 4R-1-04 (special funds created); § 4R-1-06 (regulatory authority of the State Agency); § 4R-4-05 (regulatory authority of Special Management Areas); §§ 5R-2-01 to 5R-2-03 (dispute resolution); § 5R-4-01 (inspections and other investigations); § 5R-4-03 (orders to cease or restore); § 5R-4-04 (injunctions); § 5R-4-05 (civil liability); § 5R-4-06 (civil penalties); § 5R-4-08 (liens for liquidated monetary claims); § 5R-4-09 (citizen suits).

Comparable statutes: ARK. CODE ANN. § 15-22-507 (fees and other cash received by the Commission to be paid into the Arkansas development fund); DEL. CODE ANN. §§ 6005(b) tit. 7, (administrative penalties), (d) (dedicated to the purposes of the Chapter), 6019 (voluntary compliance); GA. CODE ANN. § 12-5-52 (administratively imposed civil penalties); 455B.109 (administrative fines); HAW. REV. STAT. § 174C-15(b) (administratively imposed civil penalties); KY. REV. STAT. ANN. § 151.380(1) (all monies received to be paid into the Water Resources Fund); MASS. GEN. LAWS ANN. ch. 21G, § 14 (administratively imposed penalties); MISS. CODE ANN. § 51-3-55(3) (administratively imposed civil penalties); N.J. STAT. ANN. § 58:1A-16 (administratively imposed civil penalties and authority to compromise and settle); N.C. GEN. STAT. § 143-215.17(b) (administratively imposed civil penalties); S.C. CODE ANN. § 49-5-100(C) (administratively assessed civil penalties); VA. CODE ANN. § 62.1-252(B) (civil charges by agreement in lieu of civil penalties).

§ 5R-4-08 LIENS FOR LIQUIDATED MONETARY CLAIMS

(1) Any liquidated monetary claim arising from the enforcement of this Code and owing to the State, the State Agency, or the State Water Fund shall constitute a lien against the real property on which the withdrawal occurred or the withdrawn water was used unless the owner of the land can demonstrate that the withdrawal and use was without the knowledge or neglect of the owner.

(2) The lienholder of the lien created in this section may enforce the lien through summary proceedings for foreclosure of the lien in any court of competent jurisdiction.

Commentary: The Regulated Riparian Model Water Code provides what might be its most effective enforcement measure through a provision that any liquidated claim for money due to the State, the State Agency, or the State Water Fund from the enforcement measures under this Code shall be a lien against the real estate involved in the violation. The lienholder can obtain a summary enforcement of the claim before any competent court, greatly expediting the collection of the moneys due. This remedy has proven formidable in enforcing CERCLA. *See* 42 U.S.C. § 9607(L)(1), (2). Many states have also enacted environmental lien statutes under schemes resembling CERCLA. Serious questions have been raised about some of these, including the lien under CERCLA, on due process grounds. *See Reardon v. United States,* 947 F.2d 1509 (1st Cir. 1991).

Lien statutes are, in any event, rare in water allocation statutes. The drafters of this Code have concluded that they should form a part of the remedial repertory available to the State Agency. This section provides a measure of protection to the owners of property that might be subject to such a lien by requiring that the debt be liquidated, *i.e.,* for a definite amount no longer open to dispute. Further, the section provides that the lien is defeated if the owner can demonstrate that the violation occurred without the knowledge or neglect of the owner. These limits together should resolve the constitutional questions that have been raised about the CERCLA environmental lien statutes. Cheryl Kessler Clark, *Due Process and the Environmental Lien: The Need for Legislative Reform,* 20 ENVTL. AFF. 203 (1993).

Cross-references: § 1R-1-08 (procedural protections); § 2R-2-15 (person); § 2R-2-23 (State Agency); § 4R-1-04 (special funds created); § 5R-4-05 (civil liabilities); § 5R-4-06 (civil penalties); § 5R-4-07 (civil charges); § 5R-5-01 (crimes).

Comparable statute: KY. REV. STAT. ANN. § 151.299.

§ 5R-4-09 CITIZEN SUITS *(optional)*

(1) Any citizen of the State may obtain an injunction or other appropriate remedy in an enforcement action brought against the person responsible for any violation of the provisions of this Code or of any order, permit term or condition, or regulation adopted pursuant to

this Code if no other enforcement measures are pending based upon the same violation.

(2) No citizen shall initiate an enforcement action under this section unless the citizen shall first have given written notice of intent to initiate the action to the State Agency and to the alleged violator at least 60 days before initiating the action.

(3) The notice of intent to initiate an enforcement action shall indicate the nature of the alleged violation and of the remedy intended to be sought.

(4) A citizen action is precluded if the violation is corrected or if the State Agency initiates any enforcement measures or undertakes to provide administrative resolution of any related dispute within the 60 day period specified in subsection (2) of this section.

(5) A citizen who has given notice of the intent to initiate an enforcement action under subsection (2) of this section may intervene, as of right, in any civil legal proceeding brought by the State Agency.

(6) In any enforcement action under this section, the court shall award the costs of litigation, including reasonable attorney and witness fees, to any prevailing party.

(7) This section does not restrict any right of any person to seek relief under the statutory or common law apart from this Code for an injury caused by a violation of this Code or of any order, permit term or condition, or regulation adopted pursuant to this Code.

Commentary: The broad discretion relative to enforcement measures conferred by the Regulated Riparian Model Water Code on the State Agency creates the possibility that the Agency will fail to undertake to enforce the Code, or orders, permits, or regulations issued under the Code. To preclude this from happening under various other environmental statutes, legislatures have often made provision for citizen suits as an alternative enforcement mechanism. Such provisions are rare in water allocation statutes, although of the several that exist all are found in regulated riparian statutes. *See* Dellapenna, § 9.03(a)(5)(B). Creation of such a possibility is highly controversial in the water allocation setting for the possibility of citizen suits greatly strengthens the hand of highly committed groups (the "special interests" of political folklore), whether their commitment arises from hopes to profit from a particular enforcement action or from the highest ideals of civic and ecological responsibility. Because of the controversy about such a provision, this section is labeled "optional," unlike most other sections of this Code.

The Code offers a model provision for citizen suits for those States which might want to include such a provision in their water allocation statute. The Code's provision follows the citizen suit provisions of the federal Clean Water Act. 33 U.S.C. § 1365. As with that law, the Code seeks to keep enforcement authority securely in the State Agency, but to assure proper enforcement it confers the right to intervene in any subsequent enforcement proceeding on anyone who had given notice under this section of the intent to bring a citizen suit. Recognizing that a threatened citizen suit might be a strategy in a dispute between private parties, the section also provides that the initiation of a relevant administrative dispute resolution precludes citizen suits independently of participation in the proceeding. *See generally* BUREAU OF NAT'L AFF., ENVIRONMENTAL CITIZEN SUITS: CONFRONTING THE CORPORATION (1988); Barry Boyer & Errol Meidinger, *Privatizing Regulatory Enforcement: A Preliminary Assessment of Citizen Suits under Federal Environmental Laws,* 34 BUFF. L. REV. 833 (1985); Eileen Gauna, *Federal Environmental Citizen Provisions: Obstacles and Incentives on the Road to Environmental Justice,* 22 ECOL. L.Q. 1 (1995); Beverly Smith, *The Viability of Citizens' Suits under the Clean Water Act after* Gwaltney of Smithfield v. Chesapeake Bay Fndtn., 40 CASE W. RES. L. REV. 1 (1989).

The restriction of the right to sue to "citizens" rather than "persons" serves to prevent such suits from being brought by artificial persons. Natural persons who are not citizens of this State are also precluded. Most of the latter class will be persons resident in other States who will only seldom hold water rights under this Code.

Cross-references: § 1R-1-08 (procedural protections); § 2R-1-04 (protection of property rights); § 2R-2-15 (person); § 2R-2-24 (State Agency); § 6R-4-05 (preservation of private rights of action).

Comparable statutes: FLA. STAT. ANN. § 373.136(2); IOWA CODE ANN. § 455B.111; MASS. GEN. LAWS ANN. ch. 21G, § 13; MD. CODE ANN., NAT. RES. §§ 1-501 to 1-507.

Part 5
Criminal Enforcement

Most existing regulated riparian statutes declare some or all violations of the statute to be a crime. These provisions, common as they are, seem never to be enforced. The Regulated Riparian Model Water Code therefore does not make every or even most violations of the Code a crime, reserving such a serious enforcement measure to commensurably serious acts. If criminalization is reserved for crimes that evince an actual criminal intent, there is a greater likelihood that prosecutions will actually result and convictions will actually ensue. This Part also includes the punitive revocation of a permit, which, while not strictly criminal in nature, is closer to a criminal enforcement device than to a civil enforcement device. The final section deals with a temporary arrest power conferred on duly authorized employees of the State Agency. The latter is a highly controversial provision that, because of the uncertainty over whether it should be included in the Code, is labeled optional.

§ 5R-5-01 CRIMES

(1) Any person who knowingly makes any false statement, representation, or certification in any application, record, report,

plan, or other document filed or required to be maintained pursuant to this Code or pursuant to any order, permit term or condition, or regulation made under this Code, or who knowingly falsifies, tampers with, or renders inaccurate any monitoring device or method required to be maintained under this Code, shall be guilty of a felony, and upon conviction shall be assessed a fine of not less than $1,000 nor more than $10,000 or by imprisonment for a term of not less than 1 year nor more than 5 years, or both.

(2) Each day of a continuing violation shall constitute a separate crime.

(3) Prosecution shall be the responsibility of the prosecuting attorney for the county in which the violation occurred.

(4) The court shall set the fine or period of imprisonment imposed under this section upon a consideration of the amount of costs saved, or to be saved, by the violator through the violation, the gravity of the violation, and the degree of culpability of the violator.

(5) Fines collected under this section are to be paid into the State Water Fund.

Commentary: The only crimes under the Regulated Riparian Model Water Code are the knowing inclusion of any falsehood in a document filed or maintained under the Code or the knowing falsification of the data in any monitoring or similar device. Both acts are felonies, and each day of a continuing offense counts as a separate felony. Generally the criminal provisions in this section will have their effect during the permit application and related process, although the provisions also relate to tampering with monitoring or the like during the exercise of water rights. The criminal provisions shall also come into play if noncompliance with an arbitration order or a cease or restore order involves the knowing report of false information or the like. More routine violations will not involve the possibility of a criminal prosecution.

Civil enforcement measures all involve a considerable measure of technical expertise and technically-based discretion which is most likely to be found in the State Agency. Thus, the State's attorney-general and prosecuting attorneys play no role in civil enforcement which for them would be an occasional diversion for which they often would be ill-prepared. On the other hand, there is nothing unusual about the prosecution of the crimes set forth in this section. Therefore, the responsibility for prosecuting these crimes is vested in the officers who are expert in that process–the usual state prosecutors. As with investigations and arrests, the State Agency can initiate proceedings through its actions, but the Agency must turn the actual prosecution over to the usual governmental officers responsible for prosecuting crimes. Those governmental officers are under the general duty to cooperate with the Agency, but they remain responsible for their own duties under the laws governing their officers. The State Agency does not have the authority to control or direct the actions or decisions of these other responsible government officers.

Setting the proper amount of the fine or imprisonment for a violation remains the responsibility of the court. This section sets forth broad outer limits to the penalties that a State legislature will want to consider carefully. Existing criminal statutes as part of existing regulated riparian statutes vary widely in the penalties they authorize or impose, as well in the acts they characterize as crimes.

Cross-references: § 2R-2-15 (person); § 2R-2-23 (State Agency); § 4R-1-04 (special funds created); § 4R-1-06 (regulatory authority of the State Agency); § 4R-3-03 (duty to cooperate); § 4R-4-05 (regulatory authority of Special Water Management Areas); § 5R-2-03 (administrative resolution); § 5R-4-01 (inspections and other investigations); § 5R-4-03 (orders to cease or restore); § 5R-5-02 (revocation of permits); § 5R-5-03 (temporary arrest power); § 6R-1-05 (registration of withdrawals not subject to permits); § 6R-2-01 (contents of an application for a permit); § 7R-1-01 (permit terms and conditions).

Comparable statutes: ARK. CODE ANN. § 15-22-204(a) (any violation is a crime punishable by imprisonment of not more than six months and a fine of not more than $10,000); CONN. GEN. STAT. ANN. § 22a-376(c) (crimes are punishable by a fine of not more than $10,000); DEL. CODE ANN. tit. 7, § 6013(a) (willful or negligent violation of a permit term or condition is a crime punishable by a fine between $2,500 and $25,000 per day), (b) (knowing false statement is a crime punishable by a fine between $500 and $5,000 and imprisonment up to six months), (c) (any violation of a permit term or condition or a regulation is a crime punishable by a fine between $50 and $500); GA. CODE ANN. §§ 12-5-53 (a long list of crimes regarding surface withdrawals punishable by fines ranging from $25,000 to $1,000,000 and imprisonment from one to 15 years, depending on the crime), 12-5-107 (violations regarding underground water are misdemeanors); ILL. COMP. STAT. ANN. ch. 525, § 45/7 (most first violations are petty offenses, class C misdemeanor subsequently); IND. CODE ANN. §§ 13-2-2-13 (any violation is a class C infraction), 13-2-2.5-9(a) (violation of an emergency order is a class A infraction), 13-2-2.6-17 (same), 13-2-6.1-7 (failure to register a surface withdrawal is a class B infraction); IOWA CODE ANN. § 455B.279(2) (any violation is punishable by a fine of not more than $500 per day); MD. CODE ANN., NAT. RES. § 8-814 (any violation is to be punished by a fine between $250 and $25,000); MASS. GEN. LAWS ANN. ch. 21G, § 14 (any violation is punishable by a fine between $1,000 and $10,000 and imprisonment up to 180 days); MINN. STAT. ANN. § 105.541 (any violation is a misdemeanor); MISS. CODE ANN. §§ 51-3-45 (an unauthorized change in withdrawal is a misdemeanor punishable by a fine of not more than $200 per day), 51-3-55(2) (a knowing false statement or willful violation is a misdemeanor punishable by a fine of not less than $100 per day); N.C. GEN. STAT. § 143-215.17(a) (any violation is a misdemeanor punishable by a fine between $100 and $1,000, with the fine accruing daily for willful violations); S.C. CODE ANN. § 49-5-100(A) (any violation is a misdemeanor, punishable by a fine between $100 and $1,000; willful violations constitute separate offenses daily); WIS. STAT. ANN. § 30.298 (any violation is punishable by a fine between $500 and $10,000, and between $1,000 and $10,000 for repeat offenses).

§ 5R-5-02 REVOCATION OF PERMITS

The State Agency is authorized to revoke any permit:

(a) for any act that is criminal under this Code;

(b) for willful violation of this Code or of any term or condition of any permit or regulation issued under this Code; or

(c) when necessary to prevent an unreasonable injury to a holder of another water right pursuant to an arbitration hearing under § 5R-2-03.

Commentary: The gist of a revocation of a permit is punitive, and hence it is included in the provisions dealing with criminal enforcement. Still, the grounds for revocation are broader than those acts the Regulated Riparian Model Water Code defines as crimes. In addition to crimes, permits are also revocable for any willful violation of the Code even if not criminal or as necessary to prevent an unreasonable injury as determined in an arbitral hearing under § 5R-2-03, although neither involves a crime. *See* TARLOCK, § 3.20; Dellapenna, § 9.03.

Cross-references: § 2R-2-14 (permit); § 2R-2-30 (water right); §§ 5R-1-01 to 5R-1-05 (hearings); § 5R-2-03 (administrative resolution); § 5R-3-01 to 5R-3-03 (judicial review); § 5R-4-03 (orders to cease or restore); § 5R-5-0.1 (crimes); § 7R-1-01 (permit terms and conditions).

Comparable statutes: ARK. CODE ANN. § 15-22-204(b)(1); CONN. GEN. STAT. ANN. §§ 22a-375, 376(b); FLA. STAT. ANN. § 373.243(1) to (3); GA. CODE ANN. § 12-5-31(k)(1) to (3); HAW. REV. STAT. § 174C-58(1) to (3); IOWA CODE ANN. § 455B.271; KY. REV. STAT. ANN. § 151.125(9); MISS. CODE ANN. § 51-3-15(d); VA. CODE ANN. § 62.1-251.

§ 5R-5-03 TEMPORARY ARREST POWER *(optional)*

(1) Any employee duly authorized by the State Agency may arrest any person when the employee finds probable cause to believe that the person has committed a crime as defined in this Code if the arrest is necessary to prevent the imminent escape of the person or the destruction or loss of evidence.

(2) In the event of an arrest under this section, the arresting employee shall comply with the relevant law regarding the rights of criminal defendants.

(3) The arresting employee shall turn such persons over to proper law enforcement authorities as promptly as is reasonable under the circumstances.

(4) Immediately upon delivering any such person into the custody of law enforcement officers, the State Agency shall make a complaint in writing and upon oath before the proper court against the person so accused.

Commentary: The Regulated Riparian Model Water Code vests discretion in duly authorized employees of the State Agency to arrest persons involved in criminal violations of the Code. This follows the model of game wardens who often are also vested with arrest power when they discover crimes in the course of their duties. Even though the crimes for which the temporary arrest power is authorized are quite narrow in scope, there are other procedural protections provided to limit the scope of the arrest power. Nonetheless, the power of game wardens to arrest has often proven controversial, and the temporary arrest power in this Code might well prove similarly controversial. Because of the anticipated controversy, this section of the Code is offered merely as an optional provision. The Code will function successfully whether this temporary arrest power is included or not.

The power to arrest is hedged by several protections for the persons whom the employee seeks to arrest. First, the arrest must be based on probable cause to believe that a crime has occurred. This is a technical term from criminal law that describes a fairly high standard of evidence before an arrest can be justified. Second, the arrest must be to prevent flight or the loss of evidence. Given the crimes defined in this Code, these conditions are most likely to arise upon discovery of a falsified monitoring device or the like during an administrative inspection under section 5R-4-01. Third, even before the arrest, the arresting officer is to give the standard "*Miranda*" warnings as required for any criminal investigation. *See Thompson v. Keohane,* 116 S. Ct. 457 (1995); *Miranda v. Arizona,* 384 U.S. 436 (1966). Finally, such arrests are to be strictly temporary, with the employee to turn the arrested person over to the appropriate law enforcement officers as soon as is reasonably possible ("promptly").

One further protection of the public arises from the responsibility of the State Agency. The Agency not only must supervise the duly authorized employees to assure their compliance with this section, but the Agency can regulate their discretion through its regulations. The State Agency will also have to undertake careful training of the personnel authorized to make temporary arrests to assure they understand both the relevant provisions of this Code and any regulations adopted by the State Agency.

Cross-references: § 2R-2-15 (person); § 2R-2-23 (State Agency); § 4R-1-06 (regulatory authority of the State Agency); § 4R-3-03 (duty to cooperate); § 4R-4-05 (regulatory authority of Special Water Management Areas); § 5R-4-01 (inspections and other investigations); § 5R-4-02 (notice of violation); § 5R-5-01 (crimes); § 7R-1-01 (permit terms and conditions).

Comparable statute: DEL. CODE ANN. tit. 7, § 6017 (power to seal noncomplying equipment).

CHAPTER VI

ESTABLISHING A WATER RIGHT

The Regulated Riparian Model Water Code's most fundamental departure from the common law of riparian rights is the requirement that, with few exceptions, no water is to be withdrawn without a permit issued by the State Agency under the Code. The requirement derives from the State's police power to regulate water withdrawal and use in order to protect the public health, safety, and welfare through accomplishment of the public interest in the sustainable development of the waters of the State. The State Agency is to evaluate existing and proposed consumptive uses of water by criteria requiring the consideration of other existing or proposed consumptive and nonconsumptive uses of the water and the general public interest. *See* Dellapenna, § 9.03(a).

After setting forth the circumstances in which a permit is required, this Chapter provides the procedures and standards for implementing the mandatory permit requirement. Broadly speaking the procedures can be summarized as including the filing of an application, public notice and an opportunity for a public hearing, and the opportunity to contest issues raised by the State Agency and other interested persons. The model of this process is nicely summarized in IOWA CODE ANN. section 455B.278(1). Finally, the Chapter delineates the standards that the State Agency is to apply in determining whether to issue the permit.

If the State opts to have Special Water Management Areas as the primary agency for issuing water use permits, this Chapter, particularly parts 2 and 3, will refer to activities of the Area Water Board rather than of the State Agency. There will still need to be a statewide mechanism for assessing interbasin transfers or other transfers that will affect more than one Special Water Management Area, and for coordinating water allocation and water quality regulations. Some provisions in this Chapter, particularly section 6R-3-06 and Part 4 would thus remain as provisions directed at the State Agency rather than at Special Water Management Areas.

Part 1
The Requirement of a Permit

This Part introduces the requirement of a permit to withdraw water in this State, exempting only certain small uses. Somewhat different provisions are made for permits for withdrawals begun before the effective date of the Regulated Riparian Model Water Code and for withdrawals begun after that date. Provision is also made for temporary permits during the period a permit is being processed, and for registration of some of the uses exempted from the permit requirement.

§ 6R-1-01 WITHDRAWALS UNLAWFUL WITHOUT A PERMIT

No person not specifically exempted by this Code shall make a withdrawal from the waters of the State without first having obtained a permit as provided in this Code and without fully complying with all provisions of this Code and all orders, permit terms or conditions, or regulations promulgated pursuant to this Code.

Commentary: This section sets out the basic rule: All withdrawals from the waters of the State are unlawful unless made pursuant to a permit. Florida goes further than the Regulated Riparian Model Water Code, requiring a permit for the artificial recharge of underground water as well as for withdrawals of water. FLA. STAT. ANN. § 373.106. For analysis of permit systems in riparian States, see Dellapenna, § 9.03. *See also* SAX, ABRAMS, & THOMPSON, at 127-134; TARLOCK, CORBRIDGE, & GETCHES, at 104-21; TRELEASE & GOULD, at 349-53; Robert Abrams, *Water Allocation By Comprehensive Permit Systems in the Eastern United States: Considering a Move*

Away From Orthodoxy, 9 VA. ENVTL. L.J. 255 (1990); Earl Finbar Murphy, *Quantitative Groundwater,* 3 WATERS AND WATER RIGHTS § 24.02(a); Richard Moen, Bruce Machmeier, & John Sullivan, *A Proposal for Regulating Water Use in Minnesota,* 7 HAMLINE L. REV. 207 (1984).

The permit requirement neither creates nor destroys property rights. Rather, it is a regulation of existing property rights, as the name "regulated riparian" implies. *Nekoosa-Edwards Paper Co. v. Public Service Comm'n,* 99 N.W.2d 821 (Wis. 1959). The approach is similar to that of the zoning of land uses. Generally zoning is not a taking of property, and the several state supreme courts that have considered the question have found that the permit requirement under a regulated riparian statute does not constitute a taking of property. *Village of Tequesta v. Jupiter Inlet Corp.,* 371 So. 2d 663 (Fla.), *cert. denied,* 444 U.S. 965 (1979); *Crookston Cattle Co. v. Minnesota Dep't of Nat. Resources,* 300 N.W.2d 769 (Minn. 1981); *Omernick v. State,* 218 N.W. 2d 734 (Wis. 1974). *See generally* TARLOCK, § 3.20[3]; Dellapenna, § 9.04(a). The recent revival of interest in preventing or compensating takings of property in the Supreme Court has had an impact on the zoning of land uses. *See Dolan v. City of Tigard,* 114 S. Ct. 2309 (1994); *Lucas v. South Carolina Coastal Council,* 112 S.. Ct. 2886 (1992). *See also Los Ossos Valley Assoc. v. City of San Luis Obispo,* 36 Cal. Rptr. 2d 4th 758 (Cal. App. 1994). *See generally* James Audley McLaughlin, *Majoritarian Theft in the Regulatory State: What's a Takings Clause for?,* 19 WM. & MARY ENVTL. L. & POL'Y REV. 161 (1995); Michelle Walsh, *Achieving the Proper Balance between the Public and Private Property Interests: Closely Tailored Legislation as a Remedy,* 19 WM. & MARY ENVTL. L. & POL'Y REV. 317 (1995). This is not likely to affect the validity or cost of a permit system as established in this section.

First, there is a long-standing rule in takings jurisprudence that where one or the other of a species of property must necessarily be lost, the State can make a choice as to which one should be lost without incurring liability. *See Miller v. Schoene,* 276 U.S. 272 (1928). The power of the State to choose among competing activities, some of which must give way so that others might survive, implies the power of the State to impose the permit requirement both as a means of obtaining the necessary information for making a choice and as a means for enforcing the choice once made. The power to choose among competing activities in turn is based upon the power of the State to regulate or eliminate nuisances. *See* Gerry Cross, *Does Only the Careless Polluter*

Pay? A Fresh Examination of the Nature of Private Nuisance, 111 L.Q. REV. 445 (1995); Serena Williams, *The Anticipatory Nuisance Doctrine: One Common Law Theory for Use in Environmental Justice Cases,* 19 WM. & MARY L. ENVTL. & POL'Y L. REV. 223 (1995). The Supreme Court has expressly recognized the continuing right of the State to deal with nuisances without being held to have committed a taking. *Lucas,* 112 S. Ct. at 2900. *See* Scott Ferguson, Note, *The Evolution of the "Nuisance Exception" to the Just Compensation Clause: From Myth to Reality,* 45 HASTINGS L.J. 1539 (1994); John Humbach, *Evolving Thresholds of Nuisance and the Takings Clause,* 18 COLUM. J. ENVTL. L. 1 (1993); Serena Williams, *The Anticipatory Nuisance Doctrine: One Common Law Theory for Use in Environmental Justice Cases,* 19 WM. & MARY L. ENVTL. L. & POL'Y REV. 223 (1995).

Second, even in the recent cases resurrecting the notion of regulatory taking have included recognition of the public nature of water as a resource at least as compared to land. Thus, Justice Scalia, in the majority opinion in *Lucas,* held that a serious impairment of the value of land by a regulation of its use must be compensated, but he took pains in a footnote to comment that the State could diminish the value of a water right by as much as 95% without incurring liability. *Lucas,* 112 S. Ct. at 2895 n. 8. *See also* J. Peter Byrne, *The Arguments for the Abolition of the Regulatory Takings Doctrine,* 22 ECOL. L.Q. 89 (1995); Oliver Houck, *Why Do We Protect Endangered Species, and What Does That Say about Whether Restrictions on Private Property to Protect Them Constitute "Takings"?,* 80 IOWA L. REV. 297 (1995); Joseph Sax, *The Constitution, Property Rights and the Future of Water Law,* 61 U. COLO. L. REV. 257 (1990).

Here we definitely have a regulation of riparian rights rather than their taking. The right has long been measured by the reasonableness of the use, and that continues to be the case under the Regulated Riparian Model Water Code. What has been changed is that the initial official determination is to be made by the State Agency rather than by a court. Nothing in that determination is inherently judicial, so there is no legal barrier to vesting the decision in an administrative agency, particularly given the broad availability of judicial review of that decision. This approach not only does not constitute a taking, then, but it also does not violate "separation of powers" doctrine. If the Code in a particular broadens the right to use water to reach nonriparian locations, that also does not constitute a taking. Riparian rights were evolving in that direction anyway, and the requirement of reasonableness, the preference for existing uses, and the limited protection accorded basins of origin for interbasin transfers all provide ample protection for persons who use water on riparian land. See the commentary to section 2R-1-02.

The foregoing analysis would play out somewhat differently were a legislature attempt to displace a system of appropriative rights with this Code. Appropriative rights are defined in terms of a specific quantity of water applied to a beneficial use. *See, e.g., Imperial Irrigation Dist. v. State Water Resources Control Bd.*, 275 Cal. Rptr. 250 (Cal. App. 1990), review denied; *In re Application for Water Rights.*, 891 P.2d 952 (Colo. 1995); *Hardy v. Higgenson*, 849 P.2d 946 (Idaho 1993); *Romey v. Landers*, 392 N.W.2d 415 (S.D. 1986); *Provo River Water Users Ass'n v. Lambert*, 642 P.2d 1219 (Utah 1982); *State v. Grimes*, 852 P.2d 1054 (Was.1993). Such rights to use water clearly are vested property that could not be abolished without compensation. *United States v. State Water Resources Control Bd.*, 227 Cal. Rptr. 161 (Cal. App. 1986), *review denied*. Nor would a severe crisis forcing the abandonment of many uses due to water shortage invoke the doctrine that the state must choose among those to be destroyed when some uses must be destroyed. *Miller v. Schoene, supra*. The state has already made that choice through the temporal priority feature of appropriative rights that have become a part of the vested property right. *Sears v. Berryman*, 623 P.2d 455 (Idaho 1981); *State* ex rel. *Cary v. Cochrane*, 292 N.W. 239 (Neb. 1940). The takings clause thus would probably preclude the adoption of this Code in an appropriative rights jurisdiction.

Some eastern states have accorded a limited protection to the right to use water based upon temporal priority. CONN. GEN. STAT. ANN. § 22a-368; IND. CODE ANN. §§ 13-2-1-8, 13-2-2-5 MASS. GEN. STAT. ANN. ch. 21G, § 7; MISS. CODE ANN. § 5-3-5(2), (3); N.Y. ENVTL. CONSERV. LAW § 15-501(1); OHIO REV. CODE § 1521.16; VA. CODE ANN. §§ 62.1-248(D), 62.1-253. Whether any of these enactments would amount to the creation of such vested rights as would require compensation to change is at least debatable. Probably no temporally-defined rights to use water in eastern states are so developed as to amount to a vested property right requiring compensation before it could be altered. See Dellapenna, § 9.03(b)(3).

Although the permit neither creates nor destroys property rights, the water rights evidenced by a permit do partake to some extent of the characteristic features of a property right.

Among other things, water rights can be bought or sold, subject to the regulatory oversight of the State Agency. For another, the water right cannot be modified by the State except as provided in this Code. The State Agency's regulatory role in approving sales or other voluntary modifications, and in imposing involuntary modifications in case of water shortage or water emergency, however, is greater than one normally would expect for a property right, even under zoning statutes. This greater state involvement reflects the public and ambient nature of water as a resource, a nature that is reflected in the legal principal, found even under appropriative rights, that water ultimately is owned by the State in trust for the public. On the nature of property in water, see *Keys v. Romley*, 412 P.2d 529 (Cal. 1966); Dellapenna, § 6.01(b); Garrett Hardin, *The Tragedy of the Commons*, 162 SCIENCE 1268 (1968). *See also* JOSEPH DELLAPENNA, WATER IN THE MIDDLE EAST: THE LIMITS AND POTENTIAL OF LAW § 5.04 (1996). *See generally* J.W. Harris, *Private and Non-Private Property: What's Is the Difference?*, 111 L.Q. Rev. 421 (1995).

The next section provides a limited exception to this requirement in favor of small withdrawals that have only small effect on the waters of the State and that would be unduly burdened by requiring the water users involved to apply for and obtain a permit. Other sections exempt certain waters from allocation under this Code. No permit issued under this Code is required for withdrawals from waters exempted from allocation, although such withdrawals might be either lawful or unlawful depending on whether the exemption was intended to preclude withdrawals (sections 3R-2-01 to 3R-2-05), on whether the exemption was meant to leave a riparian owner free to withdraw without legal restraint (section 3R-1-03), or on whether the waters are exempted because withdrawals are regulated under some other body of law (3R-1-02).

Cross-references: § 1R-1-01 (protecting the public interest in the waters of the State); § 1R-1-06 (legal security for the right to use water) § 2R-1-02 (no prohibition of use based upon location of use); § 2R-1-04 (protection of property rights); § 2R-2-10 (interbasin transfers); § 2R-2-14 (permit); § 2R-2-15 (person); § 2R-2-23 (State Agency); § 2R-2-29 (water emergency); § 2R-2-30 (water right); § 2R-2-31 (water shortage); § 2R-2-32 (waters of the State); § 2R-2-34 (withdrawal or to withdraw); §§ 3R-1-01 to 3R-2-05 (waters subject to allocation); § 4R-1-04(3) (Interbasin

Compensation Fund); § 6R-1-02 (small withdrawals exempted from the permit requirement); § 6R-1-03 (existing withdrawals); § 6R-1-04 (withdrawals begun after the effective date of the Code); § 6R-1-05 (temporary permits); § 6R-1-06 (registration of withdrawals not subject to permits); §§ 6R-2-01 to 6R-2-08 (permit procedures); §§ 6R-3-01 to 6R-3-06 (the basis of the water right); §§ 7R-1-01 to 7R-1-03 (the extent of the water right); §§ 7R-2-01 to 7R-2-04 (modification of water rights); §§ 7R-3-01 to 7R-3-07 (restrictions during water shortages or water emergencies).

Comparable statutes: CONN. GEN. STAT. ANN. § 22a-368; DEL. CODE ANN. tit. 7, §§ 6003(a)(3), (b)(4), 6030 (1991); FLA. STAT. ANN. § 373.219(1); GA. CODE ANN. §§ 12-5-29(a), 12-5-31(c), 12-5-96(a)(1); HAW. REV. STAT. §§ 174C-48, 174C-84, 174C-93 (1985); IND. CODE ANN. § 13-2-2-5 (underground water only); IOWA CODE ANN. §§ 455B.268, 455B.269; KY. REV. STAT. ANN. §§ 151.140, 151.150; MD. CODE ANN., NAT. RES. § 8-802(a) (1990); MASS. GEN. LAWS ANN. ch. 21G, § 7; MINN. STAT. ANN. § 105.41(1); MISS. CODE ANN. § 51-3-5(1) 1972; N.J. STAT. ANN. §§ 58:1A-5(a), 58:1A-7(a); N.Y. ENVTL. CONSERV. LAW § 15-1501 (permits required for public water supplies, irrigation, and certain multi-purpose projects); N.C. GEN. STAT. § 143-215.15(a) (1992); S.C. CODE ANN. § 49-5-60 (underground water only); VA. CODE ANN. § 62.1-44.97; WIS. STAT. ANN. § 30.18(2) (permits required for withdrawals to restore the normal level of a stream, or for irrigation, or in excess of 2,000,000 gallons per day); WIS. STAT. ANN. §§ 144.025(e), 144.026(4).

§ 6R-1-02 SMALL WITHDRAWALS EXEMPTED FROM THE PERMIT REQUIREMENT

(1) No permit shall be required for withdrawal of less than 100,000 gallons per day from the waters from the State.

(2) Exemption from the permit requirement under this section does not preclude the application of orders or regulations adopted pursuant to this Code necessary to protect minimum flows or levels or during water emergencies.

(3) **Persons not required to obtain a permit for a withdrawal may, at their option, apply for and obtain a permit under the same terms and conditions as for other permits obtained pursuant to this Code.**

Commentary: The Regulated Riparian Model Water Code exempts certain small withdrawals from the permit requirement based on the conclusions that such small users cannot afford the expense and other burdens of complying with the permit requirement and that exempting such small withdrawals does not seriously impair the State Agency's ability to manage the waters of the State. These users might still be required to register their use with the Agency, a simple and inexpensive procedure, designed to assure that the Agency has full information about the demands upon all water sources within the State. This not only saves the exempted water user from the cost of applying for and successfully processing a permit, it also saves them from the costs of the delays often incident upon the processing of the permit. Exempting small water users also saves the State the unrecoverable costs of processing permits for exempt water users. Water users are prevented from evading the permit requirement under this section by the requirement that all withdrawals for single or related uses be aggregated when the State Agency determines whether a withdrawal is exempted from the permit requirement as well as when the Agency decides whether to issue a permit.

Several existing regulated riparian statutes exempt small users, variously defined. Other regulated riparian statutes exempt uses for particular purposes, particularly for domestic and agricultural uses. Notes in the listing of comparable statutes compiled below demonstrates the range of exemptions found in actual regulated riparian statutes. For the alternative models of exempting certain withdrawals found in existing regulated riparian statutes, see Dellapenna, § 9.03(a)(3). The most common exemption is the one selected for this section, the withdrawal of 100,000 gallons per day. This figure might not be appropriate in any particular jurisdiction; one could debate at great length the reasons for selecting any particular figure.

The Code does not provide a special exemption for domestic uses on the basis that those are properly covered by the volumetric exemption provided in the Code. Any withdrawal on a larger scale is unlikely to qualify as a domestic use, but if the use does qualify it is given a preference in a number of other sections dealing with the permit requirement. In addition to the exemption from the permit requirement in this section, the Code exempts certain small sources from allocation by the State Agency under section 3R-1-03. They are not even subject to the registration requirement. No preference is given to agricultural use as such, although the exclusion of certain small water sources from allocation under the Code will primarily benefit agricultural uses.

Simply because a particular use of water does not rely on an allocation (section 3R-103) or require a permit (this section) does not assure that these uses will not interfere with each other or with other lawful uses that do require permits. When this occurs, any ensuing disputes are resolvable under the twin principles of reasonable use and the prevention of unreasonable injury. For such disputes, the only recourse will be to go to court unless the parties voluntarily agree to arbitrate in some fashion or invoke the State Agency's power to mediate or conciliate. In any event, limitations on use based upon the location of the use–the watershed rule and the rule that uses must be on riparian land–have, however, been repealed by this Code.

Disputes between individual water users do not exhaust the problems that can arise involving those whose use is exempt from allocation or the permit requirement. Regardless how a use becomes exempt, the small exempted uses can cumulatively amount to a considerable amount of water, effectively defeating the public interest in the waters of the State and the goal of sustainable development. The problem of cumulative effects was recently shown in dramatic fashion in the arid state of New Mexico when the State Engineer determined that if all pending applications for new domestic wells were approved (60,000 to 80,000 in number), the resulting drawdown from New Mexico's aquifers would have an undue effect on appropriations from streams. The State Engineer made this decision even though each well would have been limited to only 3 acre-feet. *See Domestic Well Permits on Hold in New Mexico,* U.S. WATER NEWS , July 1996, at 16.

The legislature presumably has set the level for these exemptions at a level sufficiently low that even the cumulative effects will not be significant during years of normal precipitation. During water emergencies, however, these cumulative effects can be very important. Because of this, all exempted uses (whether the exemption is from allocation or from the permit) are subject to the

State Agency's regulatory authority for dealing with such problems and for preserving minimum flows and levels. As with other users facing restrictions on their uses because of water emergencies, users exempted from the permit requirement might find it to their advantage to have a plan for conservation in place before the emergency in order to gain some measure of control over the steps they will have to take in response to the emergency. To do so, they might voluntarily

Yet another model for exempting selected users from the permit requirement would be to authorize the State Agency to define exempted uses by regulation. A similar approach, found in the Florida regulated riparian code, authorizes the responsible agencies to accomplish much the same end through the means of "general permits" (rather than individual permits) for particular classes with "minimal adverse impact." FLA. STAT. ANN. § 373.118. If the legislature is to delegate such a broad discretion to define exemptions from the permit requirement to the Agency, the latter approach is preferable. General permits at least require the Agency to prepare a record similar to that prepared for individual permits and to renew the permit periodically. In either event, if the State Agency is to be given discretion regarding general permits or exemptions from the permit requirement, the Agency will need to cooperate with local governments to consider their needs and wants as well as the needs and wants of the State as a whole.

Simply because one uses less than some threshold amount (in this Code, 100,000 gallons per day) does not mean that these uses will not, viewed as a whole, amount to a significant total consumption during periods of water shortage or water emergency. Subsection (2) makes explicit that restrictions applicable to withdrawals of water during water shortages and water emergencies are applicable to uses for which no permit is required. This creates some potential for a significant disadvantage for small users during such shortfalls of supply as persons who have permits are able to obtain preferential treatment based upon their plans for conservation or conservation credits.

Additionally, persons who are currently using less than 100,000 gallons per day but who expect, within the reasonably foreseeable future, to pass that threshold will then have to obtain a permit. If they are coming in fairly late in the allocation process, *i.e.*, after most of the safe yield of the resource has been allocated, they might find that they cannot obtain a permit for the water sought–unless they can take advantage of the preferential treatment accorded to water developed by voluntary conservation measures. To do so, they will need to obtain a permit before undertaking the conservation measures.

Thus, either through concern to improve their position should a water shortage or a water emergency be declared, or to obtain preferential treatment in the permit process, persons who are not required to obtain a permit for their withdrawals might seek one anyway. Subsection (3) provides for such nonmandatory permits. In such case, the application is subject to the same requirements and processing as any other application for a mandatory permit, and the permit may be issued subject to the same terms and conditions as a mandatory permit.

Cross-references: § 1R-1-01 (protecting the public interest in the waters of the State); § 1R-1-03 (conformity to the policies of this Code and to physical laws); § 1R-1-5 (efficient and equitable utilization during shortfalls in supply); § 1R-1-06 (legal security for water rights); § 1R-1-10 (water conservation); § 1R-1-11 (preservation of minimum flows and levels); § 1R-1-12 (recognizing local interests in the waters of the State); § 2R-1-01 (the obligation to make only reasonable use of water); § 2R-1-02 (no prohibition of use based on location of use); § 2R-1-03 (no unreasonable injury to other water rights); § 2R-1-04 (protection of property rights); § 2R-2-08 (domestic use); § 2R-2-15 (permit); § 2R-2-17 (plan for conservation); § 2R-2-18 (the public interest); § 2R-2-20 (reasonable use); § 2R-2-23 (State Agency); § 2R-2-24 (sustainable development); § 2R-2-26 (unreasonable injury); § 2R-2-29 (water emergency); § 2R-2-30 (water right); § 2R-2-31 (water shortage); § 2R-2-32 (waters of the State); § 2R-2-33 (water source) § 2R-2-34 (withdrawal of to withdraw); § 3R-1-03 (certain small water sources exempted from allocation); §§ 3R-2-01 to 3R-2-05 (protection of minimum flows or levels); § 6R-1-01 (withdrawals unlawful without a permit); § 6R-1-03 (existing withdrawals); § 6R-1-04 (withdrawals begun after the effective date of the Code); § 6R-6-06 (registration of withdrawals not subject to the permit requirement); § 6R-3-03 (aggregation of multiple withdrawals); § 6R-3-04 (preferences among water rights); § 7R-3-05 (authority to restrict withdrawals for which no allocation or permit is required); § 7R-3-06 (conservation credits); § 9R-1-02 (preferences to water developed through conservation measures).

Comparable statutes: ALA. CODE § 9-10B-20(a) (requiring declarations of beneficial use from all users serving more than 10,000 households or withdrawing more than 100,000 gallons per day); CONN. GEN. STAT. ANN. § 22a-377(a), (b) (exempting certain small withdrawals); DEL. CODE ANN. tit. 7, §§ 6003(e) (authorizing the permit issuing authority to define exempt classes), 6029 (exempting certain small withdrawals); FLA. STAT. ANN. § 373.118 (general permits for withdrawals with a "minimal adverse impact" on the waters of the district); GA. CODE ANN. §§ 12-5-31(a) (exempting withdrawals averaging less than 100,000 gallons per day, occurring during construction of authorized facilities, and for farm uses if begun before July 1, 1988), 12-5-96(a)(1) (exempting wells withdrawing up to 100,000 gallons per day), 12-5-105(b) (special provisions for permits for farm uses); IOWA CODE ANN. §§ 455B.261 (exempting withdrawals of less than 25,000 gallons per day), 455B.268 (exempting "specific nonrecurring withdrawals for minor uses"); KY. REV. STAT. ANN. §§ 151.140 (exempting irrigation withdrawals, small withdrawals as set by regulation, withdrawals for steam power generating, and withdrawals for use in connection with the production of oil and gas), 151.210(a) (exempting withdrawals for domestic use); MD. CODE ANN., NAT. RES. § 8-802(b), (c) (exempting withdrawals for domestic uses and agricultural uses of less than 10,000 gallons per day or begun before July 1, 1988); MINN. STAT. ANN. § 105.41(1b.) (exempting small withdrawals as set by regulation); MISS. CODE ANN. § 51-3-7(1) (exempting certain small withdrawals); N.J. STAT. ANN. §§ 58:1A-5(a), 58:1A-6(a) (exempting withdrawals of less than 100,000 gallons per day); N.C. GEN. STAT. § 143-215.15(a) (exempting withdrawals of less than 100,000 gallons per day); S.C. CODE ANN. § 49-5-60(A) (exempting withdrawals of less than 100,000 gallons per day and according to certain other volumetric limits); VA. CODE ANN. §§ 62.1-44.87, 62.1-243 (exempting withdrawals of less than 300,000 gallons per month, certain withdrawals by public supply systems, and existing withdrawals); WIS. STAT. ANN. §§ 30.08(2)(b) (exempting surface withdrawals of less than 2,000,000 gallons per day), 144.025(e) (exempting wells withdrawing less than 100,000 gallons per day), 144.026(4)(b) (exempting surface withdrawals of less than 2,000,000 gallons per day).

§ 6R-1-03 EXISTING WITHDRAWALS

(1) Existing withdrawals include actual withdrawals from the waters of the State on the effective date of this Code and withdrawals made on a regular basis within the 12 months immediately before the effective date of this Code.

(2) Every person with an existing withdrawal must apply to the State Agency for a permit in a form prescribed by the Agency within one year after the effective date of this Code.

(3) A person qualifying to apply for a permit under this section may continue the existing withdrawal and its related use until the State Agency completes action on the application.

(4) The State Agency shall approve a permit for any person proving a withdrawal from a particular water source existing on the effective date of this Code for such water as is reasonably necessary to accomplish the purpose for which the existing withdrawal was made.

(5) If the aggregate of existing withdrawals exceeds the safe yield of the water source, the State Agency shall allocate the water properly available for withdrawal among existing withdrawals according to the standards applicable to the approval of an application for a new permit.

(6) Failure to file an application as provided in this subsection shall be conclusive evidence of the abandonment of any right to withdraw water based on an existing withdrawal by the person failing to apply.

Commentary: One of the most difficult issues confronting a State seeking to replace a system of common law riparian rights with a regulated riparian system is how to show adequate respect for "vested" water rights in order to avoid an obligation to pay compensation to all who have such rights. *See, e.g., Franco-American Charolaise, Ltd. v. Oklahoma Water Resources Bd.*, 855 P.2d 568 (Okla. 1993) (holding that Oklahoma's appropriative rights statute amounted to a taking of the property of owners of abolished riparian rights). *See also* M. CATHERINE MILLER, FLOODING THE COURTROOMS: LAW AND WATER IN THE FAR WEST (1993). While it is generally settled that only actual existing uses as of the effective date of the new water law system are "vested," in a mature economy, as is found throughout the domain of common law riparian rights, to exempt all existing uses of water from the permit system required by the Regulated Riparian Model Water Code would leave little or nothing for the State Agency to administer or manage. *See* Dellapenna, § 8.05(a) (analyzing the failure of the adoption of appropriative rights in Mississippi to have any effect on water usage or litigation over water during the 30 years the law was in effect). To go further and exempt all existing uses even from the registration requirement for fear of impairing vested property rights would make the gathering of meaningful data impossible and planning a mockery. *See commentary* to Alternative B in WILLIAM R. WALKER & PHYLLIS G. BRIDGEMAN *A Water Code for Virginia* § 2.03 ((Va. Polytech. Inst., Va. Water Resources Res. Center Bull. No. 147, 1985).

The Regulated Riparian Model Water Code, consistently with nearly all regulated riparian statutes, rejects temporal priority as a controlling criterion for the allocation of the waters of the State. *See* Dellapenna, § 9.03(6)(3). Therefore, the Code does not exempt existing uses from the obligation to register or to obtain a permit when a similar new use would be required to do so. Rather, the existing user will generally have to register or apply for a permit under special requirements that assure existing users of obtaining a first permit without the need to pass muster under the standards applicable to new or renewal permits. When the initial permit expires, however, the application to renew is to be judged by the same standards as for any other application to renew. In that setting, the Code provides a small preference for prior uses, but does not guarantee renewal if the State Agency determines that renewal is not in the public interest.

Failure to file for the initial permit, and thus failure to accept the regulatory scheme entailed in accepting the initial permit, is conclusively presumed to be abandonment of any claim to a water right based on the common law.

The approach set out in this section is modeled after that adopted in Florida based on the Model Water Code developed at the University of Florida School of Law. *See* MALONEY, AUSNESS, & MORRIS, at § 2.03. The Florida statute, which allowed three years to file for a permit, was upheld as constitutional in *Village of Tequesta v. Jupiter Inlet Corp.*, 371 So. 2d 663 (Fla.), *cert. denied,* 444 U.S. 965 (1979). Other statutes have opted for periods as short as a year. *See Texaco, Inc. v. Short,* 454 U.S. 516 (1982). Whether an even shorter period, say six months, would pass constitutional muster is not certain. The Code recommends the period of one year as the minimum period that one can be certain will not be found to be unconstitutional. For a general discussion of the constitutional issues involved, see the commentary to section 6R-1-01. *See generally* Dellapenna, § 9.04(a).

The Code provides the State Agency with authority to assess the validity of claims of prior use entitled to a guaranteed initial permit under this section. Furthermore, subsection (4) of this section provides a solution should the situation arise that the aggregate of existing withdrawals exceeds the safe yield of the water source. In such a case, failure to limit existing uses would be contrary to the public interest and defeat the fundamental goal of sustainable development. The Agency shall allocate the water available within the safe yield among the existing withdrawals according to the criteria applicable to new permits, *i.e.,* according to the Agency's assessment of the reasonableness of the several uses. Limiting allocations to existing withdrawals is a necessary and proper exercise of the State's police power to select among several activities, some of which in the very nature of things must cease. This reality precludes a claim that the regulation is a taking of property; indeed, the State could, under this analysis, restrict existing uses more severely than authorized by this section. *Miller v. Schoene,* 276 U.S. 272 (1928). That is precisely what is done when the time to renew the permit arrives. As with other permits, upon expiration and application for renewal, there is no guarantee for renewal and no rule precluding those who had not heretofore withdrawn from the source from applying to receive the water. Discussion of this constitutional issue is found in Dellapenna, § 9.04.

Cross-references: § 1R-1-01 (protecting the public interest in the waters of the State); § 1R-1-02 (assuring efficient and productive use of water); § 1R-1-05 (efficient and equitable allocation of water during shortfalls in supply); § 1R-1-06 (legal security for the right to use water); § 1R-1-08 (procedural protections); § 1R-1-10 (water conservation); § 1R-11 (preservation of minimum flows and levels); § 2R-1-01 (the obligation to make only reasonable use of water); § 2R-1-03 (no unreasonable injury to other water rights); § 2R-1-04 (protection of property rights); § 2R-2-14 (permit); § 2R-2-15 (person); § 2R-2-18 (the public interest); § 2R-2-20 (reasonable use); § 2R-2-21 (safe yield); § 2R-2-23 (State Agency); § 2R-2-24 (sustainable development); § 2R-2-26 (unreasonable injury); § 2R-2-30 (water right); § 2R-2-32 (waters of the State); § 2R-2-33 (water source); § 2R-2-33 (withdrawal or to withdrawal); §§ 3R-1-01 to 3R-2-05 (waters subject to allocation); § 6R-1-01 (withdrawals unlawful without a permit); § 6R-1-02 (small withdrawals exempted from the permit requirement); § 6R-1-04 (withdrawals begun after the effective date of the Code); § 6R-1-05 (temporary permits); § 6R-1-06 (registration of withdrawals not subject to permits); § 6R-2-01 to 6R-2-08 (permit procedures); §§ 6R-3-01 to 6R-3-05 (the basis of the water right); §§ 7R-1-01 to 7R-3-07 (the scope of the water right).

Comparable statutes: ALA. CODE § 9-10B-20(e), (f); CONN. GEN. STAT. ANN. §§ 22a-368(a), 22a-373(c); FLA. STAT. ANN. §§ 373.226, 373.233(1); GA. CODE ANN. §§ 12-5-31(a)(3), 12-5-105(a); HAW. REV. STAT. §§ 174C-50; IOWA CODE ANN. § 455B.265(2); MD. CODE ANN., NAT. RES. § 8-802(b), (c); N.Y. ENVTL. CONSERV. LAW § 15-1501 (no permit necessary for existing supplies); N.C. GEN. STAT. § 143-215.16(e) (existing withdrawals guaranteed a permit to the extent the water is reasonably necessary to the withdrawer's needs); S.C. CODE ANN. § 49-5-70(F) to (H); VA. CODE ANN. §§ 62.1-44.93, 62.1-243(B), (C).

§ 6R-1-04 WITHDRAWALS BEGUN AFTER THE EFFECTIVE DATE OF THE CODE

> **Any person not qualifying as having an existing withdrawal from the waters of the State as defined in section 6R-1-03(1) must apply to the State**

Agency for a permit in a form prescribed by the State Agency before initiating any withdrawal of the waters of the State or undertaking any work intended to form part of the withdrawal of the waters of the State.

Commentary: All persons not entitled to a preference as an existing withdrawal or otherwise exempt from allocation or the permit requirement under this Code must apply for a permit according to the normal procedures applicable to such new or all renewal permits. The applicant must file the necessary forms before beginning any work on the proposed withdrawal. Elsewhere, the Regulated Riparian Model Water Code provides that no equity attaches to an application because of investments of money or labor in acquiring the property or beginning the work necessary for the proposed withdrawal or used of the waters of the State.

Cross-references: § 1R-1-01 (protecting the public interest the waters of the State); § 1R-1-02 (assuring efficient and productive use of water); § 1R-1-06 (legal security for the right to use water); § 1R-1-08 (procedural protections); § 2R-1-01 (the obligation to make only reasonable use of water); § 2R-2-03 (no unreasonable injury to other water rights); § 2R-1-04 (protection of property rights); § 2R-2-14 (permit); § 2R-2-15 (person); § 2R-2-20 (reasonable use); § 2R-2-26 (unreasonable use); § 2R-2-30 (water right); § 2R-2-32 (waters of the State); § 2R-2-33 (water source); § 2R-2-34 (withdrawal or to withdraw); §§ 3R-1-01 to 3R-2-05 (waters subject to allocation); § 6R-1-01 (withdrawals unlawful without a permit); § 6R-1-02 (small withdrawals exempted from the permit requirement); § 6R-1-03 (existing withdrawals); § 6R-1-05 (temporary permits); § 6R-1-06 (registration of withdrawals not subject to permits); §§ 6R-2-01 to 6R-2-08 (permit procedures); §§ 6R-3-01 to 6R-3-05 (the basis of the water right); §§ 7R-1-01 to 7R-3-07 (the scope of the water right).

Comparable statutes: CONN. GEN. STAT. ANN. § 22a-368(b); GA. CODE ANN. §§ 12-5-31(a)(1), 12-5-96(a)(1); ILL. COMP. STAT. ANN. ch. 525, § 45/5..

§ 6R-1-05 TEMPORARY PERMITS

(1) The State Agency may issue a temporary permit for a withdrawal of the waters of the State while an application is pending under this Chapter or when an emergency arises that requires immediate action without the delays incident to the processing of an application for a permit.

(2) A temporary permit shall specify the date on which it expires, which in any event cannot be more than 6 months after the temporary permit is issued.

(3) The State Agency may renew a temporary permit upon its expiration if action on the primary permit is not yet completed or if the emergency continues, but no series of temporary and renewed temporary permits can be issued for a single purpose for total period of more than 24 months.

(4) The State Agency shall issue temporary permits on such terms and conditions as are necessary to prevent any significant impact on any other permitted use of the water or any substantial change in the water source.

(5) The notice and hearing requirements under this Chapter do not apply to the issuance or renewal of a temporary permit.

Commentary: From time to time the State Agency might find it appropriate to issue a temporary permit without requiring compliance with the full procedural requirements of the normal permit process. Two obvious examples would be unforeseen emergencies or when an existing user seeks to continue withdrawing and using water while an application to renew a permit is pending. The Regulated Riparian Model Water Code responds to these needs by authorizing the Agency to issue temporary permits, for strictly limited periods, to cover the exigency giving rise to the need for the temporary permit.

The authority to issue temporary permits poses only limited risk of mismanagement or abuse when the temporary permit is attendant to the processing of a full permit application. Somewhat greater dangers attend to an emergency permit. For a discussion of strategies for coping with water emergencies, see Dellapenna, § 9.05(d). This problem is addressed by the requirement that permit applications be processed in the order of their filing except for prompt approval of routine applications, or where the public health, safety, or welfare would be threatened by delay, or when efficient process of permits requires grouping several applications for a single evaluation. See section 6R-3-03. This section dispenses only with the requirements of notice and hearings and not with the other procedural and substantive standards provided in this and the next Chapter. These other standards therefore inform and delimit the authority to issue temporary permits as well. As with any permit, the Agency is to specify the terms and conditions applicable to the temporary permit which are then binding on the permit holder until the expiration of the temporary permit or the awarding of a primary permit.

Cross-references: § 2R-2-15 (permit); § 2R-2-16 (person); § 2R-2-18 (the public interest); § 2R-2-20 (reasonable use); § 2R-2-21 (safe yield); § 2R-2-23 (State Agency); § 2R-2-24 (sustainable development); § 2R-2-29 (water emergency); § 2R-2-30 (water rights); § 2R-2-32 (waters of the State); § 2R-2-33 (water source); § 2R-2-34 (withdrawal or to withdraw); § 6R-1-01 (withdrawals unlawful without a permit); §§ 6R-2-01 to 6R-2-08 (permit procedures); §§ 6R-3-01 to 6R-3-05 (the basis of the water right); §§ 7R-1-01 to 7R-3-07 (the scope of the water right).

Comparable statutes: FLA. STAT. ANN. § 373.244; GA. CODE ANN. § 12-5-96(c)(2); HAW. REV. STAT. § 174C-50(e), (g); MISS. CODE ANN. § 51-3-15(2)(b); S.C. CODE ANN. § 49-5-60(C)(2).

§ 6R-1-06 REGISTRATION OF WITHDRAWALS NOT SUBJECT TO PERMITS

(1) The State Agency may, by regulation, require some or all persons whose withdrawal is exempt from allocation or from the permit requirement to register their withdrawal of the waters of the State periodically, including such information as the State Agency determines to be necessary to carry out the State Agency's responsibilities under this Code.

(2) Persons who are not required to register their withdrawals may, at their option, register their withdrawals by providing the same information as is required under the regulations issued pursuant to subsection (1) of this section.

Commentary: The Regulated Riparian Model Water Code exempts the withdrawal of water from certain shared waters, from certain small surface water sources, and for certain small uses from the obligation to obtain a permit. Some States might also elect to exempt some other preferred uses from that obligation. Nevertheless, for informational purposes in fulfilling the State Agency's planning responsibilities and also in designing appropriate strategies for and responding to water shortages and water emergencies, the Agency needs information about all uses of the waters of the State. The obligation to register is designed to assure that the State Agency will obtain the necessary information. See Dellapenna, § 9.03(a)(1).

The Agency is given broad authority to define which holders of water rights that are exempted from allocation of from the permit requirement must register and what information registrants need to provide. How the Agency should define the answers to such questions will vary with the resources available to the Agency to process the registration requirement and with its assessment of the information it needs to carry out its responsibilities. Registration regulations could, for example, require the following data for the year prior to the registration:

(a) estimated average daily withdrawal;

(b) the maximum daily withdrawal;

(c) the sources of the water withdrawn;

(d) the capability of the withdrawal facility;

(e) the uses made of the water; and

(f) the volume of wastewater returned to the water source.

Probably the Agency will exempt some exempted withdrawals even from the registration requirement. The most likely examples will be the small water uses that are exempt from allocation under section 3R-1-03, or perhaps some of the small users exempt from the permit requirement under section 6R-1-02. Some legislatures might prefer to define classes exempt from the registration requirement in the statute rather than to leave it to the discretion of the Agency. Numerous actual statutes provide models for such statutory exclusions.

Some persons who are not required to register their uses might nonetheless choose to do so in order to establish a clear record of their use. This possibility is recognized in subsection (2). Such non-mandatory registration is to satisfy the same requirements as the mandatory registrations under subsection (1).

Cross-references: § 1R-1-01 (protecting the public interest in the waters of the State); § 1R-1-02 (assuring efficient and productive use of water); § 1R-1-04 (comprehensive planning); § 1R-1-05 (efficient and equitable utilization during shortfalls in supply); § 1R-1-10 (water conservation); § 1R-1-11 (preservation of minimum flows and levels); § 2R-2-15 (person); § 2R-2-18 (the public interest); § 2R-2-23 (State Agency); § 2R-2-29 (water emergency); § 2R-2-31 (water shortage); § 2R-2-32 (waters of the State); § 2R-2-33 (water source); § 2R-2-34 (withdrawal); § 3R-1-02 (certain shared waters exempted from allocation); § 3R-1-03 (small water sources exempted from allocation); §§ 4R-2-01 to 4R-2-04 (planning responsibilities); § 6R-1-02 (small withdrawals exempted from the permit requirement); § 7R-3-05 (authority to restrict withdrawals for which no allocation of permit is required).

Comparable statutes: ALA. CODE § 9-10B-20; ARK. CODE ANN. §§ 15-22-215 (surface water sources), 15-22-302 (underground water); GA. CODE ANN. § 12-5-96(b); HAW. REV. STAT. §§ 174C-26, 174C-27, 174C-83, 174C-92; IND. CODE ANN. §§ 13-2-1-6(3), 13-2-6.1-7; IOWA CODE ANN. § 455B.268(2); MASS. GEN. LAWS ANN. ch. 21G, §§ 5, 6; VA. CODE ANN. §§ 62.1-44.38(C), 62.1-44.85(13), 62.1-44.92(1), 62.1-99, 62.1-244; WIS. STAT. ANN. § 144.026(3).

Part 2

Permit Procedures

This Part sets out the procedures to be followed in processing permit applications. In addition to specifying the contents of the application, the procedures include notice and an opportunity to be heard for any person using water or likely to use water from the same source, and a right of comment for anyone. Only persons who can demonstrate an actual likelihood of adverse effect are entitled to contest a hearing application. A number of other procedural safeguards are also provided, including an obligation of the State Agency to act, and an opportunity for the applicant to remedy any defects in the application.

§ 6R-2-01 CONTENTS OF AN APPLICATION FOR A PERMIT

(1) An application for a permit to withdraw water pursuant to this Code shall contain the following information:

(a) the name and address of the applicant;

(b) the amount of the proposed withdrawal of water, including estimates of the projected daily, monthly, seasonal, and annual mean and peak withdrawals;

(c) the place and source of the proposed withdrawals;

(d) the place and nature of the proposed use of water;

(e) the place of the proposed return flow of withdrawn water;

(f) an estimate of the projected overall consumptive use of water;

(g) the anticipated effects, if any, of the withdrawal on existing or proposed uses dependent on the same water source, along with a list of the persons entitled to notice under § 6R-2-02 in so far as known to the applicant;

(h) the impact of the proposed withdrawal on other water sources hydrologically interconnected with the water source from which the withdrawal is to be made;

(i) the current operating capacity of any existing withdrawal system and the effect of the proposed withdrawals on the existing withdrawal system;

(j) any land acquisition, equipment, energy consumption, or the relocation or re-siting of any existing community, facility, right-of-way, or structure that will be required;

(k) the total anticipated costs of any proposed construction;

(l) a list of all federal, State, or local approvals, permits, licenses, or other authorizations required for any part of the proposal;

(m) a statement of whether and how the proposed withdrawal complies with all applicable plans and strategies for the use, management, and protection of the waters of the State and related land resources;

(n) the planning status and estimated timetable for the completion of the proposed project;

(o) a description of alternative means for satisfying the applicant's need for water if the requested permit is denied or modified;

(p) a description of any plan for conservation the applicant proposes to follow; and

(q) **any other information reasonably required by the State Agency by regulation.**

(2) **In any dispute regarding any fact in issue between the agency and an applicant for a permit, the burden of proof shall be on the applicant.**

Commentary: The Regulated Riparian Model Water Code authorizes the State Agency to require a particular form through regulations adopted by the Agency. This section indicates the minimum information that the Agency must include on the form. The information specified is necessary to determine what the applicant proposes to do and to facilitate the Agency's evaluation of the application. The required information should enable the Agency to consider all dimensions of the public interest and the sustainability of the development in question in choosing between competing permit applications and in undertaking its planning and shortfall management functions. *See* Dellapenna, § 9.03(a)(5)(A).

In general, the required information is what anyone carefully planning an investment in hydraulic facilities would already have gathered for that process, and thus including it on an application for a permit would not be a significant added burden, either physically or financially. For example, subsection (l) merely requires the application to list other approvals, permits, licenses, or the like that will be necessary. Rather than burdening the applicant, this could work to the applicants advantage as the Code requires the Agency to issue a combined permit representing several of these processes whenever that would improve the operation of the application or enforcement process. To the extent that this, or other information, might be confidential business information, the Code provides direct protection for that confidentiality. The only persons for whom the assembling and disclosure of the required information would be an undue burden are the very small users who are exempted from allocation or from the permit requirement under this Code.

While most of the information required by this section is self-explanatory, several points deserve a brief discussion, particularly when the information required refers to items that have a technical definition under this Code. In particular, subsection (f) requiring an estimate of the consumptive use merits some attention as sorting through the definition takes a bit of patience. Consumptive use is defined in this Code as simply any use that is nonconsumptive. Nonconsumptive use, in turn, is defined as a use that does not make either substantial qualitative or substantial quantitative changes or exacerbate a low-flow condition. In short, a consumptive use is one that render water unfit or unavailable for other desired uses regardless of the reason for that result. *See* Dellapenna, § 6.01(a)(4). Given this expansive concept of consumptive use, the permit applicant will have to estimate all significant changes the proposed project is likely to make in the quantity or quality of the water returned as compared to the water withdrawn.

Withdrawal itself is a term of art in this Code. It includes both the removal of water from its natural course or location or the control of water in its natural course of location. Thus, a withdrawal includes dams or other devices for regulating flow or percolation as well as diversion canals, pumping stations, and so on. The term is similar in effect to the appropriative rights term "diversion," and like the latter term is applied in a manner that an ordinary speaker of English would not necessarily recognize.

Finally, the required information is essential to determining the impact of the proposed project on the sustainable development of the waters of the State, as well as other aspects of the public interest such as preserving the integrities of the water source. This information, when correct, will be entered into the statewide data system, except to the extent that it might be confidential business information. That alone requires that the information be accurate, and explains why anyone who knowingly submits false information commits a felony. While one who innocently submits false data is not guilty of a crime, the Agency might take this, and the reasons it occurred, into account when decided whether to issue a permit and what terms and conditions to include in the permit. In any dispute, the burden of proof is on the applicant.

Cross-references: § 1R-1-01 (protecting the public interest in the waters of the State); § 1R-1-04 (comprehensive planning); § 1R-1-05 (efficient and equitable allocation of water during a shortfall in supply); § 1R-1-09 (coordination of water allocation and water quality effects); § 1R-1-10 (water conservation); § 1R-1-11 (preservation of minimum flows and levels); § 2R-2-02 (biological integrity); § 2R-2-03 (chemical integrity); § 2R-2-04 (comprehensive water allocation plan); § 2R-2-06 (consumptive use); § 2R-2-07 (cost); § 2R-2-13 (nonconsumptive use); § 2R-2-14 (permit); § 2R-2-15 (person); § 2R-2-16 (physical integrity); § 2R-2-18 (the public interest); § 2R-2-21 (safe yield); § 2R-2-23 (State Agency); § 2R-2-24 (sustainable development); § 2R-2-29 (water emergency); § 2R-2-30 (water right); § 2R-2-31 (water shortage); § 2R-2-32 (waters of the State); § 2R-2-33 (water source); § 2R-2-34 (withdrawal); § 3R-1-03 (small water sources exempted from allocation); §§ 3R-2-01 to 3R-2-05 (protection of minimum flows and levels); § 4R-1-05 (application of general laws to meetings, procedures, and records); § 4R-1-06 (regulatory authority of the State Agency); § 4R-1-07 (application fees); § 4R-1-09 (protection of confidential business information); § 4R-2-03 (the statewide data system); § 4R-3-04 (combined permits); § 5R-5-01 (crimes); § 6R-1-01 (withdrawals unlawful without a permit); § 6R-1-02 (small withdrawals exempted from the permit requirement); § 6R-3-01 (standards for a permit); § 6R-3-02 (determining whether a use is reasonable); § 6R-3-03 (aggregation of multiple withdrawals); § 6R-3-04 (preferences among water rights); § 6R-3-05 (prior investment in withdrawal or use facilities); § 7R-1-01 (permit terms and conditions); § 7R-1-02 (duration of permits); § 7R-2-01 to § 7R-2-04 (modification of water rights).

Comparable statutes: CONN. GEN. STAT. ANN. § 22a-369; FLA. STAT. ANN. § 373.116(1), 373.229(1); GA. CODE ANN. § 12-5-31(d); HAW. REV. STAT. § 174C-51; MD. CODE ANN., NAT. RES. § 8-805; MASS. GEN. LAWS ANN. ch. 21G, §§ 8, 9; MINN. STAT. ANN. § 105.416(2); MINN. STAT. ANN. § 105.44; MISS. CODE ANN. § 51-3-33(2); N.Y. ENVTL. CONSERV. LAW §§ 15-503(1), 15-1503(1); N.C. GEN. STAT. § 143-215.16(c), (d); S.C. CODE ANN. § 49-5-60(A); VA. CODE ANN. § 62.1-44.100; WIS. STAT. ANN. §§ 30.18(3), 144.026(5).

§ 6R-2-02 NOTICE AND OPPORTUNITY TO BE HEARD

(1) Before deciding whether to approve or deny a permit, the State Agency shall, beginning within 14 days after the filing of an application for a permit, publish a notice of the permit application once each week for four consecutive weeks in a newspaper of

general circulation in each water basin to be affected by the proposed withdrawal and in the State Register, and provide individual written notice to:

(a) every unit of state or local government with regulatory authority or other responsibility for the proposed withdrawal;

(b) each owner of land contiguous to the location of the proposed withdrawal; and

(c) each person holding a permit under this Code or under the National Pollution Discharge Elimination System for the water source from which the proposed withdrawal is to be made if such a permit holder is likely to be affected by the proposed withdrawal or use.

(2) Individual written notice shall be by any form of mail with return receipt requested.

(3) The required notice shall indicate the water source from which it is proposed to withdraw the water, the quantity and location of the proposed withdrawal, and the purposes for which it is proposed to withdraw the water.

Commentary: This section is designed to assure that any person who has an interest in the issuance or denial of a permit under the Regulated Riparian Model Water Code has a fair opportunity to be heard before a decision is made on the application for the permit. This is a common requirement in regulated riparian statutes. See Dellapenna, § 9.03(a)(5)(A), at 469. While this goal seems to impose a considerable burden, fiscal as well as physical, on the State Agency, the expense, at least, is to be passed through to the applicant under the fee schedule.

Some States might prefer to provide for publication in the State's equivalent to the Federal Register. While there is precedent for considering such publication to be constructive notice to all within the State, in reality such journals are rarely read by any except lawyers. The requirement of publication in newspapers of general circulation within the relevant water basin would appear to be better calculated to achieve the goal of notifying those likely to be affected by the issuance or denial of a permit when their names are not known to the applicant or to the Agency. For a discussion of adequacy of notice see WILLIAM R. WALKER & PHYLLIS G. BRIDGEMAN, A WATER CODE FOR VIRGINIA § 2.04 commentary (Va. Polytech. Inst., Va. Water Resources Res. Center Bull. No. 147, 1985).

Connecticut requires more than mere notice of the filing of an application. That State requires notice of the intent to file an application for a permit be given to local units of government within which the withdrawal is to occur 30 days before the filing of the application. CONN. GEN. STAT. ANN. § 22a-370. Such a requirement seems excessive and is not recommended in this Code..

Cross-references: § 1R-1-08 (procedural protections); § 2R-2-15 (person); § 2R-2-23 (State Agency); § 2R-2-30 (water right); § 4R-1-05 (application of general laws to meetings, procedures, and records); § 4R-1-06 (regulatory authority of the State Agency); § 4R-1-07 (application fees); § 4R-1-09 (protection of confidential business information); §§ 5R-1-01 to 5R-3-03 (hearings, disputes, and judicial review); § 6R-2-04 (contesting an application); § 6R-2-05 (public right of comment); § 6R-2-07 (notice of action on applications); § 6R-2-08 (opportunity to remedy defects in an application).

Comparable statutes: ALA. CODE § 9-10B-22(a); ARK. CODE ANN. § 15-22-206; DEL. CODE ANN. tit. 7, §§ 6004(b), 6006(1); FLA. STAT. ANN. §§ 373.116(2), 373.146, 373.229(2), (3); GA. CODE ANN. § 12-5-96(f); HAW. REV. STAT. §§ 174C-50(C), 174C-52; MD. CODE ANN., NAT. RES. § 8-806(a) to (c); MASS. GEN. LAWS ANN. ch. 21G, § 9; MINN. STAT. ANN. § 105.44(3), (5); N.Y. ENVTL. CONSERV. LAW § 15-0903(2); N.C. GEN. STAT. § 143-215.15(d); S.C. CODE ANN. § 49-5-60(B) to (E); VA. CODE ANN. § 62.1-44.100(g), (i); WIS. STAT. ANN. §§ 30.02, 30.18(4), 144.026(5)(e).

§ 6R-2-03 PROCESSING APPLICATIONS IN THE ORDER RECEIVED

The State Agency shall process applications in the order in which they are received except:

- **(a) where to do so would prevent prompt approval of routine applications;**
- **(b) where the public health, safety, or welfare would be threatened by delay; or**
- **(c) when the Agency undertakes joint consideration of pending applications proposing to withdraw water from the same source of supply.**

Commentary: To balance the need for fair processing of applications with the need for efficient management of the State Agency's procedures, this section provides that applications are to be processed in the order in which they are received by the Agency except if the application lends itself to a routine approval or denial without extended consideration, or if the public health, safety, or welfare requires expedited consideration, or to enable the Agency to undertake joint consideration of multiple applications to withdraw water from the same source.

Cross-references: § 1R-1-08 (procedural protections); § 6R-3-04 (preferences among water rights).

Comparable statute: IOWA CODE ANN. § 455B.265(1).

§ 6R-2-04 CONTESTING AN APPLICATION

(1) Any person who might be adversely affected by the granting of a proposed permit may, within 30 days of actual notice of the receipt of

the application by the State Agency or, if no actual notice is required or has proven impossible, within 30 days of constructive notice by publication of the final notice required in section 6R-2-02(1), submit a statement to the State Agency briefly outlining the reasons for believing that an adverse effect is likely to result.

(2) Any person submitting a statement contesting an application for a permit under subsection (1) of this section is to be provided with a copy of the permit application upon paying the costs of duplicating the application; a request for a copy of the application must be made within 10 business days of the filing of the statement contesting the application.

(3) Any person submitting a statement contesting an application for a permit under subsection (1) must file any further comments on the application within 21 days of receipt of the copy of the application.

(4) Any person submitting a statement is entitled to a hearing under section 5R-1-01 upon requesting the hearing on non-frivolous grounds not later than the last day for the submission of the further comments under subsection (3).

(5) No person who has not contested an application for a permit under this section shall be entitled to seek judicial review of the decision to grant the permit in question.

Commentary: This section specifies the burden on a person who seeks to contest the award of a permit to another person and makes clear that any one who complies with the procedural requirements is entitled to a hearing under the Regulated Riparian Model Water Code so long as the person contesting the approval of the application has alleged non-frivolous grounds. For a similar proposal, see WILLIAM R. WALKER & PHYLLIS G. BRIDGEMAN, A WATER CODE FOR VIRGINIA § 2.04(4) (Va. Polytech. Inst., Va. Water Resources Res. Center Bull. No. 147, 1985).

Cross-references: § 1R-1-08 (procedural protections); § 2R-2-15 (person); § 2R-2-23 (State Agency); § 2R-2-30 (water right); § 4R-1-05 (application of general laws to meetings, procedures, and records); § 4R-1-06 (regulatory authority of the State Agency); § 4R-1-09 (protection of confidential business information); §§ 5R-1-01 to 5R-3-03 (hearings, disputes, and judicial review); § 6R-2-02 (notice and opportunity to be heard); § 6R-2-05 (public right of comment); § 6R-2-07 (notice of action on applications); § 6R-2-08 (opportunity to remedy defects in an application).

Comparable statutes: GA. CODE ANN. § 12-5-96(h); S.C. CODE ANN. § 49-5-60(B); VA. CODE ANN. § 62.1-44.100(h).

§ 6R-2-05 PUBLIC RIGHT OF COMMENT

> **Any person may submit written comments on any application within 45 days of the publication of the final notice required in section 6R-2-02(1).**

Commentary: The Regulated Riparian Model Water Code requires the State Agency to receive written comments from any person regarding any pending application if received within the time specified. This section does not guarantee a hearing to persons not likely to be adversely affected by the issuing of the permit. The Code does not require an informational hearing on every application for a permit, leaving that to the Agency's discretion.

Cross-references: § 1R-1-08 (procedural protections); § 2R-2-15 (person); § 2R-2-23 (State Agency); § 2R-2-30 (water right); § 4R-1-05 (application of general laws to meetings, procedures, and records); § 4R-1-06 (regulatory authority of the State Agency); § 4R-1-09 (protection of confidential business information); §§ 5R-1-01 to 5R-3-03 (hearings, disputes, and judicial review); § 5R-4-09 (citizen suits); § 6R-2-02 (notice and opportunity to be heard); § 6R-2-04 (contesting an application); § 6R-2-07 (notice of action on applications).

Comparable Statute: HAW. REV. STAT. § 174C-13.

§ 6R-2-06 OBLIGATION OF THE STATE AGENCY TO ACT

(1) The State Agency shall rule upon all applications within 6 months of the initial filing of the application, unless the State Agency shall, by order, extend time for not more than an additional 6 months.

(2) Failure of the State Agency to rule upon an application within the time applicable under this section shall be deemed to be an approval of the application and the issuance of the permit on the basis of such terms and conditions as are inferable from the application.

(3) An applicant may bring an action in any court of competent jurisdiction to declare the terms and conditions of the permit as provided in subsection (2) of this section.

Commentary: In more than one regulated riparian state, the administering agency has been seriously understaffed and underfunded, so that permits either have not been issued or have been issued with inexcusable delays. At the present time, the worst examples of such derelictions are Indiana and Virginia. The Regulated Riparian Model Water Code places the burden of non-action on the State Agency rather than the applicant. This not only gives the Agency an incentive to fulfill its duties promptly, but it also protects an applicant from unreasonable delays in undertaking the withdrawal and use of water caused by the nonaction of the Agency. *See also* Dellapenna, § 9.03(a)(5)(A), at 470 n.433. This section therefore also creates incentives for the legislature to provide adequate staff and other resources to assure that the Agency can fulfill its responsibilities. On the other hand, as the Agency is bound to set fees high enough to cover its costs in processing applications, the burden of providing adequate staff and resources ultimately should not fall upon the general public fisc.

To some extent the legislature can evade the concerns expressed here by simply making the processing period prescribed in this section longer to reflect the ability of the Agency, given its staffing and budget, to process applications. The figure of 6 months provided in this section is actually at the outer edge of the periods found in existing regulated riparian statutes. The range of times allowed is indicated by the notes to the comparable statutes. An alternative would be to authorize the governor to extend the processing period or to suspend the implicit approval provided in subsection (2). If the State opts for the Special Water Management Area to issue permits, the State might, after the fashion of Florida, leave it to each Area to decide whether to issue permits. This would allow the State to concentrate the staff and the funds for the processing of permits in those parts of the State in which the need for regulation was greatest.

Cross-references: § 1R-1-08 (procedural protections); § 2R-2-15 (person); § 2R-2-22 (Special Water Management Area); § 2R-2-23 (State Agency); § 4R-1-07 (application fees); § 4R-4-06(4) (optional subsection on permit issuing authority of the Special Water Management Area) § 6R-2-07 (notice of action on applications); § 6R-2-08 (opportunity to remedy defects in an application).

Comparable statutes: ALA. CODE § 9-10B-19(3); CONN. GEN. STAT. ANN. §§ 22a-371, 22a-373(a), (d) (action required within 120 days); DEL. CODE ANN. tit. 7, § 6006(4) ("promptly"); HAW. REV. STAT. §§ 174C-50(d), 174C-53(c) (90 to 180 days depending on circumstances); MASS. GEN. LAWS ANN. ch. 21G, § 9 (within 30 or 90 days depending on the completeness of the application); MINN. STAT. ANN. § 105.44(4), (8) (within 30 days or 60 days depending on the class of application); WIS. STAT. ANN. § 144.026(5)(c) (within the time set by regulation).

§ 6R-2-07 NOTICE OF ACTION ON APPLICATIONS

(1) If the State Agency determines that an application for a permit meets the requirements for a permit, the permit shall be issued accompanied by a written statement of such terms and conditions as the Agency determines to be appropriate under this Code or regulations made under this Code.

(2) The State Agency shall provide a written explanation of its grounds for including any particular term or condition in a permit whenever the person to whom a permit is issued requests such explanation in writing.

(3) If the State Agency determines that an application for a permit fails to meet the standards for a permit, the application shall be denied and the application shall be returned to the applicant accompanied by a written statement of Agency's findings regarding the application and the reasons for its denial.

(4) The State Agency shall provide individual written notice of its disposition of each application to any other person who participated in the application proceedings pursuant to this Chapter, along with the grounds for any decision as communicated to the applicant.

Commentary: This section directs how, and to whom, the State Agency is to communicate its actions regarding an application. Subsection (1) requires that the Agency must indicate in writing the terms and conditions of the permit if it determines to issue a permit. If requested to do so by the permit holder, the Agency must provide a written explanation of the reasons for any term or condition to any permit under subsection (2). Subsection (3) further directs that if the Agency denies a permit, the Agency must return the application to the applicant along with a written statement indicating the reasons for the denial. Subsection (4) requires the Agency to communicate the terms and conditions of any permit or notice of the denial of a permit, along with any explanations provided to the permit holder, to any person who participated in the application proceedings.

The return of the application and reasons to the applicant or the issuance of the permit serves as an individual written notice to the applicant of the State Agency's disposition of the application. The requirements of this section will help the applicant or any other interested person to determine how to respond to the Agency's action on an application. An applicant might choose to file a new, amended application, or seek a hearing from the Agency or judicial review of the Agency's decision, or take some other action. Persons who contested the application might also decide to seek judicial review of the Agency's decision or to participate in any ensuing further administrative proceedings on the application. If a person seeks administrative or judicial review, the reasons for the denial as provided with the return of the application or the reasons for the terms or conditions as provided to the permit holder shall be the focus of the ensuing inquiry or the reasons for the denial as indicated in the statement accompanying the denial. For examples of statutes that spell out procedures for an applicant to appeal a decision granting or denying a permit, see Dellapenna, § 9.03(a)(5)(A).

Cross-references: § 1R-1-08 (procedural protections); § 2R-2-15 (person); § 2R-2-23 (State Agency); §§ 5R-1-01 to 5R-3-03 (hearings, disputes, and judicial review); § 6R-2-06 (obligation of the State Agency to act); § 6R-2-08 (opportunity to remedy defects in an application); § 7R-1-01 (permit terms and conditions).

Comparable statutes: FLA. STAT. ANN §§ 373.107; GA. CODE ANN. § 12-5-96(e); IOWA CODE ANN. § 455B.278(2); MD. CODE ANN., NAT. RES. §§ 8-806(d) to (h), (l) to (n), 8-807(a); MASS. GEN. LAWS ANN. ch. 21G, § 11; MINN. STAT. ANN. § 105.45 (notice by publication); MISS. CODE ANN. § 51-3-35; N.Y. ENVTL. CONSERV. LAW § 15-0903(4); S.C. CODE ANN. § 49-5-60(C); VA. CODE ANN. § 62.1-44.100(c), (j); WIS. STAT. ANN. § 144.026(5)(c).

§ 6R-2-08 OPPORTUNITY TO REMEDY DEFECTS IN AN APPLICATION

(1) The State Agency shall provide each applicant whose application has been denied a reasonable opportunity to remedy the defects in the application that caused the denial.

(2) The State Agency shall give individual written notice of any resubmission to persons entitled to notice of the action on the earlier application, and shall provide such persons a reasonable opportunity to comment on or contest the resubmitted application.

(3) The State Agency shall establish by regulation the period of time allowed for resubmission of an application, or for commenting on or contesting the resubmission.

Commentary: This section requires the State Agency to allow an applicant who has been denied a permit to resubmit the application with alterations designed to remedy the causes of the denial. The Agency should respond to a resubmission as a continuation of the earlier application process rather than the initiation of a new application. The advantage of such an approach is largely in terms of the administrative and financial burden as the earlier record compiled on the earlier application will often be sufficient to evaluate the new application except in so far as the modifications in the application might require new information or data. The Agency will also notify all persons entitled to notice under the preceding section of the resubmission, allowing them a reasonable opportunity to comment upon or contest the resubmission. The Agency, which will spell out the details of this process in its regulations, will not need to require the applicant or its own staff to assemble the complete data necessary for evaluating a wholly new application.

Cross-references: § 1R-1-08 (procedural protections); § 2R-2-15 (person); § 2R-2-23 (State Agency); § 4R-1-06 (regulatory authority of the State Agency); §§ 5R-1-01 to 5R-3-03 (hearings, disputes, and judicial review); § 5R-4-09 (citizen suits); § 6R-2-02 (notice and opportunity to be heard); § 6R-2-04 (contesting an application); § 6R-2-05 (public right of comment); § 6R-2-06 (obligation of the State Agency to act); § 6R-2-07 (notice of action on applications).

Comparable statute: VA. CODE ANN. § 62.1-44.100(c).

Part 3
The Basis of a Water Right

This Part sets forth the standards to be used in evaluating a permit application. In particular, this Part specifies the factors relevant to determining whether a particular proposed use is reasonable. Certain limited preferences are provided for use in the permit process, but that are also relevant in times of water shortage or water emergency. Special standards are provided for interbasin transfers, including the power of the State Agency to provide for generalized compensation to the basin of origin for the secondary and tertiary effects of a interbasin diversion.

§ 6R-3-01 STANDARDS FOR A PERMIT

(1) The State Agency shall approve an application and issue a permit only upon determining that:

(a) the proposed use is reasonable;

(b) the proposed withdrawal, in combination with other relevant withdrawals, will not exceed the safe yield of the water source;

(c) **the proposed withdrawal and use are consistent with any applicable comprehensive water allocation plan and drought management strategies;**

(d) **both the applicant's existing water withdrawals and use, if any, and the proposed withdrawal and use incorporate a reasonable plan for conservation; and**

(e) **the proposed withdrawal and use will be consistent with the provisions of this Code and any order, permit term or condition, and regulation made pursuant to this Code or any other statute pertaining to the use of water.**

(2) **In any judicial review of the Agency's determination under subsection (1) of this section, the burden of proof shall be on the person challenging the Agency's determination.**

Commentary: This section of the Regulated Riparian Model Water Code sets forth the standards that govern whether a permit shall be issued. Subsection (1)(a) sets forth the most basic standard, that any proposed use must be reasonable. The definition of a reasonable use requires that the use be efficient and not involve the waste of water, that the use will not unreasonably injure or otherwise burden any other individual water user or class of water user, that the use will not endanger the public health, safety or welfare or otherwise conflict with the public interest, and that the use is consistent with sustainable development. The public interest relative to the waters of the State, other than the immediate protection of public health, safety, and welfare, is found in the policies expressed in this Code. *See generally* Dellapenna, § 9.03(b). For a discussion of how courts have handled the "reasonable use" rule, see TARLOCK, § 3.12[4]; Dellapenna, §§ 7.02(d)-7.03(e). The meaning, or at least the application, of the concept alters somewhat when the decision whether a particular use is reasonable is shifted from a court reviewing the use in the context of a concrete dispute to an administrative agency reviewing the use in the abstract. Dellapenna, § 9.03(b)(1).

The full meaning of the concept of a reasonable use, which is further developed in the next section, perhaps exhausts all relevant standards for the issuance of a permit. This section highlights several other general standards, all of which relate to the reasonableness of a use but none of which are completely subsumed within that basic standard. Subsection (1)(b) indicates the second basic standard, that the withdrawal not exceed the safe yield of the water source. The concept of safe yield under this Code is not a simple mathematical calculation; it depends on a judgment by the State Agency involving the balancing of human needs against the preservation of the long-term social utility of the resource, and includes specifically the prevention of impairment of the biological, chemical, and physical integrity of the water source. The State Agency is not to issue a permit if the authorized withdrawals were to have a significant adverse impact on basic environmental or aesthetic values or seriously undermine the survival of the basics of the ecosystem–except when necessary for human survival. In a State that enacts a fully hydrologic definition of "safe yield" (*i.e.*, "safe yield" equals natural or artificial recharge or runoff), the legislature would want to add a phrase to the end of subsection (1)(b) to read "except to the preserve human life."

Subsection (1)(c) requires the State Agency to determine that all permits will be consistent, when issued, with any applicable comprehensive water allocation plan and any relevant drought management strategies. Subsection (1)(d) adds that, for each permit, the State Agency must approve a plan of conservation both for the proposed withdrawal and use and for any existing withdrawals and use. A plan of conservation is a plan developed by the applicant indicating how he, she, or it proposes to conserve water both during periods of normal precipitation and especially during periods of water shortage and water emergency. Finally, subsection (1)(e) requires the State Agency to find that the applicant will in fact be able to comply with this Code and with the regulations made pursuant to this Code, and most particularly the terms and conditions of the permit. The same applies to any other statute pertaining to the use of water. The latter category will particularly refer to water quality statutes and their regulations and caselaw, for failure to comply with a regulation issued (caselaw) under a statute is a failure to comply with that statute.

The following sections of this Part articulate more specific aspects of these standards. Additional requirements might be imposed under the regulatory authority of the Special Water Management Areas. Even for such additional requirements, however, the permit application will be evaluated by, and the decision of whether to issue or deny the permit will be made by, the State Agency unless the State enacts optional subsection (4) of section 4R-4-06 which confers the permit issuing authority on the Special Water Management Area.

Subsection (2) places the burden of proof on any person challenging the Agency's determinations under this section in a court of law. This provision expresses the usual presumption of validity accorded to administrative decisions based upon the realization that administrative bodies have a degree of expertise that courts usually will not have. The standard of proof is provided by the general law of the state. This provision could also refer to such statutes from other States or the federal government.

Cross-references: §§ 1R-1-01 to 1R-1-15 (declarations of policy); § 2R-1-01 (the obligation to make only reasonable use of water); § 2R-1-03 (no unreasonable injury to other water rights); § 2R-1-04 (protection of property rights); § 2R-2-02 (biological integrity); § 2R-2-03 (chemical integrity); § 2R-2-04 (comprehensive water allocation plan); § 2R-2-05 (conservation measures); § 2R-2-06 (consumptive use); § 2R-2-07 (cost); § 2R-2-09 (drought management strategies); § 2R-2-11 (modification of a water right); § 2R-2-13 (nonconsumptive use); § 2R-2-14 (permit); § 2R-2-16 (physical integrity); § 2R-2-17 (plan for conservation); § 2R-2-20 (reasonable use); § 2R-2-21 (safe yield); § 2R-2-22 (Special Water Management Area); § 2R-2-23 (State Agency); § 2R-2-24 (sustainable development); § 2R-2-26 (unreasonable injury); § 2R-2-27 (waste of water); § 2R-2-29 (water emergency); § 2R-2-30 (water right); § 2R-2-31 (water shortage); § 2R-2-32 (waters of the State); § 2R-2-33 (water source); § 2R-2-34 (withdraw or withdrawal); §§ 3R-1-01 to 3R-2-05 (waters subject to allocation); § 4R-1-06 (regulatory authority of the State Agency); §§ 4R-2-01 to 4R-2-04 (planning responsibilities); § 4R-3-04 (combined permits); § 4R-4-06 (regulatory authority of the Special Water Management Areas); §§ 6R-1-01 to 6R-1-05 (the requirement of a permit); § 6R-1-06 (registration of withdrawals not subject to permits); § 6R-3-02 (determining whether a use is reasonable); § 6R-3-03 (aggregation of multiple withdrawals); § 6R-3-04 (preferences among water rights); § 6R-3-05 (prior investment in withdrawal or use facilities); §§ 6R-4-01 to § 6R-4-05 (coordination of water allocation and water quality regulation); § 7R-1-01 (permit terms and conditions); § 7R-2-01 (approval required for modification of permits).

Comparable statutes: ALA. CODE § 9-10B-22(b); CONN. GEN. STAT. ANN. § 22a-373(b); FLA. STAT. ANN. §§ 373.223(1), 373.233; GA. CODE ANN. §§ 12-5-31(h), 12-5-6(h); HAW. REV. STAT. §§ 174C-49(a), (b), (e), 174C-54; IOWA CODE ANN. § 455B.265(1); KY. REV. STAT. ANN. § 151.170(2); MASS. GEN. LAWS ANN. ch. 21G, § 7; MINN. STAT. ANN. §§ 105.416 (irrigation from underground water), 105.417 ("appropriation" from surface water), 105.45 (all applications); MISS. CODE ANN. §§ 51-3-13, 51-3-15(2)(e); N.Y. ENVTL. CONSERV. LAW §§ 15-503(2), 15-1503(2); N.C. GEN. STAT. § 143-215.15(b), (c), (h); VA. CODE ANN. § 62.1-248; WIS. STAT. ANN. §§ 30.18(5), 144.026(5)(d).

§ 6R-3-02 DETERMINING WHETHER A USE IS REASONABLE

In determining whether a use is reasonable, the State Agency shall consider:

(a) the number of persons using a water source and the object, extent, and necessity of the proposed withdrawal and use and of other existing or planned withdrawals and uses of water;

(b) the supply potential of the water source in question, considering quantity, quality, and reliability, including the safe yields of all hydrologically interconnected water sources;

(c) the economic and social importance of the proposed water use and other existing or planned water uses sharing the water source;

(d) the probable severity and duration of any injury caused or expected to be caused to other lawful consumptive and

nonconsumptive uses of water by the proposed withdrawal and use under foreseeable conditions;

(e) the probable effects of the proposed withdrawal and use on the public interest in the waters of the State, including, but not limited to:

(1) general environmental, ecological, and aesthetic effects;

(2) sustainable development;

(3) domestic and municipal uses;

(4) recharge areas for underground water;

(5) waste assimilation capacity;

(6) other aspects of water quality; and

(7) wetlands and flood plains;

(f) whether the proposed use is planned in a fashion that will avoid or minimize the waste of water;

(g) any impacts on interstate or interbasin water uses;

(h) the scheduled date the proposed withdrawal and use of water is to begin and whether the projected time between the issuing of the permit and the expected initiation of the withdrawal will unreasonably preclude other possible uses of the water; and

(i) any other relevant factors.

Commentary: This section describes the factors that shall inform any decision by the State Agency regarding whether a proposed use is reasonable. Given the dual nature of the standard of reasonable use, the factors to be considered include both abstract questions of the social utility or value of the proposed use and also relational questions of the relative value of the proposed use compared to other existing or planned uses. This section also indicates that the question of reasonableness requires the Agency to consider impacts on users dependent on other hydrologically interconnected water sources, and on users in other water basins and in other States.

The abstract question of reasonableness requires examination of the proposed use for its consistency with sustainable development and other aspects of the public interest. This in turn will call into question the consistency of a proposed use with the comprehensive water plan and the drought management strategies already developed by the Agency. Even assuming a perfect fit with these standards, however, does not end the inquiry. The Agency must still consider the effect on other water users, in other words, the relation of the proposed use to other existing and planned uses.

The relational question does not rest on a presumption that existing uses are necessarily reasonable, particularly given the role accorded to more abstract questions of social utility in this calculus. For example, an application for a permit to drill a deep, high-pump-pressure well that threatens to (or does) cause shallow existing wells to go dry could still be determined to be a reasonable use if the Agency were to find that the existing wells were unreasonably shallow. Such a finding could arise when the Agency determines that protecting shallow existing wells would improperly preclude rational development of the water source to the detriment of the entire community. Balancing efficient use with prior investment is central to determining what is "reasonable." This balancing process is constrained by the existence of earlier permits. A permit is an assurance of substantial legal and administrative protection of a use for the of the permit. If the earlier wells had already received permits, the Agency's decision to award the new permit stands on a different footing. The Agency can not simply authorize interference with existing wells prior to the expiration of their permits. *See* section 6R-3-01(e). The Agency could authorize interference only if it were to undertake a dispute resolution process that could result in ordering the new applicant to compensate (in funds, in water, or otherwise) the affected existing water right holders for the remaining duration of their water rights. *See* sections 5R-2-01 to 5R-2-03. In the alternative, the person seeking to make a new use might purchase existing permits and apply for Agency approval of any necessary modification of the permits purchased. *See* sections 7R-2-01 to 7R-2-04.

Some will see the foregoing analysis as a step in the direction of appropriative rights rather than a perpetuation of the riparian approach to water management. This is not so, both because the permits will expire periodically and because of the possibility of water shortages or water emergencies. Upon expiration of a permit, the Agency can deny renewal of a permit for an existing use if it is unreasonable in light of conditions at the time of the renewal. Section 6R-3-04. While nonrenewal is not likely for an existing use that has real value to the users and to society, particularly for domestic wells, the permits can also be renewed on different terms and conditions than was formerly the case. Section 7R-1-01. If the domestic wells subject to permits are unreasonably shallow, the Agency undoubtedly will renew the permits on condition that the owners drill down to a reasonable depth.

Droughts will provide another occasion when the reasonableness principle will come into play. Existing permits can be restricted during water shortages and water emergencies. If there is a water shortage or water emergency, the Agency will restrict wells (or other withdrawals) more severely according to the reasonableness of the use. This last possibility arises even for wells or other withdrawals for which no permit is required. See section 7R-3-05. Shallow wells for domestic purposes might be protected to some extent given the priority given to the preservation of human life, yet those shallow wells will be most vulnerable to the effects of drought. The Agency will have to balance these concerns in order to manage the effects of drought reasonably. The Agency might, for example, authorize a competing deep, high pressure well to continue operating but require its owners to provide substitute water for domestic purposes to owners of shallow wells that go dry from the combined effects of the drought and the continued pumping from the deeper well. Other solutions might be found. Whatever the solution, it will be based upon reasonableness rather than upon temporal priority.

The list of factors to be considered in determining reasonableness is long, and involves features that relate to both the abstract and the relational aspects. The analysis rewards applications for permits that seek to minimize adverse impacts on other private and public values. No precise formula for combining these several factors can be devised, leaving considerable discretion in the Agency to weigh and balance these factors to determine whether a particular proposed use is reasonable. RICE & WHITE, at 27; SAX, ABRAMS, & THOMPSON, at 164-71;

TARLOCK, § 5.16; Dellapenna, § 9.03(b). *See also* Robert Abrams, *Water Allocation By Comprehensive Permit Systems in the Eastern United States: Considering a Move Away From Orthodoxy*, 9 VA. ENVTL. L.J. 255, 257 (1990); Barry Boyer, *Alternative to Administrative Trial-Type Hearings for Resolving Complex Scientific, Economic, and Special Issues*, 71 MICH. L. REV. 111 (1972). Additional requirements relating to the determination of whether a use is reasonable might be further refined in regulations adopted by Special Water Management Areas.

Cross-references: §§ 1R-1-01 to 1R-1-15 (declarations of policy); § 2R-1-01 (the obligation to make only reasonable use of water); § 2R-1-02 (no prohibition of use based on location of use); § 2R-1-03 (no unreasonable injury to other water rights); § 2R-1-04 (protection of property rights); § 2R-1-02 (biological integrity); § 2R-2-03 (chemical integrity); § 2R-2-04 (comprehensive water allocation plan); § 2R-2-06 (consumptive use); § 2R-2-07 (cost); § 2R-2-08 (domestic uses); § 2R-2-09 (drought management strategies); § 2R-2-11 (modification of a water right); § 2R-2-12 (municipal uses); § 2R-2-13 (nonconsumptive use); § 2R-2-14 (permit); § 2R-2-16 (physical integrity); § 2R-2-17 (plan for conservation); § 2R-2-18 (the public interest); § 2R-2-20 (reasonable use); § 2R-2-21 (safe yield); § 2R-2-22 (Special Water Management Area); § 2R-2-23 (State Agency); § 2R-2-24 (sustainable development); § 2R-2-26 (unreasonable injury); § 2R-2-27 (waste of water); § 2R-2-29 (water emergency); § 2R-2-30 (water right); § 2R-2-31 (water shortage) § 2R-2-32 (waters of the State); § 2R-2-33 (water source); § 2R-2-34 (withdrawal or to withdraw); §§ 3R-1-01 to 3R-2-05 (waters subject to allocation); § 4R-1-06 (regulatory authority of the State Agency); §§ 4R-2-01 to 4R-2-04 (planning responsibilities); § 4R-3-04 (combined permits); § 4R-4-05 (regulatory authority of Special Water Management Areas); §§ 5R-2-01 to 5R-2-03 (dispute resolution); §§ 6R-1-01 to 6R-1-05 (the requirement of a permit); § 6R-1-06 (registration of uses not subject to permits); § 6R-3-01 (standards for a permit); § 6R-3-03 (aggregation of multiple withdrawals); § 6R-3-04 (preferences among water rights); § 6R-3-05 (prior investment in withdrawal or use facilities); §§ 6R-4-01 to § 6R-4-05 (coordination of water allocation and water quality regulation); § 7R-1-01 (permit terms and conditions); §§ 7R-2-01 to 7R-2-04 (modification of water rights); §§ 7R-3-01 to 7R-3-07 (restrictions during water shortages or water emergencies).

Comparable statutes: GA. CODE ANN. §§ 12-5-31(e) to (g), 12-5-96(d); IOWA CODE ANN. § 455B.267.

§ 6R-3-03 AGGREGATION OF MULTIPLE WITHDRAWALS

In calculating the total amount of an existing or proposed withdrawal pursuant to a permit issued under this Code, or as qualifying for an exemption from the permit requirement of this Code, the State Agency shall include all separate withdrawals by a single person for a single use or for related uses.

Commentary: Often water right holders will apply for a succession of permits to secure increasing allocations of water for a particular use or a related set of uses. This can come about either because of expansion of the original planned operation, or because the State Agency chose initially to issue a permit for less than the applicant sought, or for other reasons. In such cases, the Agency is directed to aggregate all withdrawals for the particular use or related set of uses in determining whether the entire use is reasonable and in determining whether to issue the permit for any increased withdrawal. The aggregation requirement also applies to determining whether a withdrawal is small enough to be exempt from the permit requirement.

Cross-references: § 2R-2-15 (person); § 2R-2-33 (water source); § 2R-2-34 (withdrawal or to withdraw).

Comparable statute: WIS. STAT. ANN. § 144.026(2).

§ 6R-3-04 PREFERENCES AMONG WATER RIGHTS

(1) When the waters available from a particular water source are insufficient to satisfy all lawful demands upon that water source, water is to be allocated by permits up to the safe yield or other applicable limit of allocation of the resource according to the following preferences:

(a) direct human consumption or sanitation in so far as necessary for human survival and health;

(b) uses necessary for the survival or health of livestock and to preserve crops or physical plant and equipment from physical damage or loss in so far as it is reasonable to continue such activities in relation to particular water sources; and

(c) other uses in such a manner as to maximize employment and economic benefits within the overall goal of sustainable development as set forth in the comprehensive water plan.

(2) In processing applications for withdrawals from water sources within the scope of subsection (1) of this section, the State Agency may determine whether applications are competing by aggregating the applications by periods of time, not to exceed one year, the periods to be set by regulation.

(3) Within each preference category, uses are to be preferred that maximize the reasonable use of water.

(4) Applications to renew a permit issued under this Code shall be evaluated by the same criteria applicable to an original application, except that renewals shall be favored over competing applications

for new withdrawals if the public interest is served equally by the competing water uses after giving consideration to the prior investment pursuant to a valid water right in related facilities as a factor in determining the public interest.

Commentary: This section establishes general priorities for the issuance of permits among competing applicants in watershort areas. These same priorities are also relevant to coping with water shortages or water emergencies. *See* sections 7R-3-01(3), 7R-3-05(2). Some existing regulated riparian statutes provide for detailed and specific schemes of preferences, such as for agriculture or industry, and so on. *See* Dellapenna, § 9.05(d). This section eschews any attempt at such specific preferences as they generally reflect political clout rather than rational water management and are often not enforced in practice anyway. The criteria in this section are not to be applied in a rigidly mechanical fashion, but require consideration of the characteristics of the water source, the possibilities of alternative sources, and the interplay of various existing or proposed uses on those characteristics.

The preferences set forth in this section serve three extremely limited purposes. One is to direct the Agency in selecting among competing applications, including applications to renew a permit. The second is to guide the Agency in reviewing applications to modify a water right. The third is to guide the development and application of drought management strategies during periods of water shortage or water emergency. This section does not override general environmental and aesthetic values governed by Part 2 of Chapter III. That part provides that minimum flows and levels can be allocated only during water emergencies and only for certain limited purposes. Those minimum flows and levels will serve to protect most nonconsumptive uses, uses that are not provided a priority in this section.

The criteria reflect the social utility of the proposed uses. A separate preference is given for applications for renewal permits that favors renewal whenever the public interest would be equally served by either renewing a prior permit or by issuing a new permit to a competing use. This applies to the renewal of a permit for a withdrawal existing on or before the effective date of the Regulated Riparian Model Water Code every bit as much as it applies to a permit for a withdrawal begun after the effective date of this Code. In determining whether the public interest would be equally served, the State Agency is to consider prior investments only if made pursuant to a valid water right. Consideration of investments made in anticipation of a permit not yet issued is barred by the next section. *See* Dellapenna, §§ 9.02(b), 9.03(a)(3). This limited preference will serve as well to reinforce the view that existing withdrawals are not taken when they are required to obtain a permit, but merely that they are being subjected to reasonable regulation. See the commentary to section 6R-1-02.

Many existing regulated riparian statutes contain other preferences than those provided here. Some focus on the nature of the use, some on the quantity of use, and some on a combination of such factors. The one universal preference, found even in most appropriative rights States, is a priority for the water necessary for simple human survival. The word "necessary" indicates that inessential uses and waste alike are not to be preferred over other priorities provided in this section. This preference will generally relate to domestic and municipal uses or public water supply systems.

While the second preference is not so universal, it arises from almost the same concerns–life itself must take preference over at least temporary interruptions in jobs and economic activity. The subsection not only protects livestock and crops in the ground from death or injury, however; it also protects businesses from actual physical damage to plant and equipment from lack of water, a rather more unusual situation than the loss of livestock or crops would be. Subsection (1)(b) expressly recognizes that any of these activities might have to be phased out if shortages are chronic and the activities have, as a consequence, become uneconomic. This is made clear both by having the preference extend only to livestock, crops, plant, and equipment already existing, and by the qualifying clause at the end of the subsection. Thus this subsection will find its greatest relevance during water shortages and water emergencies.

Finally, the section provides that in watershort areas, the Agency should seek to maximize employment and economic activity in a sustainable manner. These several preferences, particularly the last preference for maximizing employment and economic activity, will be worked out in the comprehensive water plan developed by the Agency and updated every five years.

Cross-references: §§ 1R-1-01 to 1R-1-15 (declarations of policy); § 2R-1-01 (the obligation to make only reasonable use); § 2R-2-02 (no prohibition of use based on location of use); § 2R-1-03 (no unreasonable injury to other water rights); § 2R-1-04 (protection of property rights); § 2R-2-02 (biological integrity); § 2R-2-03 (chemical integrity); § 2R-2-04 (comprehensive water allocation plan); § 2R-2-06 (consumptive use); § 2R-2-08 (domestic use); § 2R-2-09 (drought management strategies); § 2R-2-12 (municipal uses); § 2R-2-13 (nonconsumptive use); § 2R-2-14 (permit); § 2R-2-16 (physical integrity); § 2R-2-18 (the public interest); § 2R-2-19 (public water supply system); § 2R-2-20 (reasonable use); § 2R-2-21 (safe yield); § 2R-2-23 (State Agency); § 2R-2-24 (sustainable development); § 2R-2-26 (unreasonable injury); § 2R-2-27 (waste of water); § 2R-2-29 (water emergency); § 2R-2-30 (water right); § 2R-2-31 (water shortage); § 2R-2-33 (water source); § 2R-2-34 (withdrawal or to withdraw); §§ 3R-1-01 to 3R-2-05 (waters subject to allocation); §§ 4R-2-01 to 4R-2-04 (planning responsibilities); §§ 6R-1-01 to 6R-1-06 (the requirement of a permit); § 6R-3-01 (standards for a permit); § 6R-3-02 (determining whether a use is reasonable); § 6R-3-05 (prior investment in proposed water withdrawal or use facilities); § 6R-3-06 (special standard for interbasin transfers); §§ 7R-2-01 to 7R-2-04 (modification of water rights); §§ 7R-3-01 to 7R-3-07 (restrictions during water shortages and water emergencies).

Comparable statutes: FLA. STAT. ANN. § 373.233(2) (preference for renewal of permits), GA. CODE ANN. § 12-5-31(f) (preference for renewal of permits); IOWA CODE ANN. § 455B.266 (detailed scheme of priorities for water emergencies); MD. CODE ANN., NAT. RES. § 8-802(d); MINN. STAT. ANN. § 105.41(1a); N.Y. ENVTL. CONSERV. LAW § 15-0105(5) (preference for domestic and municipal uses); VA. CODE ANN. § 62.1-248(D) (preference for domestic use).

§ 6R-3-05 PRIOR INVESTMENT IN PROPOSED WATER WITHDRAWAL OR USE FACILITIES

(1) The fact that an applicant has acquired, through the power of eminent domain or otherwise, any land for the specific purpose of serving as the site for proposed facilities to withdraw or use water or has

undertaken construction on such facilities, prior to the obtaining of a permit from the State Agency, is not admissible in any administrative or judicial proceeding relating to the application or permit and shall have no bearing on decisions relating to the application or permit.

(2) Prior acquisition of land or prior commencement of construction is a voluntary risk assumed by the applicant and no compensation is due for any loss in the value of the land or of the investment in facilities should a permit be denied or issued subject to terms and conditions less favorable than those sought in the application.

Commentary: On occasion an applicant attempts to bolster an application by beginning investment in the proposed project before the permit is issued, or perhaps even before the application has been received by the State Agency. This section indicates that any such investment shall not create an equity in favor of approval of the application or the issuance of a permit by barring the admission of evidence of any such investment and by barring compensation for any loss on the purchase of land acquired or for other expenses incurred in commencing construction prior to the denial of a permit or the issuance of a permit on terms or conditions less favorable than those sought by the applicant.

Cross-references: § 4R-3-05 (limitation on the power of eminent domain); § 6R-3-01 (standards for permits); § 6R-3-02 (determining whether a use is reasonable).

Comparable statutes: FLA. STAT. ANN. § 373.2235.

§ 6R-3-06 SPECIAL STANDARD FOR INTERBASIN TRANSFERS

(1) In determining whether to issue a permit for an interbasin transfer of water, the State Agency shall give particular weight to any

foreseeable adverse impacts that would impair the sustainable development of the water basin of origin.

(2) In addition to the factors set forth in sections 6R-3-01 to 6R-3-05 of this Code, in determining whether an interbasin transfer is reasonable the State Agency shall consider:

(a) the supply of water available to users in the basin of origin and available to the applicant within the basin in which the water is proposed to be used;

(b) the overall water demand in this basin of origin and in the basin in which the water is proposed to be used; and

(c) the probable impact of the proposed transportation and use of water out of the basin of origin on existing or foreseeable shortages in the basin of origin and in the basin in which the water is proposed to be used.

(3) When authorizing an interbasin transfer notwithstanding probable impairment to the existing or future uses of water in the basin of origin, the State Agency shall assess a compensation fee to be paid into the Interbasin Compensation Fund by the person granted a permit for the interbasin transfer in so far as is necessary to compensate the basin of origin for generalized losses not attributable to injuries to particular holders of water rights in the basin of origin.

Commentary: Large transfers of water from one water basin to another have become common. Often these transfers involve the transfer of water from a rural to an urban area. Rural areas fear the erosion of their tax base, the economic health of the community, and the possibility of general social disruption that might arise from an interbasin transfer that, in extreme cases, could cause land to be taken out of production or could prevent future investment in the region. Any of the foregoing impacts could also produce severe secondary economic impacts that would cripple the remaining farmers, affect businesses relying on customers formerly employed in activities directly precluded by the interbasin transfer, and even adversely affect fish, wildlife, and in-place uses. In such cases, one can question the wisdom of ravaging a small rural community in order to provide water to an expanding city. *See generally* SAX, ABRAMS, & THOMPSON, at 262-270; TARLOCK, § 10.04(2)(c); TARLOCK, CORBRIDGE, & GETCHES, at 837-39; TRELEASE & A. GOULD, at 78-80; Owen L. Anderson, *Reallocation,* in 2 WATER AND WATER RIGHTS § 16.02(c)(2); Dellapenna, § 7.05(c)(2). Protection for the water basin of origin is now a well-established part of the law of many States, particularly in the western States. *See, e.g.,* ARIZ. REV. STAT. ANN. § 45-172; CAL. WATER CODE § 1215, 10505, 10505.5; TEX. WATER CODE ANN. § 16.052.

Historically, such problematic transfers were theoretically prohibited under common-law riparian rights under the operation of rules limiting the use of water to riparian lands and to lands within the watershed of origin. *See* Dellapenna, § 7.02(a). Such common-law prohibitions have been codified in a number of States. *See, e.g.,* ME. REV. STAT. ANN. § 2660-A(1). These prohibitions have even carried over to some regulated riparian statutes despite the common purpose of those statutes of enabling non-riparian and non-watershed uses. *See, e.g.,* IND. STAT. ANN. § 13-2-1-9 (applicable to the Great Lakes watershed only); N.J. STAT. ANN. § 58:1A-7.1 (applicable to the Pine Lands National Reserve); N.Y. ENVTL. CONSERV. CODE § 15-1506 (applicable to the Great Lakes watershed only); WIS. STAT. ANN. §§ 30.18 (applicable to designated trout streams), 144.026(5)(d)(7) (applicable to the Great Lakes watershed only).

Some States that still essentially follow common-law riparian rights have enacted statutes to authorize and regulate interbasin transfers. South Carolina is perhaps the most prominent example, requiring a permit for interbasin transfers having a maximum capacity of either 5% of the seven-day, ten-year low flow of the water source or 1,000,000 gallons/day if begun after December 1, 1984. S.C. CODE ANN. §§ 49-21-20, 49-21-20(a)(2). *See also* OHIO REV. CODE § 1501.32(A) (requiring permits for the diversion of more than 100,000 gallons/day from either Lake Erie or the Ohio River for use outside the watershed of origin).

In this section, the Regulated Riparian Model Water Code recognizes the special claims that a water basin of origin can legitimately raise when an applicant proposes to transfer water out of its basin of origin for use in another basin. Under this section, the State Agency is charged to examine particularly the probable effects of a proposed interbasin transfer on current or anticipated uses of water in the basin of origin and on the subsequent development of economic and other values of the water basin of origin. On the other hand, the State Agency is to consider only actual impacts, present or foreseeable, and not vague concerns about hypothetical uses in the remote future. And this special attention to the concerns of the basin of origin is not to preclude altogether the transfer of water out of the basin, but simply special solicitude for the needs of the basin of origin in determining whether a proposed out-of-basin use is reasonable.

Subsection (3) provides for compensation to the basin of origin when interbasin transfers are approved to be paid into the Interbasin Compensation Fund. The Fund is to be used to provide benefits for the particular water basin of origin for the transfer of water out of the water basin. This Fund is not a substitute for, nor even related to, payments that a person might make to a water right holder as part of a contractual modification of a water right; rather, the Fund derives from payments intended to compensate the public generally in the basin of origin for the loss of opportunities and other costs arising from the transfer of water out of the water basin. The existence of this Fund does not preclude the State Agency from requiring compensation "in water" for the basin of origin rather than compensation in money. The State Agency is given considerable discretion in administering this Fund.

If the State opts to have Special Water Management Areas as the primary agency for issuing water use permits, there will still need to be a statewide mechanism for assessing interbasin transfers or other transfers that will affect more than one Area. The result could be a simplified version of this Part centering on this section as the operative basis of a statewide permitting authority sitting over a locally administered primary permitting authority. Chapter VIII provides an entire regime for the consideration and evaluation of proposals to transfer water across state and national boundaries that could serve as an alternative model for dealing with withdrawals and uses of water that affect more than one Area.

Cross-references: § 1R-1-12 (recognizing local interests in the waters of the State); § 1R-1-14 (regulating interbasin transfers); § 2R-1-02 (no prohibition of use based on location of use); § 2R-

2-10 (interbasin transfers); § 2R-2-28 (water basin); § 7R-1-01(k) (permit terms or conditions involving making an interbasin transfer to include compensation to the water basin of origin); §§ 8R-1-01 to 8R-1-06 (multijurisdictional transfers).

Comparable statutes: ALA. CODE § 9-10B-25; CONN. GEN. STAT. ANN. §§ 22a-369(10), 22a-372(g); FLA. STAT. ANN. § 373.2295; GA. CODE ANN. § 12-5-31(n); KY. REV. STAT. ANN. 151.200(2); MINN. STAT. ANN. § 105.417(3); S.C. CODE ANN. §§ 49-21-10 to 49-21-80; WIS. STAT. ANN. § 144.026(d)(7).

Part 4

Coordination of Water Allocation and Water Quality Regulation

This Part is drafted on the basis that the responsibility for the allocation of water under the Code is vested in a different agency from the agency responsible for the achieving and maintenance of the prescribed water quality standards. This section spells out the essential procedures that the State Agency is to follow in coordinating its allocation decisions with the achievement and maintenance of water quality standards applicable by law within the State. The process is broken into a number of discrete stages, each of which is described in a particular section. Should the State vest both responsibilities in a single State Agency, the provisions and commentary of this Part would have to be rephrased to accommodate simplified procedures that could result from such a merger of responsibilities, but substantively the provisions of this Part would need little, if any, change.

For regulated riparian States that now vest authority over water allocation and water quality in a single agency, see: CONN. GEN. STAT ANN. §§ 22a-424, 22a-366; DEL. CODE ANN. tit. 7, § 6003(a); FLA. STAT. ANN. §§ 373.223, 403.087; GA. CODE ANN. §§ 12-5-21, 12-5-31; IOWA CODE ANN. §§ 455B.172, 455B.264; KY. REV. STAT. §§ 151.040, 224.10-100(19)(a); MD. CODE ANN., NAT. RES. §§ 4-401 to 4-405, 8-101(g); MINN. STAT. ANN. § 105.39; MISS. CODE ANN. §§ 49-2-7, 49-17-28, 51-3-15; N.J. STAT. ANN. §§ 58:1A-6(a)(1), 58:10A-6; N.C. GEN. STAT. §§ 143-215.15, 143B-282; WIS. STAT. ANN. §§ 92.05, 144.025, 144.026.

Apparently no purely appropriative rights State so fully integrates issues of water allocation and water quality, although several States that have dual systems recognizing both appropriative and riparian rights have done so. *See* CAL. WATER CODE § 1610; S.D. CODIFIED LAWS §§ 34A-2-36, 46-1-1 to 46-1-9; TEX. WATER CODE ANN. §§ 11.135, 26.011; WASH. REV. CODE §§ 43,21A.020, 90.03.250.

§ 6R-4-01 PROTECTING AND PRESERVING WATER QUALITY STANDARDS

(1) The State Agency shall allocate or approve transfers of the waters of the State in such a manner as to protect and preserve the quality of those waters.

(2) The State Agency shall not allocate water to a water right for any use that appears likely to result in a violation of the water quality standards designated by the State without consulting with [*the State's water quality agency*].

(3) If [*the State's water quality agency*] objects to a proposed allocation of water to a water right, the [*State's water quality agency*] may appeal the State Agency's decision to [*the normal mechanism under State law for resolving conflicts between the resolution of inter-agency disputes*].

Commentary: This section provides the basis for coordinating water allocation and water quality pursuant to the strong policy favoring such coordination established in the Regulated Riparian Model Water Code. The Code takes the position that allocation decisions remain the responsibility of the State Agency as defined in this Code even when those decisions impact on the achievement of the prescribed water quality standards. The Agency is required to coordinate its processes with the agency responsible for those water quality standards and even to issue a single, joint permit if that would improve the operation of both sets of regulatory need. The other agency can have recourse to whatever is the normal administrative process of the State for resolving disputes between different agencies. The reasons for this structure are set forth at length in the commentary to the policy on coordinating water allocation and water quality regulation.

Cross-references: § 1R-1-01 (protecting the public interest in the waters of the State); § 1R-1-03 (conformity to physical laws); § 1R-1-09 (coordination of water allocation and water quality regulation); § 2R-2-06 (consumptive use); § 2R-2-13 (nonconsumptive use); § 2R-2-14 (permit); § 2R-2-15 (person); § 2R-2-18 (the public interest); § 2R-2-23 (State Agency); § 2R-2-24 (sustainable development); § 2R-2-30 (water right); § 2R-2-32 (waters of the State); § 2R-2-33 (water source); §§ 3R-2-01 to 3R-2-05 (protection of minimum flows or levels); § 4R-1-05 (application of general laws to meetings, procedures, and records); §§ 4R-3-01 to 4R-3-05 (coordination with other branches or levels of government); §§ 6R-1-01 to 6R-1-05 (the requirement of a permit).

Comparable statutes: HAW. REV. STAT. §§ 174C-32, 174C-66 to 68; VA. CODE ANN. § 62.1-44.89.

§ 6R-4-02 DATA TO BE PROVIDED BY *[THE STATE'S WATER QUALITY AGENCY]* TO THE STATE AGENCY

The State Agency shall include in the statewide data system the following data, to be provided by the *[the State's water quality agency)*, using that data, when relevant, in considering the allocation of water under this Part:

(a) the ambient water quality standards and effluent discharge standards for all waters of the State;

(b) the number and effluent discharge data for all point sources for which the *[the State's water quality agency]* has issued a National Pollutant Discharge Elimination System permit;

(c) all information and data on any nonpoint source of return flow as may be available to the *[the State's water quality agency]*; and

(d) changes in ambient water quality standards or effluent discharge standards for any segment of any water source in the State.

Commentary: This section requires the State Agency to gather certain data from the agency responsible for regulating water quality and to include that data in the statewide data system required by this Regulated Riparian Model Water Code. With this information available and up-to-date in the data system, the State Agency will be in the best possible position to appraise the probable quality impacts required to be considered for any withdrawal for a consumptive use. The State's agency responsible for water quality is under a duty to cooperate with the State Agency, and thus is under a legal duty to provide the information indicated by this subsection. That duty is restated in this section to emphasize its existence and to remove any grounds for disputing the point. The duty is expressed in the broadest possible terms given the goals for the Statewide Data System. As with other data included in the System, confidential business information will generally be protected from disclosure.

The duty of mutual cooperation is a legal duty. While in some States, that will imply one unit of state government suing another for failure to cooperate, in many States there will be an administrative mechanism for resolving such problems. In a State with such an administrative mechanism, the Code expects that mechanism to be used to resolve disputes about what information is to be provided under this section. In a State that assigns both the allocation and the quality maintenance function to a single agency, this section can be omitted as the State Agency will, presumably, have already included that information in its statewide data system and there will be no need to express a legal duty on another agency to provide the information.

The terms used in this section are taken from the federal Clean Water Act. 33 U.S.C. §§ 1251-1387. These terms include "ambient water quality standards," "effluent discharge standards," "National Pollutant Discharge Elimination System permit," "nonpoint sources," and "point sources." Most or all of these terms will also be addressed in the laws of the State relating to water quality.

Cross-references: § 1R-1-09 (coordination of water allocation and water quality regulations); § 2R-2-32 (waters of the State); § 2R-2-33 (water source); § 4R-2-03 (statewide data system); § 4R-1-09 (protection of confidential business information); § 4R-3-02 (cooperation with other units of State and local government); § 4R-3-03 (the duty of other units of government in this State to cooperate with the State Agency).

§ 6R-4-03 EVALUATING ALLOCATIONS FOR THEIR POTENTIAL EFFECT ON WATER QUALITY

(1) The State Agency shall establish and implement standards and procedures that include coordination with the *[the State's water quality agency]* for the issuance of permits for water rights:

(a) when a withdrawal may affect the volume of flow for waters receiving effluent discharges;

(b) when allocating water to a use that will result in a return flow, whether as a point source or a nonpoint source, that appears likely to contain any category of pollutant regulated by federal legislation or regulations, or in *[the State's water quality code or statute]* and the regulations adopted by *[the State's water quality agency]*;

(c) when the withdrawal of underground water will create a zone of depression threatening intrusion by saline waters, hazardous waste, or other pollutants; or

(d) when artificial recharge of underground water appears likely to create a risk of the introduction into the water source of any category of pollutant regulated by federal legislation or regulations, or in *[the State's water quality code or statute]* and the regulations adopted by *[the State's water quality agency]*.

(2) To determine the impact of an allocation of water to a consumptive use on water quality, the State Agency shall consider the following:

(a) the nature, size, and safe yield of the water source;

(b) the biological and chemical effects of any degradation of the quality of the water source resulting from the proposed allocation, by itself or in combination with other existing, permitted, or planned uses, and adversely affecting the water's availability or fitness for other uses;

(c) injury to the public health, safety, or welfare, or to environmental quality and integrity that would result if any expected degradation of water quality were not prevented or abated;

(d) the necessity for the withdrawal and the costs to the applicant for a permit or approval of meeting the needs through other means;

(e) the extent of adverse quality effects on other uses and the extent of remedial costs necessary to mitigate those effects;

(f) the effect on the waste assimilative capacity of a water source as determined according to subsection (3) of this section; and

(g) any other impact on the public interest and sustainable development.

(3) In order to assure that the State's water quality standards are achieved and maintained, the State Agency shall, in determining whether a proposed or existing water withdrawal or use is reasonable, determine the effect of an allocation of water on the capacity of the water source to assimilate effluent from point and nonpoint sources, balancing the cost of additional pollution control on the pollutant source against the cost of losses imposed on other actual or potential users of water as a result of the impact of the proposed effect on the water source's waste assimilation capacity.

Commentary: This section prescribes the procedures and standards the State Agency is to apply to evaluate allocations for their potential effects on water quality. That will, in the course of things, include virtually every allocation. The section requires the State Agency to create the necessary procedures and provides for the minimum substantive content for those procedures to consider. For a definition of water quality in this context, see MALONEY, AUSNESS, & MORRIS, at 45, 248. To consider such effects is merely to carry through on the policy of the Regulated Riparian Model Water Code to conform governmental decisions to the physical laws relating to water resources. Coordination of the two functions of water allocation and the regulation of water quality is essential to ensure that every potential point source discharger be identified at the earliest possible time, and that other activities affecting water quality begin to come under effective regulatory review. This is not done through the creation of yet another environmental impact statement requirement, but rather as a normal part of the determination of whether a proposed or actual withdrawal and use of water is reasonable. No person should receive a permit to withdraw water from the waters of the State without assessment of the quality impacts of the proposed activity.

Subsection (1) sets out the general requirement to consider water quality in appraising applications for a permit to withdraw water or to approve a transfer of an existing withdrawal of water. Normally, the permits for point source discharges are obtained through the National Pollutant Discharge Elimination System under the federal Environmental Protection Agency or the State agency responsible for water quality. Clean Water Act, 33 U.S.C. § 1342. Nonpoint sources, such as much drainage from agricultural activities or surface mining, also potentially degrade the waters of the State, although such uses are not subject to the National Pollutant Discharge Elimination System permit requirement. *See* TARLOCK, § 5.19[4][5]. Before allocating water to either sort of consumptive use, the State Agency must consider the effect of the proposed allocation on the general waste assimilative capacity of the water source and the extent to which any return flow from the use is likely to increase the pollutant load of the water source. The section also calls attention to the problem of excessive zones of depression on underground water sources. *See* MALONEY, AUSNESS, & MORRIS, at 73-74, 245-48. (The term "zone of depression" is used instead of the more familiar "cone of depression" because the latter refers to a precise geometric shape that, while generally characteristic of zones of depression, might not be an accurate description of the shape of the effects of dewatering an aquifer given the particular hydrogeology involved.)

As subsection (1) indicates, the impacts on waste assimilative capacity often will be more far reaching than the effect of return flows. The quality of water in point source return flows is often effectively regulated by the National Pollutant Discharge Elimination System, yet the diminution of water flowing on the surface or percolating beneath the ground can cause the water source's quality to fall below established water quality standards through altering the effect of existing return flows from other point sources, or through the "intrusion" of various pollutants into a heretofore high quality aquifer. In a State that assigns both the allocation and the quality maintenance function to a single agency, subsection (1) will be rephrased to require consideration of water quality impacts when the prescribed conditions are met.

Subsection (2) lists the factors the State Agency is to consider in evaluating the quality effects of a proposed allocation of water. The decision on whether to issue a permit or to approve a modification of a permit must be predicated on an analysis of the alternatives to satisfy the water needs of the applicant. As is generally true under the Code, the overall goal is the achievement of the public interest in the waters of the State generally, and of sustainable development in particular. Subsection (2) will not be changed by the assignment of both the allocation and the water quality maintenance functions to a single agency.

Subsection (3) requires a balancing of the several factors identified in subsection (2) to determine whether to issue a permit notwithstanding any adverse quality effects. The State Agency is to balance the costs of alternative means of satisfying the water needs of an applicant against the costs of achieving and maintaining the legally prescribed water quality standards through the alternative means available for that purpose. The costs of achieving or maintaining prescribed water quality standards is a direct function of the extent of treatment required for effluent discharges, which in turn is a function of the waste assimilative capacity of the water source at the point of discharge. MALONEY, AUSNESS, & MORRIS, at 261-64 (1972). Implicit in this is the consideration of whether the financial burden of achieving and maintaining the legally prescribed water quality standards will, or should, fall on the public purse or upon the particular water right holders, as well as other dimensions of the public interest. This subsection thus acknowledges the reality of the use of the waters of the State for effluent assimilation, making waste assimilation a use of the water that must be considered by the State Agency every bit as much as any withdrawal. Subsection (3) will not be changed by the assignment of both the allocation and the water quality maintenance functions to a single agency.

As with other aspects of the permit issuing process, a person interested in the decision can either request a hearing, make a comment, or seek judicial review as appropriate. In any of these processes, the Code does not prescribe a new standard of review, leaving that to the general administrative law of the State. The problem of purely procedural challenges by someone who really disagrees with the substance of the decision is dealt with, at least somewhat, by allowing the State Agency to deny a hearing to persons who are making merely frivolous claims.

Cross-references: § 1R-1-01 (protecting the public interest in the waters of the State); § 1R-1-02 (assuring the efficient and productive use of water); § 1R-1-03 (conformity to the policies of the Code and to physical laws); § 1R-1-08 (procedural protections); § 1R-1-09 (coordination of water allocation and water quality regulation); § 1R-1-10 (water conservation); § 1R-1-11 (preservation of minimum flows and levels); § 2R-1-01 (the obligation to make only reasonable use of water); § 2R-1-03 (no unreasonable injury to other water rights); § 2R-2-02 (biological integrity); § 2R-2-03 (chemical integrity); § 2R-2-06 (consumptive use); § 2R-2-07 (cost); § 2R-2-13 (nonconsumptive use); § 2R-2-14 (permit); § 2R-2-15 (person); § 2R-2-18 (the public interest); § 2R-2-20 (reasonable use); § 2R-2-21 (safe yield); § 2R-2-23 (State Agency); § 2R-2-24 (sustainable development); § 2R-2-25 (underground water); § 2R-2-26 (unreasonable injury); § 2R-2-30 (water right); § 2R-2-32 (waters of the State); § 2R-2-33 (water source); § 2R-2-34 (withdrawal or to withdraw); §§ 3R-2-01 to 3R-2-05 (protection of minimum flows of levels); § 4R-1-05 (application of general laws to meetings, procedures, and records); § 4R-1-06 (regulatory authority of the State Agency); § 4R-3-02 (cooperation with other units of state and local government); § 4R-3-03 (duty to cooperate); § 4R-3-04 (combined permits); § 4R-4-05 (regulatory authority of Special Water Management Areas); §§ 5R-1-01 to 5R-3-03 (hearings, dispute resolution, and judicial review); §§ 6R-2-01 to 6R-2-08 (permit procedures); §§ 6R-3-01 to 6R-3-06 (the basis of a water right); § 6R-4-01 (protecting and preserving water quality standards); § 6R-4-02 (data to be provided by *[the State's water quality agency]* to the State Agency); § 6R-4-04 (combining permits for water allocation and water quality); § 6R-4-05 (preservation of private rights of action).

Comparable statutes: CONN. GEN. STAT. ANN. § 22a-373(5); IND. CODE ANN. § 13-2-25(C) (underground water); IOWA CODE ANN. §§ 455B.267(2), (4), 455B.271(2)(d), (3); MASS. GEN. LAWS ANN. ch. 21G, § 7(9); MISS. CODE ANN. § 53-3-25 (b) (requirement of prevention of salt water intrusion); VA. CODE ANN. § 62.1-44.38.

§ 6R-4-04 COMBINING PERMITS FOR WATER ALLOCATION AND WATER QUALITY

(1) Whenever consistent with the policies and requirements of this Code, the State Agency and the *[the State's water quality agency]* shall

issue a combined permit expressing terms and conditions governing both water allocation and water quality.

(2) If the State Agency determines for any reason that a combined permit is not possible under subsection (1) of this section, the State Agency shall:

(a) publish, in a newspaper of general circulation within the county in which the withdrawal is to occur, a notice of its intention to issue a permit under this Code at the end of 30 days from the publication of the notice; and

(b) promptly send written notice to the *[the State's water quality agency]*; and

(c) issue the permit as planned unless precluded by the action of a court or other body authorized by law to review the decision in question.

Commentary: Subsection (1) of this section reiterates the general obligation that the State Agency, when feasible, combine its permits with other permits required for the use of the waters of the State, specifically contemplating the combining of the allocation permit with a National Pollutant Discharge Elimination System permit. When this proves to be impossible, subsection (2) establishes a procedure for the State Agency to issue its own permit separate from the National Pollutant Discharge Elimination System permit. Subsection (2) requires both general public notice and specific written notice to the agency responsible for water quality within the State. Should the water quality agency oppose the State Agency's decision, the water quality agency can appeal the State Agency's decision as indicated in the commentary to section 6R-4-03. Aggrieved individuals will have recourse to the general rights of judicial review provided elsewhere in this Code.

Except for the need to eliminate what would be a redundant reference to a second agency, subsection (1) would be unchanged in a State that assigns both the water allocation and the water quality maintenance functions to a single agency. Subsection (2) would be omitted in a State that assigns both the water allocation and the water quality maintenance functions to a single agency.

Some regulated riparian statutes have taken a different approach to the final authority to issue permits, requiring an application for an allocation permit to present a National Pollutant Discharge Elimination System permit as a condition to receiving the allocation permit. *See, e.g.*, VA. CODE. ANN. § 62.1-243. This approach should strongly appeal to those who favor a single "master" pollution permit covering air pollution, solid waste disposal, water pollution, and what not. Combing such a "master" permit with a water allocation permit might well make the permit process too massive for practical implementation. A state that legislatively commits itself to such a "master" pollution permit program would need, at the least, to carefully consider whether or how to rewrite this section and section 4R-4-04.

Cross-references: § 1R-1-09 (coordination of water allocation and water quality regulation); § 4R-3-01 (cooperation with the federal government and with interstate and international organizations); § 4R-3-02 (cooperation with other units of State and local government); § 4R-3-03 (the duty of other units of government within this State to cooperate with the State Agency); § 4R-4-04 (combined permits); § 6R-4-01 (protecting and preserving water quality standards); § 6R-4-03 (evaluating allocations for their potential effect on water quality).

§ 6R-04-05 PRESERVATION OF PRIVATE RIGHTS OF ACTION

This Code does not alter or abridge any right of action existing in law or equity, whether civil or criminal, nor does it prevent any person from exercising rights to suppress nuisances or otherwise to abate pollution.

Commentary: The proliferation of federal and State regulations designed to achieve and maintain the quality of the waters of the State indicate that private litigation has not been an effective means for accomplishing these ends as far as society as a whole is concerned. See Peter

Davis, *Protecting Waste Assimilation Stream Flows by the Law of Water Allocation, Nuisance and Public Trust, and by Environmental Statutes*, 28 NAT. RESOURCES J. 357 (1988). Nonetheless, these private rights of action remain an essential means for remedying individual injuries caused by activities that degrade the waters of the State. This section reiterates the general policy of the Regulated Riparian Model Water Code that it does not preempt private rights of action for injuries cognizable under laws other than this Code.

Cross-references: § 2R-1-04 (protection of property rights); § 5R-4-09 (citizen suits); § 8R-1-04 (appointment and maintenance of agent for receipt of process and other legal notices).

Comparable statutes: ALA. CODE § 9-10B-27; GA. CODE ANN. § 12-5-46; HAW. REV. STAT. § 174C-15(c); MD. CODE ANN., NAT. RES. § 1-508; N.C. GEN. STAT. §143-215.22; WIS. STAT. ANN. § 144.026(12)(a).

CHAPTER VII

SCOPE OF THE WATER RIGHT

This Chapter addresses several important questions relating to the water right created by the Regulated Riparian Model Water Code. The Chapter defines the extent of the water right through the terms and conditions of the permits to be set by the State Agency, including the duration of permits and forfeiture for nonuse. Generally, a permit confers a legally protected right to use water for the duration of the permit, so long as the permit holder complies with the terms and conditions of the permit. Other provisions of the Code detail what happens when there is a dispute between two permit holders (sections 5R-2-01 to 5R-2-03), what is to happen when an application for a permit discloses a likely conflict with existing permits (sections 6R-3-01, 6R-3-02), what happens when a permit holding seeks to renew an expiring permit, particularly if there are competing applications for the same water (section 6R-3-05(4)), and the circumstances under which the State Agency can revoke a permit (section 5R-5-02).

In addition to delineating the power of the State Agency to determine the terms and conditions of permits, this Chapter deals with the modification of water rights and the authority of the State Agency to impose restrictions during water shortages and water emergencies. The topics covered in this Chapter are at the core of the managerial scheme embodied in this Code. In particular, the Code seeks to encourage and enable voluntary modifications of water rights so they can be shifted to different uses, but also undertakes to promote such flexibility through time-limited rights and through the authority of the State Agency to restrict water rights to respond to particular crises. *See generally* Dellapenna, §§ 9.03(a)(4), 9.03(d), 9.05(d).

Part 1

Extent of the Right

This Part provides the basic provisions on the extent of the water right. This begins by providing the standards the State Agency is to apply in setting the terms and conditions of a permit, proceeds to the duration of permits, and concludes with provisions relating to the forfeiture of a water right evidenced by a permit. Other important aspects of the extent of a water right are dealt with in the remaining Parts of this Chapter relating to the modification of a water right and the authority of the Agency to restrict withdrawals or uses pursuant to a permit during periods of water shortage and water emergency.

§ 7R-1-01 PERMIT TERMS AND CONDITIONS

If the State Agency approves an application for a new, renewed, or modified permit, the Agency shall modify an existing permit or issue a new one, indicating in the permit the following terms and conditions:

(a) the location of the withdrawal;

(b) the authorized amount of the withdrawal and the level of consumptive use, if any, and required conservation measures, if any;

(c) the dates or seasons during which water is to be withdrawn, including any seasonal or shorter variations in the authorized withdrawals or level of consumptive use;

(d) the uses for which water is authorized to be withdrawn;

(e) the amount of return flow required, if any, and the required place of discharge, if any;

(f) the requirements for metering, surveillance, and reporting as the State Agency determines to be necessary to ensure

compliance with other conditions, limitations, or restrictions of the permit, including consent to inspections or investigations as provided in section 4R-4-01 of this Code;

(g) the time within which all necessary construction authorized by the permit must be completed or within which the withdrawal or use of water must begin to be made, with the delay not to exceed one-half of the duration of the permit, subject to extension by order of the State Agency for cause shown;

(h) any extraordinary withdrawals of the waters of the State necessary for the construction of any facilities necessary to withdraw or use the water;

(i) any obligation to restore the lands or waters of the State to their condition prior to the issuance of the permit upon its expiration;

(j) the date on which the permit expires;

(k) payment by a holder of a water right involving an interbasin transfer of a withdrawal fee to be paid into Interbasin Compensation Fund; and

(l) any other conditions, limitations, and restrictions the State Agency determines to be necessary to protect the public interest, the environment and ecosystems, the public health, safety, and welfare, and to ensure the conservation, sustainable development, proper management, and aesthetic enhancement of the waters of the State.

Commentary: The Regulated Riparian Model Water Code requires the State Agency to delineate in each permit the terms and conditions that govern the water right conferred by the permit. This section describes the essential terms and conditions that must be included in each permit, but does not specify what those terms or conditions should be in any particular permit. In general, these various terms and conditions are to conform to law and policies of the Code and to the physical laws that describe the behavior of water. For an example of a permit with terms and conditions, see RICE & WHITE, at 79-88. *See also* TARLOCK, § 3.20[6][b].

Most importantly, the terms and conditions will define how much water is authorized to be withdrawn and consumed at any given time, as well as the time, place, and authorized purpose of the withdrawal. The section also requires the Agency to add a number of other terms and conditions to each permit that are necessary to assure that the basic terms and conditions are met. The Agency is to limit the quantity of water permitted under a water right to that amount which can be put to a reasonable use by the right holder. By so limiting the quantity of water withdrawn and used, the permit serves to reduce or eliminate the waste of water, making more water available for others uses, including for nonconsumptive uses and to preserve protected minimum levels. *See generally* RICE & WHITE, at 27; SAX, ABRAMS, & THOMPSON, at 164-71; TARLOCK, § 5.16; Robert Beck, *Prevalence and Definition, in* 2 WATERS AND WATER RIGHTS § 12.03(C)(2). The Agency is required to indicate in each permit the date on which it expires. This serves to put all on notice without ambiguity. The indicated date triggers not only the end of the permit but also when the current water right holder needs to apply to renew the permit if the holder chooses to do so. The duration of permits is covered in the next section. *See* Dellapenna, § 9.03(a)(5)(A).

In order to administer and enforce the permits properly, the Agency must require that each water right holder install and maintain adequate metering and related devices and to report the resulting information to the Agency from time to time. The officers and duly authorized employees of the Agency have the right to inspect such devices at any reasonable time. These requirements should reduce the administrative burden on the Agency while enabling effective periodic review and verification by State officials. The Agency is also required to add appropriate conservation measures and other terms and conditions designed to protect environmental and aesthetic values. The Agency has general authority to require terms and conditions designed to protect environmental and aesthetic values in general, and the biological, chemical, and physical integrity of a water source in particular. This power also includes the power to impose, as terms and conditions of a permit, specific obligations to adopt and implement conservation measures and to restore the lands and waters to their pre-withdrawal condition when such requirements are necessary and proper.

The Agency is also charged to administer a fund to provide compensatory benefits for water basins of origin after the Agency has issued a permit for (and thereby approved) an interbasin transfer. Such benefits will generally focus upon enhancing the basin of origin's use of the water resources remaining after the interbasin transfer, but are not limited to such use. This power of the Agency is similar to, but broader than, the power of the Agency to require compensation to specific holders of water rights who are adversely affected by a proposed modification of another's water right through an arbitral hearing. The Agency might require compensation by other means than through payments to the Fund, such as compensation "in water" through provision of replacement water to the basin of origin, or through the provision of extra storage or pumping capacity in the permit holders works for the use (at nominal reduced charges) within the basin of origin, or through similar arrangements. For a discussion of protection of area of origin, see Owen Anderson, *Reallocation,* in 2 WATERS AND WATER RIGHTS § 16.02(c)(2).

Cross-references: §§ 1R-1-01 to 1R-1-15 (declarations of policy); § 2R-1-01 (the obligation to make only reasonable use of water); § 2R-1-02 (no prohibition of use based on the location of use); § 2R-1-03 (no unreasonable injury to other water rights); § 2R-1-04 (protection of property rights); § 2R-2-02 (biological integrity); § 2R-2-04 (chemical integrity); § 2R-2-05 (conservation measures); § 2R-2-06 (consumptive use); § 2R-2-08 (domestic use); § 2R-2-09 (drought management strategies); § 2R-2-10 (interbasin transfer); § 2R-2-11 (modification of a water right); § 2R-2-12 (municipal uses); § 2R-2-13 (nonconsumptive use); § 2R-2-14 (permit); § 2R-2-15 (person); § 2R-2-17 (plan for conservation); § 2R-2-18 (the public interest); § 2R-2-19 (public water supply system); § 2R-2-20 (reasonable use); § 2R-2-21 (safe yield); § 2R-2-23 (State Agency); § 2R-2-24 (sustainable development); § 2R-2-26 (unreasonable injury); § 2R-2-27 (waste of water); § 2R-2-28 (water basin); § 2R-2-30 (water right); § 2R-2-32 (waters of the State); § 2R-2-33 (water source); § 2R-2-34 (withdrawal or to withdraw); §§ 3R-1-01 to 3R-2-05 (waters subject to allocation); § 4R-1-04 (special funds created); § 4R-3-04 (combined permits); §

5R-2-03 (administrative resolution of disputes among holders of permits to withdraw water); § 5R-4-01 (inspections and other investigations); § 5R-4-03 (orders to cease and restore); § 5R-5-01(l) (crimes–tampering with monitoring devices or supplying false information); § 6R-1-01 (withdrawals unlawful without a permit); § 6R-1-02 (small withdrawals exempted from the permit requirement); § 6R-1-03 (existing withdrawals); § 6R-1-04 (withdrawals begun after the effective date of the Code); § 6R-1-05 (temporary permits); § 6R-3-01 (standards for a permit); § 6R-3-02 (determining whether a use is reasonable); § 6R-3-03 (aggregation of multiple withdrawals); § 6R-3-04 (preferences among water rights); § 6R-3-06 (special standard for interbasin transfers); §§ 6R-4-01 to 6R-4-05 (coordination of water allocation and water quality regulation); § 7R-1-02 (duration of permits); §§ 7R-2-01 to 7R-2-04 (modification of water rights); §§ 8R-1-01 to 8R-1-07 (multijurisdictional transfers).

Comparable statutes: ALA. CODE § 9-10B-22(b); GA. CODE ANN. §§ 12-5-27, 12-5-31(m), 12-5-97; HAW. REV. STAT. § 174C-54(d) (monitoring requirements); IND. CODE ANN. §§ 13-2-2-6, 13-2-2-7, 13-2-2-9, 13-2-6.1-4(6) (monitoring and reporting requirements); IOWA CODE ANN. § 455B.265 (conservation measures and related terms to be included in each permit); KY. REV. STAT. ANN. §§ 151.160 (monitoring and reporting requirements imposed by statute), 151.170 (all permits to be "specific"); MD. CODE ANN., NAT. RES. §§ 8-807(b), 8-810; MASS. GEN. LAWS ANN. ch. 21G, § 11; MINN. STAT. ANN. § 105.41(4), (5) (monitoring and reporting requirements), 105.46 (time limits on construction not to exceed five years), 105.461 (requiring the restoration of waters or lands); MISS. CODE ANN. §§ 51-3-15(2)(a), 51-3-23; N.J. STAT. ANN. §§ 58:1A-5(b), (c), 58:1A-8; N.Y. ENVTL. CONSERV. LAW §§ 15-503(4), 15-1503(3); S.C. CODE ANN. §§ 49-5-60(C)(1), 49-5-70(D), (E); VA. CODE ANN. § 62.1248(A); VA. CODE ANN. § 62.1-44.100(d), (e); WIS. STAT. ANN. §§ 30.18(6), 144.026(6)(a).

§ 7R-1-02 DURATION OF PERMITS

(1) The State Agency shall issue permits for a period of time representing the economic life of any necessary investments not to exceed 20

years, except that permits may be issued for a period reasonable for the retirement of debt associated with the construction of related facilities by a governmental or other public body or public service corporation not to exceed 50 years.

(2) Not more than six (6) months prior to the expiration of any permit, a water right holder may apply for a renewal of the permit; such an application is entitled to the renewal preference provided in section 6R-3-04(3) only if received by the State Agency before the permit expires.

Commentary: Time-limited permits maximize State control by enabling the State Agency to reallocate the waters of the State to more reasonable uses as the earlier permits expire. This approach reflects a conclusion that sales of water rights will remain relatively rare under a regulated riparian system just as they have under the more strictly private property regime of appropriative rights. *See* Owen Anderson, *Reallocation,* in 2 WATERS AND WATER RIGHTS §§ 16.02, 16.04; Steven Clyde, *Legal and Institutional Barriers to Transfers and Reallocation of Water Resources,* 29 S.D. L. REV. 232 (1984); Bonnie Colby, *Economic Impacts of Water Law–State Law and Water Market Development in the Southwest,* 28 NAT. RESOURCES J. 721 (1988); Dellapenna, § 6.01(b); Eric Freyfogle, *Water Justice,* 1986 U. ILL. L. REV. 481, 510-14; Kevin O'Brien, *Water Marketing in California,* 19 PAC. L.J. 1165 (1988). On the problems in transferring water rights under traditional riparian rights, see Dellapenna, § 7.04. Nor have the highly touted transferable air pollution emission allowances proven particularly useful in practice. *See* Sam Hays, *Emissions Trading Mythology,* ENVTL. FORUM, Jan./Feb. 1995, at 15; Lisa Heinzerling, *Selling Pollution, Forcing Democracy,* 14 STAN. ENVTL. L.J. 300 (1995); Robert McGee & Walter Block, *Pollution Trading Permits as a Form of Market Socialism and the Search for a Real Market Solution to Environmental Pollution,* 6 FORDHAM ENVTL. L.J. 51 (1994); Deborah Mostaghel, *State Reactions to the Trading of Emissions Allowances under Title IV of the Clean Air Act Amendments of 1990,* 22 B.C. ENVTL. AFF. L. REV. 201 (1995). For a defense of transferable emission allowances, see Matthew Polesetsky, *Will a Market in Air Pollution Clean the Nation's Dirtiest Air? A Study in the South Coast Air Quality Management District's Regional Clean Air Incentives Market,* 22 ECOL. L.Q. 359 (1995).

The language in this section is modeled after FLA. STAT. ANN. § 373.236. *See also* Dellapenna, § 9.03(a)(4). Following this model, if the conclusion that private sales will remain relatively rare is accurate, the Agency will be able to use the expiration of permits to facilitate the application of water to more socially valuable uses. Perhaps even more important than the outright denial of renewal of a permit is the power this gives to the Agency to revise the terms and conditions of the permits in light of changing circumstances. This power is likely to lead to ever more stringent requirements of conservation measures as well as other means of furthering the public interest in the waters of the State. Somewhat more favorable renewal terms and conditions might result if the renewal applicant has been successful in applying conservation measures or in following through on a plan of conservation. The alternative to this approach is to make market transfers significantly easier than is the case in any State today, something that could only be achieved by largely ignoring the "spill-over" effects of a market transfer.

Setting the proper duration of permits requires a delicate balancing of the need of investors for the security of right necessary to assure recovery of their investments and the need of the State to continue to manage actively an important public resource. The need for security of right would nearly always be less than the duration of economic life of the assets invested in the project, so that sets the upper limit to permit life. To simply provide that the permit shall run for the period necessary to retire any related debt would enable an applicant to extend the life of a permit by arranging ever longer periods of debt service. The normal term provided here is 20 years, which the Agency can adjust through its regulations to set a situation where 5% of the total permits will expire annually, allowing a more even and predictable workload. Depending on staffing and budget, the Agency might be able to handle some higher percentage annually, and can shorten the duration by regulation appropriately.

A legislature might prefer to set the duration directly and leave little or no discretion in the Agency on the matter. Should it do so, the legislature should allow a means for staggering expiration dates to assure an even and predictable workload. The most common duration found in actual regulated riparian statutes is 10 years, with a longer period of 50 years being provided for public investments on the theory that 50 years is the common period for bond issues used to finance public investments. This provides marginally better security for such investments (would any State Agency actually terminate a permit supplying water to thousands or millions of homes and their related economic bases?) and thus enables them to obtain slightly better interest rates from the capital market. *See generally* MALONEY, AUSNESS, & MORRIS, § 2.06. Georgia, which originally enacted the temporal limitations found in the Florida law, recently enacted a statute authorizing its administrative agency to issue permits for up to 50 years, while requiring conservation plans for permits issued for a longer duration than 25 years. The administering agency is not obligated to issue such lengthy permits, and if it does must review the operation of the permit every 10 years. *See* Julie Beberman, *Legislative Review: Conservation and Natural Resources,* 12 GA. ST. U. L. REV. 51 (1995).

Several regulated riparian States have found it acceptable to provide for shorter durations than that provided in this section, apparently without significant adverse effects on investment in water within the state. Perhaps this reflects the reality that permits will seldom be completely denied renewal when they expire, although new terms and conditions will often be attached to a permit upon its renewal. Actual regulated riparian statutes have used periods ranging from 1 to 20 years, with (as noted) 10 being the most common. Several regulated riparian statutes provide a preference of a longer period for public water projects as provided in subsection (1).

The Agency remains charged to consider all effects in deciding whether to decline to renew a permit, including the investments lawfully made in pursuance of the water right that the renewal applicant seeks to renew. In the event that the public interest would be equally served by renewal or by awarding the permit to a competing applicant, the State Agency is directed to renew the permit. The water right should be granted to another applicant only on a clear showing that the public interest generally, and sustainable development in particular, would be enhanced. The Code anticipates six months as the normal period for processing an application, and this period is selected as the window for submitting an application to renew a permit. If the water right holder does not file an application to renew a permit during this six-month period before the permit expires, the water right holder loses the water right and any subsequent application is to be treated as a new application rather than as a renewal application.

Cross-references: § 1R-1-06 (legal security for the right to use water for specified periods); § 1R-1-07 (flexibility through the modification of water rights); § 2R-2-05 (conservation measures); § 2R-1-04 (protection of property rights); § 2R-2-11 (modification of a water right); § 2R-2-17 (plan for conservation); § 2R-2-18 (the public interest); § 2R-2-23 (State Agency); § 2R-2-24 (sustainable development); § 2R-2-27 (waste of water); § 2R-2-30 (water right); § 7R-1-01 (permit terms and conditions); §§ 7R-2-01 to 7R-2-03 (modification of water rights).

Comparable statutes: ALA. CODE § 9-10B-22(c) (certificates of use to be reviewed "every 12 months or sooner"); FLA. STAT. ANN. § 373.236 (20 years for ordinary permits, 50 years for permits to public entities); GA. CODE ANN. §§ 12-5-31(h) (10 years minimum and 50 years maximum), (j) (renewal applications within six months before expiration), 12-5-97(a) (10 years minimum and 50 years maximum), (b) (renewal applications within six months before expiration); HAW. REV. STAT. §§ 174C-55, 174C-56 (not more than 20 years); IOWA CODE ANN. § 455B.265(3) (10 years of the life of the structure); MD. CODE ANN., NAT. RES. § 8-811 (triennial review); MASS. GEN. LAWS ANN. ch. 21G, § 11 (as set by regulation, but not more than 20 years); MINN. STAT. ANN. § 105.44(9) (cancellation at any time if necessary to protect the public interest); MISS. CODE ANN. § 51-3-9 (10 years for ordinary permits and as long as necessary to amortize investment for permits to public entities, renewal applications within six months before expiration); N.J. STAT. ANN. §§ 58:1A-7(b) (automatic renewal absent hearing to show cause for non-renewal), 58:1A-8(a) (permit to set the date of expiration); N.C. GEN. STAT. § 143-215.16(a) (10 years or less); S.C. CODE ANN. § 49-5-70(A) (10 years or as reasonable); WIS. STAT. ANN. § 144.026(6)(b) (review every five years).

§ 7R-1-03 FORFEITURE OF PERMITS

(1) If a water right holder wastes the water or fails to withdraw or use water as authorized by a permit for a period of consecutive five (5) years (without counting years when water was physically and legally unavailable), the holder forfeits the right and the permit becomes void.

(2) A forfeiture also occurs whenever the State Agency determines that a person to whom a permit has been issued will be unable under any foreseeable circumstances to comply with this Code or with relevant orders, permit terms or conditions, or regulations made pursuant to this Code or any other statute pertaining to the use of water.

(3) A forfeiture can pertain to the whole or any part of a water right, depending on the extent to which the water is wasted or not withdrawn or used, or the extent to which the holder of the right is unable to comply with the terms or conditions of the permit.

Commentary: The public interest in the efficient and equitable use of the waters of the State precludes the speculative holding of water rights. To the extent that any water authorized for use by a permit is not used, the water right reverts to the State. *See* RICE & WHITE, at 31; TARLOCK, § 5.18; C. Peter Goplerud, *Protection and Termination of Water Rights,* in 2 WATERS AND WATER RIGHTS, § 17.03. Forfeiture, the involuntary relinquishment of a permit and therefore of the water right evidenced by that permit, occurs through the failure to use the water or to the wasting of water. Forfeiture enables unused water or improperly used water to be reallocated by the State Agency without reference to the claims of the permit holder who failed to use the water or who failed to use the water properly. *See* WATER RIGHTS OF THE FIFTY STATES AND TERRITORIES 28, 118 (KENNETH R. WRIGHT ed., 1990).

In setting the period of years for the forfeiture, the legislature must balance the need for reasonable flexibility in developing a withdrawal and use against the risk of monopolization of water by permit holders who make no use or no proper use of the resource. *See* TARLOCK, § 3.11. The need to prevent monopolization and to enable water to be provided for more pressing needs requires that the Regulated Riparian Model Water Code deem failure to use water because it is not needed for the forfeiture period as conclusive proof that the permit was improvidently issued. The term selected here, five consecutive years, is the most common such term among similar statutes. One does not count years in which water was neither physically nor legally available; such years simply drop out of the picture. Thus, if a particular permit holder fails to use available water for three years, and then water becomes unavailable for six years, when water becomes available again the permit holder has a period of two more years to resume using the water or the permit is forfeit.

Among current statutes, the range of periods of nonuse or improper use that works a forfeiture is from three to ten years. The period chosen here must be less than the period within which permits expire, for the expiration allows the Agency to reevaluate the use and to reduce or eliminate permit for water that is not used or that is not used properly. There is simply no point to having a forfeiture provision if it comes close to the period of duration for permits, and some might prefer to leave the expiration as the sole means of evaluating a permit holder's performance under the permit. The longer the duration of a permit, however, the more important it becomes to have an interim means of evaluating a permit holder's performance and dealing with improper performance or with non-performance. Willful violation of the terms or conditions of a permit does not work a forfeiture; rather, it serves as a basis for the Agency to revoke the permit.

A risk created by forfeiture statutes is that water will be "used" merely to avoid a forfeiture. In other words, the risk arises that a particular water right holder will use the water wastefully in order to avoid a forfeiture. The Code depends on its prohibition of waste, its requirement that all uses be reasonable, and its incentives for conservation to deal with this risk. No forfeiture results if the water was not available for use during any part of the period required for the forfeiture. Water might not be available because of floods, droughts, preferences to other water rights, or other reasons. *See* RICE & WHITE, at 31; TARLOCK, § 5.18(2); C. Peter Goplerud III, *Adjudication of Water Rights,* in 2 WATERS AND WATER RIGHTS § 17.03(b).

Cross-references: § 1R-1-01 (protecting the public interest in the waters of the State); § 1R-1-02 (assuring efficient and productive use of water); § 1R-1-03 (conformity to the policies of this Code and to physical laws); § 1R-1-05 (efficient and equitable allocation during shortfalls in supply); § 1R-1-06 (legal security for the right to use water); § 1R-1-08 (procedural protections); § 1R-1-10 (water conservation); § 2R-1-01 (the obligation to make only reasonable use of water); § 2R-1-04 (protection of property rights); § 2R-2-05 (conservation measures); § 2R-2-14 (permit); § 2R-2-18 (the public interest); § 2R-2-20 (reasonable use); § 2R-2-23 (State Agency); § 2R-2-24 (sustainable development); § 2R-2-27 (waste of water); § 2R-2-30 (water right); § 2R-2-34 (withdrawal or to withdraw); § 3R-2-01 (protected minimum flows or levels not to be withdrawn or allocated); § 5R-4-01 (inspections and other investigations); § 5R-5-01 (crimes); § 5R-5-02 (revocation of permits); § 7R-2-01 (permit terms and conditions); § 7R-2-02 (duration of permits); §§ 7R-3-01 to 7R-3-07 (restrictions during water shortages or water emergencies).

Comparable statutes: FLA. STAT. ANN. § 373.243(4); GA. CODE ANN. § 12-5-31(k)(4); HAW. REV. STAT. § 174C-58(4); IOWA CODE ANN. §§ 455B.271(2)(c), 455B.272; WIS. STAT. ANN. § 144.026(6)(c), (e).

Part 2
Modification of Water Rights

The Regulated Riparian Model Water Code adopts a policy favoring the modification of water rights in order to promote the highest or best use of the resource. This approach, particularly when the modification occurs through a market, has strong supporters in the literature of water management and is beginning to be found in actual water management today. See, e.g., The Central Valley Project Improvement Act of 1992, 35 U.S.C. §§ 3401-3405 (1994); *Westlands Water Dist. v. United States,* 850 F. Supp. 1388, 864 F. Supp. 1536 (E.D. Cal.

1994); TERRY ANDERSON, WATER CRISIS ENDING THE POLICY DROUGHT (1983); DIANA GIBBONS, THE ECONOMIC VALUE OF WATER (1986); LOYAL HARTMAN & DON SEASTONE, WATER TRANSFERS: ECONOMIC EFFICIENCY AND ALTERNATIVE INSTITUTIONS (1970); BONNIE SALIBA & DAVID BUSH, WATER MARKETS IN THEORY AND PRACTICE: MARKET TRANSFERS, WATER VALUES, AND PUBLIC POLICY (1987); RODNEY SMITH, TRADING WATER: AN ECONOMIC AND LEGAL FRAMEWORK FOR WATER MARKETING (1988); JOHN TEERINK & MASAHIRO NAKASHIMA, WATER ALLOCATION, RIGHTS, AND PRICING: EXAMPLES FROM JAPAN AND THE UNITED STATES (World Bank Pol'y Pap. no. 198, 1993); TRANSFERABILITY OF WATER ENTITLEMENTS (J.J. Pigram & B.P. Hooper eds. 1990); WATER RIGHTS: SCARCE RESOURCE ALLOCATION, BUREAUCRACY, AND THE ENVIRONMENT 283 (Terry Anderson ed. 1983); WATER TRANSFERS IN THE WEST: EFFICIENCY, EQUITY, AND THE ENVIRONMENT (A. Dan Tarlock ed. 1992); Bonnie Colby, *Economic Impacts of Water Law–State Law and Water Market Development in the Southwest,* 28 NAT. RESOURCES J. 721 (1988); Arthur Dragun & Victor Gleeson, *From Water Law to Transferability in New South Wales,* 29 NAT. RESOURCES J. 645 (1989); K. William Easter & Robert Hearne, *Water Markets and Decentralized Water Resources Management: International Problems and Opportunities,* 31 WATER RESOURCES BULL. 9, 14-19 (1995); J. Wayland Eheart & Randolph Lyon, *Alternative Structures for Water Rights Markets,* 19 WATER RESOURCES RESEARCH 887 (1983); Eric Garner & Janice Weiss, *Water Management Options for the Future,* in THE NATURAL RESOURCES LAW MANUAL 330 (Richard Fink ed. 1995); Todd Glass, *The 1992 Omnibus Water Act: Three Rubrics of Reclamation Reform,* 22 ECOL. L.Q. 143, 177-88 (1995); Charles Howe et al., *Innovative Approach to Water Allocation: The Potential for Water Markets,* 22 WATER RESOURCES RESEARCH 439 (1986); Ray Huffaker, Norman Whittlesey, & Phillip Wandschneider, *Institutional Feasibility of Contingent Water Marketing to Increase Migratory Flows for Salmon on the Upper Snake River,* 33 NAT. RESOURCES J. 671 (1993); Morris Israel & Jay Lund, *Recent California Water Transfers: Implications for Water Management,* 35 NAT. RESOURCES J. 1 (1995); Jerome Milliman, *Water Law and Private Decision-Making: A Critique,* 2 J. LAW. & ECON. 41 (1959); Charles Roe, Jr. & James Rasband, *"Changes" to Water Rights,* in THE NATURAL RESOURCES LAW MANUAL 341 (Richard Fink ed. 1995); Mark Rosengrant, *Water Transfers in California: Potentials and Constraints,* 20 WATER INT'L 72 (1995); Gabriel Roth, *The Role of the Private Sector in Providing Water in Developing*

Countries, 9 NAT. RESOURCES F. 167 (1985); Paula Smith, *Coercion and Groundwater Management: Three Case Studies and a "Market" Approach,* 16 ENVTL. L. 797 (1986); Barton Thompson, *Institutional Perspectives on Water Policy and Markets,* 81 CAL. L. REV. 671 (1993); Richard Wahl, *Market Transfers of Water in California,* 1 WEST-NORTHWEST 49 (1995); Paul Williams & Stephen McHugh, *Water Marketing and Instream Flows: The Next Step in Protecting California's Instream Values,* 9 STAN. ENVTL. L.J. 132 (1990).

The lack of economic incentives in water usage has contributed to a reality in which water is frozen into its present uses and new uses must depend on developing "new" supplies rather than on conservation in existing uses or the transfer of water from low-valued present uses to higher-valued future uses. The end result of such a situation can only be significant and growing inefficiency. Markets are the usual way we factor economic incentives into decision-making, and thus arguably are the solution to many severe crises of inefficiency in water usage around the world. Yet, while the Code seeks to encourage voluntary modifications of permits to enable water to move to higher or better uses, two related problems make this ideal difficult to achieve. The first is the problem of the probability of externalities from any significant change in water use patterns. The second is the problem of "hold outs" who, in effect, can exercise a monopoly power if no voluntary modification of water use is possible without obtaining the contractual consent of every affected person related to a water source. For a detailed analysis of these issues, see JOSEPH DELLAPENNA, WATER IN THE MIDDLE EAST: THE LIMITS AND POTENTIAL OF LAW § 5.04 (1996).

This Part provides provisions detailing how the policy of encouraging voluntary modifications is to be put into effect while protecting other water right holders and the public interest. The term "modification" used in this Part as a descriptive term that captures the role of the State Agency when the water right depends upon a permit. Some of the drafters would have used the terms "transfer" or "reallocation" for this Part. The term "transfer" covers only some of the modifications included in this Part. It would not include, for example, a modification of a permit where only the time of use is changed. Some would restrict the term "transfer" to changes in the permit holder, thus excluding changes in the place or manner of use as well as changes in the time. All of these changes are included in the term "modification" as used in this Part. Furthermore, the term "transfer" referring to a sale of a water right or to a change in the place or manner of use can easily be confused with the term "transfer" used in this Code to refer to the transportation of water out of the basin of origin. If the term "transfer" suffers from ambiguities, the term "reallocation" is too clear. "Reallocation" seems to put the responsibility for the modification on the Agency, rather than, as is the case under this Part, on the private permit holders. At the very least, it suggests less weight to the interests of the parties seeking the modification than the policy of encouraging voluntary modifications requires. Similar yet narrower terms such as "alteration," "assignment," "conveyances," "market transactions," or "sales" simply fail to capture the full sense of the process and the concerns developed in this Part. The term "modification" appears better than any other to capture the flavor of the interactive process embracing private action and regulatory response.

§ 7R-2-01 APPROVAL REQUIRED FOR MODIFICATION OF PERMITS

(1) A person who holds an unexpired permit may apply for a modification of any term or condition of the permit, including the name of the person holding the permit, by submitting an application for modification on such forms as are required by the State Agency.

(2) A proposed modification, including the assignment of a permit to a person other than the current water right holder, becomes effective only upon approval by the State Agency.

Commentary: The Regulated Riparian Model Water Code enables a water right holder to apply to modify a permit upon a showing similar to the initial application for a permit. This section should be read in connection with the section requiring the State Agency to aggregate all related water uses in considering any application for a permit. If the only requested modification involves enlarging the amount of water to be withdrawn or consumed, it matters little whether the application is treated as an application to modify an existing permit or an application to receive a new permit.

Probably the most important applications to modify a permit will involve an assignment of the permit to another person, making that person the holder of the water right. Water rights are to be assignable by voluntary act of the current water right holder to facilitate the highest and best use of the waters of the State. Such transactions were rare under common-law riparianism, in part at least because of the unsatisfactory state of the law. *See* TARLOCK, § 3.18[2]; TARLOCK, CORBRIDGE, & GETCHES, at 136-43; Dellapenna, § 7.04. In so far as voluntary assignments can occur without injury to the public or to third parties to the transaction, the policy of the Code is to encourage such modifications. As the Code abolishes the traditional riparian restriction on the use of water based upon the location of the use, voluntary modifications could well include transfer to nonriparian uses. For the traditional restrictions, see SAX, ABRAMS, & THOMPSON, at 87-98; TRELEASE & GOULD, at 325-331; Dellapenna, § 7.04(a)(3).

Most modifications involving a change in the holder of the water right, particularly if it involves a change in place or manner or use, will be market-based. This Part of Chapter VII is designed to deal primarily with such voluntary assignments of water rights. This Part also reaches involuntary assignments (such as through bankruptcy or the execution of a judgment) if the modification will result in a material change or an adverse impact of the rights of another water right holder.

Whenever a proposed modification will change materially the manner, place, or timing of a withdrawal or use or adversely impact on another water right holder, there are two specific groups that need protection: other applicants for allocation or assignment of water rights, and other water right holders potentially injured by what in effect is the establishment of a new water right. Often more remote third parties and even the general public interest will also be at risk. *See, e.g., Simpson v. Yale Investments, Inc.*, 886 P.2d 689 (Colo. 1994); *C.F. & I. Steel Corp. v. Rooks*, 495 P.2d 1134 (Colo. 1972); *Beker Indus. Inc. v. Georgetown Irrig. Dist.*, 610 P.2d 546 (Idaho 1980); *W.S. Ranch Co. v. Kaiser Steel Co.*, 439 P.2d 715 (N.M. 1968); *State* ex rel. *Christopoulos v. Husky Oil Co.*, 575 P.2d 262 (Wyo. 1978); *White v. Board of Land Comm'rs*, 595 P.2d 76 (Wyo. 1979). *See generally* Dellapenna, § 9.03(d); George Gould, *Transfer of Water Rights*, 29 NAT. RESOURCES J. 457 (1989); Joseph Sax, *The Constitution, Property Rights, and the Future of Water Law*, 61 U. COLO. L. REV. 257 (1990).

In order to protect affected third parties or the public interest and to assure sustainable development of the waters of the State, the Agency must review and approve a proposed modification when there is reason to expect such effects. The Agency can deny approval of the modification, or can approve the modification without a substantial change in the original permit except to substitute a new person as permit holder or the like, or can approve the modification on condition that the permit holder accept a substitute permit revising the terms and conditions applicable to the water right as necessary to assure no injury to other water right holders, to other affected persons, or to the public interest. The breadth of these possibilities does not diminish the value or utility of existing water rights for no holder of a water right has a right to unreasonably injure another water right and the Agency cannot approve a modification that will injure the holder of another permit during the life of the permit. For discussions of the no-injury rule, see *Tanner v. Bacon,* 136 P.2d 957 (Utah 1943); RICE & WHITE, at 77-79 (1987); SAX, ABRAMS, & THOMPSON, at 245-71; TARLOCK, CORBRIDGE, & GETCHES, at 310-26; TARLOCK, § 5.17; Owen L. Anderson, *Reallocation,* in 2 WATERS AND WATER RIGHTS § 16.02(b). For the responsibility of the Agency to protect holders of existing permits, see the *Commentary* to section 6R-3-02.

The requirement that the modification of water rights be approved by the Agency applies equally to permits to transport and use water outside the State as it does to permits to withdraw and use the water in the State. Instances of modification involving permits for the interstate or international transportation or use of water will be judged according to the standards for such permits (Chapter VIII) rather than merely according to the domestic standards (Chapter VI). In either event, the application to modify a permit will benefit from the policies, statutory provisions, and regulations designed to promote conservation (Chapter IX).

Cross-references: § 1R-1-01 (protecting the public interest in the waters of the State); § 1R-1-02 (assuring efficient and productive use of water); § 1R-1-06 (legal security for the right to use water); § 1R-1-07 (flexibility through the modification of water rights); § 1R-1-08 (procedural protections); § 1R-1-09 (coordination of water allocation and water quality regulation); § 1R-1-10 (water conservation); § 1R-1-12 (recognizing local interests in the waters of the State); § 2R-1-02 (no prohibition on use based on location of use); § 2R-1-03 (no unreasonable injury to other water rights); § 2R-2-05 (conservation measures); § 2R-2-06 (consumptive use); § 2R-2-11 (modification of a water right); § 2R-2-13 (nonconsumptive use); § 2R-2-14 (permit); § 2R-2-15 (person); § 2R-2-18 (the public interest); § 2R-2-21 (safe yield); § 2R-2-23 (State Agency); § 2R-2-24 (sustainable development); § 2R-2-26 (unreasonable injury); § 2R-2-27 (waste of water); § 2R-2-30 (water right); § 2R-2-33 (water source); § 6R-3-01 (standards for a permit); § 6R-3-02 (determining whether a use is reasonable); § 6R-3-03 (aggregation of multiple withdrawals); § 6R-3-04 (preferences among applications); § 6R-3-05 (prior investment in proposed water withdrawal or use facilities); § 6R-4-01 (protecting and preserving water quality standards); § 7R-2-02 (approval of non-injurious modifications); § 7R-2-03 (procedures for approving other modifications); § 7R-2-04 (no rights acquired through adverse use); § 7R-3-05 (conservation credits); § 8R-1-05 (standards for action on applications to transport and use water out of the State); § 8R-1-06 (regulation of uses made outside the State); § 9R-1-01 (conservation credits); § 9R-1-02 (preference to water developed through conservation measures).

Comparable statutes: ALA. CODE § 9-10B-19(1) (conveyances); CONN. GEN. STAT. ANN. § 22a-368(c) (assignment of permits); FLA. STAT. ANN. § 373.239, 373.243(5) (modifications in general); GA. CODE ANN. §§ 12-5-31(i), (k)(5) to (7), 12-5-97(c); HAW. REV. STAT. §§ 174C-57 (modifications in general), 174C-59 (assignment of a permit); IOWA CODE ANN. § 455B.273 (modifications in general); KY. REV. STAT. ANN. § 151.170(4) (modifications in general); MINN. STAT. ANN. §§ 105.41(2) (modifications in general), 105.41(6) (assignment authorized only if in connection with a sale of appurtenant real estate); MISS. CODE ANN. § 51-3-45 (modifications in general); N.C. GEN. STAT. § 143-215.16(b) (assignment of permits); S.C. CODE ANN. § 49-5-70(B) (assignment of permits); VA. CODE ANN. §§ 62.1-44.91, 62.1-245, 62.1-248(C) (assignment of permits); WIS. STAT. ANN. § 144.026(d) (modifications in general).

§ 7R-2-02 APPROVAL OF MODIFICATIONS

(1) Except as provided in section 7R-2-03, the State Agency shall evaluate an application for approval of a modification according to the

procedures set forth in part 2 of Chapter VI and subject to the standards of section 6R-3-01.

(2) The State Agency may require a new plan for conservation as a condition of approval of a modification.

(3) If the State Agency approves a modification even though some adversely affected water right holders have not consented to the modificiaton, the State Agency shall condition approval of the modification upon the payment of adequate compensation to such adversely affected water right holders.

(4) Any person who is aggrieved by the State Agency's approval or denial of a modification, whether the State Agency has ordered compensation to that person or not, may seek judicial review of the order under section 5R-3-02 of this Code, but cannot otherwise litigate the validity of, or seek damages for, the modification.

Commentary: Subsection (1) of this section provides the basic rule for modifications of permits, whether voluntary or involuntary. That basic rule is that approval by the State Agency is to follow the same procedures and standards for evaluating an application for approval of a modification of a permit as apply to an application for a new permit. Compliance with the new permit process includes filing an application providing the same sort of information as is required for a new permit, paying a fee as provided by regulation that will at least cover the cost of processing the permit application, and providing proper notice to potentially affected parties. Persons who object to the transfer shall be given a similar opportunity to inform the Agency of the basis of their objections as for an application for a new permit.

The Regulated Riparian Model Water Code includes a policy of encouraging modifications of water rights so far as they do not violate the standards set forth in this part. Therefore, the Agency should seek to devise terms and conditions that will make approval of the modification possible. This section speaks in highly general terms, leaving the State Agency to flesh out the details through regulations. As with applications for a new permit, the burden of proof that no injury or other adverse impact will arise from the modification, however, remains on the proponent of the modification. The ultimate standard, as is generally true under this Code, is whether the proposed modification serves the public interest and promotes sustainable development of the waters of the State. The range of relevant considerations is potentially as broad as for a new permit, including environmental, ecological, and other non-monetary effects as well as economic impacts on other water rights. The Agency's inquiry normally will be narrower than for a new permit, focusing on the effects of the proposed change rather than on the effects of the permit generally. Additionally, the Agency normally will accept a lesser showing of no-injury from an application for a short-term temporary modification than for a permanent or long-term modification.

The problem that this section addresses is that, given the ambient nature of water as a resource, virtually any significant modification is likely to impact numerous other water rights, many adversely. If the Agency's approval is to await evidence of consent by every significantly affected water right holder, most modifications will become impossible. This problem, the "no-injury" rule, is why, in fact, major market transactions in water have been rare under any system of water law. *See* RODNEY SMITH, TRADING WATER: AN ECONOMIC AND LEGAL FRAMEWORK FOR WATER MARKETING 28-52 (1988); RICHARD WAHL, MARKETS FOR FEDERAL WATER: SUBSIDIES, PROPERTY RIGHTS, AND THE BUREAU OF RECLAMATION (1989); K. William Easter & Robert Hearne, *Water Markets and Decentralized Water Resources Management: International Problems and Opportunities,* 31 WATER RESOURCES BULL. 9, 14-19 (1995); Willis Ellis & Charles DuMars, *The Two-Tiered Market in Western Water,* 57 NEB. L. REV. 333 (1978); Brian Gray, Bruce Diver, & Richard Wahl, *Transfers of Federal Reclamation Water: A Case Study of California's San Joaquin Valley,* 21 ENVTL. L. 911 (1991); Morris Israel & Jay Lund, *Recent California Water Transfers: Implications for Water Management,* 35 NAT. RESOURCES J. 1, 21-29 (1995); Zachary McCormick, *Institutional Barriers to Water Marketing in the West,* 30 WATER RESOURCES BULL. 953 (1994); Mary McNally, *Water Marketing: The Case of Indian Reserved Water Rights,* 30 WATER RESOURCES BULL. 963 (1994); Ari Michelsen, *Administrative, Institutional, and Structural*

Characteristics of an Active Water Market, 30 WATER RESOURCES BULL. 971 (1994); Richard Roos-Collins, *Voluntary Conveyance of the Right to Receive a Water Supply from the United States Bureau of Reclamation,* 13 ECOL. L.Q. 773 (1987); Mark Rosengrant, *Water Transfers in California: Potentials and Constraints,* 20 WATER INT'L 72, 73, 85 (1995); Barton Thompson, *Institutional Perspectives on Water Policy and Markets,* 81 CAL. L. REV. 671, 708-23 (1993); Richard Wahl, *Market Transfers of Water in California,* 1 WEST-NORTHWEST 49, 49-51, 60-62 (1995). The nub of this problem, the effect of transaction costs as an impediment to market transactions, has been most famously explored in the work of economist Ronald Coase. RONALD COASE, THE FIRM, THE MARKET, AND THE LAW 1-20 (1988); Ronald Coase, *The Problem of Social Cost,* 3 J. LAW. & ECON. 1 (1960); Don Coursey, Elizabeth Hoffman, & Matthew Spitzer, *Fear and Loathing in the Coase Theorem: Experimental Tests Involving Physical Discomfort,* 16 J. LEG. STUD. 217 (1988); Chulho Jung *et al., The Coase Theorem in a Rent-Seeking Society,* 15 INT'L REV. L. & ECON. 259 (1995); Pierre Schlag, *The Problem of Transaction Costs,* 62 S. CAL. L. REV. 1661 (1989); Stephen Schwab, *Coase Defends Coase: Why Lawyers Listen and Economists Do Not,* 87 MICH. L. REV. 1171 (1989).

One could solve this problem by simply ignoring the external effects of a modification, but only at the price of considerably destabilizing the security and value of all water rights. *See* Jay Lund, *Transaction Risk versus Transaction Costs in Water Transfers,* 29 WATER RESOURCES RES. 3103 (1993). The change would so reorder the value of water rights, that it would amount to a massive and continuing, if haphazard, wealth redistribution. *See* MORTON HORWITZ, THE TRANSFORMATION OF AMERICAN LAW, 1780-1860, at 33-34 (1977); WATER TRANSFERS IN THE WEST: EFFICIENCY, EQUITY, AND THE ENVIRONMENT 178-81, 234-47 (A. Dan Tarlock ed. 1992); Robert Abrams, *Charting the Course of Riparianism: An Instrumentalist Theory of Change,* 35 WAYNE L. REV. 1381, 1394 (1989); Israel & Lund, *supra,* at 20-21; Rosengrant, *supra,* at 84; Joseph Sax, *Understanding Transfers: Community Rights and the Privatization of Water,* 1 West-Northwest 13 (1995). When one realizes that the most desirable water rights in the market will usually be the largest ones, the income from such a wealth transfer will inure to the benefit of those who already are the wealthiest (at least in terms of water). The losers in this market will be those with the least. This has been the experience in Chile, where the government prompted the creation of an active market for water rights simply be decreeing that there would be no protection for affected third parties, leaving the peasants unprotected when large landowners started selling their water. *See* K. William Easter & Robert Hearne, *Water Markets and Decentralized Water Resources Management: International Problems and Opportunities,* 31 WATER RESOURCES BULL. 9 (1995).

The policy of promoting equitable, as well as efficient, use of water would be ill-served by a blanket repeal of consideration of external effects when a permit is modified. This would be particularly troublesome when the external effects play a prominent role in the standards for the initial grant or denial of the permit which the holder now seeks to modify. The concern for social equity, if anything, becomes stronger, not weaker, when the effects are on non-market values. For these reasons, subsection (2) authorizes the Agency to require a new plan for conservation as a condition to its approval.

Regarding the need to balance protection of other water rights against the policy of promoting voluntary modifications, this section embraces a solution that in some respects resembles a private eminent domain power. A person can obtain approval of a modification if that person holds or acquires a permit, and then obtains the consent of the holders of all other significantly affected water rights. In the absence of such consent (which will be the normal course of events given the large number of affected third parties), the section expressly requires the Agency to condition approval of a modification upon adequate compensation to non-consenting third parties. In effect, the section makes the Agency the arbiter of such disputes. The Agency is authorized to do so, however, only if it has already determined that the modification is reasonable under the standards for the issuance of a new permit.

While allowing the Agency to assess the compensation due to injured third parties impairs the operation of the marketplace as the means for accessing the wisdom and social utility of the transfer of water rights, the transaction costs of organizing voluntary transactions among a potential myriad of affected persons or of managing piecemeal litigation involving similar numbers of disputants makes such the Agency's intervention essential if significant modifications are to occur at all. Persons who have been given notice and opportunity to participate in the approval proceedings are barred from litigating over the modification except through a petition for judicial review under the State's Administrative Procedure Act.

Cross-references: § 1R-1-01 (protecting the public interest in the waters of the State); § 1R-1-02 (assuring efficient and productive use of water); § 1R-1-03 (conformity to the policies of the Code and to physical laws); § 1R-1-6 (legal security for water rights); § 1R-1-07 (flexibility through modification of water rights); § 1R-1-08 (procedural protections); § 1R-1-09 (coordination of water allocation and water quality regulation); § 1R-1–10 (water conservation); § 1R-1-11 (preservation of minimum flows and levels); § 2R-1-01 (the obligation to make only reasonable use of water); § 2R-1-02 (no prohibition of use based upon location of use); § 2R-1-03 (no unreasonable injury to other water rights); § 2R-2-04 (protection of property rights); § 2R-2-11 (modification of a water right); § 2R-2-14 (permit); § 2R-2-15 (person); § 2R-2-18 (the public interest); § 2R-2-20 (reasonable use); § 2R-2-23 (State Agency); § 2R-2-24 (sustainable development); § 2R-2-30 (water right); § 2R-2-32 (waters of the State); § 2R-2-33 (water source); § 4R-1-07 (application fees); § 4R-3-04 (combined permits); §§ 5R-1-01 to 5R-3-03 (hearings, dispute resolution, and judicial review); § 5R-5-01 (crimes); §§ 6R-1-01 to 6R-1-06 (the requirement of a permit) §§ 6R-2-01 to 6R-2-08 (permit procedures); § 6R-3-01 (standards for a permit); § 6R-3-02 (determining whether a use is reasonable); § 6R-3-03 (aggregation of multiple withdrawals); § 6R-3-04 (preferences among water rights); § 6R-3-05 (prior investment in withdrawal and use facilities); § 6R-3-06 (special standard for interbasin transfers); § 7R-1-01 (permit terms and conditions); § 7R-1-03 (forfeiture of permits); § 7R-2-01 (approval required for modifications of permits); § 7R-2-03 (approval of non-injurious modifications); § 7R-2-04 (no rights acquired through adverse use); §§ 7R-3-01 to 7R-3-07 (restrictions during water shortages and water emergencies); §§ 8R-1-01 to 8R-1-07 (multijurisdictional transfers); § 9R-1-02 (preferences to water developed through conservation measures).

Comparable Statute: DEL. CODE ANN. tit. 7, § 6031 (authorizing the administering agency to order compensation for well interference); HAW. REV. STAT. § 174C-57(b) (general standards for approval), (c) (special standards for permits issued to county water agencies); IOWA CODE ANN. § 455B.281 (authorizing the administering agency to order compensation for well interference).

§ 7R-2-03 APPROVAL OF NON-INJURIOUS MODIFICATIONS

(1) In the event of a simple assignment of a permit, whether voluntary or involuntary, to a person other than the current water right holder that does not alter the place, time, or manner or use, the assignee of the permit must file a written notice of the assignment with the State Agency within 30 days of the assignment.

(2) Failure to register a simple assignment under subsection (1) of this section within the prescribed time renders the assigned permit void.

(3) An assignee who complies with subsection (1) of this section shall receive a reissue of the permit in the new owner's name for the period of the remaining duration of the original permit.

(4) The State Agency may authorize approval of certain classes of modification without specific review by the State Agency according to regulations defining the conditions under which a modification is deemed not to have a significant impact on the water source, other water right holders, and the public interest.

Commentary: Not all applications to modify a permit will involve changing the quantity of water to be withdrawn or used. Permits will contain many other terms and conditions, and the holder of a permit might seek to modify any of those terms and conditions. For example, an agreement to exchange or rotate permits within a lake where, because of the size and relative stability of the water body, any effect on third parties would be extraordinary hardly merits careful review by the State Agency. Furthermore, a simple assignment of a permit along with the sale of the entire operation of which it is a part often will not merit any greater public scrutiny than the water right would have received without the modification. So long as the new water right holder does not intend to change materially the manner, place, or timing of withdrawal or use, there is little chance of an impact not contemplated when the original permit was issued.

This section introduces the term assignment to describe the substitution of a new permit holder for a prior permit holder. The term has a well-established legal meaning that includes sales, leases, gifts, or any other similar transaction. As used here, the term includes involuntary assignments as well as voluntary assignments, as the policies addressed in this section are at stake in either event. The more specific terms simply are inadequate to capture the full range of transactions that might give rise to the problem addressed in this section.

This section addresses the need for a simplified procedure covering two related kinds of non-injurious modification without abandoning regulatory oversight of modifications generally: simple assignments that merely substitute a new holder of the permit for the earlier holder; and other modifications that cause no significant injury to any other person holding a water right. The first three subsections provide a simple procedure for validating simple assignments, resulting in a reissued permit indicating the correct holder of the water right. The section specifically exempts from full review any modification that merely substitutes a new person as holder of the permit without any other changes in the permit if the assignee registers the assignment with the Agency within 30 days of the effective date of the assignment. This requirement assures that the State Agency's records will be kept current and gives the Agency the opportunity to question whether more is involved in the transaction than mere assignment. Failure to register within 30 days voids the permit, leaving the water free for allocation to anyone (including, but not limited to, the assignee) who cares to apply for the water.

Subsection (4) authorizes the Agency to delineate, by regulation, the characteristics of other modifications that will not require specific review or approval by the Agency. This is a sort of "blanket approval" that by-passes the process generally required for modifications. Blanket approval is justified when the Agency reasonably determines that the changes will have minimal effect. This is particularly justified when the costs of review are a great deal higher than any likely injury that would be prevented by the review. *See generally* SAX, ABRAMS, & THOMPSON, at 134; Dellapenna, § 9.03(d). These regulations, like any regulations issued under this Code, are subject to judicial review under section 5R-3-01.

Cross-references: § 1R-1-01 (protecting the public interest in the waters of the State); § 1R-1-02 (assuring efficient and productive use of water); § 1R-1-06 (legal security for water rights); § 1R-1-07 (flexibility through modification of water rights); § 1R-1-08 (procedural protections); § 1R-1-10 (water conservation); § 2R-1-03 (no unreasonable injury to other water rights); § 2R-2-05 (conservation measures); § 2R-2-07 (cost); § 2R-2-11 (modification of a water right); § 2R-2-14 (permit); § 2R-2-15 (person); § 2R-2-18 (the public interest); § 2R-2-20 (reasonable use); § 2R-2-23 (State Agency); § 2R-2-24 (sustainable development); § 2R-2-26 (unreasonable injury); § 2R-2-30 (water right); § 2R-2-32 (waters of the State); §§ 5R-1-01 to 5R-3-03 (hearings, dispute resolution, and judicial review); § 7R-1-01 (permit terms and conditions); § 7R-1-02 (duration of permits); § 7R-1-03 (forfeiture of permits); § 7R-2-01 (approval required for modification of permits); § 7R-2-02 (approval of modifications); § 7R-2-04 (no rights acquired through adverse use).

§ 7R-2-04 NO RIGHTS ACQUIRED THROUGH ADVERSE USE

(1) The methods set forth in this Code are the only methods whereby a water right may be acquired under the law of this State.

(2) No water right or other right to use water can be acquired by adverse use, adverse possession, estoppel, or prescription.

Commentary: State planning and management of the waters of the State are at the heart of the Regulated Riparian Model Water Code. To allow adverse use as the basis for establishing a water right is to impose insurmountable barriers to the Agency's ability to acquire the information necessary to discharge the Agency's planning and management functions. Thus, even voluntary modifications of water rights are not allowed without review and approval by the State Agency. The Code therefore also prohibits adverse use as the basis of a water right. *See* Teressa Lippert, Case Note, People v. Shirokow: *Abolishing Prescriptive Water Rights Against the State,* 69 CALIF.

L. REV. 1204 (1981). For a discussion of prescriptive rights under common law riparianism, see SAX, ABRAMS, & THOMPSON, at 77, 78, 284, 285; TARLOCK, § 3.109; TRELEASE & GOULD, at 319, 324; Dellapenna, § 7.04(c), (d).

If a water right holder persists in failing to exercise or defend the water right, the permit holder forfeits the water right, the right reverts to the public, and the water becomes available for allocation to other uses, whether involving withdrawal or not. Only the Agency can properly decide what those substitute uses are to be. Private action simply is not allowed to override the mechanisms established in the Code for promoting and protecting the public interest.

Cross-references: § 1R-1-01 (protecting the public interest in the waters of the State); § 1R-1-02 (assuring efficient and productive use of water); § 1R-1-06 (legal security for water rights); § 1R-1-07 (flexibility through the modification of water rights); § 2R-1-04 (protection of property rights); § 6R-1-01 (withdrawals unlawful without a permit); § 6R-1-02 (small withdrawals exempted from the permit requirement); §§ 7R-1-01 to 7R-1-03 (the extent of the right); § 7R-2-01 (approval required for modification of water rights); § 7R-2-02 (approval of modifications); § 7R-2-03 (approval of non-injurious modifications).

Comparable statute: HAW. REV. STAT. § 174C-4(d).

Part 3

Restrictions during Water Shortages or Water Emergencies

One of the central purposes of a regulated riparian system of water law is to enable a State to cope reasonably and effectively with the recurring shortfalls in water supply that are becoming more frequent in the humid parts of the nation. *See* Robert Abrams, *Charting the Course of Riparianism: An Instrumentalist Theory of Change,* 35 WAYNE L. REV. 1381 (1989). As a result, water conservation permeates the entire Regulated Riparian Model Water Code, and the Code is suffused by the goal of sustainable development. The dominant mode by which water is managed during periods of water crisis under a regulated riparian system is the pairing of a comprehensive information gathering system with legal authority in the state to restrict uses during periods of shortfalls of water supply notwithstanding the permits authorizing greater use during periods of normal supply. This Part provides authority to the State Agency to respond to such shortfalls and to compel water users to comply with the Agency's strategies and decisions. This Part also deals with certain aspects of water conservation, although other aspects of water conservation are dealt with in Chapters VI and IX.

This Part, as does the Code generally, speaks solely in terms of water shortages or water emergencies. A State might choose to confer broader responsibilities on the State Agency, including responsibility for water quality, flood control, and so on. If this is done, the language of this Part would need to be rewritten to reflect these broader responsibilities, as would certain definitions, the planning responsibilities under this Code, and perhaps other provisions as well.

§ 7R-3-01 AUTHORITY TO RESTRICT PERMIT EXERCISE

(1) The State Agency may restrict any term or condition of any permit issued under this Code for the duration of a water shortage or a water emergency declared by the Agency.

(2) The State Agency is to impose restrictions according to previously developed drought management strategies unless the Agency determines that the relevant drought management strategies are inappropriate to the actual situation.

(3) In implementing restrictions under this section, the State Agency shall comply with the preferences provided in section 6R-3-04.

Commentary: In this section, the Regulated Riparian Model Water Code provides a mechanism to prevent uncontrolled conflict among water rights during periods when the water available falls short of the amounts necessary to satisfy all lawful reasonable uses. Without a hierarchical system of temporal or other rigid priorities, the Code must provide some other basis for resolving the conflicts that arise when water is overallocated or the water sources contain significantly less than their normal volumes. The language of the first subsection of this section is modeled generally after FLA. STAT. ANN. § 373.175.

The Code distinguishes between water shortages and water emergencies. The distinction raises different levels of authority in the State Agency, both regarding restricting the otherwise lawful exercise of water rights and regarding the protection due to minimum flows and levels. The details of these distinctions are provided in the remaining sections of this Part.

The Code, consistent with its general approach to the planning and management of the waters of the State, authorizes the Agency to act to reallocate water or otherwise intervene to modify the terms or conditions of permits in order to maximize the public interest during such crises. Generally, restrictions for either water shortages or water emergencies must follow the drought management strategies developed as part of the comprehensive planning process before the shortage or emergency is declared. Drought management strategies will include a set of priorities among water uses, although these priorities must reflect the preferences for certain uses of water found in section 6R-3-04.

The requirement that the State Agency follow previously established drought management strategies serves to make the actions of the Agency predictable, enabling water right holders to plan their reactions even before restrictions are imposed. Still, few actual shortages or emergencies will precisely match any set of assumptions underlying a drought management strategy, and the Agency is authorized to depart from the planned responses when rigid adherence would be inappropriate. On the relative merits of requiring adherence to planned responses or authorizing *ad hoc* responses, see Dellapenna, § 9.05(d).

Cross-references: § 1R-1-01 (protecting the public interest in the waters of the State); § 1R-1-02 (assuring efficient and productive use of water); § 1R-1-03 (conformity to the policies of this Code and to physical laws); § 1R-1-04 (comprehensive planning); § 1R-1-05 (efficient and equitable allocation during shortfalls in supply); § 1R-1-06 (legal security for the right to use water); § 1R-1-09 (coordination of water allocation and water quality regulation); § 1R-1-10 (water conservation); § 1R-1-11 (preservation of minimum flows and levels); § 2R-1-01 (the obligation to make only reasonable use of water); § 2R-1-02 (no prohibition of use based upon location of use); § 2R-1-03 (no unreasonable injury to other water rights); § 2R-1-04 (protection of property rights); § 2R-2-04 (comprehensive water allocation plan); § 2R-2-06 (consumptive use); § 2R-2-09 (drought management strategies); § 2R-2-13 (nonconsumptive use); § 2R-2-14 (permit); § 2R-2-15 (person); § 2R-2-18 (the public interest); § 2R-2-20 (reasonable use); § 2R-2-21 (safe yield); § 2R-2-23 (State Agency); § 2R-2-24 (sustainable development); § 2R-2-26 (unreasonable injury); § 2R-2-27 (waste of water); § 2R-2-29 (water emergency); § 2R-2–30 (water right); § 2R-2-31(water shortage); § 2R-2-32 (waters of the State); § 2R-2-33 (water source); § 2R-2-34 (withdrawal or to withdraw); §§ 3R-1-01 to 3R-2-05 (waters subject to allocation); § 4R-2-01 (the comprehensive water allocation plan); § 4R-2-02 (drought management strategies); § 4R-2-03 (the statewide data system); § 4R-4-05 (Area Water Management Plans); §§ 6R-1-01 to 6R-1-06 (the requirement of a permit); § 6R-3-04 (preferences among water rights); §§ 6R-4-01 to 6R-4-05 (coordination of water allocation and water quality regulation); § 7R-1-01 (permit terms and conditions); § 7R-3-02 (declaration of a water shortage); § 7R-3-03 (declaration of a water emergency); § 7R-3-04 (delineation of the area affected); § 7R-3-05 (authority to restrict withdrawals for which no allocation or permit is required); § 7R–3-06 (conservation credits); § 7R-3-07 (amendment or termination of a declaration of water shortage or water emergency); §§ 9R-1-01 to 9R-2-05 (water conservation and supply augmentation).

Comparable statutes: ALA. CODE § 9-10B-22; ARK. CODE ANN. § 15-22-217; FLA. STAT. ANN. §§ 373.119, 373.175, 373.246; GA. CODE ANN. §§ 12-5-31(k)(8), 12-5-31(l), 12-5-47, 12-5-102; HAW. REV. STAT. § 174C-62; ILL. COMP. STAT. ANN. ch. 525, § 45/5.1; IND. CODE ANN. §§ 13-2-2.5-3, 13-2-2.5-3.5 (underground water), 13-2-2.6-1 to 13-2-2.6-17 (lakes); IOWA CODE ANN. §§ 455B.265, 455B.266, 455B.271; KY. REV. STAT. ANN. §§ 151.182(2), 151.200; MASS. GEN. LAWS ANN. ch. 21G, §§ 15 to 17; MINN. STAT. ANN. § 105.418; N.J. STAT. ANN. § 58:1A-4; N.C. GEN. STAT. §§ 143-215.13 to 143-215.18, 143-354; VA. CODE ANN. §§ 62.1-44.83 to 62.1-44.105, 62.1-249; WIS. STAT. ANN. § 30.18(6m), 144.025(d)(2), 144.026(7).

§ 7R-3-02 DECLARATION OF A WATER SHORTAGE

(1) The State Agency shall declare a water shortage whenever it finds the conditions defined in section 2R-2-31 to exist.

(2) Before restricting the exercise of any right conferred by a permit under this Code because of a water shortage, the State Agency shall serve notice of the proposed action on and provide an opportunity for a contested hearing to any person affected by the proposed restriction.

(3) In any hearing or litigation relating to this section, the burden of proof shall be on the party requesting the hearing or initiating the litigation.

Commentary: The conditions that constitute a "water shortage" are set out in the definition of the term. The State Agency is given broad discretion to declare a water shortage when it judges that the necessary conditions exist. This decision is judicially reviewable for abuse of discretion.

Upon the declaration of a water shortage, the Agency can restrict any water right by modifying the terms or conditions of the permit, but only after giving all affected persons notice of the proposed change and an opportunity for a hearing. Hearings might be requested by water right holders who contend that a proposed restriction on the water right expressed in their permit is unnecessary or improper. A hearing might also be requested by a person who contends that one or more proposed restrictions are inadequate responses to the water shortage in light of probable effects on that person. The declaration itself has the status of a regulation and is reviewable as such. Any order issued to an individual under this declaration is reviewable as a final decision or order. The burden of requesting a hearing and of proving that the proposed restriction is either unnecessary or otherwise improper is on the person requesting the hearing.

Cross-references: § 1R-1-01 (protecting the public interest in the waters of the State); § 1R-1-02 (assuring efficient and productive use of water); § 1R-1-03 (conformity to the policies of this Code and to physical laws); § 1R-1-04 (comprehensive planning); § 1R-1-05 (efficient and equitable allocation during shortfalls in supply); § 1R-1-06 (legal security for the right to use water); § 1R-1-09 (coordination of water allocation and water quality regulation); § 1R-1-10 (water conservation); § 1R-1-11 (preservation of minimum flows and levels); § 2R-1-01 (the obligation to make only reasonable use of water); § 2R-1-03 (no unreasonable injury to other water rights); § 2R-2-15 (person); § 2R-2-21 (safe yield); § 2R-2-23 (State Agency); § 2R-2-24 (sustainable development); § 2R-2-26 (unreasonable injury); § 2R-2-27 (waste of water); § 2R-2–30 (water right); § 2R-2-31 (water shortage); § 2R-2-32 (waters of the State); § 3R-2-03 (effects of water shortages or water emergencies on protected minimum flows or levels); §§ 5R-1-01 to 5R-01-05 (hearings); § 5R-3-01(judicial review of regulations); § 6R-3-04 (preferences among water rights); § 7R-3-01(authority to restrict permit exercise); § 7R-3-04 (delineation of the area affected); § 7R-3-05 (authority to restrict withdrawals for which no permit is required); § 7R-3-06 (accommodating voluntary agreements relating to shortfalls in supply); § 7R-3-07 (amendment or termination of a declaration of water shortage or water emergency).

Comparable statutes: ARK. CODE ANN. § 15-22-217; FLA. STAT. ANN. §§ 373.175(1) to (3), 373.246(1) to (6); GA. CODE ANN. § 12-5-31(k)(8); HAW. REV. STAT. § 174C-62(a) to (f); ILL. COMP. STAT. ANN. ch. 525, § 45/5.1; MINN. STAT. ANN. § 105.418; N.C. GEN. STAT. §§ 143-215.13 to 143-215.18; VA. CODE ANN. §§ 62.1-44.83 to 62.1-44.105, 62.1-249; WIS. STAT. ANN. § 30.18(6m).

§ 7R-3-03 DECLARATION OF A WATER EMERGENCY

(1) The State Agency shall declare a water emergency whenever it finds the conditions defined in section 2R-2-29 to exist.

(2) In addition its powers under a declaration of water shortage, the Agency may, upon declaring a water emergency and without prior hearing, order a person who holds a permit under this Code immediately to cease or otherwise change the withdrawal or use of water as necessary to alleviate the emergency.

(3) An emergency order issued under this section shall specify the precise date and time on which the withdrawal or use must stop or change and the date, if any has been determined at the time the order is issued, on which the withdrawal or use might be resumed.

(4) Any restriction under this section shall not take effect against any person affected by the restriction until the State Agency serves the emergency order on that person.

(5) Any person affected by a restriction under this section may obtain a hearing to challenge the restriction to begin not more than 10 days after the State Agency receives the request for a hearing, and to be concluded as soon as reasonably possible after the hearing begins.

(6) In any hearing or litigation relating to this section, the burden of proof shall be on the party requesting the hearing.

(7) An emergency order remains in effect pending the result of any hearing or litigation relating to this section.

Commentary: A "water emergency" is a much more serious crisis in water supply than a "water shortage." When a "water emergency" exists is set out in the definition of the term. Just as for water shortages, the State Agency has a broad discretion to declare a water emergency, with its decision judicially reviewable only for abuse of discretion.

Because of the greater severity of a water emergency compared to a water shortage, the powers of the State Agency to respond to a water emergency are correspondingly greater. *See* Dellapenna, § 9.05(d). In particular, the Agency can restrict a term or condition of a permit without providing an opportunity for a prior hearing through an emergency order that directs the water right holder to cease or alter any withdrawal or use immediately. Due process is served by making the order effective after the order is given to the water right holder and providing a prompt hearing whenever requested by the water right holder. The time period of 10 days is near the outermost limits of what due process allows, although given the probability of complex issues being raised, the Code cannot assure that the hearing process will be completed within any particular period of time. Failure of the Agency to proceed expeditiously with the hearing process would be a basis for judicial review. A court might well draw an analogy to the obligation of the Agency to act on permit applications set forth in section 6R-2-06.

Any person affected by an emergency order to cease or change can immediately request a hearing to contest the propriety of the order. The burden of proof in such a hearing shall be on the person contesting the order. The declaration itself has the status of a regulation and is reviewable as such; an emergency order is reviewable as a final decision or order. Emergency orders remain in effect pending the outcome of the hearing or of any ensuing litigation.

Cross-references: § 1R-1-01 (protecting the public interest in the waters of the State); § 1R-1-02 (assuring efficient and productive use of water); § 1R-1-03 (conformity to the policies of this Code and to physical laws); § 1R-1-04 (comprehensive planning); § 1R-1-05 (efficient and equitable allocation during shortfalls in supply); § 1R-1-06 (legal security for the right to use water); § 1R-1-09 (coordination of water allocation and water quality regulation); § 1R-1-10 (water conservation); § 1R-1-11 (preservation of minimum flows and levels); § 2R-1-01 (the obligation to make only reasonable use of water); § 2R-1-03 (no unreasonable injury to other water rights); § 2R-2-15 (person); § 2R-2-21 (safe yield); § 2R-2-23 (State Agency); § 2R-2-24 (sustainable development); § 2R-2-26 (unreasonable injury); § 2R-2-27 (waste of water); § 2R-2-29 (water emergency); § 2R-2–30 (water right); § 2R-2-32 (waters of the State); § 3R-2-03 (effects of water shortages or water emergencies on protected minimum flows or levels); §§ 5R-1-

01 to 5R-01-05 (hearings); §§ 5R-3-01 to 5R-3-03 (judicial review); § 6R-3-04 (preferences among water rights); § 7R-3-01(authority to restrict permit exercise); § 7R-3-04 (delineation of the area affected); § 7R-3-05 (authority to restrict withdrawals for which no permit is required); § 7R-3-06 (accommodating voluntary agreements relating to shortfalls in supply); § 7R-3-07 (amendment or termination of a declaration of water shortage or water emergency).

Comparable statutes: ALA. CODE § 9-10B-22(a); FLA. STAT. ANN. §§ 373.119(2), (3), 373.175(4), 343.246(7), (8); GA. CODE ANN. §§ 12-5-31(l), 12-5-47; HAW. REV. STAT. § 174C-62(g); IND. CODE ANN. §§ 13-2-2.5-3, 13-2-2.5-3.5 (underground water), 13-2-2.6-1 to 13-2-2.6-17 (lakes); IOWA CODE ANN. §§ 455B.265(1), 455B.266, 455B.271(3); KY. REV. STAT. ANN. §§ 151.182(2), 151.200; MASS. GEN. LAWS ANN. ch. 21G, §§ 15 to 17; N.J. STAT. ANN. § 58:1A-4; N.C. GEN. STAT § 143-354(b), (c); WIS. STAT. ANN. §§ 144.025(d)(2), 144.026(7).

§ 7R-3-04 DELINEATION OF THE AREA AFFECTED

> **The State Agency, in declaring a water shortage or a water emergency, shall determine and clearly delineate the area of the State and the water sources included within the shortage or emergency.**

Commentary: This section confirms the authority of the State Agency to delineate the area of the State and the water sources subject to a declaration of water shortage or water emergency. A declaration of either status by the Agency must include a clear delineation of the boundaries of the area covered. As a regulation, the Agency's discretion in setting those boundaries is subject to judicial review only for abuse of discretion.

Cross-references: § 2R-2-23 (State Agency); § 2R-2-29 (water emergency); § 2R-2-31 (water shortage); § 2R-2-33 (water source); § 7R-3-02 (declaration of a water shortage); § 7R-3-03 (declaration of a water emergency).

Comparable statutes: ALA. CODE § 9-10B-21; N.C. GEN. STAT. § 143-215.18; VA. CODE ANN. § 62.1-44.94.

§ 7R-3-05 RESTRICTION OF WITHDRAWALS FOR WHICH NO ALLOCATION OR PERMIT IS REQUIRED

(1) During a water shortage or water emergency, the State Agency is empowered to restrict withdrawals for which no permit is required, or to allocate water to and among such uses, in order to alleviate the water shortage or water emergency.

(2) In exercising its power under this section, the State Agency shall proceed on the same bases and according to the same procedures as apply to restrictions on uses for which a permit is required.

Commentary: Users relying on certain small water sources and certain small-scale users are not subject to a permit requirement in order to withdraw or use water. It may not be, therefore, an adequate response to a water shortage or water emergency for the State Agency simply to modify permits. This section authorizes the Agency to restrict water rights not subject to the permit requirement as part of its response to a water shortage or water emergency. The same procedures regarding the nature and timing of such restrictions apply to water rights not required to have a permit as for those that do require a permit.

Cross-references: § 3R-1-03 (small water sources exempted from allocation); § 6R-1-02 (small withdrawals exempted from the permit requirement); § 7R-3-01 (authority to restrict permit exercise); § 7R-3-02 (declaration of a water shortage); § 7R-3-03 (declaration of a water emergency); § 7R-3-04 (delineation of the area affected); § 7R-3-06 (conservation credits); § 7R-3-07 (amendment or termination of a declaration of water shortage or water emergency).

Comparable statutes: ALA. CODE § 9-10B-22; ARK. CODE ANN. § 15-22-217; ILL. COMP. STAT. ANN. ch. 525, § 45/5.1; IOWA CODE ANN. § 455B.266(2); N.J. STAT. ANN. § 58:1A-4(c)(1), (2).

§ 7R-3-06 CONSERVATION CREDITS

(1) In so far as practical, the State Agency, in ordering restrictions on the withdrawal or use of water during a water shortage or water emergency, shall not order a person to do more if that person has successfully implemented conservation measures pursuant to the plan of conservation made a term or condition of the permit under which the person exercises a water right, until other permit holders shall have achieved comparable restrictions in the exercise of their water rights.

(2) When a person holding a water right voluntarily undertakes conservation measures during a period of water shortage or water emergency beyond those required by this Code, including the terms or conditions of the person's permit, that result in significant quantifiable reductions in the water that person had been using before the beginning of the water shortage or water emergency, that person is entitled to a credit for such reductions in any scheme of restrictions imposed by the State Agency as a response to the water shortage or water emergency.

(3) When a written agreement between persons holding water rights under this Code for those persons to undertake joint conservation measures in the event of an anticipated water shortfall is filed with

the State Agency before the declaration of a water shortage or water emergency and the agreement does not unreasonably impair the rights of other persons who hold water rights, or the public interest, or sustainable development, the Agency shall:

(a) register the agreement and include it in any relevant drought management strategies if the agreement is consistent with the policies of this Code; and

(b) credit any water actually conserved under the agreement to the obligations of the parties to the agreement to restrict their water withdrawals or consumptive uses during any water shortage or water emergency.

(4) When a written agreement between persons holding water rights under this Code for those persons to undertake joint conservation measures is filed with the State Agency during the declaration of a water shortage or water emergency and the agreement does not unreasonably impair the rights of other persons who hold water rights, or the public interest, or sustainable development, the Agency shall:

(a) register the agreement and authorize the parties to the agreement to implement those measures in lieu of restrictions imposed (or to be imposed) by the Agency; and

(b) credit any water actually conserved under the agreement to the obligations of the parties to the agreement to restrict their water withdrawals or consumptive uses during any water shortage or water emergency.

(5) Conservation credits and registered agreements on joint conservation measures shall be included in the statewide data system.

Commentary: The Regulated Riparian Model Water Code seeks to encourage voluntary action to conserve water generally and to respond to water shortages and water emergencies in particular. This section imposes an obligation on the State Agency to award conservation credits for voluntary actions to conserve water. Conservation is not a concern only during, or in anticipation of, water shortages or water emergencies, and thus the basic rule is set forth in subsection (1): Within the limits of practical enforcement, the Agency is not to order any permit holder to restrict her, his, or its withdrawal and use of water if that permit holder has achieved significant conservation through the plan of conservation included as a term or condition of the permit until other permit holders have made comparable reductions in their withdrawals and use. Any other policy would in effect reward waste and punish efficiency.

Consider the following example. An applicant for a permit to withdraw and use water in a particular industry might develop an innovative method that uses less water than is usual in the industry. If the person discloses its intent to use less water through a plan of conservation included in the application for a permit, that person will be entitled to be credited with already having saved water when a water shortage or water emergency arises. It would not only be unfair to treat that person equally with other, more water intensive, members of the same industry, but it would actually be counterproductive, creating a serious disincentive for applicants to undertake serious explorations of the methods available to save water when they apply for a permit. While there is already some incentive to do so in order to minimize the water use fees that one will pay, subsection (1) provides a desirable further incentive to the successful innovator by rewarding the innovation during a water shortage or water emergency. Subsection (1) also creates a strong incentive to others to be aware of how much water each competitor is using and then to try to match the best competitor's efficiency before a crisis arises. Each person using water can determine how much water a competitor is using for the amount of water withdrawn and the purpose of its use cannot be confidential, even though the techniques for using the water might very well be protected as confidential business information. *See* section 4R-1-09.

The remainder of the section addresses credits for steps taken as a direct response to a water shortage or water emergency. Subsection (2) requires such a credit for individually undertaken voluntary conservation measures, while subsections (3) and (4) accommodate agreements by permit holders to undertake joint conservation measures. This approach is an appropriate means for providing the maximum legal security for water rights by assuring persons who enter into such agreements that, if they undertake to solve their problems by agreement among themselves, the Agency will both plan on the basis of registered agreements and adhere to such agreements in its own actual responses to water shortfalls. Without some such provision, there is likely to be less voluntary water conservation, even during periods of severe crisis, as there would be no gain for the person undertaking the conservation measures and might well be a net loss if subsequently the Agency were to determine that resumption of the former use patterns would constitute a waste of water.

Agreements to undertake joint conservation measures are contracts. Neither this section nor the Code undertakes to create a special, administrative mechanism to enforce these agreements apart from the benefits that might be incurred in the operation of drought management strategies. These agreements, and individual efforts to conserve during a water shortage or water emergency, are different from plans for conservation which are required as part of the permit application process and deals with conservation during periods of normal supply and not special steps to crisis situations.

Quantification of the water conserved will involve comparing the amounts of water actually used before introduction of the voluntary conservation measures with that actually used afterward, allowances being made to variations in the use and occurrence of water caused by the water shortage or water emergency. Normally, the Agency will require actual measurements rather than estimates, but in a proper case the Agency might rely on estimates based upon sound engineering principles. Subsection (3) provides a small (but potentially significant) benefit for joint advance planning for water shortfalls by persons holding water rights. As an agreement filed after a water shortage or water emergency has been declared could not have been included in a drought management strategy, such an agreement does not benefit from the obligation of the Agency generally to conform its responses to relevant drought management strategies. Either way, the Agency's review of the agreements will generally conform to its procedures for the approval of modifications of permits.

The Agency will only approve joint conservation agreements if they appear workable and if they do not improperly impinge upon the rights of holders of other water rights or upon the public interest or upon sustainable development. The State Agency has a strictly limited power to approve actions by permit holders that will affect the rights of other permit holders during ordinary times. See the *Commentary* to section 6R-3-02. As conservation credits are applicable during periods of water shortage or water emergency, however, the possibilities for private action subject to approval by the State Agency are considerably broader for the rights of permit holders can be restricted during such times. This section provides the rules according to which conservation credits are to operate during water shortages or water emergencies.

Reference to the public interest in subsection (3) implicates, among other concerns, the requirement of protection for the biological, chemical, and physical integrity of the water sources involved in the voluntary conservation measures. The public interest also includes the obligation of the Agency to coordinate water allocation with water quality regulations. The public interest also implicates concerns about social equity. Private action under this section, whether undertaken individually or jointly, cannot become the basis for allocating the major portion of the waters of the State to one or a few large users of water to the exclusion of the public generally.

Subsection (5) requires that data on conservation credits and registered joint conservation agreements be included in the statewide data system. Such data will be available to the public, enabling persons not a party to such conservation measures to take such data into account in their planning. Like all data in the statewide data system, confidential business information will not generally be open to the public.

Few, if any, examples of the sort of direct encouragement of private responses to water shortages or water emergencies as envisaged in this section are found in actual regulated riparian or appropriative rights statutes. Virginia's law provides examples as close as one is likely to find. A proposed regulated riparian statute in Pennsylvania does provide for "conservation credits" along the lines of this section. PA. SEN. BILL. No. 351, § 507(c).

Cross-references: § 1R-1-01 (protecting the public interest in the waters of the State); § 1R-1-02 (assuring efficient and productive use of water); § 1R-1-03 (conformity to the policies of the

Code and to physical laws); § 1R-1-04 (comprehensive planning); § 1R-1-05 (efficient and equitable allocation during shortfalls in supply); § 1R-1-06 (legal security for the right to use water); § 1R-1-07 (flexibility through modification of water rights); § 1R-1-08 (procedural protections); § 1R-1-09 (coordination of water allocation and water quality regulation); § 1R-1-10 (water conservation); § 1R-1-11 (preservation of minimum flows and levels); § 2R-1-01 (the obligation to make only reasonable use of water); § 2R-1-03 (no unreasonable injury to other water rights); § 2R-1-04 (protection of property rights); § 2R-2-02 (biological integrity); § 2R-2-03 (chemical integrity); § 2R-2-05 (conservation measures); § 2R-2-09 (drought management strategies); § 2R-2-11 (modification of a water right); § 2R-2-15 (person); § 2R-2-16 (physical integrity); § 2R-2-17 (plan for conservation); § 2R-2-18 (the public interest); § 2R-2-20 (reasonable use); § 2R-2-21 (safe yield); § 2R-2-23 (State Agency); § 2R-2-24 (sustainable development); § 2R-2-26 (unreasonable injury); § 2R-2-27 (waste of water); § 2R-2-29 (water emergency); § 2R-2-30 (water right); § 2R-2-31 (water shortage); § 2R-2-32 (waters of the State); § 2R-2-33 (water source); §§ 3R-2-01 to 3R-2-05 (protection of minimum flows or levels); § 4R-1-08 (water use fees); § 4R-1-09 (protection of confidential business information); § 4R-2-02 (drought management strategies); § 4R-2-03 (the statewide data system); § 5R-2-01 (support for informal dispute resolution); §§ 7R-2-01 to 7R-2-04 (modification of water rights); § 7R-3-01 (authority to restrict permit exercise); § 7R-3-02 (declaration of a water shortage); § 7R-3-03 (declaration of a water emergency); § 7R-3-04 (delineation of the area affected); § 7R-3-05 (authority to restrict withdrawals for which no permit is required); § 7R-3-07 (amendment or termination of a declaration of water shortage or water emergency); § 9R-1-02 (preferences to water developed by conservation measures).

Comparable statutes: VA. CODE ANN. §§ 62.1-44.91, 62.1-245.

§ 7R-3-07 AMENDMENT OR TERMINATION OF A DECLARATION OF WATER SHORTAGE OR WATER EMERGENCY

The State Agency is authorized to amend or terminate a declaration of water shortage or of water emergency upon a finding that conditions justifying the declaration no longer exist as to part or all of the area included in the prior order.

Commentary: This section simply confirms the authority of the State Agency to amend or terminate any declaration of water shortage or water emergency. Such authority might be inferred from the authority to declare the shortage or emergency, but such authority should not be left to inference. As with any final decision by the Agency, an aggrieved person can request a hearing or seek judicial review.

Cross-references: § 2R-2-29 (water emergency); § 2R-2-31 (water shortage); § 7R-3-02 (declaration of a water shortage); § 7R-3-03 (declaration of a water emergency).

Comparable statutes: ALA. CODE § 9-10B-22(C); IND. CODE ANN. § 13-2-2.5-6; MASS. GEN. LAWS ANN. ch. 21G, § 15; N.J. STAT. ANN. § 58:1A-4(h).

CHAPTER VIII

MULTIJURISDICTIONAL TRANSFERS

The "dormant" commerce clause of the United States Constitution precludes the placing of an "undue burden" on the transportation and use of water in interstate commerce. *Sporhase v. Nebraska ex rel. Douglas*, 458 U.S. 941 (1982). Considerable controversy continues over the extent to which States can nonetheless regulate or even prohibit the export of water for use in another State. *See* RICE & WHITE, at 111-112; SAX, ABRAMS, & THOMPSON, at 777-90; TARLOCK, CORBRIDGE, & GETCHES, at 756-60; TARLOCK, § 10.07; TRELEASE & GOULD, at 678-80; Douglas Grant, *State Regulation of Interstate Water Export, in* 4 WATERS AND WATER RIGHTS §§ 48.01-48.03.

The issue has been less controversial in riparian rights states than in appropriative rights states. Nonetheless, such concerns have been primary concerns in the enactment of several regulated riparian statutes, particularly in the Delaware and Susquehanna Valleys. *See* SAX, ABRAMS, & THOMPSON, at 742-46; Dellapenna, § 9.06(c)(2); Joseph Dellapenna, *The Delaware and Susquehanna River Basins,* in 6 WATERS AND WATER RIGHTS 137 (1994 reissued vol.). Among regulated riparian states, Iowa represents an extreme in favoring local water users over out-of-State water users, requiring that in times of a declared water emergency the State's administering agency is to order the cessation of all "[w]ater conveyed across State boundaries" before ordering any in-state use to cut back. IOWA CODE ANN. § 455B.266(2)(a). Arkansas goes almost as far, prohibiting interstate transfers unless expressly authorized by the State legislature. ARK. CODE ANN. § 15-22-303. Statutes in other regulated riparian States draw no distinction between in-state or out-of-state water users, perhaps indicating by this silence that no preference whatsoever is to be given to in-state users. *See generally* Dellapenna, § 9.06(a).

This Chapter strikes a balance between protecting the interests of the exporting State and furthering the interests of the importing state. Such a balanced approach should withstand challenges based on allegations of a violation of the commerce clause while allowing the exporting state to take constitutional steps to regulate all uses of water originating in withdrawals within the state. As an alternative, States could seek through their cooperative efforts (an interstate compact which will also require the consent of Congress) to create a system of cooperative management according to mutually acceptable standards. *See generally* Jerome C. Muys, National Water Comm'n, *Interstate Water Compacts: The Interstate Compact and Federal - Interstate Compact* 241-322 (1971). *See also* RICE & WHITE, at 8, 13.

Existing and future decrees of the Supreme Court, federal legislation, interstate compacts, and international treaties provide the framework and the limits within which any attempt by a single State to regulate transboundary water withdrawals must function. All forms of federal law, including those mentioned in the preceding sentence, are supreme law of the land and preempt any inconsistent state law or regulation. U.S. CONST. art. VI. See JOHN MATHER, WATER RESOURCES, DISTRIBUTION, USE, AND MANAGEMENT 294-305 (1984); SAX, ABRAMS, & THOMPSON, at 644-74, 804-916; TARLOCK, § 9.05; TARLOCK, CORBRIDGE, & GETCHES, at 664-830; TRELEASE & GOULD, at 635-808; Dellapenna, § 9.06(b); Amy Kelley, *Constitutional Foundations of Federal Water Law,* in 4 WATERS AND WATER RIGHTS § 35.08; Amy Kelly, *Federal-State Relations in Water,* in 4 WATERS AND WATER RIGHTS § 36.01. Congress has generally been careful not to displace directly the State role in allocating the use of waters within a State although such allocations can be affected indirectly by the operation of any number of federal regulations. To that extent, the State allocation system, including management under this Model Water Code, must give way. The Regulated Riparian Model Water Code directs the State Agency to comply with the mandates of federal law in section 3R-1-02. *See generally Arizona v. California,* 373 U.S. 546 (1963); RICE & WHITE, at 109-114; MALONEY, AUSNESS, & MORRIS, at 162-165; Dellapenna, § 9.06(b); Douglas Grant, *Apportionment by Congress,* in 4 WATERS AND WATER RIGHTS, ch. 47. The Code also authorizes the State Agency to cooperate with the federal government even when not required to do so by any law, but only when the State Agency determines that to do so would be consistent with the policies and provisions of the Code. *See* section 4R-3-01.

In one of the more direct federal preemptions of State allocational authority, Congress has enacted that no water is to be transferred out of the Great Lakes basin without the approval of the governor of every Great Lakes State. 42 U.S.C. § 1962d-20. For a Great Lakes State then, the allocational authority vested in the State Agency by this Code would apply to water withdrawals within the Great Lakes basin as within any other water basin within the State, but no interbasin transfer could be issued a permit without the approval of the governors of the other Great Lakes States. Most Great Lakes States have in fact banned such interbasin transfers in statutes that are not, however, entirely consistent with the federal statute. ILL. ANN. STAT. ch. 19, ¶ 119.2; IND. CODE ANN. § 13-2-1-9(b); MICH. COMP. LAWS ANN. §§ 323.71-323.85; MINN. STAT. ANN. §§ 105.045(4), 105.41(1a); N.Y. ENVTL. CONSERV. LAW §§ 15-1607, 15-611, 15-613; WIS. STAT. ANN. § 144.026(5)(b), (11), (d)(4). Only Ohio and Pennsylvania have not legislated on the matter. *See generally* Dellapenna, §§ 7.05(c)(2), 9.06(a).

A large number of decisions from the Supreme Court in the exercise of its original jurisdiction over suits between States have decreed equitable apportionment of their shared waters. While most of the attention given in the secondary literature has focused on such litigation in the arid states west of Kansas City, there have been a significant number of such suits in the humid east as well. *See Wisconsin v. Illinois,* 388 U.S. 426 (1967); *New Jersey v. New York,* 345 U.S. 369 (1953); *New Jersey v. New York,* 283 U.S. 336 (1931); *Connecticut v. Massachusetts,* 282 U.S. 660 (1931); *Wisconsin v. Illinois,* 281 U.S. 179 (1930); *Missouri v. Illinois,* 200 U.S. 496 (1906). As a decree from a federal court, such an apportionment overrides any inconsistent state law. *See* Scott Anderson, Note, *Equitable Apportionment and the Supreme Court: What's So Equitable about Apportionment?,* 7 HAMLINE L. REV. 405 (1984); Douglas Grant, *Equitable Apportionment Suits between States,* in 4 WATERS AND WATER RIGHTS, ch. 45; George William Sherk, *Equitable Apportionment after Vermejo: The Demise of a Doctrine,* 29 NAT. RESOURCES J. 565 (1989); A. Dan Tarlock, *The Law of Equitable Apportionment Revised, Updated and Restated,* 56 U. COLO. L. REV. 381 (1985).

Interstate compacts must be approved by Congress to be effective, and thus are a type of federal law supreme over inconsistent State law. *Intake Water Co. v. Yellowstone River Compact Comm'n,* 769 F.2d 568 (9th Cir. 1985), *cert. denied,* 476 U.S. 1183 (1986). Generally, interstate compacts do not create mechanisms for actually managing water sources or for allocating water among particular users. *See* TARLOCK, § 10.05; Douglas Grant, *Water Apportionment Compacts between States,* in 4 WATERS AND WATER RIGHTS, ch. 46. In particular, most interstate compacts in States likely to adopt regulated riparian statutes merely call for the States to share information and to consult in formulating individual state plans and policies. The primary examples of (eastern) interstate compacts that do create a multijurisdictional commission to manage water sources with authority to allocate water among particular users during times of shortage have already been mentioned in the introduction to this chapter: the Delaware River Basin Compact, PUB. L. NO. 87-328, 75 Stat. 688 (1961), codified at DEL. CODE ANN. tit. 7, § 6501; N.J. STAT. ANN. §§ 32.11D-1 to -110; N.Y. ENVTL. CONSERV. LAW § 21-0701; PA. STAT. ANN. § 815.101; and the Susquehanna River Basin Compact, PUB. L. NO. 91-575, 84 Stat. 1509 (1970), codified at MD. NAT. RESOURCES CODE § 8-301; N.Y. ENVTL. CONSERV. LAW § 21-1301; PA. STAT. ANN. tit. 32, § 820.1. Both compacts involve only riparian states. Both create Basin Commissions that are unusual not only because of the extent of the regulatory authority conferred on them but also because the federal government is a full participant on the Commissions and is bound by most Commission decisions. The Basin Commissions are authorized to delegate their allocational authority to State Agencies if the Agencies have adequate regulatory authority to accomplish the policies adopted by the Commission. The Code is designed to enable such a delegation. *See generally* Dellapenna, § 9.06(c)(2); Joseph Dellapenna, *The Delaware and Susquehanna River Basins,* in 6 WATERS AND WATER RIGHTS 137 (1994 reissued vol.).

The ratification of the North American Free Trade Agreement (NAFTA) in 1993 highlighted for some the growing importance of international regulation of transboundary water resources. In fact, the United States entered into treaties regarding the management of its international fresh waters as far back as 1906. *See Convention Providing for the Equitable Distribution of the Waters of the Rio Grande for Irrigation Purposes,* signed May 21, 1906, Mexico-United States, 34 Stat. 2953, T.S. No. 455; *Treaty Relating to Boundary Waters between the United States and Canada,* Jan. 11, 1909, United Kingdom-United States, 36 Stat. 2449, T.S. 548; *Treaty Respecting Utilization of Waters of the Colorado and Tijuana Rivers and of the Rio Grande,* signed Feb. 3, 1944, Mexico-United States, 59 Stat. 1219, T.S. No. 994, 3 U.N.T.S.

313; *Treaty Relating to the Uses of the Waters of the Niagara River,* signed Feb. 27, 1950, United States-Canada, 1 U.S.T. 694, T.I.A.S. No. 2130, 132 U.N.T.S. 224; *Treaty for the Co-Operative Development of the Columbia River Basin,* Jan. 17, 1961, United States-Canada, 15 U.S.T. 1555, T.I.A.S. 5638, 15 U.S.T. 1555; Albert Utton, *Canadian International Waters,* in 5 WATERS AND WATER RIGHTS, ch. 50; Albert Utton, *Mexican International Waters,* in 5 WATERS AND WATER RIGHTS, ch. 51. *See also* JOHN KRUTILLA, THE COLUMBIA RIVER TREATY: THE ECONOMICS OF AN INTERNATIONAL RIVER BASIN DEVELOPMENT (1967); THE LAW OF INTERNATIONAL DRAINAGE BASINS 167 (Albert Garretson, Robert Hayton, & Cecil Olmstead eds. 1967); DON PIPER, THE INTERNATIONAL LAW OF THE GREAT LAKES (1967); SAX, ABRAMS, & THOMPSON, at 790-803; LUDWIK TECLAFF, THE RIVER BASIN IN HISTORY AND LAW (1967); Gerald Graham, *International Rivers and Lakes: The Canadian-American Regime,* in THE LEGAL REGIME OF INTERNATIONAL RIVERS AND LAKES 3 (Ralph Zacklin & Lucius Caflisch eds. 1981); Robert Hayton & Albert Utton, *Transboundary Groundwaters: The Bellagio Draft Treaty,* 29 NAT. RESOURCES J. 663 (1989); Mary Kelleher, Note, *Mexican-United States Shared Groundwater: Can It Be Managed?,* 1 GEO. INT'L ENVTL. L. REV. 113 (1988); Symposium, *U.S.-Canadian Transboundary Resource Issues,* 26 NAT. RESOURCES J. 201-376 (1986); Symposium, *U.S.-Mexican Transboundary Resource Issues,* 26 NAT. RESOURCES J. 659-850 (1986). These treaties are also part of the supreme law of the land that preempts any inconsistent state law. U.S. CONST. art. VI. Furthermore, unlike an interstate compact, a state cannot be a party to an international treaty, although a state might influence the negotiations of the federal government in this regard. Thus the role of States under a treaty is even more circumscribed than it would be under a compact.

This Chapter does not focus on the obligations imposed by these arrangements. The chapter focuses on the actions of the individual State rather than on the operation of an institution over which a State cannot individually exercise authority. The Chapter sets forth a body of law relating to the obtaining of a permit for the transportation of the waters of the State for use outside of the State in so far as the proposed withdrawal or use is not already covered by a federal decree, statute, compact, or treaty. The Chapter authorizes the State Agency to issue such permits and provides particular standards for the evaluation of applications for such permits. The

Chapter also protects the authority of the State from any implied waiver by virtue of the Code or the regulations adopted under the Code.

This Chapter draws upon the recent New Mexico legislation. Therefore the listings of comparable statutes include references to New Mexican statutes even though New Mexico is a pure appropriative rights State. The provisions of this Chapter have been adapted not only to the needs of the regulated riparian States, but also in a manner that the drafters consider more consistent with the requirements of the dormant commerce clause and other legal restraints on the ability of a State to oppose the export of water.

§ 8R-1-01 TRANSPORTATION AND USE OF WATER OUT OF THE STATE

Consistent with the State's paramount interest in the conservation of the waters of the State and the necessity of maintaining adequate water for requirements within the State, the State recognizes that under proper conditions the transport and use of the waters of the State out of the State is consistent with the public interest of the State and with the sustainable development of the waters of the State pursuant to this Code.

Commentary: The Regulated Riparian Model Water Code does not attempt to prohibit the export of water from the State. No complete ban could withstand challenge under the dormant commerce clause. *Sporhase v. Nebraska ex rel. Douglas*, 458 U.S. 941, 957 (1982). Instead, the Code sets as the cornerstone of its policy regarding the transportation of water for use out of the State the protection of the public welfare and the appropriate conservation of the water resources of the State. These two concepts are merely aspects of the ordinary standards for the issuing of a permit to withdraw water under this Code. This policy is embodied in this section.

A complete ban on the interstate transportation and use of water is lawful only if the ban has been authorized or approved by Congress. U.S. CONST. art. I, § 10, cl. 3; *Sporhase*, 458 U.S. 941, 958-960. *See also New England Power Company v. New Hampshire*, 455 U.S. 331

(1982); *Prudential Insurance Company v. Benjamin,* 328 U.S. 408 (1946). Congress has authorized such a ban for the export of water from the Great Lakes basin unless the export is approved by the governors of every Great Lakes State. 42 U.S.C. § 1962(d). Five of the eight States have adopted legislation pursuant to the Congressional authorization that prohibit such exports or restrict such exports to narrowly defined circumstances. ILL. ANN. STAT. ch. 19, ¶ 119.2; IND. CODE ANN. § 13-2-1-9(b); MINN. STAT. ANN. §§ 105.045(4), 105.41(1a); N.Y. ENVTL. CONSERV. LAW §§ 15-1607, 15-611, 15-613; WIS. STAT. ANN. § 144.026(5)(b), (11), (d)(4). Should a Great Lakes State consider adopting this Code, the legislature might want to add a further section relating to this ban. *See generally* Dellapenna, §§ 7.05(c)(2) at 337-41, 9.06(a) at 549-51.

Cross-references: § 1R-1-01 (protecting the public interest in the waters of the State); § 1R-1-02 (assuring the efficient and productive use of water); § 1R-1-10 (water conservation); § 1R-1-11 (preservation of minimum flows and levels); § 1R-1-12 (recognizing local interests in the waters of the State); § 1R-1-13 (regulating interstate water transfers); § 1R-1-14 (regulating interbasin transfers); § 2R-1-01 (the obligation to make only reasonable use of water); § 2R-1-02 (no prohibition of use based on location of use); § 2R-1-03 (no unreasonable injury to other water rights); § 2R-2-18 (the public interest); § 2R-2-24 (sustainable development); § 2R-2-30 (water right); § 2R-2-32 (waters of the State); § 3R-1-02 (certain shared waters exempted from allocation); §§ 3R-2-01 to 3R-2-05 (protected minimum levels not to be allocated); § 4R-3-01 (cooperation with the federal government); § 4R-3-02 (cooperation with other units of state and local government); § 6R-1-01 (withdrawals unlawful without a permit); §§ 6R-3-01 to 6R-3-06 (the basis of the water right); §§ 6R-4-01 to 6R-4-03 (coordination of water allocation and water quality regulation); §§ 7R-2-01 to § 7R-2-04 (modification of water rights); § 8R-1-02 (the requirement of a permit to transport and use water outside of the State); § 8R-1-03 (application as consent to authority); § 8R-1-04 (appointment and maintenance of an agent for receipt of service of process and other legal notices); § 8R-1-05 (standards for evaluating applications to transport and use water out of the State); § 8R-1-06 (regulation of uses of water made outside of the State); § 8R-1-07 (authority of the State unimpaired); §§ 9R-1-01 to 9R-1-02 (water conservation).

Comparable statutes: ARK. CODE ANN. § 15-22-303(a); N.M. STAT. ANN. § 72-12B-1.

§ 8R-1-02 REQUIREMENT OF A PERMIT TO TRANSPORT AND USE WATER OUT OF THE STATE

(1) Any person intending to withdraw any water from a water source in this State for transportation and use outside of the State or to alter the place or purpose of use from a place in this State to a place outside this State must receive a permit from the State Agency to do so.

(2) A person seeking a permit under subsection (1) of this section shall apply for a permit according to the forms prescribed pursuant to this Code for applications to withdraw or use water generally.

(3) No permit application or permit is necessary for the transportation of water out of the State in closed containers or for domestic use of the persons transporting the water.

Commentary: This section makes explicit that any person intending to transport water for use out of the State is subject to the ordinary permit process applicable to activities involving the withdrawal of water for use of water within the State. Whether this intent arises as an original matter or as the modification of an existing withdrawal does not matter. This obligation is not limited by the exception from the permit process applicable to certain small sources or to certain small withdrawals and use. *See* sections 3R-1-03, 6R-1-02. On the other hand, the permit process does not apply to the transportation of bottled liquids or other closed containers or to water transported for the domestic use of the individual or family transporting the water.

Cross-references: § 1R-1-01 (protecting the public interest in the waters of the State); § 1R-1-02 (assuring efficient and productive use of water); § 1R-1-04 (comprehensive planning); § 1R-1-05 (efficient and equitable allocation during shortfalls in supply); § 1R-1-07 (flexibility through modifications of water rights); § 1R-1-08 (procedural protections); § 1R-1-09 (coordination of water allocation and water quality regulations); § 1R-1-10 (water conservation); § 1R-1-11 (preservation of minimum flows and levels); § 1R-1-12 (recognizing local interests in the waters of the State); § 1R-1-13 (regulating interstate water transfers); § 1R-1-14 (regulating interbasin transfers); § 2R-1-01 (the obligation to make only reasonable use of water); § 2R-1-02 (no prohibition of use based on location of use); § 2R-1-03 (no unreasonable injury to other water rights); § 2R-2-14 (permit); § 2R-2-15 (person); § 2R-2-18 (the public interest); § 2R-2-20 (reasonable use); § 2R-2-23 (State Agency); § 2R-2-24 (sustainable development); § 2R-2-26 (unreasonable injury); § 2R-2-27 (waste of water); § 2R-2-32 (waters of the State); § 2R-2-33 (water source); § 3R-1-03 (small water sources exempted from allocation); §§ 3R-2-01 to 3R-2-05 (protection of minimum flows and levels); § 6R-1-01 (withdrawals unlawful without a permit); § 6R-1-02 (small withdrawals exempted from the permit requirement); § 6R-2-01 (contents of an application for a permit); § 6R-3-01 (standards for a permit); § 6R-3-02 (determining whether a use is reasonable); § 6R-3-04 (preferences among water rights); § 6R-3-05 (prior investment in proposed water withdrawal or use facilities); § 6R-3-06 (special standard for interbasin transfers); §§ 6R-4-01 to 6R-4-05 (coordination of water allocation and water quality regulations); §§ 7R-2-01 to 7R-2-04 (modification of water rights); § 8R-1-01 (transportation and use of water of water out of the State); § 8R-1-02 (the requirement of a permit to transport and use water outside of the State); § 8R-1-03 (application as consent to authority); § 8R-1-04 (appointment and maintenance of an agent for receipt of service of process and other legal notices); § 8R-1-05 (standards for evaluating applications to transport and use water out of the State); § 8R-1-06 (regulation of uses of water made outside of the State); § 8R-1-07 (authority of the State unimpaired).

Comparable statutes: ARK. CODE ANN. § 15-22-303(b); N.Y. ENVTL. CONSERV. LAW §§ 15-1505, 15-506.

§ 8R-1-03 APPLICATION AS CONSENT TO AUTHORITY

A person who files an application under section 8R-1-02 thereby submits to the laws of this State governing the allocation and use of water, and implicitly promises to comply with those laws.

Commentary: This section makes clear that any person who has sought the benefits and protections of this Regulated Riparian Model Water Code relevant to the transportation and use of water out of the State is thereafter precluded from challenging the authority of the State to make decisions regarding such activities. Such an application would apply to multijurisdictional transfers existing prior to the application for a permit or even prior to the enactment of this Code, as well as to proposed new withdrawals, transportations, or uses. On the other hand, the applicant would have the same rights as any other person to seek judicial review of regulations or final agency decisions under this Code.

Cross-references: § 2R-2-14 (permit); § 2R-2-15 (person); § 8R-1-01 (transportation and use of water of water out of the State); § 8R-1-02 (the requirement of a permit to transport and use water outside of the State); § 8R-1-04 (appointment and maintenance of an agent for receipt of service of process and other legal notices); § 8R-1-05 (standards for evaluating applications to transport and use water out of the State); § 8R-1-06 (regulation of uses of water made outside of the State); § 8R-1-07 (authority of the State unimpaired).

Comparable statute: N.M. STAT. ANN. § 72-12B-1(E).

§ 8R-1-04 APPOINTMENT AND MAINTENANCE OF AN AGENT FOR RECEIPT OF SERVICE OF PROCESS AND OTHER LEGAL NOTICES

(1) Any person filing an application for, or holding a permit authorizing, the withdrawal of water within the State for transportation and use out of the State, shall designate an agent in this State for receipt of service of process and other legal notices, and shall thereafter maintain such an agent within the State during the time the application is pending and, if a permit is received, at all times the permit is in effect.

(2) Failure to appoint or maintain the agent required under this section shall be deemed to be consent to the Secretary of State of this State to serve as such agent.

(3) Upon receipt of service of process or other legal notice pursuant to this section, the Secretary of State of this State shall promptly undertake to deliver the process or notice to the person on record as holding the relevant water right, but failure of such delivery shall not invalidate any action taken pursuant to this Code.

Commentary: This is a fairly ordinary provision to assure that a person who withdraws water for transportation and use out of the State cannot claim failure to be served with process or to receive legal notices as a basis for avoiding obligations arising under the Regulated Riparian Model Water Code.

Cross-references: § 1R-1-08 (procedural protections); § 2R-1-04 (protection of property rights); § 6R-2-02 (notice and opportunity to be heard); § 6R-2-04 (contesting an application); § 6R-2-05 (public right of comment); § 6R-2-07 (notice of action on applications); § 6R-4-03 (preservation of private rights of action); § 7R-1-03 (forfeiture of permits); §§ 7R-3-01 to 7R-3-07 (restrictions during water shortages or water emergencies); § 8R-1-01 (transportation and use of water of water out of the State); § 8R-1-02 (the requirement of a permit to transport and use water outside of the State); § 8R-1-03 (application as consent to authority); § 8R-1-05 (standards for evaluating applications to transport and use water out of the State); § 8R-1-06 (regulation of uses of water made outside of the State); § 8R-1-07 (authority of the State unimpaired).

§ 8R-1-05 STANDARDS FOR EVALUATING APPLICATIONS FOR A PERMIT TO TRANSPORT AND USE WATER OUT OF THE STATE

(1) The State Agency shall approve an application to transport and use water out of the State if the Agency finds that the proposed withdrawal, transportation, and use:

(a) are reasonable;

(b) will not impair existing water rights under this Code;

(c) are not detrimental to the conservation and sustainable development of the waters of the State;

(d) are not otherwise detrimental to the health, safety, and welfare of people of the State;

(e) are consistent with the obligations of this State under any applicable federal law, including interstate compacts or international agreements; and

(f) are otherwise consistent with the public interest.

(2) In addition to the factors set forth in sections 6R-3-01 to 6R-3-06 of this Code, in determining whether a withdrawal, transportation, or use is reasonable the State Agency shall consider:

(a) the supply of water available to users in this State and available to the applicant within the State or Province in which the water is proposed to be used;

(b) the overall water demand in this State and in the State or Province in which the water is proposed to be used; and

(c) the probable impact of the proposed transportation and use of water out of the State on existing or foreseeable shortages in this State and in the State or Province in which the water is proposed to be used.

Commentary: A New Mexico statute, N.M. STAT. ANN. § 72-12B-1, that listed six factors to be considered in issuing or denying a permit to transport water for use out of the State, was upheld against constitutional challenge in *City of El Paso v. Reynolds* (El Paso II), 597 F. Supp. 694 (D. N.M. 1984). Whether that list, or a similar one, would be upheld if the issue had been successfully appealed to the United States Supreme Court is far from clear; the New Mexico approach appears to some to discriminate against out-of-State users. *See generally* Frank Trelease, *Interstate Use of Water* – "Sporhase v. El Paso, Pike & Vermejos," 22 LAND & WATER L. REV. 315 (1987); Frank Trelease, *State Water and State* Commerce 56 U. COLO. L. R. 347 (1985). The appearance of deliberate discrimination largely disappears under a regulated riparian code given the considerable discretion vested by such laws in the administering agency. This discretion probably explains why most regulated riparian statutes do not address interstate transfers directly.

The enumeration of the entire *El Paso* list of factors actually would not add a great deal to the Regulated Riparian Model Water Code. Unlike the law in appropriative rights States, under which the review of applications to appropriate water is largely limited to assuring no interference with existing (senior) rights and only a small and not well established public interest criterion added to the process, under regulated riparianism the State Agency is already charged to consider many of the *El Paso*-approved factors when passing on any application for a permit.

See sections 6R-3-01 to 6R-3-06. The more the process for granting or denying a permit for interstate or international transportation and use resembles the process used for entirely domestic permits, the less is the likelihood of successful constitutional challenge for interfering with interstate or international commerce.

This section adapts the *El Paso* factors that are particularly relevant to the interstate context of the permit application process and presents them in a manner that assures the careful consideration of how those factors might support the granting of the permit as well as its denial. The section also adds two factors not listed in the New Mexico statute: that the withdrawal, transportation, and use be reasonable; and that the withdrawal, transportation, and use be consistent with the obligations of the State under federal law, including interstate compacts and international agreements. As with the general permit process, the entire standard is subsumed in the simple requirement that the use be reasonable, and the section specifically incorporates the general standards for a permit found in Chapter VI. This section, like those general standards for a permit, emphasizes certain key factors that are particularly relevant to the interstate and international context.

Subsection (1) provides specifically not only that the proposed development of water be reasonable, but also that the development not impair existing water rights under the law of this State, that the development be consistent with water conservation and sustainable development of water, that the development not impair the health, safety, and welfare of the people of the State, and otherwise is consistent with the public interest as defined in this Code. Subsection (1) also adds that any proposal to withdraw, transport, or use water out of the State be consistent with the obligations of federal law. These requirements are similar to, but not precisely the same as, the requirements for permits generally under section 6R-3-01.

Subsection (2) specifically adopts the standards of sections 6R-3-01 to 6R-3-06 as the standards for determining whether a proposed development of water under this section is reasonable, but again emphasizes certain particulars that are especially relevant to the interstate or international context. As this section implies, and as section 6R-3-01(c) makes explicit, the grant or denial of a permit is to be determined by its consistency with the State's comprehensive water allocation plan. Normally, that planning process is to take into account the resources and needs in this State, yet in the context of an interstate or international development of water, the planning process must necessarily take into account resources and needs outside of the State. Subsection (2) directs the State Agency is to consider the availability, need, and foreseeable problems both in this State and in the State or Province in which it is proposed to use the water.

Just as the use of the same ultimate standards for domestic and transboundary water projects–that a use be reasonable–serves to ensure that the regulatory scheme will meet constitutional requirements, so too the placing of the decision in the context of comprehensive planning will maximize the likelihood that a court will uphold the scheme as constitutional. The United States Supreme Court itself indicated that restrictions on the export of water would be upheld if the restrictions were part of a carefully planned strategy narrowly tailored to preserve the waters of the State. *Sporhase v. Nebraska* ex rel. *Douglas,* 438 U.S. 941, 956 (1982). *See* David Getches, *Water Planning: Untapped Opportunity for the Western States,* 9 J. ENERGY L. & POL'Y 1, 10-42 (1988); Peter Longo, *The Constitution and Water Policy of* Sporhase *Revisited: A West German Alternative,* 20 ENVTL. L. 917 (1990). This circumstance must not function, however, as a subterfuge for simple discrimination against out-of-state users. Hence the section directs the State Agency to consider these relevant variables, but does not direct decisions adverse to any particular class of use any more than the remainder of the Code does for particular classes of wholly domestic use.

Cross-references: § 1R-1-01 (protecting the public interest in the waters of the State); § 1R-1-02 (assuring efficient and productive use of water); § 1R-1-04 (comprehensive planning); § 1R-1-05 (efficient and equitable allocation during shortfalls in supply); § 1R-1-09 (coordination of water allocation and water quality regulations); § 1R-1-10 (water conservation); § 1R-1-11 (preservation of minimum flows and levels); § 1R-1-12 (recognizing local interests in the waters of the State); § 1R-1-13 (regulating interstate water transfers); § 1R-1-14 (regulating interbasin transfers); § 2R-1-01 (the obligation to make only reasonable use of water); § 2R-1-02 (no prohibition of use based on location of use); § 2R-1-03 (no unreasonable injury to other water rights); § 2R-1-04 (protection of property rights); § 2R-2-04 (comprehensive water allocation plans); § 2R-2-09 (drought management strategies); § 2R-2-14 (permit); § 2R-2-15 (person); §

2R-2-18 (the public interest); § 2R-2-20 (reasonable use); § 2R-2-21 (safe yield); § 2R-2-23 (State Agency); § 2R-2-24 (sustainable development); § 2R-2-26 (unreasonable injury); § 2R-2-27 (waste of water); § 2R-2-32 (waters of the State); § 2R-2-33 (water source); § 3R-1-03 (small water sources exempted from allocation); §§ 3R-2-01 to 3R-2-05 (protection of minimum flows and levels); § 6R-1-01 (withdrawals unlawful without a permit); § 6R-1-02 (small withdrawals exempted from the permit requirement); § 6R-2-01 (contents of an application for a permit); §§ 6R-3-01 to 6R-3-06 (the basis of the water right); §§ 6R-4-01 to 6R-4-05 (coordination of water allocation and water quality regulations); §§ 7R-2-01 to 7R-2-04 (modification of water rights); § 8R-1-01 (transportation and use of water out of the State); § 8R-1-02 (the requirement of a permit to transport and use water outside of the State); § 8R-1-03 (application as consent to authority); § 8R-1-04 (appointment and maintenance of an agent for receipt of service of process and other legal notices); § 8R-1-06 (regulation of uses of water made outside of the State); § 8R-1-07 (authority of the State unimpaired); §§ 9R-1-01 to 9R-2-05 (water conservation and supply augmentation).

Comparable statutes: ARK. CODE ANN. § 15-22-303(c); N.M. STAT. ANN. § 72-12B-1(C).

§ 8R-1-06 REGULATION OF USES MADE OUTSIDE THE STATE

> **In addition to the terms and conditions applicable to ordinary permits for the withdrawal and use of water under this Code, the State Agency shall include terms and conditions in any permit for the withdrawal, transportation, and use of water out of the State that are necessary to insure that the use of the water in another State or Province does not impair existing uses in this State or the health, safety, and welfare of persons in this State and is consistent with the sustainable development of the waters of this State and with the laws and regulations of the State or Province in which the water is or will be used.**

Commentary: By this section, the Regulated Riparian Model Water Code indicates that the State Agency can tailor the terms and conditions of any permit granted for the withdrawal, transportation, and use of water out of the State to the particular conditions arising from the interstate or international context of the permit. In addition to the usual terms and conditions, the Agency is charged to add terms and conditions both to protect the essential interests of persons in this State and to assure compliance with the laws of the State or States in which the water will be used. The basic standard remains the protection of the health, safety, and welfare of the people of the State and promotion of the sustainable development of the waters of the State. The condition that the permit holder comply with the laws of the State or Province in which the water is used is not meant to involve the Agency in supervising activities in the other State or Province, but to provide a legal basis for revoking the permit or finding a forfeiture, as appropriate, if the authorities in the other State or Province find a violation there. So long as the Agency exercises this authority in a manner that does not unreasonably discriminate against those who seek to use the water in another State (*i.e.*, does not "unduly burden" interstate commerce), such permit terms and conditions should be upheld against constitutional challenge. *Sporhase v. Nebraska ex rel. Douglas*, 458 U.S. 941, 957, 960 (1982).

Cross-references: § 1R-1-01 (protecting the public interest in the waters of the State); § 1R-1-02 (assuring efficient and productive use of water); § 1R-1-03 (conformity to the policies of this Code and to physical laws); § 1R-1-06 (legal security for water rights); § 1R-1-09 (coordination of water allocation and water quality regulations); § 1R-1-10 (water conservation); § 1R-1-11 (preservation of minimum flows and levels); § 1R-1-12 (recognizing local interests in the waters of the State); § 1R-1-13 (regulating interstate water transfers); § 1R-1-14 (regulating interbasin transfers); § 2R-1-01 (the obligation to make only reasonable use of water); § 2R-1-02 (no prohibition of use based on location of use); § 2R-1-03 (no unreasonable injury to other water rights); § 2R-1-04 (protection of property rights); § 2R-2-05 (conservation measures); § 2R-2-14 (permit); § 2R-2-18 (the public interest); § 2R-2-20 (reasonable use); § 2R-2-23 (State Agency); § 2R-2-24 (sustainable development); § 2R-2-26 (unreasonable injury); § 2R-2-27 (waste of water);

§ 2R-2-32 (waters of the State); § 2R-2-34 (withdrawal or to withdraw); § 3R-1-02 (certain shared waters exempted from allocation); §§ 3R-2-01 to 3R-2-05 (protection of minimum flows and levels); § 5R-5-02 (revocation of permits) § 7R-1-01 (permit terms and conditions); § 7R-1-03 (forfeiture of permits); § 8R-1-01 (transportation and use of water of water out of the State); § 8R-1-02 (the requirement of a permit to transport and use water outside of the State); § 8R-1-03 (application as consent to authority); § 8R-1-04 (appointment and maintenance of an agent for receipt of service of process and other legal notices); § 8R-1-05 (standards for evaluating applications to transport and use water out of the State); § 8R-1-07 (authority of the State unimpaired); §§ 9R-1-01 to 9R-2-05 (water conservation and supply augmentation).

Comparable Statutes: ARIZ. REV. STAT. ANN. § 45-292; COLO. REV. STAT. ANN. § 37-81-101(3); IDAHO CODE §§ 42-203A(5) - 222(1), -401; MONT. CODE ANN. §§ 85-2-141(7), 85-2-311(3), 85-2-316(4), 85-2-402(5); N.M. STAT. ANN. § 72-12B-1(C).

§ 8R-1-07 AUTHORITY OF THE STATE UNIMPAIRED

Nothing in this Chapter impairs the authority of the State to:

- **(a) undertake comprehensive water planning;**
- **(b) undertake itself large allocations or exports of the waters of the State;**
- **(c) regulate water marketing;**
- **(d) enter compacts with other States to allocate interstate waters; or**
- **(e) restrict interstate water uses in accordance with equitable apportionment proceedings or the requirements of any applicable federal law or regulation, interstate compact, or international agreement.**

Commentary: This section makes explicit that the specific powers conferred on the State Agency under this Chapter do not impair the general powers of the State, whether exercised through the Agency or otherwise, to plan and manage the waters of the State separately or in cooperation with other States or to cooperate with the federal government in allocating interstate or internationally shared waters. The exercise of these powers and obligations might lead to different results from those suggested or directed by the specific provisions of this Chapter. The provisions of this section echo relevant provisions scattered elsewhere throughout this Chapter and throughout the Code, but are gathered here for emphasis and clarity.

The ability to carry out comprehensive planning, including (perhaps) large allocations for internal use or for export and including the regulation of water marketing, will likely serve to strengthen the Regulated Riparian Model Water Code against possible challenges under the "dormant" commerce clause. See the commentary to section 8R-1-05. Such planning on a grand scale, including allocations and regulation of water marketing, are all provided for elsewhere in this Code. See sections 4R-2-01 to 4R-2-04 and 7R-2-01 to 7R-2-04.

The last two powers listed in this section relate to cooperative management with other States and with the federal government. Cooperation with Provinces of Canada and with States of Mexico are not inconsistent with this Code, but must occur through the actions of the federal government because of the international nature of such cooperation. See the commentary at the opening of this Chapter. Even the power to cooperate with other States of the United States also involves compliance with federal law because interstate compacts become federal law upon approval by Congress and are void if not approved by Congress. U.S. CONST. art. I, § 10, cl. 3; *Intake Water Company v. Yellowstone River Compact Commission*, 769 F.2d 568 (9th Cir. 1985), *cert. denied*, 476 U.S. 116 (1986).

Cross-references: § 1R-1-01 (protecting the public interest in the waters of the State); § 1R-1-02 (assuring efficient and productive use of water); § 1R-1-04 (comprehensive planning); § 1R-1-09 (coordination of water allocation and water quality regulations); § 1R-1-10 (water conservation); § 1R-1-11 (preservation of minimum flows and levels); § 1R-1-12 (recognizing local interests in the waters of the State); § 1R-1-13 (regulating interstate water transfers); § 1R-1-

14 (regulating interbasin transfers); § 2R-2-04 (comprehensive water allocation plans); § 2R-2-09 (drought management strategies); § 2R-2-18 (the public interest); § 2R-2-21 (safe yield); § 2R-2-23 (State Agency); § 2R-2-24 (sustainable development); § 2R-2-32 (waters of the State); § 3R-1-02 (certain shared waters exempted from allocation); §§ 3R-2-01 to 3R-2-05 (protection of minimum flows and levels); §§ 4R-2-01 to 4R-2-04 (planning responsibilities); § 4R-3-01 (cooperation with the federal government and with interstate and international organizations); § 4R-3-02 (cooperation with other units of State and local government); §§ 7R-2-01 to 7R-2-04 (modification of water rights); § 8R-1-01 (transportation and use of water out of the State); § 8R-1-02 (the requirement of a permit to transport and use water outside of the State); § 8R-1-03 (application as consent to authority); § 8R-1-04 (appointment and maintenance of an agent for receipt of service of process and other legal notices); § 8R-1-05 (standards for evaluating applications to transport and use water out of the State); § 8R-1-06 (regulation of uses of water made outside of the State); §§ 9R-2-01 to 9R-2-05 (atmospheric water management).

Comparable statutes: ALA. CODE § 9-10B-6; ARK. CODE ANN. § 15-22-303(d); MISS. CODE ANN. § 51-3-41.

CHAPTER IX

WATER CONSERVATION AND SUPPLY AUGMENTATION

The need to conserve water is usually one of the most important reasons underlying the enactment of a regulated riparian statute. *See* section 1R-1-10. Consequently, water conservation permeates the entire Regulated Riparian Model Water Code, yet the provisions scattered throughout the Code do not exhaust the needs of the State for water conservation. This Chapter addresses certain additional means of encouraging voluntary water conservation by water right holders above the levels that are required in the terms and conditions of their permit. Required plans for conservation and conservation measures are prescribed elsewhere in the Code. *See* sections 2R-2-04, 2R-2-17, 6R-3-01, 7R-1-01. The Code also provides that the water necessary to preserve minimum flows and levels shall not be allocated under this Code. *See* sections 1R-1-11, 2R-2-02, 2R-2-03, 2R-2-16, 3R-2-01 to 3R-2-04. The Code also makes two other provisions for encouraging the voluntary conservation of water: The Code authorizes the State Agency to contract to protect additional levels of water above the minimum levels protected by regulation (section 3R-2-05); and the Code provides conservation credits for voluntary actions to respond to water shortages and water emergencies (section 7R-3-06). Part 1 of this Chapter makes provisions for the State Agency to support voluntary conservation measures undertaken by other persons under this Code and for preferences to persons conserving water for the purpose of putting that water to other uses.

Conceptually, the augmentation of water supplies would also address the problem of water demand that approaches or exceeds the supply available. In fact, augmentation actually means the disruption of the natural hydrologic cycle or the inclusion of new sources of supply. Examples are the construction of dams or the tapping of hitherto unavailable sources of underground water. These means of "supply augmentation" are already regulated in the general requirement of permits for the withdrawal of water. *See* sections 6R-1-01 to 6R-1-06.

The only method of supply augmentation addressed in this Chapter is weather modification. Weather modification is another form of disruption of the natural hydrologic cycle, but a disruption that appears to actually bring water into use outside the normal permit process created by this Code. Time will tell if this disruption has sufficiently similar effects on other water sources as to justify including it in the normal permit process. This Chapter does not undertake to create a complete regulatory scheme for weather modification, addressing only questions of basic authority and responsibility for atmospheric water management and the possibility of obtaining a water right to the water produced from such management. For an in-depth discussion of weather modification, see MALONEY, AUSNESS, & MORRIS, at 283-349; JOSEPH SAX, WATER LAW, PLANNING AND POLICY 101-02 (1968); Ray Jay Davis, *Options for Public Control of Atmospheric Management*, 10 DEN. J. INT'L L. & POL'Y; Gregory N. Jones, Comment, *Weather Modification: The Continuing Search for Rights and Liabilities*, 1991 B.Y.U. L. REV. 1163. Two books exclusively dedicated to the issue of weather modification may prove insightful, see WEATHER MODIFICATION (Ray Jay Davis & Lewis Grant eds., 1978); WEATHER MODIFICATION AND THE LAW (Howard Tauberfeld ed., 1968).

Part 1
Water Conservation

The Regulated Riparian Model Water Code here introduces several means for the State Agency to support water conservation beyond that which is strictly required by the command of this Code, including the terms and conditions of a permit. In this Part, the Code authorizes programs of public assistance and public education as well as preference in modification proceedings as a reward for such voluntarily undertaken conservation measures. Additional means for the Agency to secure voluntary conservation of water is found in the authority of the Agency under section 3R-1-05 to contract to protect additional levels of water beyond those protected by regulation of the Agency and conservation credits required under section 7R-3-06.

§ 9R-1-01 SUPPORT FOR VOLUNTARY WATER CONSERVATION MEASURES

The State Agency shall encourage voluntary actions to conserve water by:

(a) providing technical assistance to any person holding a water right to aid in the development or implementation of conservation measures beyond those required by this Code, including as a term or condition of a permit, in so far as the resources available to the State Agency enable it to do so; and

(b) creating a program of information, in schools and otherwise, to educate the public about the State's water policies in general and any steps necessary to respond to a water shortage or water emergency in particular.

Commentary: Few examples of the sort of direct encouragement of voluntary conservation as envisaged in the Regulated Riparian Model Water Code exist in actual regulated riparian or appropriative rights statutes. No provisions similar to the provision of this section have been found in existing statutes, although a proposed regulated riparian statute in Pennsylvania does provide for programs of technical assistance as in subsection (a) and a more limited program of public education as in subsection (b). Pa. Sen. Bill. No. 351, § 507.

The funds used to support voluntary conservation and public education can be provided by the legislature out of general tax revenues, or might be drawn by the State Agency out of the Special Water fund. That fund, financed out of various fees, fines, and penalties related to this Code, provides funds to be used to promote the general environmental, ecological, and aesthetic values related to the waters of the State. Clearly, programs supporting voluntary conservation and public education, if properly designed and administered, will further those values.

Cross-references: § 1R-1-10 (water conservation); § 4R-1-04 (special funds created); § 4R-3-02(2) to (4) (technical assistance to local units of government).

Comparable statutes: ALA. CODE § 9-10B-5(15); FLA. STAT. ANN. §§ 373.026(4), (9), 373.619; GA. CODE ANN. §§ 12-5-1 to 12-5-4; HAW. REV. STAT. § 174C-5(6), (7), (12); KY. REV. STAT. ANN. §§ 151.010 to 151.040, 151.600; MD. CODE ANN., NAT. RES. §§ 3-301 to 3-403; MISS. CODE ANN. § 51-3-16(e); N.C. GEN. STAT. § 143-355(b1); S.C. CODE ANN. § 49-3-40(e).

§ 9R-1-02 PREFERENCES TO WATER DEVELOPED THROUGH CONSERVATION MEASURES

(1) When a person holding a water right voluntarily undertakes conservation measures beyond those required by this Code, including beyond the terms and conditions of the person's permit, that result in significant quantifiable reductions in the water that person has been using other than during a period of water shortage or water emergency, that person shall receive approval of a modification of the permit to enable the person to use the water in other locations or for other purposes in preference to others who might apply for a permit to use the water conserved.

(2) The preference provided in this section does not change the burden on an applicant for approval of a modification of a permit to demonstrate that the modification will not unreasonably injure other holders of water rights, other persons generally, or the public interest and the sustainable development of the waters of the State.

(3) The preference provided in this section does not apply to water developed from uses that originally involved the waste of water or are subject to forfeiture.

Commentary: In this section, the Regulated Riparian Model Water Code establishes a preference for persons who have voluntarily undertaken conservation measures beyond those required by the provisions of the Code, including beyond the requirements of any plan of conservation that has been made part of the terms and conditions of their permits. The interplay between this section and the conservation credits provided in Chapter VII can become rather complex. Conservation credits arise from fulfilling the terms or conditions of a permit or as a response to a water shortage or water emergency. The preference in this section deals with conservation measures taken neither as a requirement of the permit nor as a direct response to a crisis. The conservation credits covering those two situations relate with preferences in the context of restrictions on water use during a water shortage or water emergency. The preference in this section relates to an application to modify the use made of water under a permit.

A person using water can, to some extent, control which section a particular conservation measure comes under through the manner in which the conservation measures are disclosed to the State Agency (*i.e.*, through a permit application or otherwise). When that is possible, the person undertaking a conservation measure must then consider which sort of preference will be more beneficial. This basically comes down to how frequent are water shortages or water emergencies on the one hand, and how substantial are the opportunities to make another use of the water through a modification of a permit on the other. The risk of not disclosing fully how one intends to use the water does create a risk that the pattern of use, instead of giving rise to a conservation credit under section 7R-3-06, or a modification preference under this section, will be held to have been a waste of water and therefore not only not the basis for either a credit or a preference, but also in fact a basis for forfeiture of part of the water right evidenced by the permit. In an extreme case, the less than full disclosure could even lead to a criminal prosecution for perjury.

Subsection (1) provides for a preference relative to other persons applying for a new permit for the water conserved in any proceeding relating to an application by the preferred person to modify the permit to make a related or different use of the water conserved. Subsection (2) indicates that the preferred person must still prove that the modification would not significantly injure another permit holder, other persons generally (apart from denying them the opportunity to apply for a permit for the water), or the public interest and the sustainable development of the waters of the State. Some might fear that the sort of preferences provided here in effect negates the social benefits of the conservation by allocating the water levels to the party who conserved it. The Code proceeds on the basis that such a preference provides the best incentive to developing more efficient ways of exploiting water.

Furthermore, implicit in subsection (2) is a requirement that the person who claims the preference in subsection (1) will make a reasonable use of the water, although the relational aspects of determining whether a use is reasonable will be somewhat curtailed by eliminating consideration of the merits of competing applications. Quantification of the water conserved will involve comparing the amounts of water used before introduction of the voluntary conservation measures with that use afterward, allowances being made to natural variations in the use and occurrence of water. Normally, the Agency will require actual measurements to estimates, but in appropriate cases the Agency might rely on estimates based upon sound engineering principles.

Although broadly speaking any such conservation could be considered the elimination of the waste of water rather than conservation as such, when the initiative comes from the water user rather than from prodding by the Agency and the practices that the person changes were not egregiously wasteful, the activity should be rewarded as a means of encouraging the conservation measures. Without some such reward, there is likely to be less voluntary water conservation as there would be no gain for the person undertaking the conservation measures and might well be a net loss if subsequently the Agency were to determine that resumption of the former use patterns would constitute a waste of water. Here, subsection (3) eliminates any preference if the original permit inadvertently (or otherwise) authorized the waste of water or if the water can be "conserved" because it has not been used for the forfeiture period or is not capable of being used consistently with the terms and conditions of the permit. In other words, water must have been used in order to be conserved. Subsection (3) is essentially an anti-monopoly provision.

Cross-references: § 1R-1-01 (protecting the public interest in the waters of the State); § 1R-1-02 (assuring efficient and productive use of water); § 1R-1-10 (water conservation); § 1R-1-11 (preservation of minimum flows and levels); § 2R-1-01 (the obligation to make only reasonable use of water); § 2R-2-05 (conservation measures); § 2R-2-14 (permit); § 2R-2-15 (person); § 2R-2-17 (plan for conservation); § 2R-2-18 (the public interest); § 2R-2-23 (State Agency); § 2R-2-24 (sustainable development); § 2R-2-27 (waste of water); § 2R-2-29 (water emergency); § 2R-2-30 (water right); § 2R-2-31 (water shortage); §§ 3R-2-01 to 3R-2-05 (protected minimum levels not to be allocated); § 5R-5-01 (crimes); § 7R-1-01 (permit terms and conditions); § 7R-1-03 (forfeiture); § 7R-3-06 (conservation credits).

Comparable statute: IND. CODE ANN. § 13-2-1-3(3).

Part 2
Atmospheric Water Management

The Regulated Riparian Model Water Code does not spell out in detail the legal criteria and procedures for atmospheric water management. This Part supplements a State's regulation of weather modification through licensing and permitting laws. For a list of these provisions, see Ray Jay Davis, *Legal Regulation of Weather Modification in the United States and Canada*, 24 J. WEATHER MODIFICATION 126 (1992). *See also* Robert Beck, *Augmenting the Available Water Supply*, in 1 WATERS AND WATER RIGHTS § 3.04. The Council of State Governments has prepared a Model Weather Modification Control Act. 1978 SUGGESTED STATE LEGISLATION 9 (1977).

§ 9R-2-01 STATE AUTHORITY OVER ATMOSPHERIC WATER MANAGEMENT

(1) All moisture suspended in the atmosphere above this State is property of the State in trust for the people of the State, and is dedicated to their use as provided by law.

(2) **The State has the right to increase or authorize the increase of precipitation by artificial means for use in the State.**

Commentary: This section provides the State with the jurisdictional basis for regulating and conducting operations to manage the atmospheric water of the State if it sees fit to do so.

Cross-references: § 1R-1-01 (protecting the public interest in the waters of the State); § 1R-1-15 (atmospheric water management); § 2R-2-01 (atmospheric water management or weather modification); § 2R-2-32 (waters of the State); § 9R-2-02 (the obligations of persons undertaking atmospheric water management in this State); § 9R-2-03 (governmental immunity); § 9R-2-04 (private liability); § 9R-2-05 (water rights derived from atmospheric water management).

§ 9R-2-02 THE OBLIGATIONS OF PERSONS UNDERTAKING ATMOSPHERIC WATER MANAGEMENT IN THIS STATE

All persons engaged in atmospheric water management in this State shall take proper safeguards, record accurate information concerning such activities, and report that information as required by the State's weather control law.

Commentary: This section provides for the most basic of obligations to be met by anyone undertaking weather modification. This section presupposes a weather control statute which will provide more specific obligations regarding the reporting of information. The weather control law will usually impose further obligations on a person undertaking atmospheric water management. A State contemplating an active program of atmospheric water management should examine such statutes or the Model Weather Modification Control Act prepared by the Council of State Governments. 1978 SUGGESTED STATE LEGISLATION 9 (1977). For a list of such statutes already enacted, see Ray Jay Davis, *Legal Regulation of Weather Modification in the United States and*

Canada, 24 J. WEATHER MODIFICATION 126 (1992). *See also* 1 Robert Beck, *Augmenting the Available Water Supply*, in 1 WATERS AND WATER RIGHTS § 3.04.

Cross-references: § 1R-1-15 (atmospheric water management); § 2R-2-01 (atmospheric water management or weather modification); § 2R-2-15 (person); § 9R-2-01 (State authority over atmospheric water management); § 9R-2-03 (governmental immunity); § 9R-2-04 (private liability); § 9R-2-05 (water rights derived from atmospheric water management).

§ 9R-2-03 GOVERNMENTAL IMMUNITY

> **Nothing in this Code shall be construed as imposing any liability or responsibility on the State, the State Agency, *[the State's weather control agency, if any,]* or their employees for any injury caused by persons issued permits under the State's weather control law or exempted from a permit by that law or regulations adopted pursuant to that law.**

Commentary: If a person conducting weather modification operations under a permit causes harm to someone, the permittee is the party responsible for the damages and not the State, the State Agency, the State's weather control agency, if any, or any of their employees. This section confirms the governmental immunity from liability based on the conduct of others. The next section delineates the liability of weather modifiers and their sponsors.

Cross-references: § 1R-1-15 (atmospheric water management); § 2R-2-01 (atmospheric water management or weather modification); § 2R-2-23 (State Agency); § 9R-2-01 (State authority over atmospheric water management in this State); § 9R-2-02 (the obligations of persons undertaking atmospheric water management in this State); § 9R-2-04 (private liability); § 9R-2-05 (water rights derived from atmospheric water management).

§ 9R-2-04 PRIVATE LIABILITY

(1) An operation or research and development activity conducted under a permit issued under authority of the State's weather control law or exempted from a permit under that law or regulations adopted pursuant to that law is not an ultrahazardous or abnormally dangerous activity.

(2) The mere act of dissemination of weather modification agents into the atmosphere or clouds within the atmosphere, including fog, by a person holding a permit or a person exempted from the permit requirements of the State's weather control law acting within the scope of the permit or exemption shall not in itself give rise to a cause of action.

(3) Except as provided in subsections (1) and (2) of this section and section 9R-2-05, nothing in this Code shall prevent any person adversely affected by a weather modification operation or research and development activity from recovering damages resulting from intentional harmful actions or negligent conduct by a person conducting a weather modification operation or research and development activity.

(4) Other than in a legal action charging a failure to obtain a permit, the fact that a person holds a permit and has complied with the provisions of the State's weather control law and regulations made pursuant to that law is not admissible as a defense in any legal action that might be brought against such person for actions taken under the permit or pursuant to such law or regulation.

Commentary: Subsections (1) and (2) reject the possibility that liability arises without fault or from merely putting weather modification agents into the atmosphere. As indicated in subsection (3), when the person who puts weather modification agents into the atmosphere is at fault, either intentionally or negligently, that person is liable for any resulting damages. Subsection (4) provides that the possession of a permit and compliance with the State's weather control law is not a defense if the responsible person is at fault. The only time possession of a permit would be admissible would be if a person holding a permit were to be prosecuted for undertaking to modify the weather of this State without a permit.

Cross-references: § 1R-1-15 (atmospheric water management); § 2R-1-03 (no unreasonable injury to other water rights); § 2R-1-04 (protection of property rights); § 2R-2-01 (atmospheric water management or weather modification); § 2R-2-15 (person defined); § 2R-2-23 (State Agency); § 2R-2-26 (unreasonable injury); § 5R-4-09 (citizen suits); § 6R-4-03 (preservation of private rights of action); § 9R-2-01 (State authority over atmospheric water management); § 9R-2-02 (the obligations of persons undertaking atmospheric water management in this State); § 9R-2-03 (governmental immunity); § 9R-2-05 (water rights derived from atmospheric water management).

9R-2-05 WATER RIGHTS DERIVED FROM ATMOSPHERIC WATER MANAGEMENT

(1) Water derived from atmospheric water management becomes part of the State's basic water supply subject to allocation and regulation in accordance with the provisions of this Code.

(2) When a person successfully undertakes atmospheric water management, the State Agency shall grant that person a permit authorizing that person to make a reasonable use.

(3) The applicant for a water allocation right based upon operation of an atmospheric water management project shall bear the burden of quantification of the amount and timing of such augmented water supply.

(4) Quantification of a right based upon atmospheric water management shall be based upon consideration of such of the following factors as may be appropriate:

- **(a) physical and statistical analysis of historic streamflow and augmented streamflow;**
- **(b) analysis of precipitation data in the project area and in control areas;**
- **(c) computer simulations;**
- **(d) radar measurements;**
- **(e) chain of events research; and**
- **(f) such other technology or technique that currently exists or may be available in the future which comports with sound engineering and physical principles.**

Commentary: This section indicates that the State Agency retains the authority to allocate any water developed through weather modification. While the Agency should reward efforts at weather modification by allocating some or all of the resulting enhancement in the State's water supply to the person undertaking the atmospheric water management, the Agency can do so only to the extent that the proposed use is reasonable. Subsection (2)'s requirement that the use be reasonable requires, among other factors, that the use not unreasonably injury other lawful uses of water, that it be consistent with the public interest and the public health, safety, and welfare, and that it be consistent with sustainable development of the waters of the State. Subsection (3) requires the person seeking a permit under subsection (2) to demonstrate actual success in developing new water for the State. Subsection (4) suggests the ways in which the applicant for a permit to withdraw such water can quantify the amount and timing of the development of the water. Computer models are likely to become increasingly helpful in this regard.

Cross-references: § 1R-1-01 (protecting the public interest in the waters of the State); § 1R-1-02 (assuring efficient and productive use of water); § 1R-1-03 (conformity to the policies of this Code and to physical laws); § 1R-1-06 (legal security for the right to use water); § 1R-108 (procedural protections); § 1R-1-15 (atmospheric water management); § 2R-1-01 (the obligation to make only reasonable use of water); § 2R-1-02 (no prohibition of use based on location of use); § 2R-1-03 (no unreasonable injury to other water rights); § 2R-1-04 (protection of property rights); § 2R-2-01 (atmospheric water management or weather modification); § 2R-2-14 (permit); § 2R-2-15 (person defined); § 2R-2-18 (the public interest); § 2R-2-20 (reasonable use); § 2R-223 (State Agency); § 2R-2-24 (sustainable development); § 2R-2-26 (unreasonable injury); § 2R-2-30 (water right); § 2R-2-32 (waters of the State); § 2R-2-33 (water source); § 3R-1-01 (waters subject to allocation); §§ 5R-1-01 to 5R-3-03 (hearings, dispute resolution, and judicial review); § 6R-1-01 (withdrawals unlawful without a permit); §§ 6R-3-01 to 6R-3-06 (the basis of a water right); §§ 6R-4-01 to 6R-4-03 (coordination of water allocation and water quality regulation); §§ 7R-1-01 to 7R-3-07 (the scope of the water right); § 9R-2-01 (State authority over atmospheric water management); § 9R-2-02 (the obligations of persons undertaking atmospheric water management in this State); § 9R-2-03 (governmental immunity); § 9R-2-04 (private liability).

INDEX

B

C

E

F

G

J

L

M

N

R